THE FIRST AMERICAN ARMY

THE UNTOLD STORY OF GEORGE WASHINGTON AND THE MEN BEHIND AMERICA'S FIRST FIGHT FOR FREEDOM

BRUCE CHADWICK, PHD

SOURCEBOOKS, INC.®
NAPERVILLE, ILLINOIS

Also by Bruce Chadwick

George Washington's War
Brother Against Brother
Two American Presidents
Traveling the Underground Railroad
The Reel Civil War

"Bruce Chadwick reminds us that the Revolution was fought and won by men without general's stars or officers' commissions. It's good to see how much ordinary Americans cared about liberty and the pursuit of happiness."

—Thomas Fleming, author of *Liberty! The American Revolution*

"Although wars are fought by soldiers, they are usually described by historians writing about generals. This book puts first things first: the story of the Revolutionary War is told as it was experienced by the soldiers who waged it, those unsung patriots whose souls were tried by battle, privation, and disease. It is a look through the other end of the telescope, giving new meaning to such words as sacrifice and courage and perseverance. To understand the war, really understand it, read this book."

—Dave R. Palmer, Lieutenant General, U.S. Army (Ret), Author of *The Way of the Fox, The River and the Rock, Summons of the Trumpet, 1794, First in War,* and *Washington and Arnold*

"*The First American Army* is a most laudable and successful effort to put faces and personalities to some of the men at the knife's edge of the Continental Army. ...The author tells the stories of some long-forgotten soldiers whose individual achievements might appear small, but collectively comprised our army of independence. Through the use of anecdotes and excellent quotations from the writings of the soldiers themselves, he brings their characters to life and helps appreciate the intense sufferings and also some of the pleasures of life in the army.

"Dr. Chadwick brings clarity to a neglected, but absolutely vital, dimension of the Revolutionary War: why men choose to endure year after year of often bitter and frustrating army life. While the desertion rate among patriot soldiers was high, the fact that so many soldiers stayed and did their duty despite poor or non-existent food, clothing, and pay, reflects the remarkable commitment they had to achieving independence. Their steadfast faith and service in the cause never fails to evoke my admiration and respect."

—Joseph Lee Boyle, Author of *Writings from the Valley Forge Encampment of the Continental Army, December 19, 1777–June 19, 1778*

Published by Sourcebooks, Inc.
P.O. Box 4410, Naperville, Illinois 60567-4410
(630) 961-3900
FAX: (630) 961-2168
www.sourcebooks.com

Library of Congress Cataloging-in-Publication Data

Chadwick, Bruce.
  The first American army : the untold story of George Washington and the men behind America's first fight for freedom / Bruce Chadwick.
      p. cm.
  Includes bibliographical references and index.
  ISBN 1-4022-0506-6 (alk. paper)
  1. United States. Continental Army--Military life. 2. Washington, George, 1732-1799. 3. Washington, George, 1732-1799--Friends and associates. 4. Soldiers--United States--Social conditions--18th century. 5. United States--History--Revolution, 1775-1783--Social aspects. I. Title.

E259.C43 2005
973.3'4--dc22

                                                                    2005019866

Printed and bound in the United States of America
QW 10 9 8 7 6 5 4 3 2 1

CONTENTS

AUTHOR TO READER

The American Revolution may have been highlighted by the inspirational writing of Thomas Paine, the patriotism of the delegates to the Continental Congress, and the leadership of George Washington, but it was won by the enlisted men of the Continental Army over eight years of fighting against one of the greatest military forces in the world. It was not only their bravery under intense fire on battlefields at Trenton, Saratoga, and Yorktown that won the war, but their courage in simply staying together as an army through incredibly severe winters, smallpox epidemics, tattered clothes, and near-starvation that gained independence for America.

There have been many books written about George Washington and other generals in the rebellion and volumes about the key battles of the conflict. There have been lengthy biographies about important political figures of the revolutionary period such as John Adams, Benjamin Franklin, and Thomas Jefferson. But there have been very few works written about the ordinary soldiers of the Continental Army, America's first army, especially the enlisted men, the original grunts.

The First American Army is an effort to tell the story of the Revolution through the eyes of the common soldiers, not the generals. It is the story of eight men and their travails. Four of them—Elijah Fisher, John Greenwood, Ebenezer Wild of Massachusetts, and Jeremiah Greenman of Rhode Island—were enlisted men. I added a lieutenant, Pennsylvania's James McMichael, because he was a poet whose patriotic stanzas added much to the story. I selected a feisty thirty-five-year-old county militia captain, Sylvanus Seely of New Jersey, to explain the role of the militia units. I added a chaplain, the Reverend Ammi Robbins of Connecticut, and a physician, Dr. Lewis Beebe of Massachusetts, so that the reader could understand the spiritual and medical sides of the war.

Finding the men was not easy. Many generals and officers kept journals throughout the war, but few enlisted men wrote down their thoughts for posterity. Most of the enlisted men who did keep journals filled them with rather bland entries ("It rained . . ."). Very few infantrymen fought for more than one year, either, and I needed people who spent several years in the army to tell a complete story. I spent a long summer looking for ghosts of the American Revolution. I was lucky and found the extraordinary soldiers whose lives fill these pages. Only the diaries of Greenwood and Greenman were published in book form. Most of the others were published as magazine articles, some over one hundred years ago. Seely's journal was never published.

The book is the chronicle of each man's journey in the army, linked together to tell the overall story of the Revolution. As an example, the reader meets John Greenwood, the fifteen-year-old fifer from Cape Cod, at the battle of Bunker Hill in 1775. Greenwood's life is then recounted throughout the book as the reader encounters the other soldiers as they enter the story. All of the men move in and out of the volume as the history of the war unfolds. We see Greenwood participate in the invasion of Canada in 1775–1776, riding in a canoe alongside Benedict Arnold. We leave him to meet a remarkable pair of men, Doctor Beebe and Reverend Robbins, who become friends in the middle of the chaotic American retreat from Canada that winter during a terrible smallpox epidemic. We join Greenwood again with George Washington's army as it crosses the Delaware and makes history. He leaves the story but returns when he decides to fight the war on the high seas, not the battlefield. As he continually departs from the narrative, we pick up other soldiers' stories. Jeremiah Greenman, a private from Rhode Island, appears early when he joins the ill-fated invasion of Canada with Greenwood and is taken prisoner and held for nearly a year in Quebec. He comes back again at the bitter battle of Rhode Island in 1778 and in the hard winter of 1779–1780 at Morristown. The others follow that same revolving pattern.

The tales are never predictable. Greenman fought throughout the entire conflict and participated in many of its key battles, but he also trained one of America's first all-black military regiments, the First Rhode Island. The irascible Fisher joined the army right after the battles of Lexington and Concord and fought for eight years as a common infantryman, but spent a year as one of George Washington's bodyguards. Ebenezer Wild fought at Saratoga, Monmouth, and Yorktown and was so devoted to the army that he was one of the founding members of the Society of Cincinnati, the first veterans memorial group, at the end of the war.

Lieutenant McMichael of Pennsylvania, the poet, filled his journal with rhyming stanzas about patriotism. The real charm of this colonial Longfellow, though, was that he was married during the war and spent the rest of it doing anything possible to slip away to see his amorous young wife.

Finally, there was Seely, the head of the Morris County, New Jersey militia when the Revolution began. Seely, a married man with four children, was in love with the army, in love with the idea of independence, and, as his secret coded diary showed, in love with just about every woman he met. The story of his incessant womanizing, and the awful guilt that it brought, unfolding at the same time that he served as one of the most courageous militia leaders of the war, adds another dimension to this account of the first American army.

I then added entries from the diaries and journals of many other soldiers, mostly enlisted men, to complete the story of the battles of the war, the hard winters at Valley Forge and Morristown, and the army's constant struggle to survive.

Other than Dr. Beebe and Rev. Robbins, who became friends in the war, we do not know if the other men knew one another. We do know that they were often in the same battles. Seely's militia and Greenman's Second Rhode Island even fought side by side at Springfield. Their diaries give us fascinating views of these battles from the different perspectives of the men, amid much smoke and bloodshed. It should be noted, too, that these were humble men and I had to find other sources to fully report their courage under fire.

These were simple infantrymen. There was no brilliant political theory in the diaries of the men in this book and no majestic lines about republican government or the rights of man. The common soldiers left the oratory to Thomas Jefferson and Patrick Henry. But there was a constant call for independence and liberty. This is the story of brave men, the grunts of the first American army, who fought hard every day for a cause they firmly believed in and three main goals: 1) stay alive, 2) end the war to get home as soon as possible, and 3) kick the despised British out of the United States.

In doing that, for eight long years and against significant hardship, they not only won the war, but helped to create a unique democratic nation—the United States of America—that, despite all of its problems, has thrived as a model for freedom for the more than two hundred years since, thanks to them.

THE
FIRST
AMERICAN
ARMY

Chapter One

BUNKER HILL:
The Arrival of Private John Greenwood, Age Fifteen, Fifer

Early on the warm morning of June 17, 1775, British artillery in Boston and on Her Majesty's ships in the harbor opened fire on the Charlestown peninsula, north of the city. The peninsula contained the community of Charlestown, with its four hundred homes and some two hundred shops, warehouses, barns, and churches, plus three very high and large grassy hills, Bunker, the highest, Breed's, and Morton's. American troops had fortified Bunker and Breed's hills with earthworks, wooden fencing, and six cannon on the previous evening. General Thomas Gage, the commanding general in British-occupied Boston, was determined to clear the wide knolls to prevent the rebels from maintaining an elevated location where they would shell his army in the city or his ships in the harbor. An artillery pounding was to be followed by an afternoon attack of more than fifteen hundred troops.

Just after 1:30 p.m., a small navy of twenty-eight wide barges, each filled with more than forty armed British soldiers, and one transporting the man in charge of the operation, General William Howe, and his staff began to make its way across the harbor from Boston toward Morton's Point. As the ships moved through the water, the eyes of the men on board focused on Breed's and Bunker Hills.

At just over six feet tall, physically well-proportioned and able to remain calm under fire, the affable Howe cut an impressive military figure. He and his men landed and quickly realized that their cannon had the wrong-sized cannonballs and were inoperable. Howe sent the boats back for reinforcements and usable ammunition while the British navy and land artillery fired shells into Charlestown. The shells hit several of the wooden residences there, igniting small fires whose thick smoke drifted throughout the area. One shell hit a church steeple, setting it on fire, and it soon toppled into the street.

The British assault on the two hills was viewed by one of the largest audiences of civilians to witness any battle during the American Revolution. The British artillery had opened up earlier that morning and the cannonading awakened everyone. Hundreds of residents in Charlestown climbed to the tops of their homes and raced out into nearby streets and meadows to watch the fighting on the hills. In Boston, several thousand people stood on the roofs of their houses for a good view. Some climbed to the tops of churches. Hundreds more packed the wharves near the water where the view was clearer.

Somehow, it was Breed's Hill, a lower and less defensible knoll than Bunker, that the majority of the Americans wound up fortifying that day as the British continually shelled the area. The top of the hill was so elevated that the men there could see all of Boston's dozen or so church steeples. They could also look down on the mill pond, the north battery full of British cannon, Hudson's Point, and, barely, John Hancock's commercial shipping wharf, plus the tops of the masts of ships moored at the Long Wharf, on the other side of town. The provincial forces were led by General Israel Putnam, a veteran of the French and Indian War, and Colonel William Prescott. It was Prescott, the tall commander with the muscular build, developed from nearly twenty years of farming, who made most of the decisions. The esteemed Dr. Joseph Warren, sixty-nine, head of the Massachusetts Provincial Congress, had joined them as a volunteer in a rash burst of patriotism applauded by all.

Wrote James Thacher, a local doctor who was an eyewitness, "[The British] immediately commenced a tremendous cannonade from their shipping, their floating batteries, and from all their fortifications. Bombs and shot were incessantly rolling among the provincials during the forenoon 'til the Royal Grenadiers and light infantry could be prepared to make their formidable attack."[1]

Private Peter Brown, a company clerk in Prescott's Massachusetts regiment, had fought at Concord. He watched the sea of Redcoats in their immaculate uniforms swarm off the barges and prepare for the attack. It was an awesome sight. Brown wrote that the British had so many men that they appeared ready to surround the provincials. "They advanced toward us in order to swallow us up. But they found a choky mouthful of us, though we could do nothing with our small arms as yet for distance and had but two cannon and nary a gunner. And they from Boston and from the ships a firing and throwing bombs, keeping us down 'til they got almost round us."[2]

Howe ordered his men to march slowly in the direction of the newly dug breastworks on Breed's Hill. He sent the Royal Welch Fusiliers on a trot across a beach near the rear of the hill, toward a low stone wall and wood fence below the breastworks that seemed lightly defended because there was no firing coming from it.

Howe and his officers did not realize that Colonel John Stark and others had instructed their men behind the wall to withhold their fire until the Redcoats were close enough to hit with some accuracy. They were also instructed to shoot the officers to cause confusion and prevent orders from being heard.

When the intimidating Fusiliers, four abreast, bayonets fixed, trotted within fifty yards of the wall, the Americans opened up. The sound of the volley—it seemed that every musket was fired at once—could be heard throughout Boston.

The fury and force of the gunfire stunned the British. Stark had been right. At that close distance the muskets were lethal. Officers were hit and went down. The first line of men, instead of continuing up the slope toward the Americans, halted and tried to exchange fire with their muskets; this caused the second line to walk right into them. They were all easy targets for the Americans. Some of the British soldiers pitched forward, dead, and the men next to them fell backwards, musket balls lodged in their heads and chests, blood spurting everywhere. Those behind and around them were hit and killed or wounded and went down. Screams filled the air. Howe's vision of one single charge to drive the Americans off the hill and back to Charlestown evaporated in a roar of muskets, the air filled with the flames of the guns discharging and a rising cloud of smoke. Howe's own trousers were splattered with the blood of his men.

On the southern side of the hill, a similar outcome occurred as the Americans unleashed a thunderous musket volley that cut into the British army approaching the earthworks and the redoubt, a wooden wall that protected them. The British were decimated. Their regulars were not only easy targets, but Howe had so many of them, 1,550, and they were positioned so close together, that musket balls missing one soldier hit the man next to him or behind him.

The British were also advancing through grass that hid large rocks and deep holes. Soldiers tripped on the impediments and fell, sometimes bringing down those near them. Others tripped over their bodies as they tumbled. Their formations came apart in minutes and their legendary ability to maneuver on the battlefield was thwarted. As they tried to stand or help each other, they were hit with yet another volley of fire from the provincials behind the breastworks on top of Breed's Hill. Orders shouted by the English army officers were drowned out by the screaming of the wounded lying in the grass, the triumphant shouts of the rebels and the sounds of the muskets. Blood flew everywhere in the hot afternoon air and the British, shaken, retreated back down the hill.

The Americans had held. The enlisted men, especially, felt satisfaction in repulsing the first charge of the British up the slope with, as a spectator said with some pride, "a hot fire."[3] First Lieutenant Samuel Webb, fighting on Breed's, wrote that "cannon and musket balls were flying about our ears like hail" but that the Americans did not flinch and that, in fact, "our men were in fine spirits." Captain Samuel Ward, too, was proud of himself and his men, writing that he had been "where the bullets had flew several times without showing many marks of fear."[4]

Robert Steele, a drummer boy, wrote after that assault that "the conflict was sharp, but the British soon retreated with a quicker step than they came up, leaving some of their killed and wounded in sight of us . . . came up again and a second battle ensued which was harder and longer than the first. [There] was great noise and confusion."[5]

That was Howe's second assault, that he ordered with newly arrived Sir Henry Clinton, another general, at his side. The general had underestimated the Americans but he was certain that a second charge would succeed. It did not. His second attack only resulted in more dead and wounded British soldiers. A third charge was ordered late in the afternoon.

The third thrust up the hill was similar to the first two, but this time the British, with the right ammunition, used cannon that helped to soften American defenses. Again, the British were raked with a loud volley of musket fire followed by more throaty cheers from the Americans despite cannonballs exploding around them. Again, the English went down like red-colored dominos. On this occasion, earlier faulty planning caused the Americans to run out of ammunition and they could not continue to defend the hill. The Americans did not run out of powder slowly, but abruptly, moving a British officer to write with surprise that the provincial's fire "went out like an old candle."[6]

The British, with no resistance from the Americans, climbed to within the shadows of the redoubt, earthworks, and fences. The English, angry, were now the ones screaming in triumph. Colonel Prescott decided to abandon the fort to save his men from what he knew would be a massacre. He wrote, "The enemy, being numerous, surrounded our little fort, began to mount our lines and enter the fort with their bayonets."[7]

Out of gunpowder, the Americans fled amidst gritty hand to hand combat. Putnam unsuccessfully tried to direct them up to Bunker Hill, where others had waited. Then they also fled. Private Brown had stayed on Breed's until the last moment, and then departed. He wrote later, "I jumped over the walls and ran for about half a mile where the balls flew like hailstones and cannons roared like thunder."[8]

Those who viewed the action said the retreat was orderly and saw it as a great moral victory for the Americans, who had fought courageously all afternoon. The enlisted men firing away at the Redcoats that day believed that in killing 226 enemy soldiers and wounding another 828, nearly half the attacking troops, with far lesser losses of their own—140 dead, including Dr. Warren, whom the British contended was the head rabble-rouser in Massachusetts, and 301 wounded. They had showed both the country and the Crown that they were a resilient foe. "We . . . sustained the enemy's attacks with great bravery and resolution," wrote Amos Farnsworth, a corporal at Breed's, "and after bearing for about two hours as severe and heavy a fire as perhaps ever was known . . . we were overpowered by numbers and obliged to leave the entrenchment."[9]

And without enough gunpowder there was little more to be accomplished that terrible day. "Had our troops been furnished with a sufficient supply of ammunition, the enemy must have suffered a total defeat," wrote Thacher, who added that the battle built the confidence of the American troops and showed one and all that "we are favored with the smiles of heaven."[10]

The British agreed. One British lieutenant said that "the oldest officers say they never saw sharper action" and General John Burgoyne, watching the action from Boston, scoffed at the suggestion of a cowardly pullback. He noted that "the retreat was no flight; it was covered even with bravery and military skill." General Henry Clinton, who would be in America for six years, was glad to take the hills and get back to Boston without worse losses. He called it "a dear bought victory" and added that "another such would have ruined us."[11]

One of those at Bunker Hill that day was young John Greenwood, fifteen, a fifer who had returned to town to rejoin his family, whom he had not seen in two years. The Greenwoods were still in Boston, prevented from leaving by the British. Unable to see them, Greenwood had joined the army a few weeks before as a musician for the Twelfth Massachusetts Regiment. Captain T. T. Bliss had given him a pass to visit his aunt fifteen miles outside of Boston two days previously but, halfway there, his fife stuck in his pocket and sword dangling from his waist, the teenaged fifer had a premonition that something was going to happen in Boston. He alternately walked and ran back to the camp, sleeping at a farmhouse on the way.

"At dawn I heard the firing of great guns," he wrote in his memoirs of June 17, "which caused me to quicken my pace. I thought it was my duty to be there."

The fifer arrived at Cambridge Common, a mile from Breed's and Bunker Hill, amid unbridled chaos. "Everywhere the greatest terror and confusion seemed to prevail," he wrote. Greenwood headed through the scattered crowds of frantic, shouting residents, some on foot, some in carriages, and some reigning in their horses, and all of the wounded soldiers stumbling toward the common. Greenwood ran toward the slope of Breed's Hill while the battle was still in progress. He passed an African American soldier who had been badly wounded. "His collar being open and he not having anything on except his shirt and trousers, I saw the wound quite plainly and the blood running down his back," Greenwood wrote.

Greenwood asked the soldier if his wound hurt, and the man said that it did not and that once he had a bandage wrapped around his neck to stem the bleeding he would go back to the battle. The teenager had been frightened, but now a remarkable calm came over him. He wrote, "I began to feel brave and like a soldier from that moment, and fear never troubled me afterward during the whole war."

Greenwood left the wounded man and hurried toward Breed's Hill, looking for his regiment. In the tumult of the morning, he ran directly into his mother, who had been racing around the commons looking for him. His mother, who left Boston with a pass, begged him to return to his uncle's home on Cape Cod. "Don't go there," she said, looking toward Bunker and Breed's Hills. "You'll be killed!" Her son told her that he had to find his regiment and left.

Halfway to Breed's, he located the regiment, stationed on a road with two cannon. Captain Bliss, his commander, was surprised that the boy had returned. Greenwood explained that he had raced toward the action when he heard the sound of the guns in the early morning. The officer smiled down at him.

"I was much caressed by my captain and my company, who regarded me as a brave little fellow," wrote the teenager, whose morning amid the carnage at Bunker Hill began his long and dangerous journey as a soldier in the first American army.

Chapter Two

THE SIEGE OF
BOSTON, 1775–1776:
Private Greenwood Joins an Armed Camp

Private John Greenwood, one of the youngest enlisted men in the Continental Army, heard his first fife and saw his first British soldier at the same time. Like many Bostonians, he watched the arrival of two regiments of immaculately uniformed British regulars, the Fourteenth West Yorks and the Twenty-Ninth Worcesters. They came in their red coats and bright brass buttons at the city's Long Wharf on October 1, 1768, following a London decision to place troops there after the civil unrest of the previous few years.

The British regiments left their ship and assembled smartly on the wide, lengthy wooden pier with its long row of shops and warehouses and marched through town on the main thoroughfare, King Street, to the grassy field that served as the Boston commons. They were led by their regimental fife and drum band, which played martial music to impress the large crowd of colonial onlookers that had gathered to watch them parade to the commons.

The Bostonians, angry at their arrival, glowered at them as they walked by. In the groups of people scattered along the route to the commons stood young Greenwood, then just eight years old, who was fascinated by the men playing the high notes on the fife. He moved from block to block, following them along King and past Cornhill Street, winding his way between people or jumping up and down to see the band as it marched by.

Shortly afterwards, Greenwood obtained an old, rather tarnished fife. The long, slender instrument had a crack in it which he sealed with putty. He watched and listened to the British fifers on parade in Boston whenever he could and taught himself to play just by observing them. He became good enough to be taken in as a volunteer fifer with a local militia company. He was fifteen. While many of the men in the militia went through their routines monotonously, some there perhaps only for the beer that was served at the end of the day, the young fifer delighted in playing the tunes he had learned in music books he had purchased. The men enjoyed his music and nodded approvingly at him as he played while they drilled. The boy's love of fife music continued over the next few years, but his esteem for the British soldiers did not.

Samuel Maverick was a teenager who worked as an apprentice for Greenwood's father, a local dentist in Boston. The dentist paid Maverick small wages for his work in the dental office, but gave him meals and allowed him to live in his home, where he shared a bedroom with his son John. The two teenagers became fast friends. In 1770, Maverick, who loved to discuss politics, dined at the home of some teenaged friends, the Carys, and then went out. He and John's older brother Isaac approached troops gathered on King Street near the Customs House shortly after 9 p.m. but were separated. Maverick worked his way toward the front of the crowd that was harassing British soldiers. Residents shouted at the troops, some screaming "kill them!"

At the height of the dispute, when the frightened soldiers raised their muskets to threaten the crowd, Maverick shouted, "Fire away, you damned lobsterbacks!" They did. The musket fire killed Maverick and four others and sent fifteen-year-old John Greenwood spiraling into a deep depression over the loss of his close friend in what was quickly called the Boston Massacre by the press.[1] He not only grieved publicly, but was tormented in private. "After his death, I used to go to bed in the dark on purpose to see his spirit, for I was so fond of him and he of me," Greenwood wrote in his journal.

His father, who also experimented with early electrical inventions, was the son of a Harvard professor. He enrolled Greenwood in the city's prestigious North School, where he earned good grades. He was not in school for long, however, because his uncle asked his father to send John to live with him in Falmouth, a fishing community on the southwestern tip of Cape Cod. His uncle, a wealthy man, had recently become a widower and had no children. He needed someone to help him around the house and to run errands for his business. He also yearned for company.

The teenager arrived in Falmouth in the spring of 1773, a few months before the Boston Tea Party. He wrote, "The whole country at this time was in commotion and nothing was talked of but war, liberty or death; persons of all descriptions were embodying themselves into military companies and every old drunken fellow they found who had been a soldier was employed evenings to drill them."

Greenwood's uncle moved into one of the largest homes in Falmouth, a three-story wooden house on the south side of Middle Street, shortly after his nephew arrived. His uncle, who had grown to despise the Crown, became the lieutenant of a local Cape Cod militia company and brought his nephew along as the troupe's fifer. The boy joked that he was selected as the fifer because he was brave, healthy, and imbued with the military spirit. He added slyly that he was the only man or boy in Falmouth who knew how to play the fife.

Two years later, the men in the company, and everyone else on Cape Cod, learned of the battles at Lexington and Concord. Greenwood had not been home to Boston to see his family in two years. He wanted to return because he feared a war and was worried about the safety of his parents. "I was afraid [my parents] would all be killed by the British, for nothing was talked of but murder and war," he wrote in his journal.

His uncle was opposed to the idea, but Greenwood sneaked away early on a Sunday morning, his sword dangling from his belt. Greenwood walked one hundred miles from Falmouth to Boston, a journey of five days. Signs of war were everywhere. He followed the main highway, a narrow dirt road, that led from Falmouth northwest to Boston. It took him through small villages and past the fields of large farms toward the port city, occupied by approximately five thousand British troops. He recalled, "As I traveled through the different towns, the people were preparing to march toward Boston to fight."

Passersby marveled that such a young boy was walking all the way to the port where the Americans had the British trapped. One night on the road, he found himself in a crowded roadside tavern, playing tunes on his fife for the patrons. They sang along and toasted him with tankards of grog following numerous cheers for the men in the militia units that had surrounded the British. Waitresses moved quickly between the thick wooden benches where some sat to the square wooden tables with their brightly lit candles, the men banging their tankards on the tabletops as they belted out their time-honored choruses. Seamen sang songs of their voyages and others sang about men and their women. The crowd finally got around to inquiring about the young fifer who was serenading them with whatever type of music they requested. The room was becoming more and more heated as the men loudly lambasted the king and the Redcoats holed up on the Boston peninsula. And so was young Greenwood, who had explained earlier that he was headed to Boston to visit his parents.

"Why are you really going to Boston?" shouted one man. Greenwood, as aroused for war as the rest of them by that time late in the evening, put down his fife and yelled back, "To fight for my country."

All in the tavern roared their approval.

When he reached Boston, a bustling city of seventeen thousand residents, he discovered that his former hometown had become an armed camp. British soldiers occupied the city itself and the rebel army surrounded them, with headquarters in Cambridge. He was told he could not visit his parents, still living in Boston. Greenwood had landed in the middle of a nightmarish scene. General Gage had given approval for people to flee Boston, but there was no organization to the flight of the refugees. Some left by land, to the south, with their belongings packed in bags slung over their shoulders or stacked up in wooden carts. Others took the ferry to Charlestown that glided silently through the harbor.

The ferries were jammed with people and their possessions; the boats constantly threatened to tip over from the excess weight. Refugees included individual men and women, couples and families, some with animals, all carrying large trunks or tightly cinched canvas bags. There were so many people fleeing the port city—nearly half the population— that the overloaded ferries had to make runs all night, with their crowds of riders disembarking on docks shrouded in fog and darkness on the other side. No one knew where they would go next or when they could return to their homes. There were no plans to house them nearby.

Boston was a busy seaport in 1775, home to more than forty wharves and a dozen active shipyards. The city's vessels were involved in a profitable trade between England, Europe, and the Caribbean, with some ships bringing slaves to the southern colonies from the Caribbean. The city was the most sophisticated in America, with more than a dozen handsome churches; several theaters; a government house, Fanueil Hall, with its handsome brick and column exterior; prosperous Merchants' Row, a street along the waterfront jammed with three-story-high buildings; a good newspaper, the *Massachusetts Spy;* and more than two thousand homes and businesses. It was a city filled with popular taverns and hundreds of chimneys that could be seen for miles. The streets were filled with men on horseback, women in carriages, and workers with their small, horse-drawn carts.[2]

The city had become the colonies' leading shipbuilding port, the center of the Atlantic fishing industry, and North America's capital for hat making, the leather trade, distilled rum, hardware, and inexpensive furniture and carriages. Now it was a town under siege.[3]

The residents felt trapped. The city was under martial law and travel was severely restricted. The British army camped on the commons and commandeered warehouses, infuriating patriots. The editor of the *Pennsylvania Journal* called the Redcoats there "creatures" and wrote "the spirit which prevails among the [British] soldiers is that of malice and revenge; that there is no true courage to be observed among them."[4]

The town's loyalists constantly feared an attack by the rebels outside the city limits. One British sympathizer, Peter Oliver, wrote that "Our situation here, without exaggeration, is beyond description almost; it is such as eye has not seen nor ear heard, nor hath it ever entered into the heart of man to conceive Boston ever to arrive at . . . we are besieged this moment with ten or fifteen thousand men . . . all marketing from the country stopped . . . fire and slaughter hourly threatened and not out of danger from some of the inhabitants within of setting the town on fire."[5]

All was chaos.

Greenwood was told that many houses in Charlestown were vacant, abandoned by residents who had fled. He found one and slept there for several days, with others. One night he was in a crowded Charlestown tavern and was asked to play his fife by Hardy Pierce, the first corporal in Captain T. T. Bliss's company, after some soldiers saw the instrument sticking out of his pocket. He played several tunes, the music drowned out by the noise in the tavern, and the men were delighted. They brought him to the home of an Episcopal minister that had been commandeered as their regimental headquarters after the clergyman fled the city. The soldiers, and Captain Bliss, eventually convinced him to join their regiment as a fifer for an eight month enlistment at pay of eight dollars per month.

Most of the men in the American army slept in tents, but some, like Greenwood, were lucky. In addition to his eight dollars, Greenwood, probably because of his age, was allowed to live in the home of a local man who had left town and turned his residence over to the American army. Greenwood and several others shared a room, each sleeping on the floor with their knapsacks for pillows.

Another teenager, seventeen-year-old Elijah Fisher, from Attleboro, Massachusetts, whose six brothers all served in the war in some capacity, slept with others in the home of a local merchant named Nepven in

Jamaica Plains, four miles outside Boston.⁶ Many men were given quarters in rooms at different buildings at Harvard College. For others, luck sometimes ran out. Private James Stevens, of Massachusetts, like Greenwood, was fortunate to be given a small room in a Charlestown house for his quarters. Stevens returned from guard duty one evening, however, to discover that he had been kicked out of the room by an officer who decided that he wanted it.⁷

All of the soldiers, no matter where they lived, regretted the British occupation of Bunker Hill, territory won in the bloody June 17, 1775, battle. None saw it as a true triumph, though. As a Rhode Islander who witnessed the brutal fighting wrote a friend, they all believed that Bunker Hill was, in fact, a great victory for America. "If our people had been supplied with ammunition, they would have held possession most certainly. Our people are in high spirits, and are very earnest to put this matter to another trial."⁸

Bunker Hill was the only battle during the siege of Boston, but the Americans and British were engaged in constant skirmishes through the end of 1775 and in the winter of 1776. Detachments of troops from one side would be sent somewhere to do something—anything to draw attention—and soldiers from the other side would attempt to stop them. These mini-engagements were a part of Pvt. John Greenwood's life. One of the earliest came just after the British had seized control of Bunker Hill and hauled cannon to the top of it.

Several dozen British soldiers rowed ashore at Lechmere's Point to steal some cows, and a detachment of Americans, including Greenwood, was sent to stop them. They had to cross Willis Creek, waist-deep following several days of heavy rainfall, with their muskets held above their heads in order to reach the point. As soon as the men emerged from the creek, soaking wet, they were fired upon by British artillerists on top of Bunker Hill who had spotted them.

Greenwood wrote, "As eight or ten of us were in a huddle running up the hill, a ball from a twenty-four-pounder struck about three feet before me, driving the dirt smack in our faces. We ran on and just got down so as to get a shot at them before they pushed off."

The skirmish at Lechmere Point, won by the Americans when they later posted cannon there, was one of a dozen. One of the hottest occurred in late May, in the section of the Boston area known as Chelsea. The Americans were determined once again to retrieve livestock taken by the British. The Americans tried to sneak up on the British but were spotted. Pvt. James Stevens was caught like the rest.

"The (British) regulars saw our men and fired on them. The firing then began on both sides and the firing was very warm. There come a man and ordered us over a knoll right into the mouths of (their) cannon. We got on to the top of the knoll and the grapeshot and cannonballs came so thick that we retreated back to the road. Marched down to the ferry. The regulars shouted. Our men got the cannon and plastered them and gave them two or three gunsides. The firing then set in some measure and there was a terrible cry amongst the regulars."[9]

There were American attacks on British ships that attempted to land troops or to navigate Boston harbor near Charlestown. In one, General Israel Putnam ordered his men, hidden in a ditch, to wait until one ship, the *Diana,* and several accompanying barges were right in front of them before they opened fire. Their musket balls hit the schooner and barges like sheets of hail. One eyewitness said that the British "were engaged with great fury by our men along the shore." A few moments later, Putnam ordered two cannon nearby to fire on the *Diana.* The well-placed shot ripped into the sails and rope rigging of the ship, setting it on fire. The flames could be seen throughout Boston that night.

Greenwood recorded these daily skirmishes between the armies. The much vaunted Pennsylvania riflemen, as bored as everyone else as the occupation and siege dragged on, spent many nights taking potshots at British soldiers in the city, or anyone they believed to be a British soldier, or, sometimes, anything that moved. The marksmen did kill some soldiers and wounded others, but their aim was nowhere near as accurate as legend had it—and they all bragged—and they often shot up the homes of residents. One night a rifleman mistook another rifleman for a British soldier and shot him. One evening some artillerists lobbed shells at British fortifications in the town and a shell burst in a guardhouse, shearing the legs off of several of the ten Redcoats in it and badly damaging the legs of the others.

The British harassed the regiments of Greenwood and others in similar fashion, their regulars often firing at Continental Army sentries. Few were hit, but the shooting was relentless. One private, Sam Haws, reported that he was fired at by the "wicked enemy" just about every day that he worked as a sentry in August 1775. [10] Many of the nervous sentries, Greenwood said, bribed others into taking their post with half a pint of aniseed water, a popular liquid.

The British shot cannonballs at the Americans, too, but most of these did little damage. The cannon fire intrigued the young teenaged soldiers. Greenwood recalled, "The British were constantly sending bombs at us, and sometimes from two to six at a time could be seen in the air overhead, looking like moving stars in the heavens. These shells were mostly thirteen inches in diameter and it was astonishing how high they could send such heavy things. I have often seen them strike the ground when it was frozen, and bounce up and down like a foot-ball and again, falling on marshy land, they would bury themselves from ten to twelve feet in it."

Greenwood knew men who dug the shells, now with burned-out fuses, from the ground, ripped the fuses off, and poured the powder that was inside into kegs for musket use. Once a British cannonball arced through the night sky and landed right in front of a building housing Greenwood and about two hundred other men. One of Greenwood's teenaged friends in his company, Private Shubael Rament, seventeen, saw it coming through the air. He raced from the door of the building into the yard, stopping it as it rolled along the ground, and managed to pull the fuse out before it went off, saving the lives of the men inside.

Chapter Three

CAMP LIFE

L ife in camp outside of Boston was busy for Greenwood. George
Washington had been appalled at the disorder of both the men and
the camp when he first arrived, but within a month his tough discipline
and dozens of daily orders concerning construction and cleanliness had
turned the Boston camp into a military city. The men slipped easily into
routines that would be seen in every camp in every year of the Revolution. The enlisted men rose at dawn, and often before it when sentries
misjudged the rising of the sun. The days were filled with work, performed individually or in work gangs. Large and bulky earthworks of
dirt, stone, and wood, often constructed around camps, required long
weeks of labor.

Crews gathered and cut firewood throughout the war so that food
could be cooked and men kept warm. Huts and tents were frequently
repaired, especially during the fierce winters. Men who were quartered in
civilian homes, usually officers, were ordered to help keep those houses
clean and assist with chores. Men fed the thousands of horses that
accompanied the army. Enlisted men took turns standing guard over the
camp as sentries. Squads of men were sent to fish for food or to shoot

game. Soldiers from seafaring areas were asked to build small ships or whaleboats for transportation and battle. Some of the enlisted men cooked for the men in their homes or barracks—usually with one cook for every twelve men—and some were assigned as guards at hospitals.

All soldiers like to complain and the men of the first American army were no different. The enlisted men, who had joined what they thought was the military business, were especially unhappy toiling in construction. Later in the war, the soldiers at Morristown were ordered to spend much of their time building a huge earthworks fort to repulse a British attack that did not come in four years. The exhausted enlisted men, displacing tons of dirt, trees, and shrubs, mockingly nicknamed the structure "Fort Nonsense." One soldier involved in the construction of Fort Washington, in New York, sneered that the only wounds he had suffered during the entire war were eye inflammations from the dirt that flew into them as his shovel plunged into the earth.[1]

The Boston camp was a messy collection of badly built structures that lined crooked dirt lanes. Some men lived in private homes, some in tents, some in huts, and some in crudely formed stone, wood, and dirt enclosures. Some tents had boards for sides and some had canvas. Some huts were well built and some badly designed. Some held too many men and some too few. The construction of wooden barracks outside Boston, and huts later in the war, began as soon as Washington took command. Groups of men erected barns for horses and slaughterhouses for cattle. Artillery crews spent their day at first mounting cannon and then cleaning and maintaining them and practicing gunnery drills. Men sewed their tattered uniforms and those who had been tailors before the conflict assisted and supervised them. Cleaning crews dug, filled up, and maintained latrines. Some men drove wagons. In the early days of the war, the army sometimes loaned crews of enlisted men to the counties or villages where they were camped to help with necessary governmental work; many enlisted men were employed as workers to construct barns for towns.

In a unique labor system apparently used only during the Boston siege, commanders even permitted enlisted men to sell furniture or other things that they made in camp to civilians. Some made furniture for generals in return for favors. Private William Parker continued his shoemaking business in the military, producing footwear that he sold to soldiers.[2] Some men were even allowed to work for civilians in the community for a few weeks, walking back and forth from camp. The long-standing system of job-time swapping was honored, too, and many enlisted men had another do their work for them while they took the day off and swam or visited local women. Upon their return, at an agreed upon date, they worked the time of the man who had substituted for them.

Greenwood and all of the troops were drilled periodically during the day and much time was spent in the early months of the war simply training men how to load and fire muskets and maneuver with bayonets. Men attended prayers in the morning and in late afternoon when chaplains were on hand, usually led by one chaplain for each regiment. All were ordered to attend Sunday services and many went to those in nearby communities.

Hours were set aside for leisure. Ball games, such as lacrosse played by the Indians, proved popular and men competed against each other on the wide fields that surrounded the city. Washington saw so much merit in the ball games that he had men clear fields for them at every winter camp. Enlisted men engaged in wrestling matches in large, roughly hewn dirt areas. Sports fields were even cleared at Valley Forge. Many enlisted men, especially those from New England, delighted in ice skating on frozen ponds and rivers. Some went swimming in nearby lakes during the spring and summer. Shooting contests were allowed from time to time.

Men spent much of their time playing cards until this practice took up so much time and generated so many arguments that all gambling was outlawed in the winter of 1777. It was eradicated after a woman who permitted some soldiers to live in her Morristown, New Jersey, home reported that one of them had become ill during a card game and was placed in his bed by the others, who went back to their card game. Twenty-four hours later, she found the private dead and the men still playing cards, oblivious to his condition.

Men in the army indulged in a considerable amount of drinking, a common activity in colonial America. Beer and rum became a part of everyday life. The standard daily issue to the men included whiskey when available. It created substantial problems for the enlisted men throughout the war. Men in Greenwood's regiment and others often staged drinking contests, with predictable results. Winners and losers became quite ill. James Stevens wrote that in one legendary drinking contest in Boston on February 7, 1776, one man defeated the other by downing forty-four glasses of beer and then, an hour later, died of alcohol poisoning. One drunk private shot and killed another following a dispute in camp at Boston one evening. The ill-tempered assailant's stunning defense was that the shooting of the private was an accident; he was really trying to shoot the officer behind him.

Outside Boston, wives, girlfriends, relatives, and friends visited the soldiers in camp, sometimes staying at the nearby homes of friends for days. Some even lived with them. George Ewing's uncle James traveled to Valley Forge to visit him in 1777 and lived in his hut with him and another soldier for three days.[3] They brought extra food for the soldiers in the first American army, who quickly also became the first to complain about army food, as they have ever since. The women and friends also bought presents and clothing.

Many of the enlisted men maintained relationships with family and girlfriends far away by writing letters whenever they could. They looked forward to letters from home, too. Friends and family always asked how they were doing. Letters that arrived after a well-publicized and bloody battle usually were full of pleas for a letter back to assure family members, or wives and girlfriends, that their loved ones had not been hurt in the skirmish. An inordinate amount of correspondence that followed fierce battles, such as those that arrived in the days after the assault on Bunker Hill, started with the rather chilling line, "I realize that I may be writing to a dead man."[4]

The foot soldiers debated and greatly embellished every rumor that floated through camp, and there were many. Benedict Arnold had been killed. No, he had been taken prisoner. No, he had been taken prisoner and escaped. The British had hired twenty, forty, or fifty thousand Russian soldiers (pick any number) to help them fight the Americans. A huge

British force had secretly landed on the southern tip of Florida and had started to march up the Atlantic seaboard toward Boston (why any army would land in Florida to attack Boston, fifteen hundred miles away, was never questioned).

Some younger brothers mesmerized by the service eagerly agreed to take their older brother's place in the regiment for a few days as the brother returned home for a brief vacation, all authorized by lower-ranking officers. Joel Fisher once took his brother Elijah's place in Boston for two entire weeks.[5]

The men celebrated holidays in camp or by visiting the homes of fellow enlisted men. This was rather easy during the Boston siege since many of the enlisted men there lived in communities within thirty miles of the city and invited their friends for dinners at Thanksgiving and Christmas.[6]

The single men talked frequently about the lovely women they had met in whatever community near where the army had camped. Some in Boston were so mesmerized by the numerous beauties walking about the streets of Cambridge and Boston itself, across the harbor, that they watched them through the spyglasses that they were supposed to be using to track enemy movements.

If the girls made the men feel good, the chills of winter and various illnesses that were transported from one barracks to another did not. Some went to the doctors and were bled or given medicine that did little more than make them throw up. This medicine was so routine that one soldier wrote in his diary that he "saw the doctor and he gave me a puke."[7]

Other aspects of camp life were depressing, too. The men were called out for regimental funerals, and there were many. A long string of funerals for the men who had been killed at Bunker Hill in 1775 was followed by another wave of burials for those who had been wounded and finally died a few days or weeks later. Deaths in camp occurred prior to Bunker Hill, however. Men who had been shot in the battles of Lexington and Concord and cared for in the camp outside Boston died from their wounds and were buried. Men died of disease and the fevers that swept through the American camps that winter and in just about every winter. Some old men who had joined the service with great pride, in spite of their infirmities, died of old age, such as the patriotic James Frye, sixty-six, who insisted that his friends at home be told that he "died while in the Continental service." There were so many funerals that in June 1775, before Bunker Hill, the soldiers attended six in just three days. One enlisted man went to three in one day in the spring of 1776.

For many, the deaths they witnessed from bedsides in camp were the first they had ever seen. The experience unnerved a twenty-one-year-old chaplain, who described it in his journal in a shaky hand: "His breath was short. Sweat. And all of a sudden he contracted his body and it [distorted] the features of his face in a single, violent manner. He grinded with his teeth and his face turned black so fast, as if I could feel it. He vomited a large quantity of black water. Strangled. Nature Trembled. And he soon gave up the ghost at 6 p.m. I closed his eyes."[8] All of the men had to be wary of a new smallpox outbreak in Boston that took the lives of many citizens.

The enlisted men were called out by regiment and were sometimes joined by other regiments to witness a flogging of another enlisted man. Floggings, standard military punishment for a variety of crimes, occurred so frequently that men in the Boston camp attended them at least once a week, sometimes more often. Men were flogged for desertion, insubordination, falling asleep on guard duty, petty theft, and a variety of other charges. They were tied to wooden stakes or trees and beaten repeatedly with a heavy lash. Punishment ranged from a few dozen lashes to over one hundred.

The enlisted men sometimes had to witness the execution, by firing squad or hanging, of a multiple deserter or a man charged with other serious crimes, such as forgery, robbery, or spying for the enemy. The executions, which continued throughout the war, were not only designed to punish an offender, but to serve as preventative discipline for the entire army.

These events shook the men, but few of them believed that they would spend years of their lives witnessing them. Most were convinced that the American Revolution would be a very short war, perhaps just one large battle there in Boston, and then everyone, victorious, could go home. Virginia's Leven Powell told his wife to inform his business clients that he would be back soon. In a letter, he wrote, "It can be no great inconvenience for the people to wait for my return, which I expect is not far off."[9]

The men in the regiments of Greenwood and others sometimes annoyed each other, as men in any group forced to live and work together for long periods of time always do. Fistfights broke out between soldiers engaged in arguments and from time to time duels were threatened or actually fought by officers. Some men would steal clothing from others. Worse, men would steal the rifles of men in their own regiment. One man fumed when he heard that not only had someone stolen his rifle, but had sold it for five dollars in order to obtain money to gamble—and then lost the five dollars in a card game.

The men complained bitterly about their food. By order of Congress, each man's weekly food ration was supposed to consist of one pound of bread, one half pound of beef, one half pound of pork, or one and one quarter pound of beef if pork could not be had. Once each month the men were to be given one and one half pounds of fish instead of beef. For drinks, the allotment was one pint of milk and one pint of malt beer. Each man was also given six ounces of butter and one sixth of a pound of soap per week. The rations varied during the war and later molasses, cider, vegetables, rice, and Indian meal were added to the diet. Greenwood and others scoffed at what they were supposed to get whenever they looked down at the plates filled with the small, barely edible servings of the day.

The soldiers and officers in the militia units outside Boston, with no training or discipline, may have been long on bravado but they were not reliable. Washington was especially despondent about his officers. He was so upset about their quality that upon his arrival in Boston to lead the army he punished one colonel and five captains for cowardice and stealing money from their regimental budgets and court-martialed dozens of officers for other offenses.[10]

Even those who seemed so impressive upon their much anticipated arrivals, such as the raucous buckskin-clad riflemen from Pennsylvania, wound up disappointing the rest of the recruits in the army. They turned out to be chaotic bands of untamed frontiersmen who unnerved all who met them. They cursed throughout the day, drank as often as they worked, disdained the men from Massachusetts, and paid little attention to the rules of the newly created army. On two occasions in Boston a group of them charged a guardhouse and freed their compatriot Pennsylvanians who were incarcerated there. Emboldened by their success, the riflemen tried a third rescue, but Washington heard of it and surrounded the guardhouse with five hundred men, muskets loaded, and told them to shoot any riflemen who approached. None did.[11] One officer complained about them that "there never was a more mutinous and undisciplined set of villains that bred disturbance in any camp."[12]

The early days of the Continental Army, before Washington's arrival in June of 1775, may have been marked by soaring patriotism, but they were not filled with much administrative success in producing munitions or the development of a professional army encampment. There was very little gunpowder for any kind of a fight and at various times in the spring of 1775 men without powder for their muskets sharpened crude spears to use as substitutes for their guns if the feared British breakout from Boston took place.[13] Although there were numerous farmers and a large number of merchants in the army, no engineers could be found who could build usable earthworks and other battle fortifications. These skills were so lacking that General Charles Lee, who preceded Washington as the general in charge of American forces in Boston, quipped that "not a single man of 'em is capable of constructing an oven."[14]

Although some men knew how to load, fire, and care for muskets, others had never handled firearms before. This resulted in numerous accidents. One man held his musket a foot in front of him when he fired; the kick of the gun hit him in the chest and killed him. One man's musket misfired in a barracks and the ball sped through two sets of boards in wall partition, crashed through the wooden bottom of a bunk bed, went through the chest of a man sleeping there, killing him, and finally lodged in a chimney. On what one soldier called "an awful day," four men in one area of camp were badly wounded when guns went off accidentally.[15] At least one man in Boston stabbed himself to death while trying to mount his bayonet to his musket.[16] Another fell into a camp-fire and burned to death.[17]

The enlisted men shared many of the same hardships and com-plained about many of the same things that soldiers since the Persian wars had done and would do in the years to come. They all seemed to know short people who made up for their lack of height by trying to seem authoritative, sergeants with deep voices, happy drunks, and men who had apparently slept with every woman on the Atlantic seaboard. All had met bullies. Most were witness to a fistfight in camp. Someone always forgot the password of the day necessary to reenter the camp. Many loved to play practical jokes on others. All seemed to know some-one who had their tents burned in a campfire mishap. All enjoyed the spirits dispensed each day, any good food they could obtain anywhere, and an actual bed to sleep in after days of marching.

During their marches in the war most would, at one time or another, sleep in a field and sometimes wake up with snow on top of them. It seemed all, in some manner, had met British enlisted men, usually pris-oners of war, and while they hated them as the enemy, seemed to like them as people, especially teenaged British soldiers.

In the view of the soldiers, clothing was always badly stitched, mus-kets poorly made, ammunition always in short supply, orders never clear enough. They complained bitterly that on many of their marches they wound up in the same place where they started. They hated work designed merely to fill time. It would always be too cold in winter and too hot in summer.

The men all enjoyed devouring the honey they were sometimes able to obtain from local farmers in summer, appreciated any free mending of their tattered uniforms from older women, and any flirtatious look they received from younger ones. They often made fun of their officers, telling jokes about them or offering their comrades impersonations designed to make the officers look ridiculous.

There was a social, intellectual, and military divide between the enlisted men and the officers. In Europe, some noblemen became officers and their distinguished station in life made them superior to the enlisted man who joined the army as a career or who were drafted. There were a few nobles in the British army, such as Lord Cornwallis and Lord Rawdon, or sons of lords, such as Lord Richard Howe, but their officers had come from important families in the merchant class, families that had always enjoyed impressive social standing in British society. They, too, considered themselves above the ordinary men they commanded.

The American officer was quite different. The officers, like the men, heralded the new, independent nation they were fighting for, but saw their sudden appointment as a captain or major as immediate entry into a "new" social order in America. Some had been members of the wealthy upper class, especially the southerner planters who had become rich off slave labor, and some had come from prosperous mercantile and shipping families in the New England and Middle Atlantic states. Many, though, had simply been elected by their men or appointed by Congress or state legislatures and had this elite life thrust upon them. They embraced it because, all of a sudden, someone was paying attention to them.

The American officers rarely fraternized with the enlisted men in camp, on the march, or anywhere else off the battlefield. That was because, many of the enlisted men charged, they spent much of their time lobbying for promotions, feuding with others whom they did not see fit for command, complaining of constantly being overlooked when colonels and generals were named, engaging in duels with each other to satisfy personal honor, and becoming embroiled in disputes with townspeople, merchants, and farmers over unpaid debts.

Almost none the officers had ever been leaders of men before and knew nothing about their responsibilities. Most were young, some twenty or twenty-one, and younger than many of the men they commanded. They had no military training. They failed to follow orders to help drill their men, visit the sick, check on firearms, or supervise men who were supposed to clean their regiment's area of the camp. They were highly ineffective commanders and often performed badly in battle.

One twenty-one-year-old officer, John Lacey, defended himself by reminding critics that "we were all young and in a manner unacquainted with human nature, quite novices in military matters, had everything to learn and no one to instruct us."[18] Colonel William Richardson, of the Fifth Maryland Regiment, agreed that his junior officers were novices, but sneered that they were "but few removes from idiots."[19]

The enlisted men, who had their own jobs to fill up their days and nights, left the officers to their own lives. The privates, corporals, and sergeants did what they were told to do, but ignored the officers during much of the war except when they needed their assistance in obtaining furloughs to go home to visit their wives and family. At times, the officers and the enlisted men of the Revolution seemed like two different kinds of soldiers in two different armies.

The enlisted men never missed an opportunity to poke some good-natured humor at their superiors and the army itself, even if their barbs might land them in trouble. Some spoke to officers sarcastically. One sergeant, Joseph White, a teenager, even had the audacity to have some fun about the officers and army with George Washington himself.

White's commander sent him to Washington's headquarters with an urgent message and ordered him to deliver it personally to the commander in chief. Washington was standing with his wife Martha when White was ushered into the room. The general read the message and then looked up at White.

"What officer are you?" he said.

"I am the assistant adjutant of the regiment of artillery," answered young White proudly.

"Indeed," Washington said, "you are very young to do that duty."

White looked straight at the sharply dressed General, at six foot three and over two hundred pounds a towering presence, and told him that while that was true, in the army he was growing older every day. A wide smile, one of the few the men ever saw, spread across Washington's face and he let White go.[20]

Soldiers who became unhappy with the service went home when their terms were up, refusing to reenlist, blithely assuming that others would take their place. This practice began at the very beginning of the war, at the end of 1775, when half of the nearly twenty thousand soldiers went home when their time expired.[21] This practice confounded Congress and the generals and the troops who stayed, many of whom hissed at the groups of those returning home as they left camp. Others unwilling to wait until their time ended simply left camp as deserters, seeing no harm in it. Men deserted individually, with friends, or with small groups. They took their belongings, and sometimes their muskets, with them. No one stopped them as they marched home to Pennsylvania, Connecticut, Virginia and other states. Some even deserted to the enemy.[22] "We shall not, with all our rhetoric, be able to maintain many," Colonel Jedediah Huntington complained to his brother Jabez in November 1775.[23]

The delegates to the Continental Congress knew that the army they had raised to lead America to its promised land was beset with problems within months of its formation and that the patriotism that followed Lexington had ebbed. As early as October 1775, John Adams and other delegates found themselves bombarded with complaints about the military. He wrote to one of his state's generals, "It is represented in this city by some persons and it makes an unfriendly impression upon some minds that in the Massachusetts regiments there are a great number of boys, old men, and Negroes such as are unsuitable for the service and therefore that the Continent is paying for a much greater number of men that are fit for action or any service."[24]

Delegate Silas Deane, his desk drawer full of complaints too, wrote to his wife that "the behavior of our soldiers has made me sick, but little better could be expected from men trained up with notions of their right of saying how and when and under whom they will serve."[25] John Hancock, the president of Congress, summed up the feelings of most about the behavior of the army in a letter to the leaders of the colonies to tell them that "the situation of the army is alarming."[26]

But Congress also understood that the men had surrendered much and been given little in return. The delegates noted with pride, too, that there were soldiers just fifteen years old, such as John Greenwood, who were willing to die for their country. All of the enlisted men had their thanks. New Hampshire delegate Josiah Bartlett reminded congressional colleagues that the men faced "almost insuperable difficulties" and said in the spring of 1776 that "instead of wondering that we are in no better situation than at present, I am surprised we are in so good."[27]

Chapter Four

MOTHER AND SON REUNION

The problems of the commander in chief and the Continental Congress were far from the mind of John Greenwood, who reenlisted. His major problem was finding a way to sneak into Boston to locate his parents, especially his mother, whom he had seen just briefly on the morning of the Bunker Hill battle when she had shrieked at him to run away.

Greenwood's efforts to see her again, and to reunite with his father, were thwarted because of the travel prohibitions. What the teenaged soldier did not realize, however, was that his mother was right there in Cambridge. On the day before Bunker Hill, when he last saw her, Mrs. Greenwood had obtained a pass from the British to visit the American camp to search for her son, whom she heard had recently arrived. She took hidden money with her to pay anyone she could find to serve in Greenwood's place as a substitute. Terrified that her son would be killed or wounded, she intended to talk her youngster into going back to Falmouth, where he could stay with his uncle and where he would be safe.

Mrs. Greenwood had not returned to Boston after the battle of Bunker Hill because of the chaos and new travel restrictions, this time imposed by the Americans. She had actually been living in Cambridge for six weeks, at a friend's home, and spent her days there in sheer misery because men in the army had told her that they knew for a fact that her son had been killed at Bunker Hill in one of the ferocious British assaults. The few inquiries she had made turned up no sign of her son and, relying on information from soldiers she considered to be well informed, she drifted into prolonged mourning.

In mid-July, however, Mrs. Greenwood met Sergeant John Mills of Connecticut, who told her that her son was very much alive and living on the other side of Charlestown. An hour later, John Greenwood wrote, he was standing in front of his tent, staring out at the camp, when he heard joyful screams nearby. He wrote, "Who should I see but my mother, coming toward me in the company of Sergeant Mills."

An emotional reunion of mother and son followed, but Mrs. Greenwood could not stay. She had managed to obtain a pass from General Washington himself to return home to Boston earlier that day and had to leave right away. Mrs. Greenwood walked to Bunker Hill, where she was admitted to the fort after showing her pass, and was then introduced to a British officer, Major John Small, whom she told friends was quite friendly. She was transported to her home and then she asked Small to take her to see General Gage.

It is unknown why she wanted to see Gage. As soon as she walked into his office his aides peppered her with questions about the size of the American army and its weapons and supplies. She apparently abandoned the conversation she planned to have with the British general under the barrage of queries. Angry that the officers were trying to pry information out of her, she snapped at Gage about his soldiers, "We are ready for them any time they choose to come out and attack us!"

She had reacted as a patriot, and as any mother of a soldier. Mrs. Greenwood was, however, a lone American Daniel in the middle of a Redcoat lion's den. The officers were incensed at her reply and shouted at her, but Gage paid them no heed. He just waved them out of the room and told her to return to her home.

Greenwood and the rest of the men in the army were eager to attack the British army. "For danger, we knew none," Greenwood bragged. Washington wanted to do so badly and planned an attack across the harbor at night, but his generals vetoed the idea.

In the winter of 1776, Washington decided that he could use a battery of cannon to shell the British from Dorchester Heights, a peninsula south of Boston that looked down at the city across the harbor he faced. The army did not have many cannon and none large enough to fire heavy cannonballs that far.

To the rescue came the improbable Henry Knox. The portly Knox, who weighed close to two hundred eighty pounds, had been a bookseller before the war and had read, he claimed, just about every book ever written on artillery. He had become head of the Continental Army's artillery and told Washington that he would go to Fort Ticonderoga, in New York, with a regiment of men and transport the guns there to Boston. To do so, Knox and the soldiers had to move cannon out of the fort, cross Lake George on boats, cross the Hudson River, and take the field pieces nearly three hundred miles in winter, over snow covered roads and in severe weather. It seemed like a task of Biblical proportions, but Knox and his men did it. Using forty-two wooden sleds, eighty yoke of oxen, and a small fleet of ships, Knox transported the guns from Ticonderoga to Boston in less than three weeks and gave Washington his needed firepower.

Washington ordered the cannon, protected by hundreds of bales of hay, placed on the heights in the middle of the night so that the men doing the work would not be seen and wind up as targets for British sentries. It was an enormous job undertaken on the evening of March 4. The completion of the work took three thousand men under General John Thomas, laboring all night, but by the first light of morning the hill was completely fortified.

Greenwood was on the heights that next morning, peering down at Boston across the water, a target he believed would be rather easy to shell for the more than two dozen guns Knox had mounted on the hills. The

British were wary of the guns as soon as sentries spotted them after the sun rose that morning. They felt like sitting ducks. The English planned to storm Dorchester Heights in a flotilla of small boats, but an unforeseen storm arose on the night of the invasion and they had to give up the assault. Greenwood had looked forward to an attack. He wrote, "If they had succeeded in landing they would certainly have been overpowered, for it was a steep hill and the Americans had a number of hogsheads and barrels filled with sand to roll down upon them, and intended to sally out of the fort upon them when in confusion and they would have liked no better fun."

The British did not like the "fun" the Americans provided on the night that their insulting play, *Blockade of Boston*, written by General Burgoyne, was staged in January at their fort on top of Bunker Hill. The British army presented the drama to mock the American forces, but there was an extra, unwritten act in the script.

As the play commenced at about 9 p.m., Greenwood, fife in his waistband, was summoned along with fifty other men to march silently along a causeway belonging to Charlestown mills that ran beneath the fort. When most of Charlestown was burned on the day of the Bunker Hill battle, about ten or twelve damaged houses had been abandoned by their owners. Sutlers, homeless people, and camp followers, including people who sold merchandise to British soldiers, had moved into them. The plan was to attack the homes while the British army's amateur thespians were busy with their play and not paying much attention to anything else. Only a few men were left to stand guard over the neighborhood.

Greenwood wrote, "We surprised the sentries, took a number of prisoners, and set fire to these houses right under their very noses, the enemy at the fort being so astonished as not to fire for some time, at least not until the houses were in a light blaze."

Ironically, the fires became visible right at the key moment in the play at the fort up above. In the drama, a Yankee sentinel, dressed as a tailor with paper measures hanging over his shoulders and his large shears sticking out of his pocket, rested upon his musket. He was talking to another Bostonian and looking out toward the harbor. A British sergeant, spotting the fire, ran on to the stage and shouted, "To arms! To arms! Gentlemen, the rebels are upon us!"

Everyone assumed that the sergeant was part of the play; they cheered lustily but did not move from their seats. "The audience clapped their hands stoutly because he did so well, and it was some time before he could make them understand it was no sham. When they did, however, they tumbled downstairs, over one another, as fast as they could and broke up the Yankee play," Greenwood recalled.

Unable to storm Dorchester Heights and certain that his men could not survive continued artillery bombardment from the cannon stationed there, General Howe, who had succeeded Gage in charge of the army in Boston on October 10, 1775, decided to depart from the city and sail to Halifax, Canada, to develop a new strategy. He did not want his ships fired upon as they left. Howe struck an agreement with Washington that the British would not set fire to Boston, as they had threatened, if the Americans would let them sail away unmolested.

Newspaper editors throughout the colonies hailed the March 17, 1776, withdrawal. Wrote an editor of the *Pennsylvania Evening Post,* "This morning the British army in Boston, under General Howe, consisting of upwards of seven thousand men, suffering an ignominious blockade for many months past, disgracefully quitted all their strongholds in Boston and Charlestown, fled from before the Army of the United Colonies, and took refuge on board their ships."[1]

Bostonians, Greenwood, and thousands of other soldiers, including Private Jeremiah Greenman, who had just arrived with a Rhode Island regiment, and Elijah Fisher, who had survived Bunker Hill, watched with great satisfaction as the huge fleet of British ships raised their anchors at 9 p.m. and, their wooden hulls creaking, slowly sailed out of the harbor. The Bostonians who lined the streets and heights of the area were hoping that they were free of the hated Redcoats forever. One of them, Boston councilman Timothy Newell, wrote with satisfaction, "Thus was this unhappy distressed town (through a manifest interposition of divine providence) relieved from a set of men whose unparalleled wickedness, profanity, debauchery, and cruelty is inexpressible." Many saw their departure as an achievement for the Continental Congress. Others, such as a local minister, the Rev. Manasseh Cutler, viewed it as more than that. He saw the exodus of the Redcoats as a sign from above. "It was like the flight of the Assyrians," Rev. Cutler told friends, "It was the Lord's doing and is marvelous in our eyes."[2]

Some soldiers were hopeful that the British army would be seen no more, but Washington believed that the English would be back, if not in Boston then somewhere else, and that the American Revolution would not end until one army had soundly defeated the other in a single, bloody battle.

That was not to be for some soldiers, such as privates Greenwood and Greenman. Most of the army would be sent to the New York City area, where Washington was certain the British would strike. Greenwood and Greenman, however, would not march with them. They would embark on a perilous expedition to Canada that would bring them face to face with British forces and Indian warriors in a strange land and plunge them into one of the most dreadful nightmares in American history.

Chapter Five

THE SOLDIERS
The War

*B*y the spring of 1775, the tension between the American colonists and the
British Crown had been growing for more than a decade, ever since the
end of the French and Indian War in 1763. To cover the cost of that war and
protect the American colonies from any more conflicts, Parliament insisted
that the colonies pay higher taxes and permit the soldiers of the British army,
with their bright red coats, shiny black shoes, and haughty attitudes, to
occupy America.

The residents of the colonies that stretched along the Atlantic seaboard from
Maine to Georgia, three thousand miles from England, believed that they had
created a vibrant country of their own since the time their British ancestors
arrived at Plymouth, Massachusetts, and Jamestown, Virginia, in the early days
of the seventeenth century. Over more than one hundred fifty years, the colonists
had developed comprehensive legal, economic, and social systems. They had created their own courts, state assemblies, county governing boards, and schools
and had dozens of good newspapers. America had become a trading giant, buy-
ing and selling with England and other European powers. In addition to the
Roman Catholic and English Anglican religions, the colonies now supported the

breakaway Methodist, Baptist, and Presbyterian churches. The population of the colonies had grown continually and by 1770 stood at 2.15 million, nearly double what it had been a generation before.

Yet the Crown had little use for the Americans' treasured institutions and would not let the colonies enjoy any voting representation in Parliament. The colonists, given a little democracy by the Crown through self-governing assemblies and independent courts, constantly sought more and English leaders did not like that at all. Starting in the 1760s, Parliament passed harsh new laws to raise taxes, curtail colonial commerce, and curb political freedom to keep the Americans in line. The Stamp Act of 1765 required all newspapers and legal documents to be taxed via a stamp that had to be affixed to them. The Iron Act forbid American manufacturers from selling carriages, plows, and kitchen utensils in England. The Revenue Act of 1764, better known as the Sugar Act, placed a tax on molasses, rum, coffee, and wine. The Currency Act outlawed American paper money. The Townshend Acts of 1767 authorized taxes on tea, glass, paper, and other goods. Those acts also introduced a new tax to pay for the costs of the British army occupying America. There were even taxes on new doorknobs.

Some royal governors sneered at colonial assemblies and shut them down when they did not approve of their legislation, infuriating the colonists. The presence of British soldiers also annoyed the colonists, especially after a group of them shot and killed five Americans in Boston in 1770 in what the newspapers called the Boston Massacre.

The angry Americans felt that their economy was being crushed and their freedoms taken away—they were becoming slaves to England. They fought back. Thousands participated in boycotts of British goods and most newspapers refused to obey the Stamp Act, which had to be rescinded. The protests reached a crescendo one night in 1773 when a radical group, the Sons of Liberty, dressed as Mohawk Indians, boarded the Dartmouth, *a cargo ship in Boston harbor, and tossed its more than three hundred crates of tea into the water in the Boston Tea Party.*

British revenge was swift and harsh. Parliament passed the Intolerable Acts that further curbed freedoms and shut the port of Boston, a crippling blow to New England's economy. Americans immediately denounced the

Crown from the bustling cities to the small villages that dotted the country. People berated King George in small taverns and in large assembly halls. Some men, such as Virginia's George Washington, took charge of armed militia companies and trained them for war. Others formed Committees of Safety, secret organizations that would aid any such rebellion.

In England, the king and parliamentary leaders insisted that their actions from 1763 to 1775 had been temporary and necessary, but the Americans saw them as the precursors of even more draconian steps to destroy the new, democratic social order they had spent so many years creating. They would not give it up. Many felt, too, that, geographically, more than three thousand miles from London, they were a separate country anyway. They believed that they were a religious people and that God wanted them to free themselves from the motherland. Americans insisted fervently that they were a virtuous people who could create a virtuous nation. The British, they charged, were immoral and corrupt and no longer had the right to rule them. Their economy was surging. Who really needed England anymore?

And, too, many of them believed that they were being borne along on the currents of history and that, as Thomas Paine put it with such elegance, "time hath found us." If a war was needed to validate this virtuous land, many said, let it come. If families had to be shattered, businesses ruined and even if lives had to be given up for American freedom, so be it. None said it better than the fiery red-haired Patrick Henry when he stood in a Virginia hall and shouted, "Give me liberty or give me death."

The British never understood the anger that permeated America and the colonists did not understand the need for the Crown's stranglehold on them. Both were headed for a showdown. It arrived on April 19, 1775. British general Thomas Gage learned that the colonists had secretly stored weapons and ammunition in the tiny Massachusetts village of Concord, outside of Boston. Nearly nine hundred British troops were dispatched to seize this arsenal. The night before, silversmith Paul Revere and others rode through the countryside to warn residents of Concord, and other communities, that the British would be coming the next day. A company of armed local minutemen confronted the British regulars on the village green in the town of Lexington as the king's troops tried to march through it on their way to Concord. A single shot was fired by someone—no one knows from which side—the "shot heard round the world," and a battle followed, with the Redcoats chasing the Americans off the green. The British then continued to Concord, where they were engaged in another heated battle with militia. This time, the British fled and began a long march back to Boston, harassed by the militia all the way. The Americans, firing from behind buildings, trees, and stone walls, inflicted 273 casualties, with 72 dead, on the English force.

The American Revolution had begun.

The battles of Lexington and Concord, reported in colonial newspapers throughout the Atlantic seaboard, galvanized many Americans against the Crown. At the behest of Massachusetts leaders, thousands of men, young and old, left the security and comfort of their homes in the cities and on farms and joined local militia units. The formation of these companies was greeted with celebrations. In Williamsburg, Virginia, an afternoon of festivities was capped by a parade of soldiers attended by hundreds of cheering residents of the state capital. The editor of the leading newspaper in the colony wrote that Virginians were happy "that the domination of Great Britain was now at an end, so wickedly and tyrannically exercised for these twelve or thirteen years past."[1] These militia units then marched to Boston, where an army of nearly twenty thousand men was gathering to force the British out of the busy port city. There, under the command of several generals and later George Washington, the newly appointed commander in chief, these men became the first American army.

The militia companies were raised locally and were not national units like today's army. Residents of the same town or county joined the same militia troop, along with cousins who lived nearby. Friends and men who worked in the same stores or farms joined up together. The men went to war in their own crude uniforms, carrying their own muskets. The leader of their militia was not appointed by superior officers or strangers, but elected by his own men. The officers came from all walks of life. One British army lieutenant, accustomed to professional soldiers serving as officers, was astonished that among a group of American prisoners he found a blacksmith, hatter, butcher, tanner, shoemaker, and tavern-keeper.[2] The army included fathers and sons, cousins and siblings. All six brothers of the How family of Methuen, Massachusetts—David, Jonathan, James, Jacob, Isaac, and Farnham—enlisted at the same time.[3] The units, with popular homegrown leaders, quickly came to represent the people of a county and, collectively, the new United States in the eyes of the American people.[4] The British did not find themselves facing a professional military force, but a true people's army.

The first American army was a sight to behold as it grew at the perimeter of Boston. Men from all over the New England states poured into the army camp. Huge tracts of white tents, brightly illuminated by campfires in the evening, expanded every day as more men arrived. Some crusty forty- and fifty-year-old veterans of the French and Indian War trudged into camp, their old uniform coats and breeches a little too tight on their frames, and regaled the men with their old war stories. Wide-eyed teenaged boys, seated around campfires, listened to them with rapt attention. Everyone was ecstatic over the arrival of the bands of swaggering riflemen, in their frontier buckskin shirts, who had become legends for their marksmanship and lust for a fight. Townspeople in Connecticut, Rhode Island, New Hampshire, Vermont (then a part of New Hampshire), and the other New England states marveled at the sight of newly formed militia groups marching smartly down their roadways in the early morning, the men shouldering muskets and tucking pistols into their belts, bragging to each other about the quick destruction they would unleash on the British.

These militia units would double and triple in size as they approached the greater Boston area. Farmers watched soldiers walk down the road alongside their fields and, moved by their patriotism, dropped their rakes and hoes, kissed their wives and children goodbye, went to their houses, fetched their muskets, and ran after the army, joining the rear echelon as it moved along. Merchants in small towns, equally moved, did the same, dragging old muskets that had not been fired in years out of their closets and slinging them over their shoulders after bidding their families farewell.

Tiny bands of musicians, usually with very young drummers and fifers, serenaded the men with songs, both old and new. Enormous colorful banners filled the air, along with the throaty cheers of the men after innumerable toasts with ale. It was a time of heady anticipation.

It was a brand new army for a brand new country. It was a very different fighting force than the British army, with its perfectly turned-out soldiers standing ramrod straight, always in a precise formation, the carefully molded products of some of the best training in the world. The rebels formed an army of men from most of the colonies determined to win independence from the mother country. It was a military force that, at its best, would fight against tyranny just as other American armies would do so again and again over the next two hundred years. It was an untrained army that would rely on sheer courage, determination, grittiness, and amazing resourcefulness to not only survive, but to prevail. It was an army, the men outside Boston believed in the spring of 1775, as America would always believe, that was fighting for freedom and justice for all.

It was an army, however, cobbled together with soldiers from crowded seaports and pastoral valleys, that would rapidly become an enigma. The soldiers in the new American army, especially in the first two years of the revolt, acted in ways that dumbfounded their commanders and neighbors alike. The men who signed up to overthrow the yoke of the tyrannical King George III would fight masterfully one day and amateurishly the next. They would engender admiration and scorn from the British on the same morning. They would be belittled by their commanders on the same day for their bad behavior off the battlefield that they were extolled for their bravery on it. The men of the Continental Army and the militias that supplemented them would be sometimes brilliant and sometimes just awful. Its men would at times show unparalleled heroism in fights that would live in history and at other times disappoint all who knew them. They would spend ten minutes discussing a crucial battle but all week arguing over one dollar that another soldier owed them. They would be hailed as heroes one day and denounced as liars, embezzlers, forgers, and scoundrels the next. The military force that began to form in Massachusetts, greeted with cheers from the residents, would turn out to be an army that would delight and confound the republic, often at the same time.

It was an army of men who were uncertain what the future held for them and did not know where the vicissitudes of war would take them next. The soldiers' anxieties were well summarized by Joseph Bloomfield, an officer of the Third New Jersey, who made out his will just after he enlisted. On his birthday, October 18, 1775, he wrote in his journal, "This day is my birthday, being twenty-three years of age, old enough to be better and wiser than I am. This day twelve months ago I was engaged in my profession of the law enjoying the calm sunshine of a peaceable quiet and easy life. Now I am five hundred miles from my native place amongst strangers and exposed to all the hardships and fatigues of a soldier's life, no ways settled, not knowing where I may be destined next week."[5]

The new army of the United Colonies, as the country was called in the first year of the war, impressed the residents of Boston and the colonial representatives who gathered at the second Continental Congress in Philadelphia in 1775. They boldly predicted that an army of seventy-five thousand volunteers would be recruited within months. And then, congressional delegates predicted, the Americans would win independence in a brief clash. All appeared to agree with John Adams, who gave a toast early in the rebellion for "a short and violent war."[6]

The American army never grew to seventy-five thousand men. Washington's force of nearly twenty thousand men in Boston was about as large as it became, except for a slight swelling in size in the rather quiet autumn of 1778. Washington's main army was usually between ten and thirteen thousand men, with several thousand or so in units under other generals, but few men stayed the length of the war. They were continually replaced by others and, over the course of the eight year conflict, approximately two hundred fifty thousand Americans served in the army. That represented nearly half the adult men in the country, an astonishing percentage.[7]

The army did not impress its commander, Washington, though, who saw nothing more than a collection of untrained, undisciplined, and ill-equipped men who did not know what they were getting them-selves into by confronting the British. He was worried that the men would be unable to face the enemy with much order and that their lines would collapse under what he knew would be ferocious assaults by the Redcoats with their glistening bayonets and thundering cannon.

He was right. Many of the strengths heralded by civic leaders, min-isters and newspaper editors turned out to be weaknesses. The home-grown nature of the different militia units provided as much trouble as it did virtue. Because the militia captain was selected by his friends and neighbors, he was often quite lax in maintaining order among those whose companionship he cherished prior to the war. Some militia even had bylaws that forbid punishments by the captain.

Unrestricted drinking created unruliness in the ranks and was unchecked by the hometown officers. The public areas of camps were messy; stacks of garbage and old food could be found everywhere. Men ignored the common latrines and relieved themselves wherever they chose. This practice became so prevalent that the mayor of Philadelphia complained in 1776 of the local army barracks that they were "as dirty as a pigsty, with ordure in cellars, outhouses, yards, etc. the stench of which is intolerable."[8]

The farmers and merchants had no military training upon arrival and many did not believe they needed any. Soldiers rebelled at the drills that they were forced to undergo, certain that their ability to shoot scamper-ing squirrels with their bulky rifles in the forest was all the skill they needed. As their friends and ministers had told them repeatedly, many believed that the war would be over and the British chased back to London, their tails between their legs, within a few weeks. Why train? All were reluctant to take orders from their local leaders, their friends, and were certainly in no mood to take them from newly arrived colonels and generals, all strangers, some from states very far away and some with British accents.[9]

The militiamen loathed the mundane and often distasteful work that camp life required, such as repairing huts, mending canvas, building fires, completing precision drills, or cleaning latrines, and they hated the brand-new discipline imposed upon their lives even more. They resented the higher accord in the army given to their captain, higher pay for the officers, and the lesser punishments meted out to officers for a common offense, such as stealing wooden fence rails from local farmers to make fires. Their resentment grew as the army grew and all whined when new orders forced them to scramble out of their tents at 4 a.m., before sun up, to dress, eat, and then work until nearly noon.[10]

The men in the state militias often squabbled among themselves. Men from city militias balked at living next to men from rural units. Ethnic groups resented each other. Men from the middle states mocked men from New England. There was considerable resentment early in the war that Congress often replaced Massachusetts men with Virginians, giving the army an unbalanced southern look. At the same time, the Virginians complained bitterly that despite a few promotions, they had to serve under hundreds of Massachusetts officers who gave the army an unbalanced Northern look. In the early days, this animosity often resulted in fistfights among the enlisted men. The infantrymen who battled each other sometimes struck officers and many times threatened to kill them. When they were court-martialed for such offenses, the enlisted men complained that the disciplinary board, made up of officers, was unfairly stacked against them. Thousands refused to pay attention to firearms training and, as a result, dozens killed or wounded themselves and others by accidentally discharging their muskets.[11] Many who joined the army to participate in what they saw as the great adventure of their lives became homesick within weeks.[12] All of this created chaos.

The militia units were separate from the regular troops of the Continental Army. Men volunteered to join the Continental Army and served from between one and three years. Soldiers in the militia volunteered, or were drafted, by their states for short-term enlistment, usually three months but sometimes eight or twelve. None had to reenlist when their time was up.

Militiamen were extremely parochial. They were fighting for the United States, to be sure, but they were really fighting for their state and county. Their allegiance to their home areas was so great that regiments and artillery units sometime left camp to travel home to defend their native state against an attack or rumored attack, as did a Pennsylvania artillery unit in the winter of 1777. No one stopped them. This localism was so great that troops from Pennsylvania continually referred to their colony not as their "state" but as their "country." Most states elected governors during the war years, but the leaders of some states were elected as "presidents."[13] Disputes became heated when clothing shipments for the soldiers of a particular state arrived in camp but nothing arrived for soldiers of another state quartered nearby. Some states provided chaplains for the men's spiritual needs and others did not. Doctors accompanied some state units and others had no medical services at all. The men became bitter over these discrepancies, too.

Despite the frequent complaints of the commander in chief in the early days of the war, scathing criticism from Congress and the press, and the considerable frustration of the people, the Continental Army not only survived but conquered. The soldiers were able to do so despite eight long years of brutal winter camps and heated summer battles, and the deaths of over ten thousand men. For nearly a decade, the Continental Army was battered, ill-equipped, undermanned, badly funded, raggedly clothed, and poorly fed. They consisted of a collection of enlisted men, militia volunteers, Indians, black freedmen, slaves, fifers and drummers, sixty-six-year-old grandfathers and thirteen-year-old kids, artillery specialists, French infantrymen, Prussian drill instructors, and Polish cavalry leaders. And ultimately they defeated the greatest army on earth.

They achieved their historic victory because in George Washington they had a superb leader, to be sure, but they also did it because they were brave men. Even their most strident critics recognized that. Throughout the war, from the firestorm of Bunker Hill to the final assault on Lord Cornwallis's army on the banks of the York River at Yorktown, Virginia, congressmen, generals, and their officers always praised the fortitude and raw courage of the foot soldiers in that first American army.

When it came to fighting, the men were eager. One soldier preparing for a fight against the British near Bristol Ferry, in Rhode Island, rammed two cartridges down his musket barrel instead of one as a friend looked on. When asked why he double-loaded, the soldier answered proudly, "I'll be damned if I don't give them a good [fight]." George Fleming, a captain in the Second Artillery Regiment, wrote to another officer who had gone home on furlough in the middle of the war about the enlisted men that "the company continue much as when you went away—always ready to go through fire and water."[14]

In a letter to a newspaper, one soldier bragged that "[we will] bring thousands into the field, push the enemy with vigor, drive them from our towns, storm them in their strongholds, and never pause until we force them from our shores."[15]

They were proud of what they had suffered. Some men who had been shot during the war, such as Lt. James Monroe, later the fifth president, hit in the chest at Trenton, refused to have the musket ball removed, telling friends and family that the ball would be a reminder of their service to the United States all of their lives.

And they were proud, as the amateur songwriter from New York said, of what they had done. Young Private Granger was with the American army that defeated the British at Saratoga in one of the major victories of the war. Upon returning home, he met inquisitive neighbors in his village asking about the engagement, and he described the battle at length, then recounted all of the wagons, cannon, gunpowder, and muskets the British had given up at its conclusion. He paused, sighed, and then added with great satisfaction that it was "the first British army that had ever surrendered to any nation, it was said."

And most of all, they were proud that they had fought for the United States. One soldier was thrilled that his younger brother was going to join the army late in the war. He wrote to his father that "the profession of arms in such a cause as we are now engaged, is both just and honorable, and I am persuaded it would be a piece of injustice to deprive a young man of an opportunity of having it in his power at some future period, to look back on the present and enjoy the heartfelt satisfaction flowing from a consciousness of having done his duty."[16]

This attitude rarely flagged, even under the most depressing conditions in winter camps and under heavy musket fire. The nadir of the soldiers' war was undoubtedly the winter camp at Valley Forge, where over two thousand of the fourteen thousand American troops died of disease and wounds. Yet the tenacity of those who survived touched the hearts of all. In one lengthy letter to Congress outlining the condition of the army during that treacherous winter, a group of generals at Valley Forge wrote of the common soldiers that "there is no difficulty so great but that the troops are willing to encounter. There is no danger so imminent but they despise in comparison to the freedom of America . . . They delight in discipline, subordination, and perseverance: with these they expect to triumph over lawless domination and welcome the returning sweets of peace and plenty."[17]

Chapter Six

WHY THEY FOUGHT

The motivations of the men who enlisted in the Continental Army were numerous. All soldiers in all wars believe that God is on their side, and the enlisted men in the United States military felt that way, too. The Great Awakening was an evangelical movement that had swept through America in the colonial era. Its advocates, usually Presbyterian, Methodist, and Baptist ministers, told Americans that the old preaching of the Anglican church that all were condemned to hell at birth was wrong. They insisted that men and women could attain heaven by leading good lives and helping mankind. They also preached that God was not within the official church, but within the souls of the people.

By the 1770s, the idea of doing good for mankind and establishing a new and better moral order came to mean for many defeating the British Army.[1] This was constantly instilled in the men by hometown preachers and later chaplains in the service. This pulpit crusade began as soon as the war commenced. Less than two weeks after the engagements at Lexington and Concord, Corporal Amos Farnsworth jotted in his journal about a sermon by Rev. William Emerson, "[He] encouraged us to go and fight for our land and country, saying we did not do our duty if we did not stand up now."[2] Many of the men pouring into the Boston area at the start of the war did not see themselves as just soldiers in the Continental regiments, but God's army. They fought for the independence of their nation and with it the salvation of their souls.[3]

Army recruiters stressed the manliness of the soldier. Men who fought in the army, they told the young men gathered around them in villages throughout the colonies, were true men while those who stayed home to tend to their families and run their farms and businesses were not. Recruiting agents in Pennsylvania frequently used the phrase "manly resistance" to the Redcoats in their enrollment speech.[4] Part of this argument contended if you were not a brave man you must be a coward; there was no middle ground. Soldiers believed it and saw soldiering as a magnificent chance to show not just their friends but the whole world that they were real men. One wrote home at the beginning of the war that "the dangers we are to encounter I know not but it shall never be said to my children your father was a coward."[5]

Men were eager to protect their homes and families. It was very personal. Army recruiters did not dwell on political theory when trying to sign up their infantrymen. The war, they said, was being fought by men to defend their loved ones, especially their wives and girlfriends, and their land. Recruiters and politicians always emphasized the need for men to fight for their women. Letters from women urging men to join the army were printed in newspapers throughout the Atlantic seaboard. Some newspapers routinely printed stories about the courage of wives at home while their husbands were off fighting for their country. Other stories stressed the patriotic feelings of single women who similarly wanted the men of their town to fight in the service.[6] Recruiters from Thompson's Rifle Battalion of Pennsylvania even told men that if they did not join the army all would witness "our towns laid in ashes and our innocent women and children driven from their habitations."[7]

There were financial reasons. Most young men in the colonial era did not earn much money as subsistence farmers, laborers, or apprentices. They believed that they could earn more in the army, even if, like New Hampshire's William Scott, they had no opinion about the Revolution.

"I know nothing of it," said Scott, "neither am I capable of judging whether it was right or wrong."[8] Later, as the war dragged on, soldiers volunteered to collect cash and land bounties that were paid for recruits, bounties that added up to a considerable amount of money for men who could barely make ends meet.

There were soldiers who were just hungry for fame, such as George Morison, a private in one of the Pennsylvania rifle companies, who signed up because "the eyes of all mankind were upon us . . . I panted to partake in the glory of defending my country."[9]

Many young men who joined the army had never left their counties. For them, a lengthy trip to far away cities was the journey of their lives. "Most of us had not . . . been twenty miles from home. We were now leaving our homes, our friends, and all our pleasant places behind and which our eyes might never again behold," wrote Connecticut's Dan Barber.[10]

The Virginians saw sights that amazed them, such as the vast beauty of Lake Champlain in New York. The Pennsylvanians saw sights that befuddled them, such as their very first moose, spotted in Maine, that they described to friends in rather comical terms, admitting with great embarrassment that they had assumed that moose only lived in Russia. Soldiers delighted in traveling to legendary places they had only read about in books. The enlisted men who accompanied Benedict Arnold to Canada told friends that they were excited to be in a foreign country. Some, such as Lt. James McMichael from Pennsylvania, wrote of other states as if they were faraway lands, decrying the language of German-Americans that he could not understand, describing the complexions of residents in those other states as "tawny" or "ruddy" and concluding, like an amateur anthropologist, that the people of New Jersey resembled those of Great Britain.[11] One group of young enlisted men just outside of Boston had been ordered not to visit the city because of smallpox, but sneaked into the town anyway just so that, one awestruck private wrote, "We could say, if we lived, that we went to Boston."[12]

Some were excited to spot famous people, the celebrities of the era. Some enlisted men wrote home with delight that they met Benjamin

Franklin in Canada. Others met John Adams in Boston. Most at one time or another met the governor of a state. Some encountered foreign diplomats who visited camp. The supreme thrill, though, was any sighting of George Washington. Men would write home of glimpsing Washington even if they had merely seen him gallop down the road on his handsome horse. An actual meeting with him would make for a story told and retold for generations.

Some saw the war as the adventure of a lifetime. That was certainly the reason Joseph Plumb Martin signed up in Connecticut's fifth battalion two days after the signing of the Declaration of Independence in 1776. He wanted to become, he wrote, "what I had long wished to be, a soldier."[13]

And when the various enlisted men formed into neat lines on their village greens and marched off to war to the applause of their friends and neighbors they felt not just pleased but, as a company, something very special. They were, as a young chaplain wrote of his comrades, "an elegant regiment."[14]

For some, the war was very personal. John Greenwood joined the army as a fifer because of his friend Samuel Maverick, killed by the British in the Boston Massacre. Some students at Princeton University joined after the British ruined university buildings when they marched through the town. Sam Shaw joined because for months hated British troops had been quartered in his Boston home. Elisha Bostwick of Connecticut fought because the British hanged Nathan Hale, his friend and neighbor. Dan Granger, just thirteen, walked into the American camp in Boston and talked a colonel into letting him take the place of his brother because he feared the brother, very ill, might die if he did not return home. Doctor Lewis Beebe signed up, in part, to flee the grief he felt following the death of his young wife. Jeremiah Greenman of Rhode Island, a seventeen-year-old with no job or future, wrote that he joined "to make myself a man."

The men in the army also saw themselves as the military extension of the political and social revolution taking place around them in America and embraced their role. Wrote one philosophical soldier to a newspaper,

"We fight to rejoice that the Almighty Governor of the universe hath given us a station so honourable and planted us the guardians of liberty, while the greatest part of mankind rise and fall undistinguished as bubbles on the common stream."[15]

And some, like Lemuel Roberts, joined the service in a simple burst of patriotism. He wrote, "The whole continent now became attentive to the call of liberty; the alarm was universal and feeling my bosom glow with love for my country, I turned out on the first alarm."[16]

That exuberance exhibited by Roberts and so many others was evident to the British. One of Her Majesty's soldiers wrote that "what religion was there [during the Huguenot wars in France] liberty is here, simply fanaticism, and the effects are the same."[17]

Some of the better educated men in the army believed they were casting the foundation not just for a new political system in the 1770s, but a new democratic order that would last forever and become a model for republics throughout the earth.

And they fought because they had good reason to do so. Americans had not gone to war since the oppressions of the Crown had begun in the early 1760s because no one seemed to believe that there was a significant reason for a military engagement. The British had not attacked any of their militias and the navy had not bombarded any colonial port. Even the occupation of the British army, the quartering of soldiers in colonists' homes and the Boston Massacre in 1770 did not seem like justifications for an armed rebellion. There had been many reasons to wail about the British in newspapers and magazines and to stage rallies to protest restrictive trade laws and rising tax levies and to damn the king in round after round of beers at taverns, but none to actually fight a war. The brutal, bloody battles of Lexington and Concord changed all that. The Americans had been attacked by the British army and had to defend their country. It was that simple.

Newspapers from Georgia to Massachusetts hailed the brave soldiers of the brand new Continental Army. Despite the many vexations that the enlisted men caused them, Washington and his staff would always be proud of them. "I cherish those dear, ragged Continentals, whose patience will be the admiration of future ages and glory in bleeding with them," wrote Colonel John Laurens, one of Washington's top aides.[18] The generals who fought with them the longest, such as Nathanael Greene, respected the foot soldiers more than anyone else. "Our men are better than our officers," he wrote.[19]

The soldiers who stayed with the army returned the confidence placed in them, assuring all that when it came time to fight they would be ready. Many felt just like a Connecticut private who wrote home of the men in arms just before the crossing of the Delaware River on Christmas Day in 1776 that "You would be amazed to see the fine spirits they are in. The . . . troops are really well disciplined and you may depend will fight bravely . . . we shall do honour to ourselves."[20]

MARCH
TO
QUEBEC

Chapter Seven

PRIVATE JEREMIAH GREENMAN AND BENEDICT ARNOLD

The War

anada. The northern neighbor of the thirteen colonies was so vast that it could not even be properly charted on existing maps. The members of the Continental Congress, flush with successes at Lexington, Concord, and the valiant stand atop Bunker Hill, plus the ongoing siege of Boston, coveted Canada. Why not conquer it and annex it as the "fourteenth colony," more than doubling the size of the "united colonies," and removing the British from most of North America?

The idea was not a new one. In 1690, New England colonists, tired of raids by the Indians and their French allies, launched a two-pronged assault on the country, one on land to capture Montreal and another by sea to take Quebec. Men in both had to turn back when a smallpox epidemic struck the region. Again, in 1740, New England troops under the Crown's flag captured

Fort Louisbourg, on Cape Breton Island, but had to cede it back to France. The British, with American volunteers, had captured Quebec and Montreal during the French and Indian War, which was waged between 1756 and 1763.

Now, in the fall of 1775, Canada beckoned once again. Congress feared an invasion by the British down the Richelieu River into Lake Champlain and then, following an overland march to Albany, on down the Hudson River to New York. It would permit the British to separate New England from the other colonies. Members of Congress had invited Canadians favorably disposed to the Revolution to sit in on some of their meetings concerning their country in an effort to gain their support for an invasion of Canada. That effort never materialized, but the delegates always believed that these men, and thousands of other Canadians, would lock arms with the Continental troops and rise up against the Crown as soon as the American army was within sight of their communities.[1]

The delegates were eager to strike Canada and so was George Washington, who saw the conquest of the country as a sure way to block any land or sea assaults on America from the north. Any full-scale invasion of Canada was complicated, though. How do you take another country? What if the local residents did not rise up and join the Americans? Would soldiers who had marched a few miles to Boston down well-traveled highways be able to march more than two hundred miles through treacherous mountain terrain to Canada? How could such a venture be supplied?

And who would lead such a dangerous mission?

Jeremiah Greenman, seventeen, from Newport, Rhode Island, was one of nearly seven hundred privates in a force of eleven hundred soldiers walking up gangplanks onto the decks of a fleet of eleven ships at a wharf at Newburyport, Massachusetts on September 18, 1775. He had enlisted in the army just a few weeks before and had arrived in Cambridge just in time to be assigned to the Canadian expedition.

Greenman was impressed by the spirit of the men boarding the boats that day and even more taken by the rousing send-off they were given by a large and boisterous crowd of citizens gathered near the docks of the fishing town. He wrote of the scene in the journal he kept for the duration of the American Revolution, "Colors flying, drums a-beating and fifes a-playing, the hills and wharves covered [with people] bidding their friends farewell."

Greenman and the Rhode Islanders, and the other soldiers, were confident, too, because they would march north under the leadership of one of the early heroes of the Revolution, Colonel Benedict Arnold. Washington needed a man of great fortitude and endurance who could command men on a wilderness trek as well as on the battlefield, a man the troops could trust and someone the people admired. That was Arnold.

Arnold was the man of the hour. The feisty colonel from Connecticut had earned headlines when, with Ethan Allen, he captured the "impregnable" Fort Ticonderoga on the southwestern shore of Lake Champlain earlier that spring. Arnold seemed to be everywhere during the early days of the war. Following his audacious conquest of Ticonderoga, he sailed up Lake Champlain and captured the British garrison at the Canadian town of St. John's, seizing the British warship *George* anchored there.

He returned to Massachusetts surrounded by some minor controversy because he had become involved in a contentious dispute with Congress over the reimbursement of his personal expenses—he had few receipts—during his heroics at Fort Ticonderoga. At the time, few thought much about it.

Arnold, the son of a shipowner and great-great-grandson of the colonial governor of Rhode Island, had always thirsted for the military life. He joined a local militia company in New Haven, where he lived, in the early 1770s following years of traveling on land and on sea as a trader and was soon elected its captain. Arnold led his seventy-man company to Boston to join the army after the battles of Lexington and Concord. He was easily noticed. Colonel Arnold was about five feet, eight inches tall and possessed a compact, muscular frame. He had jet-black hair, blue-gray eyes and a hooked nose. He was extremely well dressed, a persuasive speaker, and had arrived as the commander of six dozen men. He was ready to fight, right now. In short, he was just the kind of man the Continental Army needed.

Later, Colonel Henry Livingston wrote of Arnold's possible departure from the service in 1777, just after the battle of Saratoga, "I am
much distressed that General Arnold's determination to retire from the
army . . . He is the life and soul of the troops . . . to him and to him alone
is due the honor of our late victory."[2]

People who met him grumbled about his egotism, hot temper, and
self-congratulatory airs, but none of that really mattered because the
army was woefully short of men with any military acumen at all. That
experience was evident in his masterful planning for the assault on
Ticonderoga and his leadership in the actual attack.[3] Benedict Arnold got
things done.

Washington wanted to take Canada. His initial plan was to send
General Philip Schuyler there from Albany at the head of a fifteen hundred man force to launch a two-pronged attack. Arnold insisted on showing him another plan and the commander in chief was intrigued. As a
trader, the colonel told Washington, he had visited Quebec by ship and
sailed up and down the coast of New England and knew well the Kennebec River, in Maine, then part of the Massachusetts colony. He had
obtained copies of journals and maps drawn in the French and Indian
War by British colonel John Montresor, including Montresor's charts of
water and land routes between the Kennebec and Quebec, charts with
which the commander in chief was familiar. With Washington listening
intently, Arnold proposed journeying to Quebec via an unusual route up
the Kennebec—from its mouth in the Atlantic Ocean to the Chaudière
River, past the ominously named Dead River, to Quebec. His requested
force of one thousand men would have to cover about one hundred
eighty miles on land and water and trek across several low mountain
ranges, but they would surprise the British at Quebec and conquer the
walled-in city.[4] On paper, the plan seemed feasible.

There were weaknesses. It would take seven or eight weeks to reach
Canada and the men would have to march through the mountainous
regions in early winter, a season that could bring numerous snowfalls and
freezing temperatures for soldiers who had never marched that far in
inclement weather. An army might live off the land in summer, but it

could not do so in winter. No one took into consideration the snow in the mountains and the flooding of the rivers and lakes in the area following lengthy and often ferocious rainstorms. The maps did not indicate the many churning rapids and high waterfalls around which the men would have to carry sixty-five tons of supplies and their two hundred bateaux— flat-bottomed boats that carried eight men each. Maps of the area were not accurate and the distances between places in the country were actually far greater than they appeared on them. The charts showed rivers and ponds, but did not note their true depths. There were hardly any villages, farms, or people in that northeastern area of New England who could provide supplies if necessary.[5] If the expedition became lost or trapped by snowstorms, they would be too far away from any towns for rescue.

General Schuyler never made it to Canada. His army of fifteen hundred began its journey on August 30, but Schuyler fell ill with scurvy and rheumatism halfway there and was forced to return to Fort Ticonderoga, replaced by his second in command, the energetic General Richard Montgomery.

The charismatic Montgomery, thirty-seven, was the son of a member of the Irish parliament who had served in the British army for years before moving to America in 1772 and marrying the daughter of wealthy New Yorker Robert Livingston. He was determined to spend the rest of his life as a gentleman farmer, but joined the Continental Army when the war began. Assisted by reinforcements, Montgomery, an experienced commander, defeated British and Canadian forces at Chambly and St. John's in Canada and on November 13 seized Montreal. The city only had one hundred fifty men in it; most were captured. The head of the province, Governor Guy Carleton, a British general, had left Montreal two days before it surrendered. He raced to Quebec to help fortify that city. Montgomery left men in Montreal to hold the town and marched toward Quebec, the first part of the plan a great success.

As they traveled up the Kennebec River, Benedict Arnold's eleven hundred men immediately ran into difficulties. The boats of green pine were not well built. "Our canoes proved very leaky," Arnold complained in his journal.[6] Just ten days into the expedition the men were forced to carry supplies and their boats more than one mile around a series of fast-running rapids on the Kennebec River, a much greater distance than indicated on the maps. It would not be the first time. Private Jeremiah Greenman wrote that they had bigger problems. "We were obliged to draw our boats over shoals; in many places up to our arms in water and so swift that we could hardly stand." He added that the terrain in the region surrounding the Kennebec was dreadful. "Nothing but rock and roots and a swamp."

The trip became even worse during the first week of October. Greenman wrote on October 6, "Carried [boats] . . . one mile and a quarter over roots and rocks and mud . . . got some oxen to carry a few of our barrels over the carrying place." With no local farmers to ask for directions and the maps confusing, the next day the army took a wrong turn and became utterly lost. On the following day, it rained continuously as the men walked for eight long miles. Private Greenman and the other enlisted men, heads down, trekked forward the best they could, feet stumbling on rocks at times, plodding through six inches of mud at others, rain coming down on them in thick sheets. Greenman, fed up with the trip already, scrawled in his journal that he and the soldiers had "entered an uncultivated country and a barren wilderness."

It was a striking wilderness, though. When they were old men, Greenman and the others talked with awe about the gorgeous waterfalls, lakes, and mountaintops they passed on the expedition. On that first day they stopped to gawk at Three Mile Falls, one of the loveliest the men had ever seen, and after that there were more, climaxed by the falls at end of the Chaudière River that tumbled 135 feet down into the rushing waters of the St. Lawrence. Once the Kennebec ran over Three Mile Falls it became quiet for a few miles and then rumbled down into a mountain gorge with high stone walls and collections of heavy rocks for several hundred yards, the water creating a thunderous roar as it rushed through.

The men marched through meadows of waist-high grass and looked up at the chain of mountains that surrounded them, tops covered with snow. They followed narrow paths through thick forests of evergreen trees and traipsed over the leaves that had fallen from oak, maple, and beech trees.

They found that the roads that appeared on the maps did not exist and they had to build them. Wrote Greenman, "Employed ourselves in making a sort of a road through the woods so that we might get our bateaux and provisions along." An added difficulty the entire army faced was the lack of expertise in tasks like constructing roads. Arnold had three hundred frontiersmen from Virginia and Pennsylvania under Colonel Daniel Morgan, but the rest were simple farmers. Now, in the middle of nowhere, they had to perform tasks with which they were not familiar; their labors became time consuming and frustrating. The men from New England were accustomed to snow, but the temperatures that winter were far below normal and in the mountain ranges of the area they remained low for days, freezing the snow on the ground. The earth was slippery to walk over for weeks. The soldiers from Virginia had never seen snowfalls or cold spells such as the ones they encountered on the trip.

Much of the food the soldiers carried to sustain them was ruined during those first few weeks because of misplanning and misfortune. Large supplies of cod fish were all left in the bottoms of the boats and the fresh river water that spilled into the craft from the Kennebec destroyed them. Shabbily built barrels of dry bread were similarly ruined when the water seeped into them, as were barrels of peas.

The bateaux had been manufactured in haste for the invasion and constantly sprung leaks. Complained George Morison, a private from Pennsylvania, "Many of the bateaux were so badly constructed that in them or out of them, we were wet. Could we have then come within reach of the villains who constructed these crazy things, they would fully have experienced the effects of our vengeance."[7]

The men began to fall sick; some died. Dr. Isaac Senter, the physician accompanying the expedition, reported on October 12, a week's marching time before the men would reach the aptly named Dead River, that many soldiers had come down with dysentery and diarrhea and that the water in their barrels had gone bad. He wrote, "No sooner had it got down than it was puked up by many of the poor fellows."[8]

Greenman fought his way through clusters of bushes and trees. The clearings were littered with stones and the paths that did exist were covered with fallen trees and brush. One clearing they traversed at the bottom of a ridge was very swampy and strewn with lengthy rotted-out logs that they had to step over. When they approached the Chaudière River, they had to push their way through jungles of spruce, cedar, and hemlock trees and cross deep and winding ravines that nature had slashed into the slopes of the hills near the water.

Their grittiness and determination, hallmarks of the entire American army throughout the Revolution and in the years to come, was evident to Arnold, who marveled at the way the enlisted men plunged through the forests. "Our men," he noted, "are very much fatigued in carrying over their bateaux, provisions. The roads being extremely bad . . . They appear very cheerful . . . Their spirit and industry seem to overcome every obstacle."[9]

The divisions of troops became easy victims of the terrain. Dozens of bateaux had been so badly damaged that they had to be left behind. Supplies had to be put in all of the boats and about half the men on the expedition were forced to walk, not ride, as the army moved ever northwards toward Canada. Their coats were ripped by branches and soon could not protect the men from the wind and cold. Their shoes were cut up, too, by the jagged rocks in the streams they traversed, and by the time they approached the headwaters of the Dead River many had become barefoot.

Exhausted upon their arrival at the Dead River, an extension of the Kennebec, on October 20, the men were drenched by a heavy rain that grew in intensity all day and by nightfall, aided by south by southwest winds, became a full-blown storm. Meandering nearby creeks began to overflow and swiftly running water surged over the banks of the river and shores of the ponds and tore through the woods. The strong winds knocked over dozens of large trees. The men scrambled into clearings to avoid falling trees but were afraid to put up tents for fear that the winds would knock them over and injure the inhabitants. Many simply laid on the open ground in clearings, huddled against each other, hats pulled down over their heads, coats wrapped tightly around them, and sat out the storm. Despite gallant effort to save them, the soldiers lost dozens of barrels of flour, pork, and other supplies that were carried away by the badly flooding ponds.

The men found themselves in the center of a calamitous natural disaster when the sun rose over the rain-soaked countryside in the morning. The ponds, now lakes, and the overflowing Dead River flooded out many of the landmark trails and creeks on Arnold's previous maps and the men did not know what direction to take. Several divisions, including Greenman's, became lost, some for as long as a day, before backtracking to the main army.[10] Others ignored Arnold's orders to walk on high ground, above the new shorelines created by the overflowing water. To save time they waded through the three feet deep waters of the "ocean swamp," as Greenman called it. The freezing waters soon made their legs and lower bodies numb and they had to leave the water, find high ground, and then dry off. They all rested to regain circulation in their legs, which caused further delays.[11]

Dissension over the weather, lack of food, bad maps, and general mismanagement of the army had grown throughout the trip, especially among the last two divisions in the expedition, led by Lt. Col. Christopher Greene and Colonel Roger Enos, whose divisions had suffered the most from lack of food, sickness, and lost bateaux. A few days after the Dead River flooded, on October 25, following a storm that dumped several inches of snow on the ground, the officers of both divisions called a council of war to determine whether they should go on or turn back, an action that verged on mutiny. Many of the officers and men were panic-stricken following the series of natural disasters that had befallen them.

After a lengthy discussion at the council, held in a wide clearing, Greene and Enos urged the men to catch up with Arnold, regardless of the dangers. Others vigorously argued that they should go home because to advance meant certain death. Greene, angry at the men who wanted to depart, reminded them that both he and Enos had received letters that very day from Arnold assuring them that they would arrive in Quebec within fifteen days. Greene reminded them that it would take them more than fifteen days to get back home.

The colonel's strident lecture did little good. The officers in Greene's division voted to go on, but Enos's officers decided to go home. Enos's companies, totaling three hundred men, or nearly one-third of the entire force, left the following morning and made it back to the coast in eleven days. Enos was brought before a court of inquiry for desertion, but acquitted following emphatic testimony by his officers that they firmly believed that, under-supplied, they would perish in the wilds of Maine.

The men who remained in the expedition, knowing that the departure of Enos's men weakened their forces, were angry. The men of Captain Henry Dearborn's company even prayed out loud that the men going back with Enos would die on the way as punishment for abandoning them in the middle of the wilderness.[12]

It was here, too, that the unhappy men, with nothing left to eat, first discussed killing the dogs that had accompanied them, many of them personal pets, in order to stay alive. It was a disturbing conversation, but one they felt necessary, even though they did not think they would actually do so. Surely they would find food.

The Dead River was the halfway point on the trip, and when he reached it on October 25, Arnold was furious that it had turned out to be twice the distance from the mouth of the Kennebec that the maps showed. Quebec, too, was not one hundred eighty miles from the sea, but closer to three hundred sixty miles. They were already seven days behind schedule and had consumed most of their provisions, which were soon cut to half rations. Arnold, ever cautious, had, in fact, feared problems with supplies and taken along 50 percent more than he believed he would need. The additional supplies were now nearly gone, too.

The Dead River began with a series of ponds much farther apart than Montresor's maps indicated. All in all, the men, now reduced to about seven hundred with the loss of Enos's troops, had to carry their boats and remaining supplies nearly eight miles between two of the ponds and it debilitated them. Greenman was done in. He observed, "[Men] were greatly fatigued by carrying over such hills, mountains, and swamps such as men never passed before."

Life did not improve when they reached the Chaudière River, the watery path to Quebec, eighty miles away. It, too, ran too fast for the leaky bateaux and exhausted men. The bateaux with the sick troops loaded into them could not be maneuvered by the healthy men assigned to pilot them and had to be taken out of the river. The sick then had to walk several miles and help carry their boats. One man was lost, along with dozens of guns and several thousand dollars stashed into a sack, when his bateaux overturned with two others in one of the rapids in the Chaudière.

The men began to kill and eat their dogs that same night, during their fifth week on the expedition. Greenman was so hungry that he put the animal cannibalism out of his mind. Greenman wrote of the dog, "I got a small piece of it and some broth that it was boiled in with a great deal of trouble." On the following day, the men learned that those in another company, and in a third, had also killed and devoured their pet dogs. By November 1, Greenman was writing in his journal that food was so scarce "there was nothing to eat but dogs."

But there was, as the hungry men discovered. Some men boiled their cartridge pouches and others their moccasins and ate them. The men in one division removed all of the candlesticks they had been carrying for light in the evening and had them for dinner. Others gleefully consumed lip salve and slender chunks of shaving soap that they carved off the bars with their knives.

It was the lowest point in their lives and they feared dying in a grim, desolate wilderness hundreds of miles from their loved ones. Private Abner Stocking walked through the camp that morning and saw men "so weak that they could hardly stand on their legs." They were despondent, he wrote, "many sitting wholly drowned in sorrow, wishfully placing their eyes on everyone who passed by them, hoping for some relief. Such pity-asking countenances I never before held. My heart was ready to burst and my eyes to overflow with tears when I witnessed distress which I could not relieve."

Private Morison observed that "the universal weakness of body that now prevailed over every man increased hourly on account of the total destitution of food; and the craggy mounds over which we had to pass, together with the snow and the cold penetrating through our death-like frames made our situation completely wretched and nothing but death was wanting to finish our sufferings."[13]

Finally, on October 30, forty-two days after they began their journey, Benedict Arnold, leading an advance scouting party searching for food, arrived at the first of several houses near the Chaudière. There he was able to procure from a local farmer a number of cattle for his men, which they first saw a day later when they encountered the advance scouts on their return. The men were delirious with happiness. Greenman wrote, "It was the most joyful sight I ever saw and some could not refrain from crying for joy. Some of the men were so hungry before the creatures [cattle] were dressed that they had the skin and all entrails guts and everything that could be eaten on the fires a-boiling."

Two days later, they passed a farmhouse where the residents offered to sell Arnold more food. Greenman wrote, "There was beef and bread for us, which we cooked plenty of. Some of the men made themselves sick eating so much." He added that it snowed that night as they lay on the ground, but, thanks to the food, "we slept very hearty."

On November 12, Arnold's expedition, fortified by more food from farmers they met, arrived on the banks of the St. Lawrence River, one of North America's major waterways, which connected the Atlantic Ocean to both Quebec and Montreal. Their journey was nearly over. The enlisted men and their officers, and Arnold, had accomplished quite a feat; they had walked and sailed through three hundred fifty miles of some of the most difficult terrain in the United States, traveled up three rivers, crossed two mountain ranges, survived a severe storm, a treacherous flood, and several snowstorms and made it to the gates of Quebec City with 675 men, losing just 55—dead, sick, or deserted—not counting the three hundred men who turned back with Enos.

In letters he wrote to his superior, Schuyler, back in Albany, Benedict Arnold praised his men. "Short of provisions, part of the detachment disheartened and gone back, famine staring us in the face, an enemy's country and uncertainty ahead. Notwithstanding all these obstacles, the officers and men, inspired and fired with the love of liberty and their country, pushed on."[14]

But Arnold's praise for the enlisted men under his care paled in comparison to the admiration they had for him for leading them through the wilderness. Private Stocking, who feared death on the trip, told friends, in remarks repeated by all of the enlisted soldiers, that Arnold was "beloved by his men."

Congress was euphoric. One delegate wrote that the journey through the wilds of New England was "thought equal Hannibal's over the Alps."

Chapter Eight

JEREMIAH GREENMAN:
Prisoner of War

Quebec City was a walled-in fortification that an army could not conquer unless it was starved out, battered it with cannon in a lengthy siege, or stormed it with several thousand troops. This did not worry either General Arnold (he had been promoted on January 10, 1776) or General Montgomery, who arrived there with his army on December 3 and took charge of the entire operation. Both men had said earlier that the inhabitants of Quebec and the towns around it, both French and English, would rise up and join forces with the Americans as soon as the fighting began. This idea had been part of the overall plan for months and this anticipated love of the Americans was reaffirmed for Arnold in conversations with Frenchmen from whom he purchased provisions as his army marched closer to the St. Lawrence.[1]

The two generals were wrong. The inhabitants had no intentions of assisting the Americans. That realization led Montgomery to suggest a short siege of the city and its eighteen hundred defenders to soften up its defenses, followed by a storming of the walls. The siege did not last long because it was ineffective, as the American forces totaled around

1,325 men; Montgomery then planned a direct assault. He would wait until a snowstorm hit and then launch a surprise attack, using the blanket of falling snow as a cover. The generals knew that they could not attack the city directly across what was called the Plains of Abraham on the western side of the city because the walls overlooking the wide plains were too well fortified. They had to go around the city and attack from the rear, near the river. That would be a difficult task.

The central part of Quebec, with its military garrison, administrative officials, and cathedral, was inside a stone fortress that could only be entered through heavily guarded gates. The only feasible assault would have to be a concentrated charge against one of the large gates protecting the city or an attack in which men mounted the walls with ladders. To do so, the Americans would have to charge through the streets of what was called the lower town, a series of neighborhoods in front of one gate that overlooked the St. Lawrence. Two narrow roads led to it.

Everything fell into place on December 31 when a storm began. The attack was a disaster. Montgomery and Arnold underestimated the fire-power of the British inside the town. Very few local residents rose up and joined Montgomery, but the overwhelming majority helped the British hold Quebec against the Americans. The snowstorm did not act as a cover and, in fact, made it difficult for the advancing lines of Americans to see where they were going. The nearly one foot of snow on the ground made it impossible to carry cannon caissons on sleds and some had to be left behind. The roads into Quebec were much narrower than they appeared on maps and the troops found that they had to advance in double, and at times in single file, and became easy targets for British musket fire. The British had suspected a night assault and were prepared with artillery. A single cannon burst killed Montgomery and two of his top aides shortly after his wing of the army reached the town. Benedict Arnold, advancing from another direction, was shot in the leg and went down, cursing loudly. His wound prohibited him from any movement, slowing his column of troops.

Several companies of men managed to force their way into the lower town after subduing the enemy at barricades at one of the wharves defended by several cannon. Wrote Private Morison, "We fired into the portholes with such effect that the enemy cannot discharge a single cannon." One company of riflemen led by Daniel Morgan surprised a company of British, taking them prisoners. Morgan was uncertain about what to do next. He had heard that Arnold was wounded, but he had no idea what was happening to Arnold's main troop. Morgan took command, but did not know the fate of Montgomery and his men, either. His officers insisted on waiting for the general. Instead of moving forward, Morgan opted to wait for Montgomery, who never came. He and his men were eventually confronted by the British in the town. Morison continued, "A furious discharge of musketry is let loose upon us from behind houses; in an instant we are assailed from different quarters with deadly fire. We rush on to every part (of the neighborhood) rouse the enemy from their covert and force a body of them to an open fight; (but) now attacked by thrice our number."[2] Morgan's men were forced to surrender.

The musket fire from the walls proved deadly. Private Stocking wrote of "a tremendous fire from the windows" that halted the attack of his company. "Thirty of our privates being killed and thirty-five wounded," he wrote of the enlisted men, "and surrounded as we were without any relief, we were obliged to surrender ourselves."[3]

A Rhode Island company lost several men in a heavy musket fire from the ramparts as they advanced through the lower town but did not make it into the inner city. William Humphrey, a private in the regiment, wrote of the frustration of its members: "We rallied our men and tried to scale the second barrier, and not withstanding their utmost efforts, we got some of our ladders up but was obliged to retreat, our guns being wet, as not one to ten would fire; then we was concluded to retreat, which we did to the first barrier that we had took, and when we came there we found we could not retreat without losing all our men or at least most of them."[4]

Jeremiah Greenman was in one of the other companies that fought their way into the lower town. He wrote, "With hearts undaunted to scale the walls we march on down to St. Roche," and then to the lower town area of Quebec. They were easily spotted. "Alarm sounded and bells rang. They soon turned out and formed themselves along the ramparts.

They kept a continual fire on us but we got up to their two-gun battery after losing a great number of men. We soon got into their battery, which was two nine pounders. We got in and took seventy prisoners. Then our men's arms got wet and we could not do much."

Greenman's unit was trapped. They soon learned that Montgomery had been killed and Arnold wounded. The attack had failed. Surrounded, they were forced to surrender to the British, as did between three and four hundred other Americans (fifty-one were killed and thirty-six wounded in the assault). Greenman was first marched to a Jesuit college in Quebec, opposite the cathedral there, and then to a convent, where he was put under guard, with others, as a prisoner of war.

At first, Arnold did not know what happened to anyone after he was shot and went down in the snow. The general was carried back to a makeshift American hospital at St. Roche, where he received reports of the fighting. Despite the setbacks he had seen all around him in Quebec, he refused to order a retreat. The feisty Arnold was treated by Dr. Senter and did remain in the hospital, confined to bed, but he took two pistols with him and told Senter that he would fight it out with the British from his bed should they arrive.

Prisoner of War

Upon his arrival at the convent on the evening of January 1, 1776, Greenman had to chuckle when his jailers presented him with a cup of rum and a biscuit and wished him a happy New Year. Some New Year.

The prisoners there, all enlisted men, were given one pound of bread, a half pound of meat and six ounces of butter once a day, and a half pint of boiled rice each day. A resident of the town gave them a cask of wine for New Year's.

The enlisted men were kept in very cramped quarters. "Very uncomfortable," wrote Greenman, "Not enough room to lay down to sleep."

He wrote too soon. A few days later the enlisted men were taken to another room in the convent that was smaller than their original chamber. The men tore up some partition boards in the new cell and burned them to give themselves more room. Two men didn't need more room;

they were clamped in irons following a conversation about escaping that was overheard by a guard. The promised food allowances had been forgotten and the men were served salmon, or "stinking salmon," as Greenman put it.

Some of the troops were housed in a jail that overlooked a square through which wooden wagons carried the blood-soaked bodies of dead Americans. They had been tossed on top of each other, their limbs splayed this way and that, and their wounds fresh. They were driven on the way to the "death house," where the slain American soldiers would be dumped in a pile with their compatriots. Pvt. John Henry, somberly watching a procession of the wagons, began to cry when one drove past his cell window carrying a friend. He wrote, "Poor Nelson lay on top of half a dozen other bodies, his arms extended beyond his head, as if in the act of prayer."[5]

Greenman found himself in such a tawdry prison because neither side planned for a long war. Neither the Americans or British constructed prisons and prisoners of war were marched into whatever large structures either side could find. The British put several thousand captured soldiers in New York City prisons that were formerly sugar warehouses. Prisoners taken in the Philadelphia battles found themselves in the Walnut Street jail in that city. Many American sailors were taken back to England and tossed into Dartmoor, Old Mill, and Forten prisons and even incarcerated in the Tower of London. Those captured in the Caribbean, usually from privateer vessels, were put into small jails or homes converted into jails on nearby islands. British and Hessian prisoners were held in jails and warehouses. Some Hessians were put to work as laborers in ironworks.

The worst jails were the dreaded prison ships of the British navy, anchored in Wallabout Bay, off Brooklyn. The British needed large spaces to house three thousand American soldiers captured in the New York battles in 1776 and decided to refit several transport ships for confinement. The men were dumped into hopelessly overcrowded and badly managed ships, such as the *Jersey, Hunter,* and *Stromboli.* They slept side by side on wood planks in the badly ventilated holds of the ships with terrible food, infrequent exercise, and severe punishments for small infractions of the captain's haphazard rules. The *Jersey*, a real hellhole, was renovated as a prison after it was determined to be unfit for service in the early 1770s. The men considered it the worst prison. Thousands died on the prison ships and their bodies were buried on beaches of Wallabout Bay. In 1808, American authorities decided to dig up the skeletons of prisoners buried there and found eleven thousand, some of whom were British and Hessian dead. Several thousand more were buried elsewhere and never found. No comprehensive records were kept on either side, but it is likely that more than ten thousand Americans perished as prisoners of war.[6]

One solution to prison overcrowding for the British, particularly early in the war, was parole. Officers who were captured were held in private homes at night and allowed to walk about the city during the day; some even struck up friendships with residents and conducted romances with local women. These prisoners were usually kept between six months and a year and then sent home.

Prison exchanges were another means of obtaining freedom. The British would free several dozen prisoners following a similar release by the Americans. This was often done by rank, one general for another or three lieutenants for three lieutenants. Enlisted men exchanged were grouped together.

Captivity was depressing for soldiers, but it also had profound effects on their families back home. Men held prisoner could not help with their family farm or business. Their imprisonment placed enormous stress on their wives and family. Few were as upset, and held up as well, as Abigail Johnson, whose husband, Colonel Thomas Johnson, was held captive in Canada. She was eight months pregnant when he was captured; her sister was staying with her for the birth that her husband would miss. She was steadfast, though, and in her letters never worried about her health, only his. "It gives me great satisfaction to hear that you are well," she wrote, "for I was very anxious for you."[7]

Many were harmed more by what they perceived as abandonment by wives, friends, and neighbors than by their terrible living conditions. Caleb Foot was taken prisoner in the winter of 1780 and incarcerated in the dreary confines of Forten Prison, in Portsmouth, England. In letters to his wife, he complained about the terrible food, cold, and lack of clothing, but he saved his real anguish for her and the others back home, telling her that "I must lie in prison 'til the wars are over and not have the pleasure to receive one letter from home; for I find by unhappy experience that friends in America are very scarce. It is very surprising that I cannot find one friend to write to me. This mystery is very dark to me, and I cannot account for it" (most likely Mrs. Foot, like many others, simply did not know where her husband was being held).[8]

The windows of the convent where Jeremiah Greenman was housed did give the men good seats for the weeks-long, rather feeble siege of the town that Arnold tried to oversee from his hospital bed. Greenman regularly observed fires in St. Roche's, outside the city, and at distant farmhouses that he surmised were caused by British bombardment. He and the men were certain that another American attack on Quebec would begin shortly and that they would soon be freed. Greenman noted, "We live very happily and contented, though we are in such a dismal hole, hoping the first dark night that our people will be in and redeem us." The chance to watch the war ended in a few days when their jailers nailed thick wooden planks across their windows to prevent any further viewing.

By March 1, a smallpox epidemic had raced through the convent, as it had struck throughout the Quebec area. Greenman wrote that nearly sixty men had been afflicted (actually, by that time several hundred prisoners as well as American troops outside the city had come down with the pox). They were taken to the hospital to fight it. In a discriminatory and cruel decision, Governor Carleton had permitted officers, but not enlisted men, to be inoculated by Quebec doctors, so Greenman and his fellow enlisted men in the convent were constantly at risk.

"Very cold and disagreeable," he wrote of his days in confinement. The seventeen-year-old Greenman did not have to remain in prison, though. A miraculous opportunity presented itself on March 1. An American loyalist who was a trader, Captain James Frost, arrived at Quebec with his small fleet of ships that had just sailed up the St. Lawrence River. He was given a tour of the prison, along with several British officers who had arrived with him. Frost was allowed to walk past some of the cells and look at the prisoners. He was startled to see Jeremiah Greenman in one. Frost had been a friend of Greenman's father before the war and knew the boy, too.

Frost asked the guards to remove Greenman from his cellblock for a conference and pulled him far away from the officers, a firm hand on Greenman's by now rather weak arm, turning to shield his actions from the jailers. Frost reached into his jacket and gave Greenman some money. Then he carefully explained to the teenager that if he would sign a king's pardon, or admission of guilt, the captain, who had friends in high places in Quebec, could not only have the boy set free, but released into his custody. Then, as his guardian, he could put him on board one of his ships as a general seaman and take him home to his family in Rhode Island.

An undernourished but proud Greenman looked right at him, thrust the money into his pocket, and nodded his thanks. But he refused the extraordinary offer. "I told him I had entered the cause of my country and meant to continue in it until our rights was declared." The officers laughed at him but Frost did not. The teenager turned, summoned the guard, and went back into confinement, ignoring his chance to go home.[9]

Greenman and the others passed their time in prison with ingenious inventions. They played every word game they had ever learned and told endless war stories. When they ran out of stories they discussed every girl each of them had ever met. Needing some musical entertainment to perk up their downtrodden spirits, they tore the buttons off their coats and somehow turned them into a fife that a musician among them played to cheer them up.

On most days the prisoners discussed the many rumors that floated through the convent. The two that received the most dissection were that 1) Benedict Arnold would personally lead a charge on the town to free them, and that it would come that night or the next, and 2) George Washington, furious that they had been held in prison, had assembled an army of two thousand of his best soldiers and had sent it to Quebec weeks before; it would be arriving to storm the city at any moment.

The days dragged on. Every few days someone would be put in irons for offenses such as trying to talk to a sentry or discussing escape. Every few nights an alarm would be sounded and a cannon would be rolled into place in front of Greenman's cell to prevent an escape if an attack from outside the walls commenced. "They are afraid of us," he wrote proudly.

The soldiers were moved again on March 13, forty-three days after their capture, to a secure army barracks they nicknamed the Dauphin Jail, because the British, hearing the same rumors as the prisoners, were certain that Arnold would lead an attack on March 15.

There were so many prisoners in each room at the overcrowded barracks that they had to sign a sheet that was nailed to the door to identify them. Greenman joked that at least the new jail was so strong, with its high ceiling and thick stone walls, that it was "bomb proof" and they would be safe from cannon fired by either side.

The new jail had windows that no one bothered to board this time and the men had an ample view of the city and, beyond it, if they stood on their toes, they could see the colors flying over the tops of the tents of the American forces. The enlisted men confined with Greenman began to think that they might be able to escape from the jail, which was not as secure as the convent. "Most of the prisoners thought best to get out then," Greenman said.

The larger problem was to escape from the walled-in city with its enormous gates. An escape from the barracks would be noticed and the men would have little time to make it to the walls and scramble over them to freedom. There were British soldiers everywhere, in addition to the jail guards and sentries on the walls, and the Americans would be shot.

The planning of the escape took days, and as the men talked they came up with an ingenious scheme to not only escape from the confines of the Dauphin Jail, but seize Quebec itself. The plan, as Greenman outlined it often in later years for eager listeners, went like this: all of the prisoners would quietly leave through the main door of the barracks, which they were certain could be jimmied open. One group of escaping soldiers would subdue the Redcoats guarding the perimeter of the Dauphin Jail and everyone else would follow them out. One group of prisoners, containing artillerists, would race to the cannon on the ramparts, running up the narrow stone stairways, disabling soldiers in their way, turn several cannon around, and then shoot at any building in the town in order to set it on fire. At the same time, anticipating the confusion the artillery would cause, another group of men would storm St. John's Gate, the main entrance to the city, kill or knock out any guards there, and quickly open it. Anyone who subdued a British soldier would grab his musket and fire at other soldiers, or fire anywhere, to make noise.

Their comrades outside the city, spotting the fires and hearing the cannon and muskets, and seeing the gate raised, would then surely attack the town. The ensuing battle that Greenman and the other escapees envisioned would not only result in their freedom, but the capture of Quebec.

And the complicated and daring plan might have worked, too, except for one, tiny, unforeseen problem: ice. The main barracks door was continually stuck shut by ice that formed on the floor within the jail every day. Two teenaged soldiers were assigned to discreetly chip away at the ice, to allow the door to swing open when necessary, but they were spotted by guards. The two teenagers were grabbed and locked in irons and interrogated, as were other prisoners. One frightened man divulged the entire scheme.

The revenge of their British jailers was swift. All of the men were confined in thick, heavy leg irons or handcuffs, which Greenman wrote were "very uncomfortable." Head counts were now taken twice a day to make certain that no one had escaped. Rations were cut and a new kind of biscuit was given to the men. "We think they was poisoned," Greenman said of the biscuits after most of the men became sick shortly after eating them.

The men demanded medical care after vomiting up the biscuits. They received it, but the only medicine they wound up with was the common physic that doctors on both sides gave men to make them purge themselves. "[It] proved that we was poisoned," insisted a bitter Greenman, who, like the others, vomited even more after taking the medicine.

Here, again, the men, miserable in their irons, talked endlessly of the attack by Arnold that they were certain would be launched at any moment. It was their only hope, but as March faded into April and then early May, Greenman abandoned that dream and lamented. "We are almost ready to give up, fearing they will not come."

Any hopes they maintained of an American attack to free them were ended harshly on May 6. Just after the sun rose that morning, the prisoners looked out their windows on an astonishing sight—three large British warships (the frigates *Surprise* and *Iris* and the sloop *Martin*) majestically sailing up the St. Lawrence right at them, their big canvass sails unfurled and billowing in the Canadian wind, the first of fifteen ships in a fleet. Greenman observed, "Three ships came into the harbor with reinforcements of about one thousand men at which time all the bells in the city rang."

The troops did not disembark and march into Quebec, as Greenman expected, but, in a preplanned, surprise maneuver, charged directly at the American camp on the Plains of Abraham, shocking the Continental Army. Governor Carleton directed a force of two hundred men from the ships and seven hundred of his own soldiers in the charge. The Americans fled in confusion after a short battle that the men in the Dauphin Jail watched in utter depression. Their last hope for salvation seemed to flee along with their army.

Greenman was dejected and angry at his comrades at the same time. He wrote, "If they had only known how bad it was to be a prisoner they would never have retreated [without] giving battle."

The twelve warships behind the *Surprise, Iris,* and *Martin* arrived the next day, with more troops and cannon. Throughout the month, additional vessels landed in Quebec; some troop transports and some supply ships. Their jailers told them that the new army was led by Britain's best general, the flamboyant "Gentleman" Johnny Burgoyne, and that he rode at the head of an army of over seven thousand men. First they were going to chase and destroy the American troops, now under the command of General John Thomas, and then turn toward Montreal and wipe out the Americans holding it. The city was under the command of Arnold, who had moved there in early May.

The news crushed Greenman. "Here we live very discontented and quite out of hope of ever being relieved," he wrote in late September, adding later that "they are keeping us in such a hole not fit for dogs much more for men."

He was certain that he would never go home and might spend years in the Dauphin Jail, but he was wrong. Governor Guy Carleton decided that he was better off without the prisoners because it was too costly to house, feed, and guard them. During the first week of June, Carleton walked into the Dauphin Jail, surrounded by his armed guards, and stood a few yards from Greenman as he addressed the men.

They could go home, and shortly, he told them, as long as they promised to remain there and not rejoin the American army and fight against the British. It was that simple. By now, the men just wanted to leave and almost all signed a promise to remain at home, including Greenman. They left Canada nine weeks later on British ships that eventually took them to New York for their release. The night before they were to be freed, the British on board hosted them to a "night of carousing and dancing," as Greenman gleefully noted in his journal.

The private, by then eighteen, was set free the next morning, September 25, 1776, after nine months as a prisoner of war. He and several other soldiers walked from New York toward New England and home, more than two hundred miles, reaching Rhode Island on November 9. He luxuriated in "clean clothes" and "new shoes" and was happy to be home.

Jeremiah Greenman's war appeared to be over. After all, the teenager had promised Governor Carleton that he would remain at home and never take up arms against the British again.

He lied.

Chapter Nine

A HARROWING RETREAT

John Greenwood traveled to New York with the bulk of George Washington's army following the British evacuation of Boston, certain that he would defend that city. He would not. Greenwood's regiment was among several designated to provide reinforcements for the ill-fated invasion of Canada. Greenwood's Twelfth Massachusetts was dispatched to Canada after the men had spent just three weeks in New York. It was a happy layover for Greenwood, who had been promoted to senior fifer, because he was able to have new fifes made for the regiment by a skilled New York instrument maker. His fifes in his bags, he boarded a ship headed up the Hudson for Albany with his regiment. There, they would go overland and sail up Lake Champlain to Montreal. In the Canadian city, Greenwood assumed, they would march east and stage another attack on Quebec.

The Twelfth Massachusetts reached Montreal, still held by the Americans, a few weeks later. The teenager was apprehensive about any battles the regiment might find itself in, complaining in his diary that the five hundred men of the Twelfth Massachusetts were badly equipped. They carried muskets and blunderbusses of different sizes, possessed little ammunition, and had no bayonets. The men did not have swords either, although some had procured tomahawks. They had heard reports that hundreds of Indians were fighting with the British.

Exactly what they all feared—a battle involving Indians—took place only days after their arrival. A combined force of five hundred Indians and one hundred fifty British had surrounded an American outpost west of Montreal called the Cedars on May 19, 1776, forcing its interim commander to surrender. Some of the American soldiers there were executed by the Indians when they seized the garrison. The commander of the Cedars had left before the attack to plead for reinforcements from Arnold at Montreal. On May 17, Arnold sent one hundred forty men under Major Henry Sherburne of Massachusetts to assist the troops at Cedars, not knowing it was now held by the Indians. Sherburne brought the leader of the Twelfth Massachusetts, Captain Bliss, and some of his men with him.

Bliss asked Greenwood if he wanted to accompany the men or appoint other fifers to travel with them. Greenwood decided to remain in Montreal and sent two other fifers. "Off they all marched," he wrote, "[I] little thinking what a time they would have of it."

Greenwood, who had made the most fortunate decision of his life, could not know that Sherburne and his men would march right into a well-orchestrated ambush when they were within four miles of the Cedars on May 20. Six men were executed that night and the next day; the rest were held prisoner.

News of a second debacle reached Montreal quickly and on Saturday, May 25, Arnold left that city with the remainder of the Twelfth Massachusetts and five hundred additional men from other regiments to rescue those taken prisoner. To accomplish that task, the small army would have to do battle with the British and the Indians. Greenwood and the other enlisted men were worried about being taken prisoners by the Indians; none of them wanted to be killed or mutilated. Wrote Greenwood, "It is the custom of the Indians always to carry their prisoners with them . . . have them lie on the damp ground in the open air without the least covering except the heavens. [They were] often well soaked with rain and with little or nothing to eat. [Men] are generally much debilitated and weakened and subject to attack of flux and fever. As soon as one poor fellow is not able . . . to travel with them, the Indians knock him in the head more for the sake of getting his scalp than of getting rid of him, for the scalp is their trophy of war and he who has in his possession the greatest number is accounted the bravest warrior."

Arnold sent a scout to find Indian advance war parties and told Greenwood to go with him because, someone had told Arnold, Greenwood was "a brave little fellow of some intelligence." It was here that the fifer became the soldier, carrying a gun and a sword he had procured in Montreal for the first time. That night, in search of Indians, the two men found a small two-story, two-room stone farmhouse in a thick forest. The scout, wearing a buckskin shirt, went in, leaving Greenwood hiding behind a wooden rail fence. Greenwood noted, "He was afraid my regimental clothing, blue coat turned up and trimmed with buff and silver lace, would cause suspicion."

The man and his wife inside seemed harmless, so the scout waved Greenwood to join him. Fifteen minutes later, the two soldiers and the couple were startled to hear a series of loud Indian war whoops coming from the woods outside the home. They assumed that the Indians had been in a skirmish with Arnold's army, had lost, and were running from it. The scout and Greenwood dove underneath a bed in one of the rooms in an effort to hide. "In a minute or two the house and the entire road were ensconced with Indians, making a most hideous noise and retreating as fast as they could toward Fort Anne, some twelve miles off. In about an hour, they passed by without discovering us. Had they found us, we would have been burned alive."

Greenwood and the scout left the farmhouse and made their way through the woods, avoiding roads or clearings to remain unseen, and emerged several hours later outside of Fort Anne. The scout had changed clothes at the farmhouse and, looking like a Canadian trapper, ventured into the fort to gather information. He told Greenwood to hide behind another fence of round wooden poles a few hundred yards outside the fort. The teenager was nervous. He wrote, "I began to think what a situation I was in, standing in a nook between two posts of the fence within hearing of the savage Indians. Every minute appeared an hour; sometimes I heard them walking by me in the road. Then again, I would fancy they were looking after me; in short I had but a very unpleasant time of it."

Finally, after what seemed an eternity, the scout returned to tell him that the Indians were crossing the St. Lawrence and planned to ambush Arnold's army of eight hundred men in a day or two. They had to hurry to inform the general of the danger. They began to run away from the fort through some thick underbrush, unable to see much on the ground in front of them in the dark. Greenwood fell climbing over a stone wall and cut open the heel of his right foot. He had lost the shoe for that foot earlier as they scrambled through some bushes and had to limp the two miles to the village of Lachine, on the St. Lawrence, where Arnold had told them he would stop to camp. The teenager's foot continued to throb.

Arnold, never one to wait, decided to attack the Indians preparing to ambush him and moved the army westward right after he received the information from Greenwood and the scout. Greenwood, unable to walk, was placed in the front of a boat, put in charge of a blunderbuss, and sailed toward Fort Anne with others against the current of the St. Lawrence as the bulk of the army marched along the shore. Arnold rode in a birch canoe close to Greenwood in the middle of the river.

Along the way, the boats passed a naked man on the shore of a small island, who stumbled to the banks of the river. He was an American soldier who had escaped from the British and Indians that had taken the fort at the Cedars. He eagerly agreed to lead Arnold's army to the Indian camp at Quinze Chiens, on the St. Lawrence.

There, Greenwood wrote, they received a warm welcome. "The landing place was covered with woods, and behind every tree were three or four Indians who poured or showered their bullets upon us as thick as hailstones. General Arnold thought proper to give the signal of retreat to the other side of the river, so back we went."

They did so as fast as possible. From out of the woods appeared two field pieces operated by British soldiers that began to fire at the fleeing Americans in their canoes, the cannonballs hitting close to the boats and sending splashes of water high into the air. The Indians fighting with Arnold were terrified. Greenwood observed that the cannon "made our Indians fly with their birch canoes like so many devils; they do not like to see large balls skipping over the water in and out until their force is lost, for a single one would knock their paper boats to pieces in a moment."

To Greenwood's surprise, there was no battle that night or on the following morning. The Indians and the British under Captain George Forster had decided that Arnold's forces were too large and well equipped for them and made the general an intriguing offer: they would give him almost all of their American prisoners, several hundred, if he would let them leave without firing a shot, and agree to free some British prisoners. After both sides scouted each other for six days, Arnold, as worried as anyone about leaving hundreds of his soldiers in the hands of the Indians, agreed.

The prisoners the Indians turned over to Arnold the next day were pathetic looking. "Poor fellows, they looked as if they had been dragged by the heels for a hundred miles over the ground," Greenwood noted.

On May 6, reinforcements from England sailed up the St. Lawrence and had arrived at Quebec; nine hundred British troops on the ships attacked the Americans there as soon as the ships dropped anchor, driving them west toward Montreal. Then they marched west toward an even rosier target—Arnold and his army at Montreal.

Arnold felt that the city could not be held. Upon his return he raced through Montreal to organize a massive and hasty American evacuation of the city on reports that the newly arrived British troops were within two days march of his army. With authorization from Congress, he bought up supplies from local merchants and farmers with practically worthless Continental currency. Arnold told his men to order residents to accept it, and then, in a maneuver that was to become a trademark, Arnold seized vast supplies of booty—rum, molasses, clothing—"for the army" that some later charged were for himself.

When the Americans fled Montreal on June 15, they barely managed to escape. The evacuation itself was a scene of complete disorder, graphically described by Greenwood: "Down we scampered to the boats, those of the sick who were not led from the hospital crawling after us. Camp equippage, kettles, and everything were abandoned in the utmost confusion—even the bread that was baking in the ovens—for we were glad to get away with whole skins. When halfway across the river, it began to grow very dark and down came the rain in drops the size of large peas, wetting our smallpox fellows, huddled together like cordwood in the boats, and causing the deaths of many."

They crossed the St. Lawrence as speedily as possible. "It was a very cold rain and as the boat struck the shore I, being but a boy, and wet through and through, tried to take care of myself, at which I had a tolerable good knack, and so left the rest, dead and alive, to do the same. An old barn being near, I went in and soon found that others had discovered the retreat as well as myself and were lying on the floor close together like hogs, so I contentedly pigged it down with the rest."

A fatigued Greenwood and the men did not get much rest because officers came looking for them. "Turn out or we'll fire upon you!" shouted one at the groaning soldiers in the barn, who were too tired and drenched to move. "We'll fire upon you!" the soldier yelled again, brandishing his musket in the middle of the crowded barn. "Fire away!" a demoralized and exhausted Greenwood thought to himself as he stared at the officer.

Arnold, fearful of the British behind him, led a forced march of three miles and then let the men sleep. Greenwood spotted an old wooden windmill and slept inside it, awakened in the morning by the beat of the drums, the early morning light and calls to move out. He watched as General Arnold ordered priests in the village to give him all of the wagons and carts nearby so that he could transport his stores and the sick. An angry Arnold told them that if they refused he would burn down the village; the clergymen agreed.

At St. John's, along the route toward Sorel, the Americans passed piles of warehouse stores from Montreal that Arnold had taken in the name of the army. They sat on the roadside or in yards; some of the wooden crates had been opened. The supplies, or the "plunder," as Greenwood called it, had created a major problem for Arnold. He had been given approval from Congress to take whatever he needed from the merchants and swore that he had written down a list of the goods, supplying the name of each contractor or merchant from whom it was purchased—and the cost—for verification. He told Congress, though, that the rush of the retreat prevented a complete listing. He wrote to them, "It is impossible to know one hour beforehand the necessary steps to be taken. Everything is in the greatest confusion, not one contractor commissary or quartermaster; I am obliged to do the duty of all."[1]

Arnold had sent the goods to St. John's and ordered Colonel Moses Hazen to sign for them and post a guard to insure their safety until his army arrived. Hazen, who did not like Arnold, noticed right away that there were no lists of what was in the crates or from whom they had been purchased. Despite what Arnold claimed were orders, Hazen refused to sign and to post a guard and his men opened the wooden crates and removed items from them, further muddling the paperwork on the goods.[2] It appeared that Arnold did not have receipts for most of the supplies, either. This "official" removal of captured or commandeered goods, incomplete and questionable paperwork, lack of receipts, and shoddy bookkeeping would be a hallmark of Arnold throughout the war.

Arnold's army began to approach Lake Champlain in the middle of June. At the same time, an American force of one thousand men under the command of Generals John Sullivan and William Thompson was badly defeated at Three Rivers on June 8. The survivors of that battle were also forced to turn around and retreat toward Sorel in a helter-skelter fashion after losing hundreds of men.[3] That expedition had been authorized by Congress, thanks to Arnold's gloomy letter in April that he ended by warning them that "everything is at a stand for want of resources and, if they are not obtained soon, our affairs in this country will be entirely . . . ruined."[4] Congress was so startled by the letter that it sent a congressional committee all the way to Montreal to meet with Arnold to see what could be done to take Canada. The delegation, led by Benjamin Franklin, was wined and dined by the wily general; they were convinced that they had to send Arnold all the reinforcements they could and that Canada had to be conquered—despite the newly arrived British force.

The country could not be taken, however, and the three separate expeditions of Montgomery, Arnold, and now Sullivan had ended as fiascoes and in hasty exit from Canada. The retreat from Montreal and other Canadian posts had been so badly planned that the group of Americans fleeing ahead of Arnold's army—moving as fast as it could to leave the hell that Canada had become for its soldiers—believed that the men behind them were not Americans, but the British, and had set fire to a bridge they had crossed to prevent the "Redcoats" from following. Greenwood and the others had to cross the bridge while it was still burning, running through the flames as fast as they could.

The Redcoats that Greenwood thought were behind him, however, were the *real* Redcoats and they were so close that they terrified him. He wrote, "We could plainly see the British on the opposite shore; so close were they upon us that if we had not retreated as we did, all would have been prisoners."

Arnold had his boats destroyed after the men crossed to the southern side of the St. Lawrence to prevent the British from seizing them and the men had to march southward on foot. The soldiers in Greenwood's regiment, in the rear, found themselves walking by the seriously wounded American soldiers and smallpox victims who had died on the way and had been left on the side of the road so as not to slow down the column. Their corpses made haunting mileposts.

Since he was a boy, no one asked Greenwood to do the same work that the men in the army performed. He did not have to carry heavy supplies, assist in the rowing of the boats or stand watch as a guard. He wanted to do his share to help the army, though, and so he did what he knew best—he played music. Each evening on the retreat from Montreal, Greenwood took out a new fife he had made in New York and entertained both officers and the enlisted men with tunes. He had a standard repertoire of songs that he performed and then played any personal favorites that the men requested. These included both rousing drinking tunes they had heard so often at taverns and slow romantic ballads that reminded many of loved ones at home. Then, risking his health, Greenwood walked over to the temporary camp hospitals to visit the sick, including the men afflicted with smallpox, and played songs for them on his fife. They were all grateful for some lively melodies on those terrible nights on the run.

Finally, the vast waters of Lake Champlain were in sight and the soldiers in Arnold's army were loaded into a flotilla of large sailboats, all equipped with oars for rowing when there was no wind. They had a scorching sun above them and more than a hundred miles of open water in front of them—and the British army close behind them—before they would reach their destination, Fort Ticonderoga.

Champlain, named after the French explorer Samuel de Champlain, was a natural wonder. It was the largest lake in what was the United States then, except for the Great Lakes, whose shores were shared by the U.S. and Canada. Champlain was one hundred seven miles long and fourteen miles across at its widest and just one mile at its narrowest. At some junctures at its northern tip, where it flowed into the Richelieu River near some islands, the lake was just a few hundred yards wide. The lake, which formed part of the border between New York and Vermont, covered a total of 435 square miles. It was 399 feet deep in some places, but near the shorelines, and in some places near Valcour Island to the north, it was just a few yards deep and only shallow bottom vessels could sail there. Lake Champlain was nestled between the Adirondack Mountains to the west and the Green Mountains, in Vermont, to the east.

Most of Champlain was surrounded by low terrain, marshy at times, and at many points on any boat trip on its waters travelers could see the majestic mountain ranges in the distance. The Green Mountains hugged the coastline of the northeast sections of the lake. The mountains contrasted starkly with the lake, too, and some soldiers in the retreating American army, now under the command of John Sullivan, reported sweating in the boats as they peered up at the snow-covered Adirondack Mountains in the distance. The weather on the lake, and in the region surrounding it, changed frequently and sudden summer rainstorms were common. The winds shifted with little notice or died suddenly. The waters of the lake could be flat for days and then produce ocean-sized waves when high winds swept over and churned up the water. The uncertain weather made sailing on the waters of the lake difficult. The weather shifted quickly, too, in uneven patterns. Hot days in summer were followed by chilly nights. It snowed early in winter toward the northern part of the lake, which cut into Canada, and on many Thanksgiving days those who lived there found themselves snowbound. In 1776, the snows came very early, in the third week of October.

The journey of Greenwood's regiment down the lake was slow and languid. At its narrow sections they could see deer and a wide array of small animals on the shores and some of the birds that lived off the lake, such as the great blue heron, bald eagle, and the marsh wren. Osprey occasionally flew overhead.

From time to time, when the men were tired from rowing on calm days, or when it became very hot as the sun was reflected off the lake, Greenwood pulled out his fife and played some music. As always, the men appreciated it and, after a few moments of rest, rowed again, the splashing sounds of their oars dipping into the lake accompanied by some lively tunes on the fife and the squawks of a bird soaring high above them.

Chapter Ten

THE HEALERS:
The Reverend, the Doctor,
and the Smallpox Scourge

The Rev. Ammi Robbins's journey toward the valley of death began on March 18, 1776. His departure from his home near Canaan, in the northwest corner of Connecticut, for service as a chaplain in the Continental Army could not have been more pleasant. He met friend and fellow minister Rev. Farrand in Canaan and together they rode six miles north to Sheffield, Massachusetts, just over the Connecticut state line, to the home of Robbins's sister, who was also married to a minister, the Rev. John Keep. The three ministers and Robbins's sister enjoyed a lengthy dinner and then prayed together. On the following morning, Rev. Robbins left the comfort of friends and family and headed into the heart of the American Revolution.

Robbins was a thirty-five-year-old Presbyterian minister from a state that had sent thousands of young men to war. He had joined the Continental Army because he hoped that as a chaplain he would be able to heal the hearts and souls of the men in the service who were risking their lives every day in the battle for independence that had lasted for nearly a year.

He was one of the many spiritual healers who volunteered to serve in the army after the Revolution began in the spring of 1775. The military had no difficulty signing up ministers. The men of God, who received officers' pay, were eager to join the army because they saw the rebellion as not just a political and military revolution, but a campaign to redeem men's souls, the logical extension of the Great Awakening.

George Washington believed that it was important to have many chaplains in the service. He believed that the comfort they could provide the men was as important as military leadership and that a fear of God helped to maintain discipline. The chaplains were not asked to do much more than they did for their congregations back home: they were charged with offering two prayer services on Sunday and one daily service during the week, if they so chose. They were to visit the sick and dying in the field hospitals when and if they could. They were to comfort anyone who sought them out. Some chaplains were good and some were bad, just like some doctors and officers.

Some ministers offered just one Sunday service and some faked illness to avoid Sunday work at all. Others offered a service every day in addition to their Sunday chores. Some ministers never visited the sick and some visited the hospitals all the time. Most of the army's chaplains in winter or summer camps were local ministers who added army duties to their congregational responsibilities; others traveled with the army twelve months a year. Only a few served for more than one year; Rev. David Avery served for five. They all believed that they were appreciated by the troops, especially the enlisted men and the homesick young soldiers far from their villages and loved ones.

The men of God put their lives at risk. Some chaplains died of illnesses during the war and some were killed in accidents. At least one committed suicide. Others came down with smallpox and died or had their faces scarred for the rest of their lives. Still others became ill in the service and wound up dying at home, or being weakened for life. Some lost their positions in churches back home by refusing to leave the army when called back by the church elders.

Rev. Ammi Robbins did not realize the magnitude of the nightmare he was traveling toward when he reported to Albany in the middle of that cold and blustery year. Traveling up to Canada a few weeks later would be Dr. Lewis Beebe, a Yale graduate from Sheffield, Massachusetts. Beebe was one of the hundreds of doctors who had left their private practice to save the lives and tend to the wounds of the soldiers in the first American army. He would be the healer of their bodies as Robbins would be the healer of their souls. Neither of the healers knew each other, but would meet and become friends in the middle of the terrible chaos that now engulfed Canada.

The journey to Canada became nothing short of macabre as each day passed and the army moved farther and farther north. At each stop, the minister would discover some reminder of death and catastrophe. His uncle had been killed during a battle in the French and Indian War outside of Albany two decades before and one day Robbins went out with another man to visit his uncle's grave. It was one of many in a small cemetery. He found his uncle's resting place and "dropped a tear over it" and went back to camp. It was the first of many graves over which he would cry during his journey to Canada.

The starting point for the trip, Albany, was a city full of both patriots and Tories as well as several thousand Continental Army soldiers, but it was also a boisterous city of taverns and prostitutes, and the language of the people that the righteous minister met was laced with loud and graphic profanity. The city from whence his journey would begin was, he wrote in his journal, an American Sodom and Gomorrah, "a wicked city," and he said that he deplored the "wickedness of the people [in it]."

There, prior to the beginning of the march toward Canada, Robbins offered prayers in the morning and in the evening each day, doing more than most men of the cloth in the army. The minister visited the sick in army hospitals that had been created out of residences and barns. He was encouraged by the large assemblage of soldiers that turned out to pray with him and listen to him read from the Bible and preach.

He noted in the daily journal that he kept that there was a growing awareness of death around him that was triggered by his visit to his uncle's grave in the cemetery. One afternoon he prayed with two young soldiers, weakened by fever, nearly motionless on their beds, who soon died. The next day he was summoned to the community of Stillwater, several miles from Albany, to pray for a man whose time, it was said, was growing short. It was. The man, suffering greatly in his bed, died as Robbins sat next to him on a wooden chair reading scriptures aloud.

His sermons to the congregation of several hundred troops and a collection of townspeople who lived nearby, who traveled by horse and carriage to listen to him, were long and powerful and even then people praised his preaching style. He quoted from Hosea, "I will go and return to my place until they acknowledge their offense and seek my face," and Micah, "And this man shall be the peace."

There were overtures in some of his sermons, though, unintended at that time, that provided an unsettling foreshadowing of the debacles to come on the journey they were all about to embark upon. In one ominous sermon, he talked of a God who had abandoned his people, reading a passage from the Bible that said, "If thy presence go not with me, carry us not up hence."

Robbins attended the funeral of yet another soldier who died the day before the army began its march. The entire journey north was a trip filled with somber reminders of war, destruction, and death. One day into the march, north of Saratoga, the men passed Fort Edwards, a burned-out stockade used during the French and Indian War, which Robbins reported "moldering down" like a slowly collapsing ghost. A day later, at the southern tip of Lake George, he was given a tour of the ruins of Fort William Henry. It was there, in 1757, that the British surrendered to the French, under the Marquis Louis Montcalm, only to have hundreds of his Indian troops attack their caravan as they left the fort, killing sixty-nine soldiers and women and taking two hundred away as prisoners. As Robbins finished that tour, he met two companies of Pennsylvania troops on their way to Canada, carrying their sick. They told the minister that they had left men who had died on the march on the sides of the road. "How easy 'tis for God to bless or blast our designs," a saddened Robbins wrote in his journal that night.

He was told by all, officers and enlisted men, that his sermons helped the men feel better about life in the army. This encouraged him. Robbins was ebullient on April 20, when he stood in front of two regiments of seven hundred men each on the shores of Lake George, the beautiful wide body of water with its thickly forested shoreline his backdrop, and led them in loud prayers and spirited hymnal singing before they boarded their boats for another leg of the journey north.

Robbins lived with officers in small tents that accommodated from two to four men. He did not care for some of them, continually complaining about their profanity and "wickedness" and writing that "it would be a dreadful hell to live with such creatures forever."

For the men, though, the dreadful hell was illness. "'Tis terrible to be sick in the army," Robbins lamented. "Such miserable accommodations. It is enough to kill a man's spirit when first taken to go into the hospital."

Robbins and the men with him sailed north on Lake George, thirty-three miles long and from one to three miles wide, and then on to Fort Ticonderoga on the southern shores of Lake Champlain. None of them were prepared for the grotesque specter that greeted them as they were shown the cemetery there. The very upset minister wrote, "[We] saw many holes where the dead were flung in, and numbers of human bones, thighs, arms, etc. above the ground. Oh, the horrors of war. I never so much longed for the day to approach when men shall learn war no more and the lion and lamb lie down together."

The army sailed across Lake Champlain, ever closer to Canada and Quebec, in "gondolas," sixty-foot-long, two-masted schooners with open decks to carry supplies and troops. The chaplain joined the men in rowing the boat when the winds died down. They all talked of the coming battles and their fear of dying in them. Many were frightened. The minister knew that he might lose his life, too, despite his clergyman rank. Robbins prayed for his own safety and asked God to give him strength to be brave, to survive, and to help others make it through the storm ahead. "The prospects at Quebec look very dark," he wrote. "Oh, that I might be able to trust in God and not be afraid."

What Robbins and everyone else feared was not just fighting the British and the hundreds of Indians they had enlisted as their allies, but the smallpox epidemic there. The American army had become a victim of the fatal disease in December, just before the failed assault on Quebec. Those in Arnold's army who had survived the trek to Canada were exhausted, hungry, and wore tattered and damp clothes that they rarely took off. Their huts and tents held more men than they should have. These conditions created an ideal climate for smallpox. General Richard Montgomery, who had smallpox as a young man and was immune, commandeered a building owned by the East India Company in Montreal and he appointed Doctor Isaac Senter as its administrator with orders to turn it into a six-hundred-bed hospital to house smallpox victims. They increased every day. Dr. Senter noted then that "the smallpox still very rife in the army."[1] A field hospital set up between the towns of Sillery and Cove to handle smallpox victims filled up quickly and doctors there said 10 percent of the army had the disease.[2]

General Thomas, a physician prior to the rebellion, had gone to Canada as the American commanding general on May 1. Thomas, fifty-one, was a fierce patriot and a member of Boston's Sons of Liberty. The doctor was a well-dressed and distinguished man. He tried to isolate the men with smallpox in hospitals, but he had also permitted many of his men to live in private homes throughout the area. They became infected and the disease moved rapidly from them to others, and then to many more. Many deserted from the army after the January 1 defeat at Quebec, some with the pox, and promptly infected anyone they encountered in the Quebec area, and those people infected other soldiers whom they met later.[3] Ultimately, over five hundred soldiers would die because of the pox.

General David Wooster arrived to take command of the army from Arnold in March and by the end of the month approximately one third of the 2,505 Americans had come down with the dreaded pox. Arnold wrote that "smallpox at this juncture" might result in "the entire ruin of the army."[4] The Americans who fled when British reinforcements arrived in Quebec on May 6 left hundreds of sick, including recovering smallpox victims, in hospitals and many more, unable to travel, along the sides of roads (fortunately for them, Governor Guy Carleton ordered his men to bring them back to Quebec where hospitals were set up to house them and many were saved).

Smallpox was the scourge of the eighteenth century. Epidemics in London that arrived between 1718 and 1746 had killed tens of thousands of people. Several thousand died in similar epidemics in Geneva and Berlin in those years. Forty thousand perished in a smallpox attack in Belem, Brazil, in 1750. The 1721 epidemic that reached Boston claimed the lives of 15 percent of the population of the city.

The disease struck quickly and usually took the lives of between 10 and 15 percent of the population of a city, but sometimes claimed as many as one-third or 40 percent of the residents. Those struck suffered severe fevers, throbbing headaches, aches of the loins and limbs, fast pulses, and painful vomiting. After several days, ugly pus-filled eruptions appeared on the skin all over the body, often completely disfiguring the face. Victims' heads often turned blue and those who did die perished within a week.

The standard procedure to prevent smallpox was diet and inoculation. Doctors prescribed ten to fourteen days of rest and a light diet, plus purging, followed by the injection of the smallpox pustules into the skin with a one-eighth-inch-wide lancet. The diet usually consisted of pudding, milk, ripe fruit, carrots, cabbage, potatoes, and vegetables.[5]

Smallpox would break out on the skin several days later, accompanied by a fever. The patient walked about outside and drank generous amounts of very cold water to assist the virus injected into his system in fighting off the pox. The diet and purging were considered mandatory to cleanse the body for the inoculation and introduction of the virus into the system.[6]

Ironically, these doctors, who saved so many lives, terrified residents in nearby neighborhoods because they inoculated people, giving them smallpox to fight smallpox. They feared the introduction of the disease could infect those not immune to smallpox who lived nearby. A hospital in Boston where smallpox patients were treated was burned down by neighbors who feared those inoculated there would infect the entire city.

Someone threw a bomb into the room of a man recovering from his inoculation in an attempt to kill him to prevent him from spreading the disease. Dr. Boylston, a genuine medical hero, had been frequently taunted for inoculating people; he once told friends he was concerned about his safety.[7]

No one, however, understood the magnitude of the crisis about to envelope the Americans stationed along Lake Champlain in forts at Ticonderoga and Crown Point as well as at their camps in the Canadian villages of Sorel, at the intersection of the St. Lawrence and Richelieu Rivers, and Chambly farther south on the Richelieu. None of these places was equipped to handle several thousand smallpox victims, and those infected with other diseases, such as typhus, in addition to the wounded men retreating from the military defeats in Canada. There were not enough hospitals, beds, medical supplies, or doctors. Like a tidal wave, smallpox was headed toward Rev. Robbins and all of the Americans in the northern area of New York.[8]

Robbins's regiment soon arrived at Chambly, a small village in Canada, a Catholic country that Robbins referred to as "the dwelling place of Satan." The minister, who loathed Roman Catholics, visited a Catholic church there and was appalled by what he saw: three crucifixes, a holy water font, and an altar. As he looked around, a young man walked down the center aisle, knelt in front of the altar, and began to pray. Robbins was indignant. "Oh, when shall Satan be found and the Anti-Christ meet a final overthrow?" he wrote of the visit to the church.

Just three days later, he and the soldiers sailed up the Richelieu River past the village of St. Dennis. A strong wind carried them at a rapid rate down the river. The Protestant minister was irked to see a long string of small homes with crucifixes on their roofs and a Roman Catholic church. In a macabre scene, a group of curious nuns in their black and white habits emerged from the church and stared at the American army, looking directly at Rev. Robbins, as their flotilla of vessels moved past them and headed toward the war.

On Tuesday, May 7, Robbins and the soldiers in his regiment met dozens of men who were returning from Quebec by land; part of the

general route that had commenced the day before when British reinforcements had arrived at Quebec. Some of the soldiers had been
wounded and bled through their clothes as they half walked, half
limped southward, trying to bear up under the hot sun. Many, trembling as they appeared, were badly infected with smallpox and other
diseases and the men with Robbins all feared the disease would spread
throughout the boat.

Shortly after the arrival of the infected soldiers, a flotilla of British
ships suddenly appeared. The warships sailed ever closer and began to
shell the Americans when their cannon were in range. The U.S. boats
and the hundreds of soldiers that had been walking along the river were
both targets of the British cannon that raked the water and the shoreline. Some of the smallpox victims had managed to scramble on board
Robbins's gondola and other vessels, and stayed there, overcrowding the
open decks of the ships, but dozens of others, still on land, were hail-
ing the vessels with their arms and yelling for help. Left behind, they
were taken prisoners as the army tried to outrun the British ships and
head south to Sorel.

General Thomas had sent out orders that all of the Americans fleeing
the Quebec area, and those headed north, such as Robbins's regiment,
were to rendezvous at Sorel, a busy fur-trapping community, and await
further orders. Robbins and the men in his boat raised their sail and
helped pick up speed by manning the oars, too, as the shelling continued
and numerous cannonballs crashed near the hull in the water, creating
huge splashes of water close enough to soak the men on the boats. Robbins
was frightened, his head swiveling from side to side as he watched shells hit
in the water and explode on land, knocking down trees, sending tons of
dirt soaring into the air, destroying huge clumps of bushes and leaving
craters in the ground.

He wrote, "Three [British] ships came near us, firing as they came,
and our boats and people in a scattered condition. Distress and anxiety
in every countenance, the smallpox thick among us. This is the most terrible day I ever saw. God of armies, help us."

A Doctor Far from Home

Robbins and the men in flight with him reached Sorel, forty miles away, five days later, the day after Doctor Lewis Beebe had arrived there. He knew from information they received on the passage north that many American troops had been killed in Quebec and three hundred taken prisoner. He knew, too, that many of those still there and many in flight were badly wounded—and had been infected with smallpox. The men he greeted as they staggered into the American camp were in bad shape. He wrote in his journal, "Those who come safe to Sorel were obliged to leave all their baggage and bring nothing away but the clothes on their backs. No person can conceive the distress our people endured the winter past, nor was it much less at the time of their retreat."

Private Lemuel Roberts began his retreat just as hundreds of the pus-filled pocks exploded on his skin, even growing inside his ears. He wrote in his journal that he was racked with pain and misery. By the time his regiment reached safety in Sorel by boat, "my pock had become so sore and troublesome that my clothes stuck fast to my body, especially to my feet; and it became a severe trial to my fortitude to beat my disorder and assist in managing the boat."[9]

Lewis Beebe found himself in Sorel at the opposite end of the world from his former life. The bright, twenty-six-year-old doctor had, in just a few short years, achieved some distinction as a general practitioner in Sheffield, where he had moved after graduation to start his practice. Life was good. Beebe had become a welcome member of the community. He had married Lucy Allen, the sister of the fabled Ethan Allen, head of the Green Mountain Boys, on September 20, 1774.

His golden life unraveled rather quickly once the war began. His wife, in her early twenties, died on June 10, 1775, and he plunged into a lengthy depression. Ethan Allen had gained fame by capturing Fort Ticonderoga from the British with Benedict Arnold in the spring of 1775, but shortly afterwards Allen was captured in a daring but failed attack on Montreal and sent to England, where he was hailed as Britain's most illustrious prisoner of war. Beebe decided that leaving his home-town, and memories of his wife, for a stint in the army might help him recover emotionally and he volunteered in the spring of 1776. It seemed like a logical choice. His patriotic brother-in-law was surely an inspiration for the doctor. Beebe had also been friendly with John Brown, a political radical at Yale. He joined a Connecticut regiment and was assigned to join forces en route to reenforce an American army already reeling from a severe defeat at Quebec in the winter.

Beebe and Rev. Robbins might have met in Sorel, rapidly filling up with sick troops, that first day that Robbins arrived in May 1776. If not, they met shortly afterwards because both of their journals, and the journal of Rev. David Avery, another chaplain, indicate that Beebe and Robbins became friends and often traveled and dined together at the homes of local residents or with officers in their tents. Beebe wrote that he listened to and admired Rev. Robbins's sermons; Robbins wrote of his meals with the doctor. Both men were healers. Robbins, a man of God, had arrived in war-torn Canada to spiritually heal the souls of men who were fighting and dying. Beebe had reached Canada not only to physically heal the men badly wounded in the battles there, but to attempt to save soldiers trapped in a brutal smallpox epidemic. Now, caught in the middle of a landmark military disaster and a massive, uncoordinated, frantic retreat, with dozens of men arriving in Sorel with their bodies ravaged by the smallpox and other illnesses, the two young healers would have their hands full.

The other doctors were pleased to greet Beebe. They had been overwhelmed by the volume of soldiers being carried into their hospitals. Surgeons used to treating a few men each day found themselves standing in the middle of temporary hospitals set up in barns or large tents with several hundred men around them and more being carried in each hour, many groaning from their wounds and illnesses.

Dr. Beebe began his work on a Wednesday, three days after his arrival, treating fifty patients in the general hospital at Sorel, where within weeks a total of more than thirty-three hundred sick men would be in hospitals, taking up all of the narrow wooden beds and laying on blankets spread on the floors. He treated most with the bloodletting that was so popular in the colonial era. Doctors firmly believed that many illnesses were caused by infected blood and that simply bleeding the victims, sometimes draining several pints from their bloodstream, would cure them. He gave others medicines such as tarts, antimonies, or jalap. A good doctor and a physician always trying to learn about disease, Lewis Beebe realized quickly that the dozens of different wounds the men had suffered, their diseases, ailments, and the smallpox afforded him a unique chance to study medicine, opportunities that never existed back in tiny Sheffield. "The camp is one of the finest schools in the world," he noted.[10]

The next day a controversy erupted over how to treat the smallpox victims. There were more each day and soon infected men would total nearly two thousand in medical wards at Sorel and nearby in the towns of St. John and Chambly. At the time, there were inoculations, but the "ten days rest and diet" procedure for inoculation was slow and men came down with the disease before the inoculation could take effect.

Doctors urged high ranking officers to authorize inoculations upon arrival so that the men could be treated quickly and their lives saved. It seemed like an obvious decision. Benedict Arnold, who had been watching his men die of the pox since December, understood the need for the inoculations and ordered all of the men in Sorel to undergo them. The first regiment, Colonel Porter's, was inoculated that day. The doctors made plans to inoculate everyone else within the next week or so. But then General John Thomas, who had seen men and women die of smallpox in Boston earlier in the year, disagreed and upon his arrival at Sorel the following day, May 16, ordered a halt to the inoculations that Arnold had just approved. Not only did Thomas override Arnold, but said that any soldier who received an inoculation would be shot. Thomas had decided that mass inoculations, and the recovery period, would render too many soldiers unable to fight should the British catch up to the Americans. Despite his reasons, the doctors in camp were astonished that a former physician would bar inoculations, especially since this was an obvious emergency.

So was everyone else. After Thomas's orders halting all inoculations, men who did not want to be shot but wanted to survive smallpox secretly inoculated themselves between their toes, so there would be no physical evidence of cuts in their skin. Officers even told the men to do so and suggested areas of the body where cuts could not be easily detected. Everyone was scared. "The smallpox strikes terror into our troops," wrote Rev. Robbins, who had seen the ravages of the disease in hundreds of men in Sorel, a place, he added, that had poor leadership and was in a daily state of confusion. (It is not known whether Robbins was immune to the disease).

On the following Tuesday, Dr. Beebe was visited by an aide to General Thomas who told him that the commanding general wanted to see him right away; the general did not feel well. The physician, uncertain what the general wanted, accompanied the officer to Thomas's large command tent. Beebe was taken aback by the deteriorating condition of the man standing in front of him. Beebe knew what Thomas's problem was right away. "He evidently had the smallpox," a startled Beebe wrote, wondering how someone ill with the pox would prevent others from being inoculated. It made no sense.

Beebe's own life would now be put in danger because Thomas, who knew he was sick and needed expert medical care, ordered the doctor to travel with him and treat him in Chambly, fifty miles away, where he planned to recuperate from his illness while continuing to run the army from a different base of operations as it withdrew south.

The two men, accompanied by a few soldiers, left Sorel on Tuesday and throughout their two-day journey down river to Chambly encountered many troops who were in flight from the Quebec area. They learned of a disastrous engagement between a Rhode Island regiment of seven hundred men led by Henry Sherburne, and several hundred Indians. According to early reports, everyone in Sherburne's regiment had been killed in the battle. The men spreading that news had no reports of Arnold's rush to rescue Sherburne's men with soldiers including John Greenwood.

Just after sunset, after two days of slow and arduous traveling, Dr. Beebe and General Thomas arrived in Chambly. Thomas felt well enough to walk a half-mile to his lodging, listening to an array of both news and rumors about the trouble at Quebec as he moved. Doctor Beebe was at his side. The next morning, following more treatment from Beebe, General

Thomas told the physician that he felt much better, and over the next few days his pustules began to shrink and his condition visibly improved. Beebe began to think that the general might survive the attack. His spirits were lifted at the new health of his most famous patient.

The condition of others with smallpox did not improve. Dr. Beebe began to treat more soldiers trying to fight off smallpox while laying in horse barns amid dirty hay and dung. The large wooden barns that creaked at night from the wind and were overwhelmed by heat in the daytime appeared to be large ovens in which men were roasting from the heat and dying of the pox. There was a nonstop cacophony of weeping, moans, and sheer misery that surrounded the doctor as he worked throughout the day in the barns. Beebe wrote of the men there ceaselessly groaning from pain:

> The most shocking of all spectacles was to see a large barn crowded full of men with this disorder, many of which could not see, speak, or walk—one, nay two, had large maggots, an inch long, crawl out of their ears. [Pustules] were on almost every part of the body. No mortal will ever believe what these suffered unless they were eyewitnesses. It was almost sufficient to excite the pity of brutes.

Rev. David Avery was an obstinate man who would ask Dartmouth College for his tuition back because, he charged, he received no education there. The chaplain had traveled to Ticonderoga and Crown Point with Beebe in the winter. Avery possessed an iron constitution and was never sick, despite being surrounded by illness. He visited those barns at Chambly, too. He wrote, "The sick were in horse stables just cleared of dung . . . laid on the floors of the stinking stables."

Those who survived those barns, and other wretched hospitals, described their illnesses and desperate efforts to overcome them in graphic detail. Simon Fobes survived his pox in a Quebec prison. He wrote, "When the pock was coming out in seventy to eighty of our number, a fever very high and no water to drink, the men drank their own urine which made the fever rage too violently to be endured. Our flesh seemed a mass of corruption. At the same time, we were covered with vermin. When we were a little recovered, we were moved back to our former prison without any cleansing or changing of our apparel. Our clothing was stiff with corrupted matter."[11]

Many of the men coming down with the smallpox were in mid retreat in the region and could neither rest or obtain inoculation. They were stuck and had to fight their way out of Canada and out of the grips of the epidemic. One was Bayze Wells, of Connecticut. He started to break out on May 7 while staying overnight at a farmhouse. He did not want to remain, ill, and be taken prisoner, so the next morning he climbed into a bark canoe and, with others, paddled several miles downriver to meet his regiment. He remained there for a week, becoming sicker, and then they had to flee. The entire group left in canoes and Wells, like the others, had to paddle as fast as he could all night. He felt dizzy throughout the evening and into early morning and, just after dawn, fainted in the canoe. He had to be carried the rest of the day in a cart and finally managed to make it to a hospital.

Many died on the retreat. One soldier, Charles Cushing, estimated that thirty captains alone had perished from the pox. Cushing's friend, Colonel James Reed, of New Hampshire, told him that he expected to lose an entire third of his regiment to the disease.[12]

Others had to fight on while the smallpox festered in their bodies. Bayley Frye, a novice soldier who was made a colonel in order to get him to volunteer for a dangerous mission, found himself coming down with pox during the first week of May. Pustules began to appear on May 10. A few days later, very sick, he was ordered to take a village of four houses that held thirty-three men, women, and children. In the fight that ensued he nearly fainted from the pox several times. He could not move quickly and was badly injured.[13]

Dozens of men fleeing the Quebec disasters arrived in Chambly daily. New orders countermanded old ones within hours. Many had been wounded and others had smallpox.

Dr. Beebe, overworked and overwhelmed, was an angry young physician. He had nothing but disdain for the officers in the Continental Army that he had met in just two weeks at Sorel and Chambly. On the day when the officers ordered as many men as possible to parade at Chambly, over twelve hundred, most of them barely able to walk, Beebe scrawled sarcastically in his journal, "Had we a Washington or a Lee to take the command from a set of haughty, ambitious aspiring miscreants who only pride in promotion and honor, we might have hopes of regaining Quebec."

He was even unhappier about his treatment of General Thomas, who had taken a turn for the worse after all the outward appearances of recovery. Thomas suddenly became ill and died of the pox in his bed at Chambly just after the sun rose on the morning of Sunday, June 2, a distraught Dr. Beebe at his bedside. What enraged Beebe was that the general, a doctor, might have been saved by being a recipient of the very smallpox inoculations that he had outlawed.

On the day after Thomas's death, Beebe took a count of the men in the Chambly barns suffering from smallpox and put the number at just over three hundred. He and others had apparently secretly inoculated them, against Thomas's wishes, while the general was in bed and Beebe hoped that they would all survive. They would not. On the very next day, a man died of the pox, his entire body covered with pus-filled pocks. No one would go near his corpse for fear of catching the disease themselves and the man had to be buried without a coffin. The standard set of pall-bearers could not be found to carry the body to a grave and it had to be dragged there. "The stupidity of mankind in this situation is beyond all description," wrote Beebe, who watched the way that the soldiers passed from the earth—without any dignity.

The next day Dr. Beebe visited an officer who had become his friend, Colonel Reed of New Hampshire, who had lost so many men in his regiment to the pox. Now he found to his dismay that Reed, too, had the small-pox. On his way back to his lodging, Beebe encountered a soldier whom he despised, a "little, great, proud, self-conceited, foppish quack." The man haughtily asked Beebe if he had any physic [medicine] to give him because he did not feel well. The doctor, angry about all of the men sick and dying under his care, and now Colonel Reed, too, snapped at the soldier, "I have plenty of physic, but God damn my soul if I'll let you have some."

Then he turned abruptly and walked away.

Two days later, on Friday, one man died of smallpox, one of colic, and one of a fever. Beebe and other doctors struggled to keep the soldiers in the barns alive. He was furious about the spartan, temporary hospitals, the dearth of medicine, and the uselessness of traditional medical practices. He wrote that night that he was "moved with compassionate feeling for poor, distressed soldiers; when they are taken sick, are thrown into this dirty, stinking place, and left to take care of themselves, no attendance, no provision made, but what must be loathed and abhorred by all, both well and sick."

On Sunday, two men under his care died of smallpox and two more passed away from the disease on Monday. That same fatal day was also the one year anniversary of Lucy Beebe's death and the memory of his late wife's passing sent Beebe into a deep depression. He sadly wrote in his journal that night: "Oh fleeting time, who dost make no delay, but with rapid force sweeps all without distinction to one common grave. Let me remember that the same thing must take place with respect to me as it did to her."

The good doctor then learned that a regiment badly afflicted with smallpox—the majority of the men were sick and barely able to walk—had just been ordered to travel by boat to Sorel, a distance of fifty miles. Beebe called the decision "ridiculous" and then scrawled at the end of his journal entry for that long and melancholy day, "It is enough to confuse and distract a rational man from becoming a surgeon to a regiment."

Chapter Eleven

DEATH BECOMES A
DAILY VISITOR

During the second week of June, Dr. Beebe continued his medical practice—treating the sick, extracting teeth, watching men vomit after he gave them purge-inducing medicine, and inoculating hundreds of soldiers arriving at Chambly. He heard dozens of macabre stories from the men in the beds under his care. One dying enlisted man told him that he had been an ordained minister back home, but had been dismissed from his congregation over a sexual affair he had conducted with his maid. Disgraced and afraid to face anyone in his community, he joined the army. And he would soon be dead. "This is the fate of war," Beebe wrote, "one rises and another falls."

The camp was thrown into chaos by the sudden arrival of Benedict Arnold, who was still smarting from his losses in Canada and the chaotic retreat. Arnold now walked with a pronounced limp from the leg wound he suffered in the attack on Quebec on January 1. The physician saw him as an egomaniacal incompetent and one of the main causes of all the sickness and dying that surrounded him.

"The great Arnold arrived here yesterday and began to give his inconsistent orders," Beebe wrote. With great cynicism, he added that "with his great pity for the sick," Arnold ordered food allowances for those ill or with smallpox in the barns to be cut in half, along with reduced rations for the rest of the army as a food-supply crisis emerged. Arnold said that food was low, but his edict infuriated the physician. "In this order is discovered that superior wisdom which is necessary in a man in his exalted station," Beebe sneered.

The following day the camp at Chambly was hurled into confusion when news arrived that the two-thousand-man army under William Thompson had been badly beaten on June 8, 1776, at the battle of Three Rivers and was in full retreat, all of the men scrambling toward either Sorel or Chambly, chased by both the British and hundreds of Indians. The British were able to recruit Indians in Canada and New York because the Indians feared losing their homes and land if the colonists were victorious. On June 14, John Sullivan ordered Sorel evacuated. Sullivan ordered the army to retreat one hundred miles south to Île-aux-Noix, an island in the Richelieu River just north of the entrance to Lake Champlain.

Dr. Beebe wrote sarcastically that he had no fear now that Benedict Arnold was in charge. "Being favored with such superior men for generals, what may not be expected from this army, when so much attention has been paid by the Continent to make their circumstances so agreeable and comfortable under all their disadvantages in this wilderness? Surely conquest, victory, and glory must attend us."

On Monday, June 17, Dr. Beebe, with his boats full of sick soldiers and hundreds more infected with dysentery, malaria, and smallpox, arrived at Île-aux-Noix at 3 p.m. as part of the mad dash south into New York state. Île-aux-Noix contained one large farm at its center, but the rest of it was filled with insect-infested swamps. It was wholly unsuitable to any military compound, much less home for an entire army on the run. Beebe and everyone else who landed on the island were shaken by what they found there. He wrote in his journal, "I was struck with amazement to see the vast crowds of poor, distressed creatures. Language cannot describe nor imagination paint the scenes of misery and distress the soldiery endure. Scarcely a tent upon this isle but what contains one or more in distress and continually groaning and calling for relief, but in vain! Requests [for help] are as little regarded as the singing of crickets in the summers evening."

Île-aux-Noix was filled with fleeing Americans, healthy and sick, plus their equipment, baggage, and boats. At one point that month, it was estimated that a total of eight thousand American soldiers were living on the tiny spit of land. It was so jammed with military that those soldiers arriving later could not even find space to erect tents for the night and were forced to sleep outdoors, on the ground, at the edge of the water near their boats, the only piece of land left.[1]

The sick and their doctors did not remain at Île-aux-Noix long as the British force of nearly ten thousand men rapidly moved south in a relentless effort to destroy the entire American army. The American camp at St. John's, twenty-five miles north of Île-aux-Noix, was burned and the troops there also evacuated toward the hopelessly overcrowded Île-aux-Noix. Beebe and others were afraid that the army would not be able to move quickly enough to escape the grasp of the hard-pressing British troops and the always-feared Indians. The next day it was determined that everyone should be taken from Île-aux-Noix to Crown Point, nearly one hundred miles south on Lake Champlain.

Beebe was as stunned by the scenes at Crown Point as he had been at Île-aux-Noix, Chambly, and Sorel. Boats carrying dozens of sick soldiers arrived hourly in a huge, watery traffic jam. It was now reported that between thirty and fifty men were dying of smallpox each day in hospitals at Crown Point. Many had died in the boats on their way to Crown Point, falling dead in the ships. Beebe quoted the Bible when he asked himself about the wisdom of his commanding officers and their decision to undertake this massive evacuation, "Oh fools, when will ye be wise?"

Back home, word of the smallpox frightened civilians and it would soon become difficult to recruit new soldiers, as Connecticut governor Jonathan Trumbull warned George Washington. He wrote, "The smallpox in our northern armies carries with it greater dread than our enemies."[2]

Crown Point was a rather large frontier fortress. Its signature was a wide entrance protected by a pair of huge iron doors. Doctor Beebe toured the camp at Crown Point in exceedingly hot and humid weather and was crestfallen; he told friends there that his own headcount showed that about five hundred men had smallpox and hundreds of others were suffering from other diseases or recovering from wounds suffered at the battles of the Cedars and Three Rivers. Many with smallpox were developing abscesses in all parts of their bodies because there was no medicine to stop their illness from spreading.

"Death has now become a daily visitor to the camps," he wrote, adding that so many were dying that doctors, chaplains, and soldiers alike had hardened themselves to it and showed little emotion at the passing of a friend. Every time that he left the hospitals, Beebe told others that he was frustrated that there was little he could do except offer comfort. He lamented, "I can effect greater cures by words than by medicine."

By the end of June, the number of fatalities was so great—four a day in Beebe's regiment alone and fifty a day at Crown Point's hospitals—that most of the men who were healthy spent almost all their time digging the graves of those who were dying. One regiment buried one hundred men in just eight days. "Death visits us every hour," the doctor wrote.

Many of the enlisted men who died were single, but some were married and had children. Beebe was an eyewitness to the passing of Captain Shortridge, a middle-aged man who had been accompanied in the service by his two young sons. The boys were there with Beebe at Shortridge's deathbed as he expired. Beebe was distraught by the tragedies that unfolded daily and on June 29 his spirits sank to their lowest point during the entire time he spent in the military.

"What will become of our distressed army?" he wrote in his journal that night. "Death reigns triumphant. God seems to be greatly angry with us. He appears to be incensed against us, for our abominable wickedness and in all probability will sweep away a great part of our army to destruction. 'Tis enough to make human nature shudder only to hear the army in general blaspheme the holy name of God. This sin alone is sufficient to draw down the vengeance of an angry God upon a guilty and wicked army . . . ripening fast for utter destruction."

Much of this he blamed on Benedict Arnold, and in a scathing note in his journal hoped for his death: "I heartily wish some person would try an experiment on him, to make the sun shine through his head with an ounce ball; and then see whether the rays come in a direct or oblique direction."

Beebe was so upset at conditions that he did not even think the chaplains he saw at Crown Point could do any more for the souls of the dying soldiers than he could for their bodies. And he saw few. He remembered fondly the lengthy morning and evening prayers in Albany; now he was lucky to find a chaplain offering one single prayer a day. He noticed very few walking through the smallpox wards.

Chapter Twelve

THE COMPASSIONATE MINISTER AND THE ENRAGED DOCTOR

The chaplain that he missed the most was the engaging man he had met when he first arrived at Sorel, Rev. Ammi Robbins. The chaplain had become very ill just when Beebe moved to Chambly with General Thomas. Robbins was so sick that the commander who replaced Montgomery upon his death, General David Wooster, had approved his request to leave the army and return home to Connecticut. Robbins joined a regiment of men from Massachusetts on their way back to that state. After a perilous journey down Lake Champlain and Lake George by boat and across approximately one hundred forty miles of land, by wagon, he arrived home on June 5, obviously happy that his service in the war was at an end and that he had lived to talk about it. Like the other chaplains, he often wondered if diseases or the British would kill him. His buoyant journal entry for Wednesday, June 5, summed up his feelings: "Rode home and found my dear family well, after having experienced and seen the most abundant displays of Divine goodness and mercy. O for true gratitude."

The compassionate minister apparently remained obsessed with the woes of the army and the need of the soldiers for God's help. Just one month later, on July 2, 1776, the day that most of the delegates signed the Declaration of Independence—with no explanation in his journal—Ammi Robbins not only reenlisted in the Continental Army, but requested that he be sent back to his regiment at smallpox-infested Crown Point. On Tuesday, July 9, Rev. Robbins arrived back at Crown Point to rejoin his regiment. He wrote in his journal that the men, officers, and enlisted soldiers were surprised and quite pleased at his return. They were "exceedingly rejoiced to see me," he wrote. None was happier to welcome him back than Dr. Lewis Beebe, who ended the misery of his daily journal with the very happy tidings that "last evening Rev. Robbins returned to his regiment in a comfortable state of health." Robbins, recovered from all of his ailments, was full of energy and once again eager to do the Lord's work.

Dr. Beebe attended Robbins's sermon that Sunday afternoon. It began at 4 p.m., right on time, as did all of Robbins's sermons. The minister had his largest audience yet. He spoke inside the garrison, near the barracks, before General Wooster, dozens of officers, and more than a thousand troops gathered from several regiments. Well-rested from his month-long stay at home, he was in the best of health; his voice was strong and passionate. He turned to Isaiah 8, 9, and 10 in his Bible, held in front of him, for his sermon.

Dr. Beebe was thrilled by his friend's preaching that day. He wrote that "it was a most animating and encouraging discourse, delivered with spirit and warmth; he gained the most strict attention of almost every hearer present and was universally admired as an orator and divine." In it, the minister tried to be hopeful for his soldier audience, reading from the eighth verse of Isaiah: "Also I heard the voice of the Lord, saying, whom shall I send, and who will go for us? Then said I, here am I, send me." Many people came up to the minister afterwards and congratulated him on his powerful sermon. Robbins shrugged off the praise, telling them, "May I be more concerned to please God and less to please men."

Robbins's return seemed to infuse some life and hope into the death-ridden camp. The minister now prayed with the men every single morning and in the afternoon as well. He toured the different hospitals at Crown Point each day and, when he entered a large ward, asked the sick and infected soldiers there to pray along with him. He either stood or knelt, Bible in hand. He led dozens of men in prayer, sometimes a hundred in a large ward, especially the overburdened smallpox ward. Then, if the men seemed strong enough, he encouraged them to join him in singing loud and rousing religious hymns that could be heard throughout the fort and from great distances beyond its high walls.

Two days later, the minister was ordered to Fort Ticonderoga, ten miles south on the same western side of Lake Champlain. Ticonderoga was in need of chaplains. Late in the afternoon, he landed on the shore near the fort and walked directly to a small garrison hospital, one of several, to visit and comfort the sick. Most were smallpox victims. Robbins put off dinner and asked officers to call several regiments of men together for a special sunset prayer service. He dined much later after leading hundreds of men in prayer and song on the parade ground of the fort.

The following morning the energetic Robbins returned to Ticonderoga's west hospital, a large facility, and planned to spend the morning visiting men in all of the other medical facilities, too. That plan was scuttled by the misery he felt as soon as he walked into the west hospital and saw more than one hundred men there and the terrible condition that most of them were in. He was stunned. "Never was such a portrait of human misery as in these hospitals," he wrote in his journal. He asked the men to pray with him in the large, open ward. His sermon began with a phrase that he felt himself as he looked out on the groaning, diseased patients. "Be ye therefore sober and watch unto prayer," he began.

That night he was back in the fort's hospitals, seeing patients in their beds and leading hundreds of wounded and dying men in two prayer services. He felt that he needed all of his resilience, and the hand of God, to continue. He noted, "Applied myself to my duties. Indeed, it is too much, but I am carried along."

The pain that the chaplains felt, that all of the men of God felt, at Fort Ticonderoga and elsewhere in the Revolution, was very personal. They found themselves face to face with dying men every day and every night. They were there to comfort them as they prepared to leave the earth, to hear their last words, and to make promises to send their possessions to their loved ones. It was hard.

Several times over the next two days, Rev. Robbins found himself emotionally wrought. On Tuesday he was summoned to visit the son of Colonel Mann, a teenaged soldier who was dying and desperately sought some kind of religious comfort. On Wednesday he went to see his and Dr. Beebe's friend, Colonel Reed, who had been battling smallpox for over a week. Reed, covered with the pus-filled explosions, looked and sounded pathetic. "Fear he won't live," Robbins wrote after a visit in which he tried to console Reed.

It was a grueling day for the minister. He made his daily rounds of the hospitals and conducted four different prayer services, some with the loud singing of hymns and some just solemn prayers. By nightfall, he was fatigued and emotionally spent. His day was not yet over. An officer told him he had to visit Baron Frederick William Woedtke, a Prussian officer who had joined the Continental Army as a brigadier general, whom the officer thought was dying. So did Robbins.

"I felt that he was deluded," he wrote about his first impression of the general, whom the enlisted men charged was a hopeless drunk. "A very singular trial I had," he wrote of the visit to the dying Woedtke. "He most earnestly requested that I administer the sacrament to him, that he had made his peace with God, and nothing remained but to do his last command."

Woedtke, thrashing about in his bed, began to mumble some last religious desire but Robbins could not understand what it was. He stopped him from rambling with a comforting hand and told him that "if he only believed in the Lord Jesus Christ he would be accepted," and then left him, certain he would die within hours. He did.

Robbins's own health had deteriorated badly again after his arrival at Ticonderoga, just as it had during his last tour of duty. He had taken medicine to purge himself on Tuesday night and spent hours in bed, dragging himself out to conduct a prayer service. By Thursday, he was much worse. "I need a constitution of brass to tarry here . . . utterly unable to go through the hospitals," he wrote.

Very ill, Robbins sought the help of Jonathan Potts, the first surgeon of the army, who was visiting Ticonderoga and Fort George that week. Potts gave him a solution of manna, cream of tartar, senna, and aniseed, but it did not help. The minister felt even worse.

Potts was shocked by what he saw, writing that the sick were "without clothing, without bedding, or a shelter sufficient to screen them from the weather . . . we have at present one thousand sick . . . laboring under the various cruel disorders of dysentery, putrid fever, and the effects of a confluent smallpox."[1]

On Friday, Robbins went to see his friend Lewis Beebe, whom he knew he could trust for a solid medical appraisal of his condition. Dr. Beebe gave him a thorough examination but did not offer any more medicine. He told his friend that the exposure to the disease and sickness at the fort was making him ill and advised him to spend time far away from Ticonderoga. Beebe himself was sick with a fever and, not placing much faith in his fellow doctors at the fort, had made up his mind to journey all the way to Stockbridge, Massachusetts, near his home, to see a friend who was a physician and find a cure. He was just as concerned over his friend Robbins's health. He told him that he would take him to Fort Edwards, caring for him on the trip, leave him in good hands with doctors there, and then finish his own journey to Massachusetts.

Beebe procured a wagon and rode with the minister and another doctor south to Fort Edwards, where he put him to bed with an even higher fever. Beebe explained his condition to doctors there and they told Beebe that Robbins should go on to Saratoga for more medical advice and then to Stillwater, a few miles from Albany. Beebe drove the wagon all the way to Saratoga and then Stillwater, where a doctor told Dr. Beebe his friend was critically ill. The minister probably had an advanced case of the putrid fever, which brings a fever as high as 104 degrees, terrible headaches, nausea, vomiting, and a rash. The doctor told Robbins to go home for at least a month—away from anyone suffering from an illness—before he could return to his duties, and that, in fact, he was so ill that he might never be able to return to the army.

Robbins was distraught at the physician's urging that he retire from the service. Robbins wrote that night, "I would not shrink from the work. Our war is a righteous war; our men are called to defend the country; whole congregations turn out and the ministers of the gospel should go and encourage them when doing duty, attend and pray for and be with them when sick, and bury them when they die. I hope to return to my work." The next morning, extremely weak, he walked slowly to Beebe's wagon, climbed in, and headed home for what Beebe and the doctors in Stillwater were certain was a permanent stay.

Lewis Beebe apparently drove Robbins all the way home—distance of one hundred forty miles from Ticonderoga in a simple wagon over narrow dirt roads—and either bought, rented, or borrowed a horse. He rode the rest of the way to Stockbridge, Massachusetts, and visited Dr. Sergeant, his personal physician, who cured him with five days of treatments with vinum antimonial, administered three times a day, and plenty of rest. Dr. Beebe never thought of staying home for good, as he might have, and returned to the army as soon as he felt better. He did so despite his growing attraction to Margaret Kellog, the daughter of a prominent family in Sheffield, whom he must have seen again on his medical leave.

Endless Misery

Beebe's journey back to Fort Ticonderoga was constantly halted by rainstorms. He shrugged them off, starting to think like the soldiers he was treating. "The bravery of good soldiers consists in enduring hardships and fatigue with patience," he said of his travails. On Wednesday, July 28, he was stuck at Fort George, where he visited the hospital and found it jammed with seven hundred men. Officers then took him to the fort's graveyard. There were three hundred fresh graves, all dug within the last month. "It was melancholy, indeed, to see such desolation made in our army," Beebe wrote.

The staggering number of dead in the graveyard, most from small-pox, was the first sign that the American army's situation had grown much grimmer in the weeks that the doctor had been away. He was greeted by even starker sights when he made it back to Ticonderoga. More men had arrived there and the death rate had climbed to ten per day. He learned, too, that Horatio Gates was fearful of a British attack and had ordered Benedict Arnold to build a small navy to battle British warships if they ventured onto Lake Champlain.

Beebe told his superiors that half the men in his own regiment were unfit for duty not just with smallpox, but dysentery, jaundice, diarrhea, rheumatism, scurvy, piles, lumbago, and putrid fever, and that for many their situation was "truly dangerous." Dysentery raged throughout the camp, he told them, and yet he had run out of medical supplies to treat it and had to listen to the troops yell at him, and other doctors, because they could not obtain any help.

It was the smallpox that worried Dr. Beebe, though. He warned, "It has brought many to the grave and will many more unless immediately dis-charged." The number of sick had swollen so much that it was no longer possible to treat all of them in the hospitals at Ticonderoga. Small villages of tents were set up outside the fort where those with diseases, fevers, and smallpox were sent until beds were available in the hospital, made so when men died and were dumped in the graveyards. Now there were no more open graves, but merely open pits into which a dozen or more corpses were tossed every morning. "Hard fortune to have so many sick on hand at one time. But harder for those who are sick to be crowded into dirty, lousy, stinking hospitals enough to kill well men," he seethed in early August.

One soldier who had been very ill, and convinced he would die, hid the knife from his dinner plate and, a few hours later, took his life by slit-ting his throat. One evening Beebe watched men carry a corpse out of a tent. They told him that the man had been eating dinner. He took one long breath, then another, then he fell forward, dead, his face hitting the beefsteak on his plate.

Beebe was convinced now, after yet another depressing tour of his hos-pitals, that the men with smallpox, even though put in special wards, were infecting everyone else. He suggested simply sending them home to die with their loved ones. He also had to contend with the lack of medical manpower to treat the sick and dying. The doctors who had labored so courageously were coming down with fatal illnesses themselves. Some died and some were laid up in bed, unable to work. The few doctors remaining now had to take on all of the work, which grew in intensity each day. During the last week of August, several more doctors were bedridden and Beebe wrote angrily in his journal that all of the medical work had now fallen on his shoulders. He now had to treat doctors as well as soldiers on his daily rounds, serve as an administrator, beg generals for medical supplies, and complete endless paperwork. He was overwhelmed.

Soldiers remembered the deceased with great reverence. Lamenting the loss of the majority of privates in a company, Private John Henry wrote that "they were originally as elegant a body of men as ever came into my view . . . beautiful boys." Men fondly recollected the elegance of the last rites of the Catholic church and the comfort the priests gave to those about to take their last breath. James Melvin, a private from Massachusetts, survived the smallpox. He was quartered with other Americans in a Quebec monastery following the failed attack there. On January 19, the evening after a day-long snowstorm, Melvin watched as the last rites were administered to a French soldier he knew who had been ravaged by the disease.

He recalled, "The nuns came and read over him, afterwards the priest came in; then they fetched in a table covered with a white cloth and lighted two wax candles about three feet long, and set them on the table. The priest put on a white robe over his other garments and the nuns kneeled down, and the priest stood and read a sentence and then the nuns a sentence and so they went on some time; then the priest prayed by himself; then the nuns, and then the priest again, then they read all together a spell, and finally the priest alone; then the priest stroked the man's face and then they took away their candles and tables and the man died."[2]

The parents of those who passed away were not angry, but proud. Matthew Patten, of Bedford, New Hampshire, said of his son John, who died along with so many others at Île-aux-Noix, "He was shot through his left arm at the Bunker Hill fight and now was dead after suffering much fatigue to the place where he now lies in defending the just rights of America to whose end he came in the prime of life by means of that wicked, tyrannical Brute of Great Britain."[3]

Dr. Lewis Beebe had become bitter and raged about everything that he saw. In his nightly journal he complained that amid all of the suffering at Ticonderoga men stole money and food from sick soldiers and that officers argued over promotions as men were buried. He said the officers, whom he had come to despise, had established themselves as national champions at swearing. "In short," he angrily observed, "they laugh at death, mock at hell and damnation and even challenge the deity to remove them out of this world by thunder and lightening."

The doctor was just as unhappy with the drunkenness he found everywhere, among officers as well as the enlisted men. He never criticized enlisted men whom he loved, saving his barbs for the officers. "Drunkenness is a great beauty," he wrote of the officers, "and profanity an ornament in an officer. The whims, caprice, and vanity of this set of beings is ridiculous to the last degree. Children are not often guilty of such scandalous behavior."

He found several targets for his most sarcastic remarks. One officer he loathed was Major Joseph Cilley of New Hampshire, whom, he said "rightly named, is a very silly man." He lambasted most of the chaplains, calling the Rev. Ichabod Fisk, a former school classmate, "a great blunderbuss of the gospel." He condemned others for spending their time trying to land better-paying jobs at larger parishes back home instead of tending to the sick. He wrote of one boring chaplain that if he stayed away longer, "They will in all probability regain their former health and spirits."

But there was one minister whom he did admire, his friend Rev. Ammi Robbins, who remarkably was back again for a third tour of duty. Robbins had recovered at home and waved off pleas from his own doctor and friends that he remain there and forget about the war. They had warned him that he had somehow managed to escape death from the putrid fever and should not take any more chances by returning to the army. Robbins ran into a very surprised Dr. Jonathan Potts when he stopped at Saratoga en route to his regiment. Potts had heard about the large number of doctors who had died at the forts along the shores of Lake Champlain. He begged Robbins not to return to the dangerous fever- and smallpox-ridden fort. "He told me it was at the risk of my life to go into the hospitals. But if the physician goes, why not a minister of the Great Physician?"

On his way to Ticonderoga, Robbins stopped at Fort Edwards. The hospitals were full, so sick men at that garrison were housed in the fort's bakery. The minister had apparently written to Lewis Beebe that he was on his way back, despite the grave warnings of Dr. Potts about risking his life. Dr. Beebe greeted Robbins upon his arrival at 7 a.m. and had a bread and cheese breakfast with him. He then gave Robbins a tour of the Ticonderoga hospitals and the medical tents outside the fort. One large camp was at a nearby post named Mount Independence, across the lake from Ticonderoga, where hundreds more lay ill. The Fifteenth Massachusetts, with fifer John Greenwood, was camped there.

The minister was eager to hold a large prayer meeting in order to preach the word of God. On Wednesday night, September 4, after much planning and at his urging, officers gathered a huge crowd of several thousand men, healthy and sick, on the parade ground in the middle of the fort. Lit torches surrounded the area. There were so many men in the crowd, including his friend Dr. Beebe, that those at the rear could not see the minister. They shouted at him that their view was blocked by the huge assemblage of troops. The drummers from the regiments there volunteered to stack up their drums in two long lines, on top of each other, to form two pyramids about ten feet in height. The men then carried out a wooden platform and placed it on top of the two rows, connecting them.

The Rev. Robbins was pleased with the ad hoc stage, certainly the largest and highest he had ever stood on. Holding his Bible with great care, he then carefully climbed up the wall of drums to the top of the platform and there, with all able to see him, both his feet planted gingerly on the wooden platform, he preached the word of the Lord, his voice loud and vibrant, his figure illuminated by the dozens of burning torches against the star-filled sky. Thousands listened in rapt attention, their eyes looking upwards at the minister, his voice booming and his arms flailing in his animated sermon, the heavens themselves his backdrop.

Nonplussed, Robbins decided to give another robust sermon to another large crowd to calm the men the following night. He scribbled in his journal that day, "Enjoy through great mercy good health in the midst of sickness and death all around me," and in the evening preached with great power to his assemblage of soldiers. He read from the prophet Joel: "A day of trouble and distress, a day of wasteness and desolation, a day of darkness and of gloominess, a day of clouds and thick darkness, a day of trumpet and alarm." Then, adding a small touch of politics and patriotism to his preaching, he exhorted the men to be brave, that "we could rejoice in the Lord, who could turn our mourning into joy."

The sermon did little good, however, and two days later, after visiting the ever-mounting number of sick in the rancid hospitals and listening to enlisted men grumble about the war, he wrote in his journal that "our regiment is in a most miserable condition; I could wish they were all dismissed." By Friday, September 13, the situation at Ticonderoga had deteriorated even further in Robbins's eyes, just as it had for his friend Beebe. "The groans of the distressed in the camp are real affecting," Robbins wrote, adding that out of 237 men in one regiment, 197 were sick and unfit for duty. Robbins then jotted down notes about his meeting in a hospital ward with a young man from Massachusetts who was dying. Robbins wrote, "He asked me to save him and said he was not fit to die."

"I cannot die . . . Do sir, pray for me. Will you not send for my mother? If she were here to nurse me I could get well. Oh, my mother. How I wish I could see her. She was opposed to my enlisting. I am now very sorry. Do let her know that I am sorry," the boy pleaded with the minister and then, later that night, expired.

One thing that both Beebe and Robbins noticed was that substantially more soldiers turned out for the evening prayer service as the number of dying increased. Perhaps they were seeking God's protection. Robbins did not know, but he began to offer longer and stronger sermons. He asked the drummers to build his ten foot high platform with their instruments each evening and preached from the platform on top of them to ever larger congregations. Now, too, the minister noticed, his sermons in the evening attracted civilians who lived nearby, as well as the enlisted men and officers. The men not only listened to his readings from the Bible and his sermon, but joined in the loud and exuberant singing of rousing hymns, with a fifer and drummer adding music, as the torches burned around them on the parade ground and the moon rose over Fort Ticonderoga.

Robbins's exhilaration was limited, though, because the garrison was hit with a succession of bad news. First, Washington's forces had suffered a terrible defeat on Long Island, New York, during the last week of August. Second, the British army, thousands strong, had begun a march toward Ticonderoga.

Worst of all, Benedict Arnold's navy had been defeated. The British had beaten Arnold's hastily created sea force in a battle that commenced near Valcour Island at the northern tip of Lake Champlain on October 11 and lasted three days. The British sunk or disabled eleven of the sixteen ships, killing eighty or more of Arnold's men and taking more than one hundred prisoners in a sea battle that continued thirty miles southward on the lake. Arnold and the rest of his men abandoned their ships, burned them, and escaped to Crown Point. Fearful of being destroyed there by a much larger British force, Arnold had the fort burned and the men headed south again, toward Ticonderoga. Arnold wrote to his superior, General Schuyler, that he was happy to be alive. "On the whole, I think we have had a very fortunate escape and have great reason to return our humble and hearty thanks to Almighty God for preserving and delivering so many of us from our more than savage enemies."[4]

Finally, on October 15, 1776, the men from Arnold's battered navy arrived in terrible condition. Arnold was satisfied that his fleet had inflicted enough damage to several of the British warships to force their repair. But he was exasperated by the losses of his ships and men. Through sheer coincidence, Robbins and Arnold met at the hospital, where the minister was offering comfort to Arnold's men who fought in the lake engagement. The angry Arnold told Robbins to join a company of wounded men that he was sending to Fort George in the morning; Arnold decided that in addition to medical assistance, they needed all of the heavenly help they could obtain. Robbins agreed, but reluctantly. Face to face with the very insistent general, he had no choice.

The trip to Fort George, at the southern end of Lake George, nearly cost the reverend his life, and the lives of all the men in his boat. There was little breeze and the men were forced to row. The lake was smaller than Champlain and, closer to the shore, they had the opportunity to look out from the boat at the gorgeous scenery that surrounded them. Autumn had arrived in upstate New York. The green leaves on the hundreds of thousands of trees that the soldiers could see on shore had changed to their customary fall colors of red, orange, and yellow. This rainbow of turning leaves gave the woods a painter's palette of vivid color. They had pulled on their oars hard all morning, their hands callused from dragging them through the waters of the lake, but the uncertain weather of Lake George struck hard in the afternoon.

Just after 2 p.m. a fierce wind whipped across the lake and snapped the rudder band on the boat as the helmsman tried to push the rudder in order to steer forward in the severe northwest gale. The rudderless boat was then adrift and floated directly at a cluster of large, jagged rocks near the shore of a small island. The boat, moving quickly with the wind, was about to be smashed to pieces when the breeze shifted at the last moment and sent the craft sailing harmlessly into a small cove. The men dropped anchor and decided to remain there, sleeping on deck. No one took a close look at the darkening sky. Rain began to fall just after the sun went down and continued, hard, all evening. The men were drenched.

Robbins and the sick men, all of them soaked from the torrents of rain they had endured all evening, managed to fix the rudder in the morning and rowed to Fort George. There, Robbins, whose health had been restored during his latest return to the front, came down with yet another fever. Despite his ailments, he visited every ward in the hospitals at Fort George and prayed with the men. The minister had been hardened by the war. He wrote in his journal that he had tended to the spiritual needs of three men as they died in their beds in front of him that day and yet felt no great sadness; the deaths he had been witnessing for months seemed to have made him immune to suffering.

There was no sermon by the Rev. Robbins the following Sunday. The fever and bad cold he had developed on the trip from Ticonderoga to Fort George had made him so sick he could not preach. He was emotionally and mentally distressed, and on the verge of a nervous breakdown. Dr. Potts had warned him that one more tour of duty at Ticonderoga would kill him, and now, perhaps, his fatal prophecy would come true. Robbins was finished and he knew it.

On Thursday, October 31, a week after the first snowfall on Lake Champlain, a very sick and despondent Rev. Ammi Robbins arrived home in Connecticut yet again. More than five thousand Americans, half the original force, had been lost—killed in battle or by smallpox, disease, and fever, or captured—in the ill-fated expedition to Canada. Among the dead in the mismanaged, ill-advised incursion into Canada were many doctors, chaplains, and musicians who never lifted a musket, drew a sword, or fired a cannon. Rev. Robbins had survived, though, he imagined, as he wrote on the day that he arrived home for the last time, thanks to "Divine mercy and favor."

By the end of October, the smallpox scourge had faded. Arnold's navy had inflicted far more damage on the British warships on Lake Champlain than was initially suspected and Governor Guy Carleton decided to return to Canada for the time being and abandon his pursuit of the reeling American army. Even though he lost the lake battles, Arnold's ability to halt the British advance southward was critical to the war. If Carleton had moved south he might have been able to defeat the Americans at Ticonderoga and move on to join Howe in New York, splitting the colonies in two and perhaps winning the war in the spring of 1776.

This pause in the fighting gave Beebe and the other doctors inside the garrisons time to let the soldiers wounded in the summer campaign heal. Men who contracted typhus, the putrid fever, and other ailments slowly recovered. The hospital tents came down and the medical wards were soon emptied. With great bravado, General Horatio Gates, whom Congress had chosen to succeed Schuyler in that region, declared an end to the smallpox epidemic and pronounced the army in good health once again.

On December 4, Dr. Lewis Beebe—his enlistment ended and still alive despite another bout of fever—yearned to see girlfriend Margaret Kellog. Hopeful of resuming the life of a civilian, he began the long journey home to Sheffield, Massachusetts, a journey of one hundred fifty miles. He traveled with his regiment and on his own by wagon, horseback, and sleigh on a circuitous route down through New York, into Pennsylvania, east across New Jersey, north into New York again, and finally to Connecticut and Massachusetts. Upon his arrival home, he would write a final line, one of great solace, in his journal, "I once more returned to my father's house," happy at last to be among those he loved.

The two healers, the man of medicine and the man of the cloth, had survived their journey into and out of the hell of the Canadian disaster and made it back to their hometowns alive. While the doctor had fretted that he had lost so many lives, he had saved many, too. And while the minister lamented over and over again that he was unable to offer God's help to enough men, he had to know that whether it was sitting next to the bed of a dying soldier or standing on top of his high drum platform surrounded by torches, he had brought the word of God to the soldiers of the Revolution and in doing so had eased their fears.

As Beebe was headed home by sleigh to Sheffield, Massachusetts, the week before Christmas, he and the others traveling with him learned all the details of the crushing defeats George Washington's army had suffered in the New York area during the previous three months. Following the debacle on Long Island, the British followed the Americans to Harlem, forcing them to retreat. Washington withdrew his forces to White Plains, where he suffered another loss and had to withdraw still farther north.

General Howe turned his attention on another target, the garrison of three thousand Americans at Fort Washington in Manhattan. The British and Hessian force of thirteen thousand men overran the fort, forcing nearly all three thousand of its defenders to surrender. Howe and Lord Cornwallis then went after Washington's main army, pursuing it across

New Jersey. Washington had lost many of his cannon at Fort Washington. He had suffered more than five thousand men lost in casualties and desertions. The British chased him westward and now, as Beebe rode home in late December, Washington found himself on the western shore of the Delaware River in Pennsylvania, about to be crushed.

Chapter Thirteen

CHRISTMAS, 1776:
Private John Greenwood
Crosses the Delaware

The War

*J*ust before Christmas, 1776, George Washington and the soldiers of his main army of twenty-five hundred found themselves at the brink of extermination on the snow-covered western shore of the Delaware River in Pennsylvania. Washington correctly guessed that following the evacuation of Boston, General Howe would return to America and attempt to capture New York. He had met Howe head-to-head in four disastrous encounters there. The British then pursued Washington's remaining force across New Jersey to the Delaware. The Americans crossed into Pennsylvania on December 7 and the British remained on the New Jersey side. Another two thousand American troops arrived a week later. The army possessed only eighteen cannon and was short on supplies. The substantial militia promised by Pennsylvania's government never materialized.

Washington had to contend with the main British army of some nine thousand troops, and its fifteen-hundred-strong force of Hessians that were left to keep an eye on him in Trenton, New Jersey, just across the river. He feared they would cross the river and crush his army. He then concocted a daring plan to cross the Delaware at night, on Christmas Day, and take the Hessians in Trenton by surprise. Most of his generals disapproved of the idea and its chances of success were slim. Washington wrote himself a note, "Victory or death!" and then rolled it up into a ball and tossed it into a corner of the room in the building he was using as his headquarters. The attack would either be a stunning victory that would give the Revolution new life or it would be a disaster that would end it.

John Greenwood, the teenage fifer turned soldier, stood alongside the other men in his regiment, the Fifteenth Massachusetts, commanded by John Patterson, on a snow-covered parade ground near the Delaware River at 4 p.m. as the snowstorm that General Washington had predicted began to move toward the region. The snow would not arrive until later, but the men searched the darkening skies for the first falling flakes this frigid Christmas Day of 1776. The air was bitterly cold and the wind had started to move sharply through the trees along the river near Samuel McKonkey's ferry slip. The slip complex consisted of a two-story, grey stone house on the Delaware with a wide wooden dock for the ferry that traveled some two hundred yards back and forth across the river at that point.

The late afternoon chill made Greenwood even more uncomfortable than he had been for days. Like many others who had marched south from Fort Ticonderoga to Albany, and then to the Delaware, the sixteen-year-old soldier was suffering from scabies, or "the itch," the chronic soldiers' affliction that caused itching, scabs, and irritation. The teenager obtained some ointment from a doctor which he rubbed over the irritated areas of his thighs. The salve had helped, but he still ground his legs against each other as he walked, trying to make the itch go away. He had no idea where the army was headed this day as he looked out on the bleak, white countryside with its forests of barren trees broken by a few clusters of evergreens.

"None but the first officers knew where we were going or what we were going about," he wrote in his diary. "For it was a secret expedition and we, the bulk of the men coming from Canada, knew not the disposition of the army we were then in, nor anything about the country. This was not unusual, however, as I never heard soldiers say anything, nor ever saw them trouble themselves, as to where they were or where they were led. It was enough for them to know that wherever the officers commanded they must go, be it through fire and water, for it was all the same owing to the impossibility of being in a worse condition than their present one and, therefore, the men always liked to be kept moving in expectation of bettering themselves."

Greenwood had truly become a soldier by the winter of 1776 and no longer only played the fife for his regiment, except to amuse himself and his friends in camp. Today he bore his heavy musket, sixty rounds of ammunition stuffed into his pockets, and three days of cooked rations. Like the others, he was ready for battle, wherever and whenever it came.

From where many of the men stood they could see large, thick, flat sheets of ice float down the river in the distance, just as they had for the past week in sub-freezing temperatures. Tree branches full of ice hung over in wide arcs, some touching the ground. The land was still covered with one or two inches of snow that had fallen in small storms during the previous weeks. Freezing temperatures had prevented it from melting.[1] He and the other men in the regiment, standing amid their brigades, rubbed their hands together and stomped their feet on the frozen ground in a feeble attempt to stay warm.

The soldiers had reached the site after varying journeys. Some, such as Sgt. Joseph White of Massachusetts, who had become famous with the men for his comical encounter with the commander in chief in Boston, and Lieutenant James McMichael from Pennsylvania, had crossed the Delaware earlier in the month with Washington following the disheartening losses in New York and Long Island; others had arrived later with General Sullivan. Sgt. Thomas McCarty had marched all the way from Virginia.

Some Pennsylvanians, such as John Smith, had marched into camp with General Thomas Mifflin just a few days before. Smith told others that they had been repeatedly refused food and cider by Pennsylvania men and women whose farms they passed on their way to camp and had been forced to steal some to feed themselves.[2]

Sgt. White told soldiers he met that he had the same experience. General Israel Putnam ordered him to buy food for the men at a tavern at nearby Newton, but the proprietor refused to take Continental scrip (paper money), claiming that it was "rebel money" and worthless. White told him that he had orders. "I placed two men at the cellar door, as sentries; let nobody whatever go down," he said to those listening. "I called for a light and two men to go down the cellar with me. We found it full of good things; a large pile of cheeses, hams, bacon, a large tub of honey, barrels of cider and cider royal, which was very strong. Also, all kinds of spirits." The proprietor would not let them take any food, so White went back to Putnam, who accompanied him to the tavern. "I do not like your rebel money," the tavern keeper told Putnam. "The General flew round like [a] top," laughed White, nineteen, who had enlisted just before Bunker Hill. "He called for a file of men, a corporal, and four men came and [said] 'take this Tory rascal to the main guard house.'"

Sgt. Thomas McCarty had his own woes. He told men he met that on December 13, the hut he had been sleeping in burned to the ground and he had lost all of his clothing in the fire. Then a week later, the men in his regiment had been forced to sleep on the ground and awoke buried in two inches of snow that had fallen during the night.[3] There were mortifying tales, too, that enlisted men had heard. Sgt. Elisha Bostwick, who had survived the New York battles, told the men that his friend had been shot in the thigh and was too badly hurt to retreat with them; he was left to be taken as a prisoner. While leaving the field, they saw a British soldier grab his friend's musket. He used the butt of it and "broke and pounded his skull to pieces" and then looted him. Another British soldier murdered a second wounded American left for, Bostwick sneered, "British clemency."[4]

No one had a more vivid memory of English brutality than Bostwick. The twenty-seven-year-old Connecticut soldier stayed with the army despite a severe fever that had rendered him helpless for nearly two months during the spring. Still sick, he fought the best he could but had been badly shaken by the battles in New York. His regiment was hit with cannon fire early in the battle of White Plains. He wrote that "[cannon] ball first took the head of Smith, a very stout man, and dashed it open. Then it took off Chilson's arm which was amputated. It then took Taylor across the bowels. It then struck Sergeant Garrete of our company on the hip and took off the point of the hip bone. Smith and Taylor were left on the spot. Sergeant Garrete was carried off but died the same day. What a sight that was to see within a [short] distance, those men with their legs and arms and guns and pack all in a heap."[5]

The breath of the men froze in the air that afternoon as the soldiers talked among themselves. One of their officers moved in front of them and opened a pamphlet that he had carried in his hand. It was one of the dozens of copies of Thomas Paine's *The American Crisis* that General Washington had suggested be read to the men by their leaders before they boarded the boats to cross the turbulent Delaware.

The general knew from John Honeyman, a friendly local farmer who had been selling food to the Hessians—and spying for the Americans while doing so—that the Hessians planned a holiday feast on Christmas Day. They would eat too much. He knew, too, that their commander, Colonel Johann Rall, liked to drink and play cards in the evening and enjoyed sleeping late in the morning, often not rising before 9 a.m. and then not bathing and dressing until 10 a.m.

The Continental Army soldiers stood in formation as the boats were lined up in the water for the departure. To preserve secrecy, they had not been told about the Christmas Day strike until they arrived at the parade ground. They did not fear the weather or the Hessians. Many deserters had given up all hope in the Revolution and gone home, but those who remained trusted George Washington. He had driven the British out of Boston and managed to get those soldiers that survived the Redcoat onslaught at Long Island out of Brooklyn Heights via a daring, secretive, late-night escape in boats across the East River to Manhattan. The men still with him, those who had not fled after the New York debacle, would follow him where he would lead them. "We loved him," said one after the war had ended, "We'd sell our lives for him."[6]

The freezing officer opened his copy of *The American Crisis* pamphlet, which had been distributed throughout the colonies and had met with much praise from military personnel and civilians. "These are the times that try men's souls," the officer began and Greenwood listened intently. "The summer soldier and the sunshine patriot will, in times of crisis, shrink from the service of their country; but he that stands *now* deserves the love and thanks of man and woman. Tyranny, like hell, is not easily conquered; yet we have this consolation with us, that the harder the conflict, the more glorious the triumph."

Following the reading, and some encouraging words from their superiors, the men began to board the small flotilla of the sixty-six-foot-long, eight-foot-wide, three-foot-deep flat-bottomed Durham boats, named after a nearby iron furnace that used the craft to transport iron ore and freight to Philadelphia, northern New Jersey, and Pennsylvania river towns. Washington believed that the Durhams could carry men just as easily.

Greenwood's regiment was one of the first to cross. The young soldier carefully walked across the wide wooden slats of McKonkey's ferry dock, making certain that he did not slip on the already icy structure. He moved into his assigned boat with the others, unsmiling, shivering, and sat down. When all of the men were in the Durham, the boatman poled the boat away from the dock and headed out into the darkness of the river. As their boat cut silently into the water and the ice, Greenwood looked back and watched the twenty-four hundred or so remaining men awaiting their turn to cross. All heard the booming voice of Henry Knox shouting at the men loading the cannon into their separate boats to hurry along and secure the field pieces carefully.

The journey across the river was perilous. Wide, flat sheets of ice slammed into the sides of the Durhams and the boatman struggled. "The force of the current, the sharpness of the frost, the darkness of the night, the ice, and a high wind tendered the passage of the river extremely difficult," said Major James Wilkinson of the crossing later. A light wind slashed into the faces of Greenwood and the others as the boat made the agonizingly slow trip across the water. Then, just after 11 p.m., the predicted snow began to fall. It soon began to accumulate—one, two, three, four inches—and kept falling. On the other side of the Delaware, Washington, with his dark blue cloak wrapped tightly around his chest and neck, watched Greenwood and the others complete the treacherous passage. Greenwood and the soldiers in his regiment were freezing. "The storm was increasing rapidly," wrote Greenwood. "It rained, hailed, snowed, and froze and at the same time blew a perfect hurricane."

"It was as severe a night as I ever saw," agreed Captain Thomas Rodney, of Delaware, whose men shivered along with Greenwood and his Massachusetts comrades. "The frost was sharp, the current difficult to stem, the ice increasing, and the wind high. It was only with the greatest care and labor that the horses and the artillery could be ferried over."[7]

To ward off the snow and cold, Washington ordered the Fifteenth Massachusetts, Greenwood's regiment, to scour the surrounding area for downed trees and fence posts in order to make a series of bonfires. Greenwood said that the wind was at full force and that "in a moment" it cut in half the wood he tossed onto the fire. The fierce wind made it impossible for him to turn in any direction for warmth. "When I turned my face toward the fire, my back would be freezing. However, as my usual acuteness had not forsaken me, by turning round and round I kept myself from perishing before a large bonfire." The men were in good spirits, despite the deplorable weather conditions. "The cheerfulness of my fellow comrades encouraged me beyond expectation and, big coward as I acknowledge myself to be, I felt great pleasure," Greenwood said.

He and others waited on the eastern banks of the river until just before 4 a.m., when the last boats carrying men and cannon crossed. By that time, the temperature had dropped to about twenty degrees, the snow fell even harder, and a biting wind from the northwest whipped through the countryside. Sergeant Joe White, who had been with him in Boston, called it "a violent snowstorm." The army was now two hours late. It would not be able to reach Trenton at dawn, as planned. If the men were able to move quickly, marching through more than four inches of snow, they might make it by 8 a.m., when it was light, but risk losing the element of surprise that Washington had counted upon. What the soldiers did not know was that the other half of the army, under General John Cadwalader and General James Ewing, could not make it across the Delaware River further south, as planned, in order to trap the Hessians in a vice, leaving Greenwood and the others on their own north of Trenton.[8]

The eight-mile march took place amid a ferocious sleet storm. Greenwood and others could barely see in front of them as the snow fell heavily and the wind blinded them. Newspapers later recorded the storm, which first struck in Virginia and quickly moved its way up the Atlantic seaboard, as one of the worst in years. Two feet of snow fell on Virginia and snowfalls between a foot and six inches were recorded in Maryland, Delaware, New Jersey, and New York as the storm moved north by northeast. About four inches fell on the Delaware River basin.[9]

The officers walked and rode next to the men, moving them along. Every half hour or so Washington himself passed Greenwood and his regiment and quietly, but firmly, urged the soldiers to speed up the pace. "Keep up with your officers," he said in a deep voice. He warned them not to stop because they might freeze to death, as two men had done just after they crossed the river.[10] Greenwood had not been surprised at that news when he learned it later. He wrote that the men "were nearly half dead from cold for the want of clothing . . . many of our soldiers had not a shoe to their feet and their clothes were ragged as those of a beggar."

And Greenwood might have died, too, if it was not for the sharp eyes of Sergeant Madden. "At one time when we were halted on the road, I sat down on the stump of a tree and was so benumbed with cold that I wanted to go to sleep. Had I been passed unnoticed, I should have frozen to death without knowing it. But as good luck always attended me, Sergeant Madden came and, rousing me up, made me walk about. We then began to march again, just in the old slow way."

As men who saw him wrote later, Washington, more determined than ever, realized that while he might lose the early darkness for his attack, he would be able to approach Trenton unseen, because his entire army was cloaked in a blanket of snow. The gale would also drive the snow into the face of the Hessian soldiers. They would face northwest, right into the wind, as they fought.

Greenwood and the army trudged southward on Bear Tavern Road for four long hours, their feet getting colder and their faces nearly numb from the wind and snow. The army was divided along the way, with Washington taking half of the men down on Princeton Road and John Sullivan taking Greenwood's regiment and the rest southward on River Road. The men grumbled about the slow pace of the march. "We began a circuitous march, not advancing faster than a child ten years old could walk, and stopping frequently, though for what purpose I know not," Greenwood complained.

Just before 8 a.m., the American forces approached the outskirts of Trenton. Every man was ready for the battle, despite the sleepless night, snowstorm, and wearying eight-mile march.

The men told each other that the general had been right. No one was waiting for them. Colonel Rall had not sent out night patrols because of the storm and the early morning sentries who normally walked down the roads north of town remained inside their quarters, unwilling to emerge into the teeth of a bad snowstorm. The first single shot of the engagement was fired just north of town when Lt. Andreas Wiederhold, a Hessian picket, saw men coming across a field. He walked out of the guardhouse to greet them, thinking they were his early morning sentries. They ran toward him, muskets raised, and he realized, he wrote later, that it was not a few German sentries, but "the enemy vanguard."

Wiederhold ran back into the house, yelled for his seventeen men to awake and grab their arms. They stumbled outside and were greeted with three successive volleys from the Americans. The Hessian said that he ordered his men to fire but in the process was "passed by several battalions" of Americans. He knew right away that they were the victims of a sneak attack and, with his men, fled into the town with the Americans firing after them.

Rall, still sleeping as the Americans moved into position, never feared an attack. He had been told by his men that the Americans they saw rowing in the river over the last few weeks, or walking on the other side, looked hungry, wore tattered clothes, and seemed unable to engage in any kind of battle. His immediate superior, General James Grant, now in New Brunswick, had agreed with him, sneering that the Americans had no stockings or shoes and "were dying and cold, without blankets and very ill-supplied with provisions."[11] Besides, how could an entire army cross a major river and launch an attack without being seen? Rall had been so confident that his position was impregnable that he even ignored the advice of Cornwallis to build defensive earthworks around Trenton—just in case.

Just after the volleys fired at Wiederhold, the American muskets and cannon opened up on the western side of town. It was a few minutes after 8 a.m. As soon as the roar of the gunfire was heard, Washington ordered his men on the eastern side to fire into the village. Rall, after being summoned three times by an underling, hastily put on his clothes and ran outside into the snowfall. Throughout the town, the Hessians, grabbing what muskets they could, stumbled out into the still-raging storm, uncertain where the enemy was positioned. Rall was not able to rally his men and chaos ensued for the stunned Hessians.

Some Hessians raced into the snow-covered fields that surrounded the town's two streets, some pulling cannon into a nearby apple orchard. Others regrouped in a churchyard but could not see the enemy clearly in the wind and snow and the smoke from the heavy and continuous musket fire. An unintended consequence of the early morning assault was that the civilian residents of the town were just as surprised at the attack as the Hessians had been. The men and women and children of Trenton ran out of their homes into the streets, yelling. Their screams drowned out the futile commands of Hessian officers, who tried desperately to organize their men into formations. They also had to shout orders above the martial music being played by the small band that Rall always brought with the regiment and had ordered to play during any battle. Rall, when he was finally dressed, managed to get on his horse and rode into the field, toward several hundred of his men, to take command. A moment later, he was shot and fell from his horse into the snow, mortally wounded.

Some Hessians reached two of their cannon, turned them northward, and fired a single shot at the American artillery but hit nothing. Knox ordered some men to fire away with their muskets at the Hessians near the cannon, but the snow and rain had rendered many of their guns useless. Knox then ordered as many men that could do so to charge the caissons and kill the Hessians manning them in any manner possible. A dozen or more infantrymen led by Lieutenant James Monroe, who would go on to become the nation's fifth president, rushed the Germans near the cannon, waving their swords and running as fast as they could. One of the men with Monroe, Sgt. Joe White, said that "I [yelled] as loud as I could scream for the men to run for their lives right up to the pieces."

Halfway there, the Germans manning the cannon raised their muskets and fired a volley of shots at the charging Americans. One shot hit Monroe squarely in the chest. The lieutenant fell instantly into the snow, his sword crashing to the ground next to him. He was badly wounded and bleeding profusely, his blood turning the snow around him crimson.[12]

Sgt. White, howling at the top of his lungs and running next to Monroe, turned and saw him fall as the crackling of the Hessian muskets filled the chilly air. White, now leading the attack, his adrenaline flowing, started to scream even louder, waving his sword wildly above his head. "I was the first to reach the [cannon]. One man was . . . tending. 'Run, you dog!' I yelled. He looked up and saw [sword] and ran. We put in a canister of shot and fired [at the fleeing Hessians]."[13]

The battle did not begin for Greenwood and his regiment, moving slowly west of Washington's divisions, until just after 8 a.m. as their artillery group reached the northern end of town. A Hessian six-pound cannon fired wildly into the snow and a cannonball exploded just in front of Greenwood's cannon caisson. He would recall, "The ball struck the fore horse that was dragging our only piece of artillery, a three-pounder. The animal, which was near me, as I was in the second division on the left, was struck in its belly and knocked over on its back. While it lay there kicking, the cannon was stopped and I did not see it again after we had passed on."

Everything after that seemed a blur to Greenwood. He noted, "It was dark and stormy so that we could not see very far ahead; we got within two hundred yards of about three or four hundred Hessians who were paraded two deep in a straight line with Colonel Rall, on horseback, to the right of them. They made a full fire at us, but I did not see that they killed anyone."

Greenwood moved toward the Hessians, proud that he was brave and forlorn that he was risking the loss of a perfectly good suit and brand new shirt, with lacy ruffles on the shirt, folded up in his backpack (the men never retrieved the packs). He was also distressed that the snow and rain had rendered their muskets useless; none were able to fire. As he contemplated the loss of his shirt and soaked musket, Sherburne ordered them to rush the Hessians in front of them and to use their bayonets for weapons.

"And rush we did," said a grim Greenwood, noting that only one in five men had bayonets. The rest waved their swords and simply ran and yelled as loud as they could. "Within pistol shot, they fired point blank at us; we dodged and they did not hit a man, while before they had time to reload we were within three feet of them," he wrote. The Hessians, with the howling Americans right in their faces, turned and stumbled backwards. "They broke in an instant and ran like so many frightened devils into the town. We went after them pell-mell," Greenwood added.

Some of the Hessians had given up and were herded inside a building by the Americans. Others had been cornered in a home and seemed about to surrender. Greenwood kept moving toward the sounds of the battle with others. "I passed two of their cannons, brass six-pounders, by the side of which lay seven dead Hessians and a brass drum. This latter article was, I remember, a great curiosity to me and I stopped to look at it, but it was quickly taken possession of by one of our drummers, who threw away his own."

Greenwood bent over and pulled a sword out of the sheath of one of the dead Hessians. As he rose he saw George Washington, on his horse, moving slowly down the street. "March on, my brave fellows, after me," the commander in chief told the men, apparently looking right at Greenwood. Greenwood described how his regiment moved down the street in remarkably calm order for men in a heated battle. They saw five hundred Hessians on their right and, in columns of two, marched down the road and turned to face them, just a few yards away. The men raised their guns and prepared to fire directly at the Hessians. Suddenly, Greenwood said, as the muskets were lifted, someone yelled out, "They have no guns! They have no guns!" Others shouted the same warning.

Greenwood and the others lowered their weapons and realized that the men in front of them had already surrendered. They had piled up their weapons on the ground and stepped back some fifteen feet. The Americans, in the snowfall, had by chance marched right between the prisoners and the pile of guns, looking to the right and not the left. Initially, the snow prevented them from realizing that the Germans had dropped their muskets. An accidental massacre was averted because several infantrymen noticed that the men were unarmed.

The attack had been a surprise, as the men hoped, and the vaunted Hessian army never had time to organize and fight back. The battle ended less than an hour after it commenced. The Americans had killed about thirty Hessians and captured nine hundred twenty. The Continental Army also confiscated six cannon and one thousand muskets, plus, the soldiers delighted in telling friends later, all of the instruments from the German band that Rall had loved so dearly. In fact, on the Fourth of July, 1777, the captured Hessian musicians used those instruments to serenade a Philadelphia crowd celebrating the first anniversary of independence.[14] The soldiers were pleased. Captain John Polhemus wrote, "We whipped them terrible."[15]

The snow-covered village of Trenton was a somber scene. "I took a walk over the field of battle and my blood chilled to see such horror and distress, blood mingling together—the dying groans and garments rolled in blood," said Sgt. White, who took an elegant sword from a slain Hessian officer lying in the snow as a souvenir of the fight. It was one of the few times that General Washington expressed some joy and broke his usual calm demeanor. "It is a great day for our country," he said to some of the enlisted men as he rode through the fields around the village.[16] He later wrote to General Cadwalader that "the officers and men who were engaged in the enterprise behaved with great firmness, poise, and . . . bravery."[17]

Greenwood was as relieved as White, McCarty, Bostwick, and the others but they had little time to savor the victory. The inability of Cadwalader and Ewing to transport their men across the Delaware meant that the three hundred Hessians who escaped southward would soon reach the British outpost at Burlington and riders from there would bring the news to Lord Cornwallis twenty miles away in New Brunswick. The British would soon be in hot pursuit of the Americans. Following his original plan, Washington led the army up the Delaware, with the nine hundred prisoners of war, and marched into Pennsylvania, again crossing the icy river, this time with boatloads of prisoners as well as his own soldiers.

Some of the enlisted men dawdled in Trenton, to the dismay of the American generals. One was White, proud that he and his comrades had taken the disabled Hessian cannon. They insisted on fixing the axle and pulling it all the way back on snow-covered roads to Pennsylvania, which they did despite an exasperated Henry Knox constantly haranguing for them to hurry up. White was so exhausted when the men, with their prize, reached the crossing point at the Delaware River that he laid down in the snow and took what he considered a well-deserved nap as the troops began to pile into the boats for the return crossing.[18]

Others spent much of their time remarking on how ordinary the much-feared and highly publicized Hessians, "the greatest soldiers in the world," actually appeared. They were not supermen after all. One enlisted man noted that they were "moderate in stature, limbs not of equal proportion, and their hair cued as tight to the head as possible, sticking straight back like the handle of an iron skillet."[19]

Greenwood found much humor in the way the Americans treated the once vaunted Hessians. Many men had taken the ornate brass helmets from slain Hessians and placed them on to their heads, smiling at each other as they did so. He noted, "With these brass caps on, it was laughable to see how they would strut, fellows with their elbows out and some without a collar to their half-shirt, and no shoes."

With at least a few days to think, Washington decided that his army was in just as precarious a position as it had been before. Now pride and revenge would be added to the usual reasons for the British to cross the river and attack him. To thwart them, he boldly crossed the river into New Jersey again. He did so for another reason, too. The general was afraid that the lone victory at Trenton might be seen as a fluke, but a second victory, this time over a large army of British regulars led by William Howe, not hired German mercenaries, would show the world that the Americans could win the war. It would also encourage the militiamen who were at home to join the fight and increase support for the rebellion throughout the colonies.

There was still one more reason, a more ominous one. Many enlistments were up on December 31 and many of his men—cold, sick, weary, and clothed in tattered uniforms—told their officers they could not wait to go home. They admired Washington and embraced the cause, but they were weary. Their departure, with no replacements in sight, would mean the end of the Revolution. Washington had to move fast. The commander in chief had decided to establish a one month emergency service enlistment. Those who remained for the emergency period of four weeks would be given a $10 bonus, more than a month's pay.

The second crossing of the Delaware took place as planned on December 30, when most of the army crossed with Washington. Another wing had crossed three days earlier with General Cadwalader. That night, Washington sat on his horse in front of an assemblage of several hundred troops in formation in Maidenhead, now Lawrenceville, just north of Trenton, New Jersey. He made a plea for the men to stay for thirty days, with a $10 bonus, and then waited for what he hoped would be mass agreement. Washington moved to the side of the field, expecting the men to step forward. No one moved. Crestfallen, Washington, who despised speaking in public, reined in his horse and walked him forward a few yards and again addressed the troops lined up in front of him.

"My brave fellows," he began in that deep, steady voice of his. "You have done all I have asked you to do and more than could be reasonably expected. But your country is at stake; your wives, your houses, and all that you hold dear. You have worn yourself out with fatigues and hardships but we know not how to spare you. If you will consent to stay but one month longer you will render that service to the cause of liberty and to your country which you probably never can do under any other circumstances. The present is emphatically the crisis which is to decide our destiny."[20]

For several moments that seemed like hours, no one took a step toward the general. Then a soldier in his forties shrugged, turned to the man next to him, and said that he would stay. He walked toward the general. Then, singly and in small groups, others walked toward the commander, too. Within a few minutes, the great majority of the men in front of him accepted his offer for just one more month in the army. Washington leaned forward in his saddle as he watched the men coming forward. He felt a great sense of relief.

Other generals issued the same plea to their men, some in front of dozens of local townspeople from nearby villages who had turned out in the freezing weather for the speeches; their appeals had the same thankful results. Private John Smith remembered that the appeal he heard was far more direct. Smith wrote simply that his general "begged them to tarry one month longer."[21] Few of the generals delivered very powerful speeches, either. White called the plea of General Knox "pathetic." To the surprise of the soldiers, the area residents in attendance burst into sustained applause when the men agreed to continue fighting.

Sgt. Joe White, whose original enlistment ran until March 1, 1777, was happy to remain in the military, but there were those who were tired of the war. John Greenwood, whose time was up, was one of them. His superiors begged him to stay in the army, but he was finished. "I was determined to quit as soon as my time was out," he said. "I told my lieutenant I was going home." "My God!" cried the lieutenant, stunned at the decision of a teenager who had started the war at Bunker Hill in a fife and drum unit, traveled to Canada, braved the smallpox epidemic there, and become one of the best soldiers in the army. "You are not going to leave us, for you are the life and soul of us."

Greenwood could not be swayed. He had recently turned sixteen. The lieutenant then began to promise him promotions. "I would not stay to be a colonel," Greenwood said and, with others, began the long march north to Boston the following morning, New Year's Eve, as the army moved south toward a confrontation with the Redcoats. He and the others did not feel that they had abandoned the army or let down the United States. They had served their time and fought hard for independence and their country. Now it was time for new recruits to fight. Greenwood had, in fact, served two consecutive enlistments. He had done his share and it was time to go home.

But he would be back.

Chapter Fourteen

THE VICTORY
THAT SAVED THE
REVOLUTION

The Redcoats that the Americans were looking for were not under the command of Howe but rather Lord Cornwallis, considered by some to be a better general than Howe. Cornwallis had split his force into two armies, leaving one with about twelve hundred men in Princeton. He took the other, with some fifty-five hundred men, south toward Trenton to engage the Americans. They did not expect Cornwallis to close in on them. This time, they left their boats at the Delaware and had no escape route over the river this far south. Cornwallis, arriving on January 2, 1777, had maneuvered adroitly, boxing the Americans in against the river with his much larger and better equipped army arrayed in front of them.

The weather, which had helped them in their first attack on Trenton, was of no benefit this time. The temperature climbed to a very unseasonable fifty-one degrees on New Year's Day and the warm weather, plus a low-pressure system that moved into the region, turned the fields and roads throughout the region to muck. The Americans were unable to move their cannon or march with much speed. By the time Cornwallis arrived, the entire American army was immobilized in a sea of mud.

The expected British attack came outside of Maidenhead, a village of just a few buildings, on the afternoon of January 2. The overwhelming British infantry, backed up by an enormous barrage of cannon fire, forced the Americans back across Assunpink Creek, their first defensive line, following a four-hour battle. There was only one bridge over the creek and as he scampered toward it, musket in hand, Sgt. White saw General Washington anchored in front of the bridge, a reassuring figure for the men as they rushed across the bridge to safety on the other side. White and the others were amazed that Washington, unflinching, was not hit by any of the hundreds of musket balls that whizzed through the afternoon air.

After the men had crossed the bridge, with Washington following the last of them, the British reached it. The Continental artillerists then peppered the bridge and the land beyond it, filled with the advancing British troops, with a long, loud, and devastating cannon fire. Joseph White, one of the artillery gunners, said that the Americans remained steady in the face a British column of troops that extended for nearly one mile and filled the horizon. Sgt. White wrote, "We loaded with canister shot and let them come nearer. We fired all together again and such destruction it made you cannot conceive. The bridge looked red as blood, with their killed and wounded and their red coats."

Inexplicably, Cornwallis did not order his men to cross the creek and chase the Americans, despite superior numbers and more cannon. As he called off an assault late in the afternoon, he told his officers that he had no fear of destroying the Americans, whom he had trapped, the next day. Referring to Washington, Cornwallis said his men would "bag the old fox in the morning"[1]

No one doubted that he could. The Americans were immobilized, hopelessly outnumbered, and had their backs to the river. The morning attack would bring about hundreds of casualties for the Americans and would end the war. White and the other soldiers firmly believed that would happen. Massachusetts's Sam Shaw wrote that "Even the most sanguine among us could not flatter ourselves into thinking with any hope of victory."[2]

To a lieutenant sitting next to him, Captain Stephen Olney of New York outlined all of the obstacles in the way of the men surviving the anticipated British onslaught in the morning. When he finished, the lieutenant shrugged his shoulders, stared at him, and said, "I don't know; the Lord must help us."[3]

White and the others were awakened from their sleep shortly after midnight with startling news; the army was going to evacuate the area. They realized that something had changed dramatically since they laid down on the fields to sleep. It was much colder and the ground was hard.

General Washington was an amateur meteorologist as a planter in Virginia. A working knowledge of weather patterns helped him to grow and, at times, save crops. He had watched the sky all day as the temperature held at 39 degrees and began to drop as a northwest wind began to build. He told his aides that these were all signs of a cold front and a frost headed their way. If so, the ground might freeze hard enough for the men—and artillery—to travel on it. Time would tell.

He was right. By midnight, the ground had frozen enough to support heavy cannon caissons. Ever the trickster, Washington then concocted an elaborate ruse to fool the British. He ordered the men to slowly evacuate, regiment by regiment, as quietly as possible, while sentries remained on duty and others continued to stoke the campfires to make it appear that the entire army was sleeping. Men carefully wrapped the wagon wheels of the cannon caissons in rags to muffle the ordinary creaking sound they made as they were pulled quietly away from the camp. Collections of rags and blankets covered the wheels of supply wagons that were sent south to avoid slowing down the army as it moved north with as much speed as possible. The men were told in whispers to move out speedily but noiselessly and in an orderly fashion. The men who had fought in the series of New York disasters told others that Washington had saved the army once before with a midnight evacuation, at Brooklyn Heights, and trusted him to be successful this time, too.

Wrote Lt. William Young later, "As soon as night fell, our people lined the woods, made large fires. As soon as I could I came to them with the wagon, with the provisions and blankets and stayed with them until twelve o'clock. Then we loaded our wagon, set out, and joined my two sons whom I left in the wood with some of our men. One o'clock. Ordered to move out with the baggage . . . such a hurry skurry among all our wagoners."[4]

By dawn, the American army of some five thousand soldiers had left the field at Lawrenceville and moved up a narrow, little-used, uneven dirt highway, Quaker Bridge Road, north toward Princeton. For several hours, many soldiers did not realize where they were headed, believing that they were traveling to Trenton and a morning attack on the British from the south. Several hundred sentries and the men who watched the campfires fled quietly and followed them just as morning arrived. As the sun rose high enough to bath the region in light, the British soldiers rose, dressed, and marched in formation toward the now-dying American campfires, wondering why there was no noise coming from the other side of the creek or the slopes beyond. They trudged over the bridge, their heads snapping from side to side. The rebels were gone.

Miles to the north, the Continental Army was able to march quickly on the frozen dirt highway. "The road which the day before had been mud, snow, and water . . . had become hard as pavement," said Stephen Olney.[5]

The men were not only pleased that they had escaped certain annihilation at the hands of the British, but had done so with such an ingenious plan. William Thompson, of Virginia, wrote to a friend of Washington's tactics that "you may expect something clever will be done."[6]

On the way to Princeton, where Cornwallis had left his other army under Lt. Col. Charles Mawhood, a captain rode up to Sgt. White, who was walking with the artillery corps, and told him that he was to command one of the field pieces when the army reached its destination. The young soldier, just turned eighteen, asked why he had been put in charge and was told that General Knox had been impressed by his bravery at Trenton ten days before and wanted him to do so. "I am not capable. The responsibility is too great for me," he told the captain. The officer said he understood, but that Knox had faith in him because he had been so brave when he led the charge against the Hessians after Monroe had been cut down. "I began to feel my pride rising," White wrote later.

The Americans again had surprise on their side when they approached the Princeton area. Lt. Col. Mawhood, accompanied as always by his two dogs, was leading two regiments of several hundred English foot soldiers out of Princeton toward Trenton. He and another officer sat on their horses watching the Continental Army move up the road toward them for a minute or more, thinking it was Cornwallis's army, fresh from annihilating Washington to the south, as everyone expected. Mawhood must have thought the war had ended. The Continental Army was very close when Mawhood finally realized that he was facing the Americans. He had to act quickly to alert his English troops, who scrambled to fall into position.

As the Americans raced across the fields and orchards of the Clark farm southwest of Princeton, Joseph White took charge of his artillery team and its large six-pound cannon. Shouting out orders over the noise of the battle, the eighteen-year-old yelled, "Fire!" and the cannon roared, along with others, cutting into the long line of British grenadiers and Highlanders that had formed in front of them. Their fire was answered by a burst of cannon fire from the British. White, shouting at his men, managed to get off one more shot as the Americans, led by General Hugh Mercer, ran within striking distance of the British.

Lt. James McMichael was one of those soldiers. "We boldly marched within twenty-five yards of them and then commenced the attack which was very hot," he said. The Americans opened up with a loud volley of musket fire that was met with a British volley. "We kept up an incessant fire," McMichael continued. It was an eerie scene and Major James Wilkinson wrote later that "the smoke from the discharge of the two lines mingled as it rose and went up in one beautiful cloud."[7]

McMichael, constantly reloading and firing his musket, was frightened. Just to his right four men fell dead in one volley and two more died to his left in the next roar of the English muskets. He could not believe that he had not been hit as he stood right in the middle of a murderous series of volleys and "thanked the kindness of Providence" for it.

There were three volleys and then the British, in larger numbers, came across the field, their bayonets gleaming in the early morning sun, and overwhelmed the Americans. Mercer was caught by several Redcoats who, instead of capturing him, stabbed him several times and left him for dead (he would die a few hours later).

Mercer's men had retreated amid the loud sounds of musketry and cannon. As they swarmed away from the enemy they met George Washington, on his horse, who rallied them. He commanded them to turn and fight and as they did Washington moved ahead of them on his horse, leading them toward the regrouped British line. Leaning forward on his horse and waving his hand at the men, he shouted, "Fire!" and the soldiers, who felt defeated just seconds ago, fired directly into the enemy, killing dozens. A second later, a raucous British volley followed. Washington had not moved from his horse and told the men to prepare to fire again. Everyone was certain the British fire would kill the commander in chief. His aide John Fitzgerald was so certain that Washington would be slain that, unable to watch his commander die, he lowered his head.

"Come on!" they suddenly heard Washington encourage them as the fire subsided. Fitzgerald and the others saw that he had not been hit. The men loaded and fired again. Washington then waved his sword and led them across the field. The enemy, watching the American commander and his men coming right at them, panicked, turned, and ran. Washington led the pursuit on his horse. "It's a fine fox chase, boys!" he yelled and the men, shouting as loud as they could, chased the enemy across the orchard fields.[8]

"His personal bravery, and the desire he has of animating his troops by example, make him fearless of any danger," wrote Sam Shaw. Another soldier wrote that the men were all proud of "our brave general."[9] Lieutenant Charles Wilson Peale, the artist, led his men in three assaults that morning. He said of the enlisted men there that they "stood the fire, without regarding the balls, which whistled their thousand notes around our heads."[10] One soldier described the musket volleys from the British "as thick as hail" and reported that three balls had grazed him, one hitting his hat, a second tearing off the sole of his shoe, and the third ripping through the sleeve of his coat and hitting the musket of the man standing behind him.[11]

In another part of Princeton, General John Sullivan's men defeated the English fifty-fifth regiment. Alexander Hamilton's artillery battery set up several cannon in a wide yard opposite Nassau Hall, the two-story, main stone building of the College of New Jersey, which later became Princeton University, and began blasting it. One ball ironically smashed into a painting of King George I that hung on a wall. The more than two hundred British soldiers holed up inside Nassau Hall soon waved the white flag of surrender outside a window.

The trauma of the pitched battle was so great that some of the men that had been hit did not even know it. One man reached into the knapsack strapped over his shoulders for a piece of bread a day later. When he pulled out the loaf he found a musket ball in it. Pvt. Elisha Bostwick then helped him take off his clothes. They discovered that he had been shot in the shirt and that the ball, just missing his body, had ripped through the shirt, his coat, and the side of the knapsack before lodging inside the piece of bread.[12]

The fighting at Princeton had been fierce. It had been brutal, too, and the Americans there that morning never forgave the British for bayoneting to death men they could have simply captured. The American enlisted men, from raw privates to sergeants like Joseph White, had held their own. They had withstood bayonet charges and cannon fire and had defeated some of the best regiments in the British army.

The Americans paid a heavy price for the victory. Two homes in Princeton were commandeered for several hours as American doctors tried in vain to save General Mercer, several other badly wounded officers, and enlisted men. Among the American dead that morning were fourteen officers and thirty enlisted men. Although disheartening, American casualties were a remarkable contrast to the British losses. The English had lost some three hundred dead or wounded and three hundred captured.

Sergeant White, who had annoyed officers nine days before at Trenton when he took a nap in the snow, remained his playful self in Princeton. Just as the battle ended he entered a building and found a rather delicious-looking breakfast of a British soldier who had been called to battle—toast, eggs, and a teapot—and, hungry from the marching and fighting, he wrote, "I sat down and helped myself." When he finished, "highly refreshed," he left, taking the absent officer's coat, silk shirt, shoes, and Bible with him. The soldier then strode into a local resident's home, musket in one hand, coat, shirt, and shoes in the other, and a wide smile on his face, and said good morning to the frightened woman who lived there. He asked her to bake him some cakes and returned a few moments later, after rummaging through a nearby house (not known if it was home to an American family or occupied by British troops), to retrieve them.

"Do you have any daughters?" Sgt. White said, posing the most dangerous question for any mother in a war confronted by an armed soldier. "Why do you ask?" she said with great hesitation. He laughed at her, immediately sensing her fears of sexual attack. "I'm just a pious old deacon," he said, reassuring the women, and told her that in return for the cakes he had presents for her daughters.

Sensing that she could trust the young soldier, she asked her daughters to come down. The first, Sally, descended halfway down the stairs, saw the American soldier and halted, too scared to continue further. "Sally, come down, here is a present for you," said the young sergeant as he walked to the bottom of the staircase and held up a fine petticoat. The mother nodded and the daughter walked down to the bottom of the stairs and accepted it. White gave the other daughter a pair of shoes. "Try them on and if they fit, keep them," he said, smiled, thanked the mother for the cakes once more, and left, looking for his regiment.

Again, the weary troops of the Continental Army had no time to celebrate or to rest. It had not taken Lord Cornwallis much time to figure out where the American army had gone after it vanished from the Trenton area during the night. Cornwallis and his army had marched toward Princeton as rapidly as possible after they found the American camp vacant and were within an hour of the town by noon, scouts told Washington. The commander in chief had considered moving from Princeton to New Brunswick, where the British had stores of ammunition and over two million dollars in gold, but imminent arrival of the main British army ruined that plan. Washington settled on his main plan, to move north to the tiny village of Morristown, in the middle of Morris County, twenty-five miles west of New York City, to set up winter quarters.

And so, in the early afternoon, following two fierce battles on successive days, most of the five thousand tired American foot soldiers headed north out of Princeton toward Morristown and what they hoped would be better lodging and a bit of rest (others took prisoners to Pennsylvania). Spies soon relayed the news that Cornwallis had marched to New Brunswick. The main British army would leave New Jersey shortly and return to New York, leaving just small garrisons at New Brunswick, Elizabeth, and Perth Amboy.

The foot soldiers did not yet know, or comprehend, what they had accomplished in their two brutal battles at Trenton and Princeton within that brief ten-day span. They had soundly defeated the best troops of the British Empire, killing over three hundred and taking over twelve hundred prisoners. They had freed most of the state of New Jersey of the main British army and prevented the occupation of Philadelphia. The Continental Congress was now free to return to the city of brotherly love and reconfigure the national government and the New Jersey state legislature was able to meet again.

Foreign powers, especially France and Spain, now believed that it was entirely possible that the Americans might win the war and began to think seriously of coming into the conflict as allies; the French even ordered four ships stocked with gunpowder and muskets to set sail for America. The British government was rocked by the dual defeats. Lord George Germain, head of the colonial office and director of the war effort, realized that the conflict would last much longer than he and his generals had anticipated. Many Americans who had been either sympathetic to the Crown or neutral about the war now changed their mind and embraced the Revolution. The American press, split on its support for the Revolution at the start of the conflict, now sided with the rebels and, in effect, became propaganda sheets for Washington and the army. None explained it better than a doctor traveling with the army, who wrote home that the double victories "have given new life and spirits to the cause."[13]

There was much praise for George Washington, but there was also substantial praise for the common soldiers in the American army. British historian George Trevelyan wrote of them, "It may be doubted whether so small a number of men ever employed so short a space of time with greater and more lasting effects upon the history of the world." And the proud editor of the *Freeman's Journal,* an American newspaper, wrote of the troops that "the men behaved with the utmost bravery."[14] George Washington, riding at the head of the column trudging northward to Morristown, may have thought of all the consequences of the dual triumphs, but Sergeant Joe White had neither the time or the inclination to do so. As he walked along the highway north toward Morristown he devoted his attention to pulling from his knapsack one of the cakes that woman in Princeton had baked for him and thinking about how pretty her daughters were.

Chapter Fifteen

NEW JERSEY AND PENNSYLVANIA, 1777–1778:
Lieutenant James McMichael: A Poet Goes to War

The War

*T*he Continental Army struggled through the winter of 1777 at Morristown. Following the twin victories at Trenton and Princeton, the army marched north to the small community in the heart of northern New Jersey to establish a winter camp. The town was protected by the Watchung Mountains to the east, intersected by two main highways, home to a large militia, run by patriotic public officials and close enough to New York that Washington could keep an eye on the British army there.

It was a winter of discontent for the American army. Hundreds of men either deserted or went home after their enlistments were up, and at one point Washington had only fourteen hundred regulars and militia left. Another smallpox epidemic hit America that winter, threatening not only the existence of the army but the lives of thousands of civilians. Washington took the unprecedented step of immediately inoculating all of the troops and any civilians who chose to participate. His bold step saved the army and thousands of citizens.

There was nothing but bad news. Just before the arrival of the army at Morristown in December 1776, the British attacked and occupied Newport, Rhode Island, a key seaport. Throughout the winter, U.S. currency continually depreciated in value, making it difficult for the army to purchase needed supplies.

Most of the troops in Washington's main force remained in Morristown until the end of May, but some regiments were assigned elsewhere.

Lieutenant James McMichael's Pennsylvania State Regiment of some five hundred men (renamed the Thirteenth Pennsylvania Regiment in late 1777), remained at Morristown all winter. In April 1777, the regiment was sent to Liberty Island in the Delaware River just south of Philadelphia to protect the city in case of a British attack, which George Washington fully expected. The capture of Philadelphia—the capital of the United States and the home of Congress and a major port—would be a major military victory for the British.

On May 1, a Sunday, a local band arrived on Liberty Island, the musicians carrying their instruments from boats to a compact parade ground to entertain the troops stationed there. Among them were the three companies of Lieutenant McMichael's regiment. They needed entertainment.

The Pennsylvanians had been through some of the most dangerous battles and hardest marches of the American Revolution. The men had no sooner left their villages in Pennsylvania on May 27, 1776, to applause and cheers from their friends and neighbors, then they, and McMichael, in his early twenties, found themselves on the front lines of the battles to defend New York. The enlisted men were thoroughly beaten at the battle of Long Island on August 27. There, in the early afternoon, the Pennsylvanians found themselves cut off from the army. They fought courageously but were hopelessly outnumbered. At first, under McMichael's direction, a line of enlisted men attempted to make a stand. In the first round of volleys the man positioned right next to McMichael had his head blown off. McMichael was badly shaken. The regiment's only chance to escape was to swim or wade through a large mill pond behind them with the enemy in hot pursuit.

McMichael, his musket held above his head, plunged into the pond, exhorting his men to follow him. Some of the men, their clothing, packs, and muskets too heavy for them, could not make it through the waters of the pond and drowned. The advancing British troops made it impossible for McMichael or other officers to go back to save them. McMichael himself was astonished that he reached the far shore of the pond. "It was the will of providence that I should escape," he wrote.

Separated from the rest of the army, he and his men did not learn until later the extent of the devastation the army suffered in the Long Island battle. McMichael later wrote that his regiment and those fighting nearby lost two colonels, nineteen officers, twenty-three sergeants and three hundred ten enlisted men, all taken prisoner (total American losses that day were 312 killed, 1,097 captured[1]). The lieutenant had survived one of the most severe engagements of the Revolution. "My preservation I only attribute to the indulgence of God," he wrote. "For though the bullets went round me in every direction, yet I received not a wound."

The Americans continued to lose in their confrontations with the British in New York and were forced to pull back from a position on Harlem Heights. The army retreated north to White Plains and formed a three mile defensive line that cut through the village.

On the morning of October 28, Howe's army, consisting of nine thousand British regulars plus four thousand Hessians, advanced on the town after crossing the Bronx River. McMichael's company and several militia units marched two miles to meet the enemy and test the Redcoats' strength. There, McMichael described a furious Redcoat and Hessian assault against the American advance party.

He wrote, "We were attacked with [their] right wing being all Hessians. We kept up an incessant fire for nearly an hour when being informed from our flanking party that the [British] light horse were surrounding us. We were necessitated to retreat to the lines." The Pennsylvanians, ordered back, joined the main line of defense later in the morning as General Howe's entire force moved forward.

"Their left wing attacked a party of ours at an advanced post on a hill," McMichael continued. "Our troops behaved with great fortitude but being overpowered by numbers were at last obliged to retreat to the lines. The enemy attempted to force our right wing in the lines but were put to a precipitate retreat back to the hill. The attack continued from 9 a.m. until 2 in the afternoon." Finally, the left side of the American line collapsed when the Massachusetts militia units broke and fled. That was the beginning of the end and Washington soon ordered another general retreat north, beyond the Croton River.

Word spread that American losses were light (actually, they had lost only one hundred fifty men, killed or wounded) and that the enemy had lost six hundred (actually 313), but McMichael, at the center of the action that day, knew that regardless of numbers, the field in front of him was covered in blood.

A wing of the American army that was sent to hold Fort Washington in Manhattan was defeated. The main army was forced to run for its life across New Jersey toward Pennsylvania, with the British in pursuit. All felt the end was near. "Our army now being reduced to a small number gives us less hope of victory," McMichael wrote.

The soldiers were bitter about the lack of public help for an army that was on its last legs. There was no assistance with food, shelter, or clothing from the New Jersey towns through which the army retreated. No local militias marched into camp to swell the ranks and, in fact, continued desertions badly depleted the army. The cheers the troops remembered in Boston had faded rather abruptly in New Jersey. In New Brunswick, a town on the banks of the Raritan River halfway across the state, McMichael watched two thousand soldiers whose time was up march home. He wrote that "the Tories now began to look at us with a disdainful countenance, wishing the enemy may drive us shortly out of town."

The Pennsylvania state regiment moved to Morristown for winter camp, but McMichael managed to talk his commanding officer into granting him a furlough to return to Pennsylvania. His request was among many granted by lower-ranking generals who did not check with the commander in chief, who agreed to furlough men, but did not want all requests approved. Washington did not realize they had been sent home until it was too late. Those soldiers who left included men such as McMichael. The furloughs, along with desertions and the departures of men whose enlistment was up, plus those whose emergency ten-day enlistment ended, left Washington with an army of just twenty-five hundred men in Morristown, his winter camp.

McMichael, who may have had smallpox earlier in life and was immune, did not get sick when the epidemic struck that winter. In fact, his health remained hearty throughout the winter. That was good, too, because his sturdy constitution permitted him to spend his time off in the village of Stony Brook, New Jersey.

It was in Stony Brook, just one mile from Princeton, where McMichael had met Susanna Vetnoy, twenty-five, the previous winter and was hopelessly smitten with her. He scribbled in his diary that it was there "when first I beheld the face of my dear Susanna." They were married on March 4, 1776, after a steamy, whirlwind courtship of just ten days.

And so, on May 1, 1777, almost a year later, McMichael listened to the musicians on that fine spring day at his army camp on an island on the Delaware River and enjoyed their songs. But it was visions of his new wife Susanna, not the tunes of the lively band, that filled the lovesick lieutenant's head.

McMichael had been seeing Susanna on short furloughs and, like so many soldiers in the Revolution, missed her terribly when he had to leave her embrace and rejoin the army. He had spent his last furlough, from

April 2 through April 7, in bed with her for six days of "conjugal bliss." The satiated young groom, like all young grooms, probably could not sleep for several days afterward, just thinking about his new bride and her enduring charms.

At the Delaware River outpost, his yearning for her grew even greater and then, on May 3, he received a steamy letter from Susanna that was full of lustful suggestions and a plea to him that she had physical "needs" that had to be satisfied. He wrote that her letter "exhilarates my animal spirits," adding that "every sentence thereof was so pleasing and so calculated to render me happy that language fails to express the dictates of my mind."

That letter sent poor McMichael reeling. It was then that he turned to poetry to express his feelings for Susanna for the first time in the war.

> Amidst alarms my love is placed
> On my Susanna, Dear
> Whilst her sweet charms is by me traced
> As well remote as near
> But when the war is at an end
> To visit her I do intend
> And with her spend the rest of life
> For hope she'll prove a good wife

McMichael fell sick after he sent that poem, as he had from time to time during his nearly two years of combat, but learned just a few weeks later, in early June, that he might obtain another furlough. The thought of traveling to see Susanna, and attending to her "needs," sent the lieutenant into another spate of poetry:

> I now thought I was in her arms
> And drowned in bliss amidst her charms
> And though not well yet I seemed all alive
> For pleasing thoughts did me revive
> Then I thought were I but at Stonybrook
> That on my dear Susanna I might look

Her smiles to me would a physician prove
We did each other admire with ardent love
I will with speed a visit pay to she
Who of all others most pleasing is to me
That when her charms I do behold
Which are as if formed in a mold
I may be happy whilst I do enjoy
Her truest love without the least annoy

The furlough did come through, but Susanna's ardent young husband was forced to cool his heels for two long days in Philadelphia before the next ferry sailed to Trenton. He crossed the Delaware with a group of officers he knew who persuaded him to join them for some "refreshments" at a tavern in Trenton that afternoon, further delaying his arrival at Susanna's house. Finally, just after sundown, he wrote in his journal, he was in the arms of his amorous wife, "which filled my mind with all the delights possibly able to flow from the transitory enjoyments."

In addition to his romantic desire for Susanna, McMichael had other reasons to ride to her home. It was a chance to live in a warm house, and not a cold tent, for a week or more. His wife surely cooked better meals than the army. Susanna, like all wives in the war, probably sewed his torn clothing. She **might** have sewn him new leggings or purchased new clothing for him. The diary indicates that they spent time with friends and her family, too, surely a comfort.

Again, duty called, and after a few days the lieutenant had to return to the military. There, he learned that his regiment was going into battle. McMichael then surprised his fellow officers and the enlisted men when he seemed overjoyed at the news. He was not thrilled about facing the British; he was ecstatic because the battle, he was told, would take place somewhere near Somerset Court House, in New Jersey. The highway to that town from Pennsylvania went through Ringoes, a New Jersey town just thirteen miles northwest of Stony Brook.

The regiment traveled to Fort Mercer, a fort on the Delaware, and then dawdled at Philadelphia. Time passed and McMichael's frustrations grew. Would this be just one more of the hundreds of false alarms the regiment had been through? Would they again sleep on their arms all night and then do nothing in the morning? Would they be marched back to their island? Finally, on June 24, they crossed the Delaware at Coryell's Ferry (today New Hope, Pennsylvania) and headed east, first for Ringoes and then toward Somerset Court House, a sleepy little village in the center of the state. The Americans there were nervous because General Howe's main army of some eighteen thousand troops had left New Brunswick. Several of Howe's regiments started to engage American units in northern New Jersey. They expected him to attack them.

What happened next is not clear. McMichael either decided to go AWOL so that he could see his wife or he talked his commanding officer into letting him sneak away from the regiment for a romantic tryst. He jumped on a horse shortly after noon on June 25 and left the column of troops as they marched down the dirt highway through Ringoes. He rode as quickly as he could, taking every shortcut he knew, crossing meadows and streams at full gallop, and reached Stony Brook, and his young wife, who was *very* happy to see him, at 2 p.m.

McMichael did not have much time with his spouse and presumably after a day and night of heated lovemaking he left her home at 2 a.m., climbing back on his horse in total darkness. McMichael rode through the night to Somerset Court House where, sleepless and physically drained, he trotted into camp astride his horse as the men rose at 6 a.m. He had nothing to fear if he had worried about being ready for battle after an evening with his wife, though. There was no encounter with the British that morning. The Redcoats were nowhere to be found.

Then, in what was a familiar pattern to the soldiers by then, the army marched about, looking for the British, but not finding them. The men finally arrived two weeks later at Morristown. The one night stand with his wife fresh in his mind, and sleepless once more thinking about her, he went to headquarters and asked for yet another furlough to return to Stony Brook, but was denied. With time on his hands,

McMichael wrote another poem to Susanna, lamenting his inability to receive a pass to visit her:

> This has my patience almost tired, and filled with regret
> Because for to go see my friends, I now no time can get
> Farewell dear creature I must go, away to the wars
> And for sometime quit Venus far, and join myself to Mars
> Whose thundering noise does fill the ears of those which do be bold
> And undergo his difficulties which scarcely can be told

The lieutenant was a lucky fellow, however. No sooner had he sent the poem off than he was ordered to return to his home state of Pennsylvania to hunt down deserters. He was ordered to ride to Bucks and Chester Counties—back via the highway through Ringoes—and track down men from his regiment who had left the army, and men from other regiments in those counties, arrest them, and return them to camp. It was made clear his mission was of the utmost urgency.

Desertion and the refusal of men to serve more than a single enlistment had been a constant problem in the Continental Army since the siege of Boston in the winter of 1775–1776, when Washington lost half his army and when men whose terms were up decided to simply walk home. Now, in the summer of 1777, Washington worried about the loss of troops once again.

Most of the men left for what they believed to be good reasons— their farms and businesses were falling apart in their absence and their loved ones needed them. "In some parishes but one or two men are left," one colonel wrote to the governor of Connecticut, explaining the mass departures that had taken place during the summer of 1776. "Some have got ten or twelve loads of hay cut and not a man to take it up; some five or six, under the same circumstance; some have got a great quantity of grass cut, some have not finished hoeing corn; some, if not all, have got all their plowing to do, for sowing their winter grain; some have all their families sick and not a person left to care for them . . . It is enough to make a man's heart ache to hear the complaints."[2]

And, too, these men had tired of reading letters written to them by friends and neighbors back home who told them they had not joined the army precisely because they did not want their farms and businesses to lapse into ruin.

The soldiers departed for any number of reasons: they were tired of the cold, lack of clothing, and lack of pay; hungry; angry that promises of bonuses were not kept. Some were fearful of catching smallpox in camp. Some did not like the Frenchmen who had joined the army. Many simply did not like their officers. One group of four hundred men whose time was up refused to stay following a dispute with their commander, Lord Stirling. One complete militia unit from Massachusetts left en masse, despite a personal plea from Washington to remain.

Officers, like the enlisted men, left the service to return to their farms and families or departed because of illness. Some officers were jealous of the higher rank and pay of others whom they deemed incompetent and went home when their time was up. Many of the men who had agreed to remain for one more month for a $10 bonus, at Washington's urging prior to the battle of Princeton, left exactly thirty days later, at the end of January. Their departure angered Washington, who had begged them to stay. But he was even more unhappy that troops from his native Virginia were leaving too, some after just a few weeks in camp.

The number of deserters, officers as well as enlisted men, became so great that Washington wailed to Congress in the early years of the war that "we should be obliged to detach one half of the army to bring back the other."[3] One general smirked that so many officers had left the military that when the next battle came, the army sent to meet them would just consist of George Washington and the enlisted men.

Washington complained to everyone he knew about the soldiers who would not reenlist unless they knew the identity of their officers. He wrote to former aide Joseph Reed that "such a dearth of public spirit and want of virtue, such stock-jobbing and fertility in all the low arts to obtain advantage of one kind or another in this great change of military agreement I never saw before and pray God I may never be witness to again . . . Could I have foreseen what I have and am likely to experience, no consideration upon earth should have induced me to accept this command."[4] Washington warned Congress and his generals that if thousands of new troops were not recruited the Revolution would collapse.[5]

Those close to the commander in chief understood his frustration, but told him that he had wrongly assumed that everyone, from privates to colonels, shared his noble vision of the Revolution. Nathanael Greene, who would later become one of Washington's closest confidants, put it diplomatically when he wrote early in the war that "His Excellency has been taught to believe that people here are a superior race of mortals, and finding them of the same temper and disposition, passions and prejudices, virtues and vices of the common people of other governments, they sink in his esteem."[6]

Many new to the military agreed with Washington's grim assessment of the troops. One lieutenant, Alexander Graydon, a well-educated Pennsylvanian, sneered at the American force, calling it "the motley army." He wrote that "the appearance of things was not much calculated to excite sanguine expectations in the mind of a sober observer. Great numbers of people were indeed to be seen, and those who are not accustomed to the sight of bodies under arms are always prone to exaggerate them. The irregularity, want of discipline, bad arms, and defective equipment in all respects gave no favourable impression of its prowess."[7]

There was little Washington could do to stem the departure of men who had served their time, but he instituted a series of steps to stop the mass desertion that threatened to ruin the military. Officer furloughs were ended so that regimental leaders could watch over their men; they were also ordered to be kind to all unhappy soldiers. Newspapers were asked to publish physical descriptions of deserters and their readers were urged to turn them in for a $5 reward. He also convinced Congress to order states to have deserters arrested and brought before local magistrates before being returned to the service. Deserters were usually given one hundred lashes and some were even executed.

That's where James McMichael's assignment originated. He and many other officers were sent to their home counties to seek out deserters and arrest them. McMichael did as he was told, but on the way was delayed at Stony Brook. The ardent young lieutenant was in such a hurry to reach his wife there that he rode all day, arriving at Susanna's home at 9 p.m. He stayed with her that night and for two more nights and days, finally departing for Pennsylvania on July 14. Susanna, unable to let her new groom go, accompanied him as far as the Delaware and then McMichael headed into Pennsylvania and she reluctantly returned home. He reasoned the outcome of the war and the history of the world had not been changed much by his secret, joyous little stopover at Stony Brook.

There were other times when McMichael would sneak off to see his beloved. Sometimes he rode to Stony Brook and on other occasions he met her for trysts at the homes of her friends in Amwell, a community several miles north. Once he had to leave Susanna to catch a ferry back to camp and missed it. McMichael promptly decided to spend two more days with Susanna. The lieutenant then invented a lengthy tale about his Herculean but unsuccessful efforts to travel up and down the Delaware for days to find another ferry to reach camp, an explanation his commanding officer grudgingly accepted.

His poems to Susanna inspired Lt. McMichael to write more poetry and throughout the revolution he penned dozens of poems, some long and some short. It was not unusual for soldiers to write a four line ditty to a wife, girlfriend, or family member every once in awhile, but following his summer trysts, McMichael turned to rhyme to describe his feelings not just about his passion for Susanna, but the Revolution itself. His poems grew from four lines to eight lines to several pages. Later, they would become Homeric in length. He found rhymed stanzas an easy medium to express himself and did so often. He wrote during warm, pleasant summer days but also turned to poetry during his bleakest hours at Valley Forge.

Infused into his poetry was the same gritty determination to win the war, unite the country, and secure independence from the hated Redcoats, a conviction felt by many who wrote poetry or the songs that regiments sang throughout the conflict. In all of McMichael's stanzas, there was a disdain for the Tories:

We are now unto Chester County came
In which some people lives that are of fame
But some are Tories to their great disgrace
Numbers of them reside near to this place

He had little use for the antiwar Quakers of Pennsylvania either, describing them harshly in one of his poems:

By Tories we are now surrounded
Either marching or rebounding
But Tories still are pusillanimous
And can't encounter men magnanimous
We made us merry at their expense
Whilst they wished we were all gone hence
These were the people called Quakers
And in war would not be partakers
To liberty's sons this seemed but light
We still allowed that we could fight

He wrote of his own hopes to fight well, expressed the night before an anticipated engagement with the enemy:

I am now nearly sick of marching
But for the enemy must be searching
When we do meet we'll surely fight
And try which party is most right
This must be decided, by arms,
By thundering Mars' most loud alarms
I'll take my post amongst the rest
And act the manner which I think best

McMichael, like all soldiers, feared death. They all knew that their lives could end at any moment on the battlefield, that they could fall from a musket ball or bayonet. It was the fear that soldiers carried within their hearts for centuries and would continue to carry long after the Revolution. During the blackest hours of the rebellion, McMichael, ever apprehensive about his safety, wrote poems about being killed, such as one he finished the night before a battle:

> When I lay down I thought and said
> Perhaps tomorrow I may be dead
> Yes I shall stand with all my might
> And for sweet liberty will fight.

It is not known if the young lieutenant sent these poems to his wife or whether he only mailed her his love sonnets. There were plenty of those and they gave the soldier renewed energy every time he finished one. He gained even more sustenance when one of Susanna's letters, especially the sultry ones, arrived and he could sit down and read it—over and over and over.

Chapter Sixteen

WOMEN OF THE REVOLUTION

McMichael's yearning to see his beloved was a common feeling among the soldiers, whether officers or enlisted men. Many had wives or girlfriends back home to whom they wrote as frequently as possible; they treasured letters from them that they received in camp. All attempted to win furloughs to visit them and made their way home as quickly as carriages or horses—or for some their feet—could take them when they obtained a pass. Soldiers bombarded their commanding officers with requests to go home specifically to see those they loved.

Wives often begged their husbands to stay home for awhile. These requests were not strictly for romantic trysts. Many men had left farms and small businesses that did not prosper during their absence. Others were the heads of families with six or more children and the responsibility to run the family and care for the children alone placed a heavy burden on their wives. Some women were also left to supervise laborers, or in some cases dozens of slaves, and found that a difficult task. Others had to run stores. The return of a husband, even if only for a few days or weeks, would prove helpful.

Some women traveled with the army to be close to their husbands, but not many. These were usually high-ranking officers' wives, who lived with them in huts, tents, or houses. A few wives of enlisted men marched with the army and were in the group called "camp followers." It consisted of several hundred people, including women who worked for the army as piece-work laborers, washing and repairing clothes, and sutlers who sold goods to soldiers and nurses. The camp followers also included several prostitutes.

The men in the army always seemed to have one eye on the Revolution and one eye on the ladies, and sometimes both eyes on the ladies, a long-standing military tradition. And the men soon discovered that no matter where they traveled in America, rural farms or bustling seaports, there were plenty of good-looking women.

The arrival of the Continental Army in any town in the colonies brought out the girls, to the delight of the soldiers. The women of the community would welcome the soldiers with decanters of wine, cakes, and cheeses—and soothing smiles. The army could not march through a village without women cheering on the men and waving to them with great enthusiasm. Soldiers walking down a street would see a window fly open and behind it a woman with a platter of cakes for them that they took with a thanks and a wink as they marched by.[1]

During the first year of the war, enlisted men were sometimes quartered in the homes of residents of the communities where they stayed overnight or camped for periods of time. They had a chance to become quite friendly with the daughters of the household and their female friends and neighbors. Then, as now, women loved men in uniform. "The women here are quite amorous," one man wrote with glee upon his arrival at Morristown in January, 1777. McMichael himself, before he met Susanna, marveled at the attractive women he met wherever the army traveled. In his diary, he wrote of the Continental Army's disastrous defeat at the hands of the British regulars and the Hessians at the battle of White Plains, but remembered, too, that it was a village that was home to "a multiplicity of beautiful young ladies." One soldier wrote of Mount

Holly, New Jersey, that it was a "compact and pleasant village, having a great proportion of handsome women therein."[2]

Men camped in one area for a long period of time sought out women wherever they could find them, and they knew where to look. Private Jabez Fitch and others went to the Punch Bowl Tavern, in Boston, "to find some white-stockinged women."[3] Sentries searched for women with their spyglasses.[4]

Sometimes the women found the soldiers. McMichael wrote that just after the army arrived near Germantown, a community just outside of Philadelphia in 1777, a group of several dozen good-looking local women marched into the American camp laughing and shouting to personally greet the soldiers. The men, needless to say, loved the attention.

Songs were written about the women that the troops met during the war, regardless of the length or seriousness of the relationship. One often-sung tune went like this:

> A soldier is a gentleman, his honor is his life
> And he that won't stand by his post will never stand by his wife
> In shady tents and cooling streams with hearts all firm and free,
> We'll chase away the cares of life in songs of liberty . . .
> So fare you well, you sweethearts, you smiling girls adieu
> For when the war is over, we'll kiss it out with you."[5]

Some soldiers encountered so many pretty girls that their fantasies were not simply kissing it out with a lovely woman, but with many of them. All were surprised at how many gorgeous women there were in America and some were astonished that certain towns were filled with them. Private Joseph Martin was one. He wrote when he marched through Princeton, New Jersey, with his regiment on the afternoon of June 24, 1778, "The young ladies of the town . . . had collected and were sitting in the stoops and at the windows to see the noble exhibition of a thousand half-starved and three-quarter-naked soldiers passing in review before them. I had a chance to be on the wing of the platoon next to the houses, as they were chiefly on one side of the street, and had a good chance to notice the ladies, and I declare that I never before nor since saw more beautiful, considering the numbers, than I saw at that time. They were all beautiful."[6]

Many of the soldiers flirted with girls they saw, but some could be downright bawdy in their eagerness to meet those of the opposite sex. Dozens of men in Charlestown, Massachusetts, spent the summer of 1775 bathing naked in the Charles River near one of the busy bridges that crossed it to show off their physiques for the women that walked across the span; some men sashayed nude across the bridge to draw even more attention. Their antics always drew complaints from local residents. George Washington had to outlaw the practice.[7] Just a year later, other soldiers swam naked in a mill pond on Long Island, New York, to entice young women from the nearby village; General Nathanael Greene ended this practice with a similar order.[8]

Some of the soldiers married the women they encountered. Some they romanced and some they never saw again. Some women that they never expected to see again they found, sometimes to the woman's chagrin. Lt. Walter Finney, of Pennsylvania, was a prisoner of war in New York City for eighteen months, but was one of hundreds of men held in residential homes and permitted to walk about the city during the day. Finney apparently struck up a romance with a woman, Mrs. Lovat, whose husband was also in the Continental Army. He gave her an expensive watch to sell in order to have money to purchase food and clothing. Finney saw neither the watch or the loving Mrs. Lovat again and he became the butt of numerous jokes among his fellow prisoners for losing his timepiece and his paramour at the same time.

Three years later, Finney was stationed at West Point and while on patrol one morning spotted none other than Mrs. Lovat and a man traveling to Newburgh on a highway. He stopped them and demanded either the watch or his money back. She said that the watch was gone; she had sold it to some officer in the American army and had no idea where he was and had spent the money long ago. Finney was furious. He had her arrested, but his superior officer let her go.

Finney, resigned once again to the loss of the watch, went about his business and began the ride back to West Point later in the afternoon. Unable to make much headway before darkness fell, he stopped at a farmhouse for lodging and was startled to find that Mrs. Lovat and her friend were staying there, too. Finney prepared for another argument about the watch, but the woman told him with a nervous smile that by incredible coincidence they drove past an army regiment just after they left him earlier in the day and spotted the soldier to whom she had sold the watch. He had given it back to her companion and, after a search of his bags, the companion produced the watch and handed it to a grateful Finney.[9]

Soldiers who could not travel home to wives or girlfriends, or had none, could always rely on prostitutes for sexual gratification. The ladies of the evening fell into three groups: women who worked out of their own homes; girls who plied their trade at taverns, as either visitors or barmaids; or the women who lived among the camp followers.

It is unclear when the first members of the world's oldest profession began working in the New World, but court records exist describing "lewd women," as they were usually called, being jailed, fined, and booted out of cities as early as the 1730s. By the 1770s, it was easy to find women who sold themselves in the taverns of the large cities such as New York, Philadelphia, and Elizabethtown. Business was brisk in cities during the Revolution. In addition to their usual clientele of merchants, seaman, businessmen, and the community's male residents, the women serviced the many American soldiers far from home. As a bonus, their source of income increased when the occupying British army arrived. Business proved so profitable during the war that prostitutes looking to move into a higher income bracket left their homes in the towns surrounding New York and set up shop along the streets and lanes of Manhattan, now bustling with soldiers.[10]

Prostitutes could be problematic, though. During the brief American occupation of New York City in the spring and summer of 1776, officers on nightly patrols reported rounding them up, usually following bar disputes or street brawls between the women and soldiers who did not pay for their services. It was not unusual for half a dozen or more prostitutes to be tossed into a New York jail each night. One officer who conducted nightly round-ups found them a menace; he referred to them as "bitch-foxy jades, jills, haggs, strums, and prostitutes," but admitted that "their employ is very lucrative."[11]

Worse, angry and drunk ladies of the evening armed with knives that they concealed in their dresses would wound or murder soldiers who did not pay up or who physically abused them. Dead and dismembered bodies of U.S. soldiers were found in a meadow just north of Trinity Church in Manhattan, a favorite clandestine meeting place for soldiers during the war.

There was class distinction, too, involving women attracted to the soldiers whether for love or money, especially in Philadelphia. After the British army left that city in May 1778, following an occupation of nearly eight months, one gossipmonger chattered that many of the well-bred young women in town were walking about quite pregnant from their liaisons with Redcoat officers, explaining that "the British officers played the devil with the girls." The wag then noted that "the privates, I suppose, were satisfied with the common prostitutes."[12]

The women who traveled with the camp followers made most of their income from the enlisted men in the army, but also profited from American officers and those from foreign countries, such as France, whom they hoped would pay them more.

Prostitutes who lived among the camp followers were not very discreet, either. They thought nothing of having sex with clients in an army tent where other men were sleeping, recalled Sergeant Benjamin Gilbert. He noted, "At night Marcy was at our tent and lay all night with Sgt. Phillips and went home at gun firing in the morning."[13] Generals usually overlooked the "working girls," but when their activities proved detrimental to army discipline they were drummed out of the camp in public ceremonies, just like soldiers were dismissed, to discourage similar overt sexual behavior among other women.[14]

Prostitutes descended on the seventeen thousand men in the army outside Boston in the spring of 1775 and caused such commotion, and distracted so many men from camp duty, that General Artemas Ward, the Continental Army's first commander prior to Washington, issued an order that "no lewd women" were to remain in the camp; two prostitutes were subsequently chased out of Charlestown.[15]

George Washington banned the "lewd women" of Philadelphia from descending on his winter camp at Valley Forge in the winter of 1777–1778 after doctors told him many of those piling into the over-crowded hospitals there suffered from venereal disease probably caught from local prostitutes during the previous months.[16] Word of the sexual cavorting in the American camps, whether with "amorous" women or prostitutes, became so pronounced that the wives of British officers, cap-tured following one battle, feared that they would be handed over to the enlisted men for their sexual enjoyment (it never happened).[17]

The wives and girlfriends of the enlisted men who trailed after the army were respectable, but were always segregated from the army when it moved, walking together and not with the soldiers. However, the "lewd women" were not seen as very respectable and caused quite a scene wher-ever they went. Washington was so embarrassed by them that he some-times ordered them to march at the rear of his army and to take side streets when the army paraded through a town so that the residents would not notice them. Once, when the army arrived in Philadelphia, the prostitutes, angry at the prudish commander in chief's wishes, refused to follow orders and paraded in a rather bawdy manner through the main thoroughfares of the city with the troops, skipping, howling, and brazenly lifting their skirts at spectators as they went.

Thomas Paine insisted that one of the major threats to unity among Americans was prostitution. He wrote in number III of *The American Crisis* that "the whole race of prostitutes in New York were Tories" and that like-minded Loyalist hookers in Philadelphia laced the pillow talk they conducted with their patriotic clients there with malicious pro-Crown propaganda.[18]

Lieutenant James McMichael had no need of prostitutes, though, because he had his passionate wife Susanna and visited her whenever he could. McMichael spent the rest of the summer of 1777 on routine work as his regiment camped in New Jersey and saw little action. He was sent on several more missions back to Pennsylvania to hunt for deserters, trips that were unproductive. On one in July, he spent the night at the Spread Eagle Tavern, in Chester County, following an afternoon ride that took him "past the Valley Forge," a remote ironworks twenty miles northwest of Philadelphia. He rode by the small forge and the wide plateau adjacent to it, on the banks of the Schuylkill River, and thought nothing of it.

Chapter Seventeen

SARATOGA, 1777:
The Arduous Journey of Sergeant Ebenezer Wild, Nineteen

The War

*E*ngland's most flamboyant General, "Gentleman Johnny" Burgoyne—fashion plate, gambler, playwright, dancer, raconteur, much-in-demand London dinner guest, and daring military leader—was given command of the large force gathered in Canada in the summer of 1777 and ordered to travel south to New York. He was to sail down Lake Champlain and capture Fort Ticonderoga and any other American garrisons he passed, sink any American ships he found, and then move south to smash the Continental force's northern army, headquartered at Albany. Generals Howe and Clinton would then travel north up the Hudson River to meet him, and with their combined army would split the colonies in two, using part of their force to render New England helpless to the north and another part to chase and destroy George Washington's main army to the south. If all went well, the American Revolution would be over before Christmas.

General Horatio Gates planned on halting the march of Burgoyne's army somewhere along the western banks of the Hudson River, using the farms and hills of the area, plus earthworks his men would build, to form a defensive line. To stop Burgoyne, aided by several thousand Hessians, Gates knew he had to bring in more men. He also had to deal with the obstinate Benedict Arnold, now one of his commanders.

E benezer Wild's journey to Saratoga had been a difficult one. No soldier in his regiment, the First Massachusetts, was happier to pitch his tent in a field that overlooked headquarters at Bemis Heights, a plateau south of the village of Saratoga, than the nineteen-year-old sergeant when he arrived with the rest of the men just after 5 p.m. on July 31, 1777.

Wild had left his home in Braintree, Massachusetts, to rejoin the Continental Army in Boston on April 9 following a furlough. His commander, Colonel Joseph Vose, let his men spend an enjoyable afternoon drinking at the Punch Bowl Tavern, the crowded, raucous, popular Boston bar, before they began marching southwest to meet up with the northern army commanded by General Gates. An overweight, ruddy-faced, former British officer who wore thick glasses, he was called "Granny Gates" by some of his men.

Congress awarded Gates the command in mid-August, replacing General Philip Schuyler after some nasty army infighting and the loss of Ticonderoga. Gates claimed that Schuyler was not capable of commanding a large army. Schuyler, though, said that Gates had engaged in an underhanded scheme to replace him.[1] Gates's scheming would soon result in nearly tragic consequences for the army when he would become connected to a duplicitous plan to supplant Washington as commander in chief. Gates moved swiftly to enlarge the size of his forces and to improve morale upon assuming command. He issued general orders for more and better training, increased cleanliness, and pushed officers to persuade their men to work harder. He told his soldiers that they had to build "confidence in themselves."[2]

It was a long and arduous trip to Saratoga for Wild's company. The men sometimes marched as much as twenty miles in a single day in hot weather and in rainstorms. They rose before seven on most mornings to march and sometimes traveled at night, stumbling along darkened dirt highways before halting to make camp in nearby fields for the evening. They slept wherever they could. Wild and the others found themselves spending the nights in private homes, barns and, if no shelter was available, open meadows. When they reached Litchfield, Connecticut, the state capital, the regiment slept in the rooms and halls of the statehouse.

On April 27, an express rider handed Colonel Vose orders to proceed with as much speed as possible to Bedford, New York; the British army was supposed to be camped near the town. The Redcoats had just raided Danbury, Connecticut, and destroyed a large quantity of supplies. After a forced march, the army discovered, as it often did, that the reported British arrival in Bedford was yet another rumor. It was in Bedford that Wild became seriously ill. He wrote, "I felt so sick that I was obliged to stop and lodged in a barn about three miles to the rear of the party." His condition did not improve the next day and he had great difficulty trying to keep up with the regiment. He remarked, "I traveled as fast as I could, but was obliged to stop every little ways."

He never revealed his ailment in his journal, but Wild fell so sick that he remained in the care of the Tomkins family in the Bedford area for nine weeks as the regiment remained in Westchester County. He rejoined the army on July 24 to find that arrangements had been made to put all of the troops in his company on a sloop so that they could sail up the Hudson and save some time in their journey to Saratoga. The ship was overcrowded—the soldiers filling every room and the cargo hold below the decks—so Wild was told to sleep on the open deck of the vessel, exposed to the night wind on the waters of the Hudson, a blessing in the heat.

Finally, on July 29, the First Massachusetts disembarked and began a long march north up the western shoreline of the Hudson toward Saratoga. Wild was struck by the beauty of the Hudson River Valley, the creeks that flowed into it, the gently rolling hills that ran parallel to the waterway, the thick green forests of trees, deep valleys, ravines, jagged rock formations, and wide ponds.

The majestic beauty of America touched the hearts of all the soldiers. In hundreds of journals and letters, that love of the land is described frequently. The war sometimes carried them into hell, but it also brought the soldiers through the gorgeous bounty of the United States. The vistas they saw, often for the first time in their lives—Lake Champlain, the Blue Ridge Mountains of Virginia, the Hudson River valley, the waterfalls of Maine, the low country of South Carolina—reminded them of the extraordinary country for which they fought.

Some admired the cities as well as the tiny villages through which they passed. Pennsylvanian McMichael remembered both in July of 1776, when he marched off to war following his commission. The troops paraded through Philadelphia—the largest city in the colonies, with thirty-four thousand residents—on the Fourth of July, and McMichael was awed by it. "This city for uniformity and a beautiful situation is equal to any I have ever seen," he wrote. Four days later, his company reached New Brunswick, in the center of New Jersey. He was as impressed by the small river town as he was by the large city in Pennsylvania, calling New Brunswick "a pretty little town situated in a valley on the western bank of the Raritan River."

Many soldiers were so struck with the beauty of the countryside that they asked for and obtained permission from their officers to climb to the tops of nearby mountains so they could have a view of the plain or forest through which they were marching.

Lieutenant Walter Finney guarded prisoners on a march through Orange County, New York, near the Hudson, and was enchanted by the serene ponds he passed along the way. He wrote, "The most remarkable objects were two ponds of water apparently on the highest ground in the settlement . . . [in the first] the water remarkably clear and sweet, the bottom a beautiful white gravel, no stream to supply it with water or any to carry it off . . . [the] second abounds with all sorts of freshwater fish, a small stream makes out of this pond."[3]

Even the weary men on Arnold's ill-fated expedition to Canada found the wilderness they crossed on their way through Maine and the lower section of Canada lovely. Many told friends back home about the roaring whitewater rapids and the deep, jagged rock gorges they traveled through, and they described in great detail the many cascading waterfalls they passed. One soldier remembered walking along the Chaudière River one chilly morning: "The marching this day better than we have had. The river grows wider and runs very quick, and some places very shallow. We passed this day several small islands—the weather this day exceedingly fine, clear and as warm as ever I saw it in New England."[4]

Several of the men on General John Sullivan's campaign against the Indians in 1779 remembered the quiet beauty of the lands where the Indians lived in western New York, recalling them lovingly to their friends when they returned home. "We crossed a large brook near the town, then entered into a most beautiful and extensive plain, which afforded an unbounded prospect; here was almost a perfect level and nothing to obstruct the sight but a few spreading oaks beautifully interspersed and plenty of grass that grew spontaneous on every part and full six feet high," wrote Robert Parker of a meadow near Genesee, New York.[5]

Soldiers often braved bad weather to reach the tops of the mountains to gain a view. In the autumn of 1777, Dan Granger, fifteen, who had replaced his sick older brother in the army camp at Boston, led a group of soldiers to the top of Crow Mountain, a precipice that overlooked the Hudson near West Point.

We set out and accomplished the task. On the way up, oil nuts lay in the crevasses of the rocks in bushels, which had fallen from the trees growing on the declivity of the mountain. We feasted [on the nuts] and then went to the summit. While on the summit, there was a thundercloud of great volume and density that came over us, rushing over with the most tremendous lightening and rain. We had to stay and take it. We could see but a very short distance and were wet as rain could make us. The thunder was tremendous and lightening vivid about us, running along on the ground as attracted by the rocks. The dense cloud passed over and fell below the mountain and spread over the plain, covering it entirely from our view. The sun shining upon it, presented a spectacle truly sublime and terrific, not easily described.[6]

The soldiers saw architectural and mechanical wonders that amazed their young minds: the rapid construction of naval vessels to engage the British navy on Lake Champlain, the mammoth iron gates of Crown Point, the thick iron chain across the Hudson, army wagons turned into sleighs for winter attacks, canoes turned into gunships as blunderbusses were attached to their bows. Several soldiers who traveled through the Hudson River Valley with Wild remarked on an inventive farmer who had constructed a large wooden barn with a retractable roof.[7]

"Gentleman Johnny" and the British at Saratoga

John Burgoyne was given his nickname of "Gentleman Johnny" by his troops, who admired him for treating them humanely in an era when British soldiers were treated badly by their officers and often flogged for minor offenses. The flashy Burgoyne, a graduate of Westminster, one of England's finest schools, had eloped with the daughter of a wealthy lord. Upon his return to England and the army, Burgoyne earned a seat in Parliament and later rose quickly in the military ranks.

During a second term in Parliament, he was offered membership in several of London's most fashionable clubs. There, in addition to witty conversation and political savvy, he became infamous as one of the city's most notorious gamblers. Bored at times, he took up acting and starred in several plays. In 1774, two years after promotion to general, Gentleman Johnny even wrote a play that was staged at the well-known Drury Theater.

He had been frustrated in Boston, where he had spent nine months as second in command to Howe and idled the time away writing plays, including *The Siege of Boston*. The general had returned to England and convinced Lord Germain to let him lead an attack from Canada into New York that would smash the rebels and end the war in a matter of weeks. He took command of Guy Carleton's army of 7,863 regulars plus Indians and Canadian volunteers. He also led three thousand Hessians, under the command of Baron Friederich von Riedesel, who was accompanied by his young, attractive wife, three children, and two servants. The army moved southward on June 21, 1777.

Burgoyne's plan to sail down Lake Champlain, conquer all before him, and seize Albany seemed foolproof. At the same time, part of his army under Colonel Barry St. Leger would travel the Mohawk River valley to Albany. Nothing went according to plan, however. There was no American navy; Arnold never rebuilt the ships that Carleton had battered and sank the previous year. The Americans had evacuated Ticonderoga and left an empty fort.

Burgoyne's march east was impeded by hundreds of trees felled by Americans to slow down his progress. Bridges were destroyed so that the British had to spend precious time rebuilding them. Burgoyne only advanced twenty miles in twenty-two days. Then, when he was within sight of the Hudson River the British commander, in no hurry, halted and waited for his baggage to be delivered, wasting more time.

When he finished dallying, Burgoyne crossed the Hudson and headed for Bennington, in the newly declared state of Vermont, to confiscate supplies and find food for his large army. There, he was turned back by Massachusetts militia led by Colonel John Stark, one of the heroes of Bunker Hill.

Burgoyne was stunned by the fast mobilization of militia and the ferocious patriotism they exhibited. In a letter that showed a far deeper understanding of the Americans' determination to win the war than any other British general exhibited, he wrote to Lord Germain, "The great bulk of the country is undoubtedly with the Congress in principle and in zeal, and their measures are executed with a secrecy and dispatch that are not to be equaled. Wherever the King's forces point, militia to the amount of three or four thousand assemble in twenty-four hours. [They are] the most rebellious race . . ."[8]

Burgoyne was worried about his loss at Bennington, but he knew that he would soon hook up with St. Leger's army of two thousand men, half of them Indians, further south. The British forces of Sir Henry Clinton would also join him. They had remained in New York after Howe took his larger army by boat to capture Philadelphia.

As Burgoyne pulled back from Bennington and headed south toward Albany, Barry St. Leger was stalled in the Mohawk Valley. An Indian chief placed within St. Leger's camp by Arnold engineered a mutiny among the Indians, who left the British. St. Leger then retreated toward Canada, chased for miles by Arnold.

Ebenezer Wild had become a veteran by the time he and the men of the First Massachusetts pitched their tents in Saratoga. He had enlisted as an eighteen-year-old corporal in Colonel Jonathan Brewer's Regiment in 1775 and was probably in the battle of Bunker Hill. He had seen much in his first tour of duty, which ended in December 1776. The company had been inoculated for smallpox in August 1776, when an epidemic of it hit the Boston area, an inoculation that may have saved his life.

Wild's regiment stayed in Boston when Benedict Arnold led the expedition to Canada, but those soldiers were sent to Fort Ticonderoga after that invasion failed. That trip, Wild's first excursion outside of the Boston area, was plagued with problems. One town, upon hearing that the men had been inoculated for smallpox and that one man had just come down with it, refused to let the soldiers spend the night sleeping in the local church for fear that the dreaded illness would spread throughout the community. The troops had to sleep in a field.

The regiment became lost at one point and spent an entire day wandering through a wooded area before stumbling upon the cabin of a man who sent them back in the proper direction. They completed several hazardous crossings of fast-running creeks and rivers in Massachusetts and New York. They had to pile all of their baggage onto rafts and pole their way across a turbulent Connecticut river; the crossing took five exhausting hours. It was impossible to simply ford one creek and the men had to spend an afternoon chopping down trees to lay across it as a bridge and then carefully walk across the round logs. Many of the men could not sleep on some evenings because the howls of wild animals kept them awake. At one point they ran out of provisions and in order to stay alive were forced to eat only green corn that they found in a field. The trip had been filled with rain, and it poured all night on August 31, the day they finally arrived at Ticonderoga, where Wild served as a guard and, already inoculated, was safe from the smallpox that killed so many troops there.

Finally, on December 22, his enlistment up, Wild was furloughed and sent home to Braintree. He arrived on January 2, 1777. The corporal spent nine weeks at home and decided to rejoin the army, in Vose's First Massachusetts regiment. This time he was promoted and made a sergeant and began his journey to Saratoga.

Burgoyne's large army arrived on the heavily wooded eastern bank of the Hudson River on September 13. By now, most of his Indians, unreliable throughout the trip, had departed, leaving him with few natives who knew the area and who could scout the enemy without drawing attention. The Americans had plenty of scouts, however, and they had been watching the British commander for days with their spyglasses. They could not miss him. As usual, the highly visible, flamboyant British general was marching with all of his troops together, his flags unfurled and flying high in the autumn breeze. His bands played British military music loud enough to be heard from some distance.[9] His column of supply wagons, cannon, and nearly eight thousand troops stretched for several miles. He moved slowly, too, because the Americans had wrecked nearly every bridge on his route, forcing him to continually stop to rebuild them.

General Gates, with seven thousand men, had blocked any route down the western side of the Hudson by building a series of earthworks around a camp that extended westward past land owned by a farmer named Freeman. The earthworks formed three sides of a square, with the open side on the south guarded by a deep ravine. Each side was about three-quarters of a mile in length. The area was thickly forested, except for a few large, open meadows within the confines of local farms, such as

Freeman's. With plenty of time, the Americans had also positioned their cannon where Gates believed they would have the most effect. The American camp lay on what was known as Bemis Heights, named after a local tavern keeper, and was two hundred feet above the Hudson, giving the Americans excellent location.[10] The general was prepared for a defensive battle and awaited Burgoyne's arrival.[11] On September 15, two nights after the British crossed, all the American troops were put in readiness. "We had orders to lay upon arms and not pull off any of our clothes," wrote Wild.

Few slept. At 2 a.m., Wild wrote, his regiment was awakened and ordered to construct even more earthworks in the dark. The officers were certain that Burgoyne would attack them that day. The British did not and three more days passed. Burgoyne hesitated because he only had a vague idea of the terrain around him and the strength of the enemy. He did not know Gates's position and had, in fact, practically marched right into the American forces after he crossed the Hudson.

On September 16 and 18, Wild wrote, more earthworks were dug in front of the camp that contained the First Massachusetts, Wild's regiment, under the command of General Ebenezer Learned. Wild's regiment was in the center of the camp and would face the brunt of the fighting. In the middle of the morning, Wild assumed the battle was about to commence. "About ten o'clock we left work and got in preparation to receive the enemy. Soon after we heard a number of guns fired, supposed to be our advanced party. About eleven o'clock we marched from the place of our encampment to the top of an eminence about a half mile from the camp."

But, again, there was no attack and the men remained on alert, apprehensive and with little sleep. They all knew that this would be a major engagement of the revolution and that Burgoyne had a large army with a long line of cannon. From Gates and Arnold down to the enlisted men like Wild, all were certain that if they did not stop the English commander he would continue to march directly south to Albany and capture it. Then he could move to New York.

The First Battle of Saratoga

Wild rose at daylight on the following morning, September 19, to find the entire western bank of the Hudson, Bemis Heights, and the forests around it covered with a thick fog. The soupy fog was so thick men could not see more than a few yards in front of them. The fog did not lift until noon, Wild said, and it was just after that when the battle began. "About one o'clock we were alarmed by the enemy. We marched from our encampment and manned the [earth]works above us. About two o'clock, an engagement ensued between their advanced party and ours which lasted fifteen minutes without cessation. Our people drove them and took some prisoners," he wrote of the heated battle.

Wild's regiment found itself facing Burgoyne himself. The British general had decided to split his army into three columns. General Simon Fraser's was sent far west in an attempt to flank the Americans. Burgoyne led a central assault that stalled at Freeman's farm. Baron von Riedesel was ordered to attack along the river road on the banks of the Hudson.

Fraser's force found itself stumbling about in thick woods and contributed little to the battle at first. The bulk of Burgoyne's column inched its way toward the farm, moving very slowly through tangled forests, following an advance guard. Von Riedesel was ordered to bring nearly a thousand men and cannon from the river to support the British commander. On top of Bemis Heights, Benedict Arnold fumed. Arnold told Gates in heated language that he was going to be attacked by all three British columns if he did not send men out to attack them first. It was now, Arnold believed, that the Americans had the advantage.

Gates, like so many other officers, did not like Benedict Arnold. His hatred for Arnold was based on Arnold's loyalty to Schuyler. Gates and Schuyler had smeared each other in letters to congressional delegates and personal appearances before Congress. It was one of the uglier feuds of the war.[12] Finally, tired of Arnold's haranguing, Gates sent Morgan's riflemen, the best sharpshooters in the army, along with Henry Dearborn's light infantry, with Arnold's wing of the army, to attack Burgoyne at Freeman's. Arnold rode off at a furious gallop to join his men.

Morgan's riflemen, with extraordinary accuracy and even better luck, killed most of the officers in the advance guard at Freeman's in several volleys and steady sharpshooting. The rest of the British fled back into the forest behind Freeman's cabin. The Americans, shouting, chased them, but ran directly into the main British force under Burgoyne, advancing quickly upon hearing the sound of the guns. Morgan's men fled, dispersed, and regrouped on the other side of the meadow, where they were joined by Arnold and other American regiments. Arnold surveyed the situation quickly and took command, barking orders over the sound of gunfire. Burgoyne's forces were joined shortly by Fraser's men, emerging from the thickets.

What followed was one of the most furious battles of the Revolution; a hot, four-hour-long fight with each side attacking and retreating and volley after volley fired across the field in the warm afternoon. The fighting involved volleys fired from just a few dozen yards, bayonet charges, and hand to hand combat. Burgoyne, later joined by Riedesel's troops who saved the day for the English, led the overall British attack. Arnold, frantically giving orders and riding back and forth between companies, led the Americans. Gates had sent several more regiments to assist at the farm and they rapidly responded to Arnold's commands.

By the time the sun went down, the grass in the meadows of Freeman's farm was covered in blood. British casualties were horrific. Overall, the enemy suffered a total of six hundred casualties that afternoon. Of the men battling the Americans back and forth at Freeman's, 44 percent were killed, wounded, or captured. American casualties were far smaller, 319, with 57 killed.[13]

"Both armies seemed determined to conquer or die. [There was] one continual blaze without any intermission 'til dark," wrote Massachusetts general John Glover at the scene. "The enemy . . . were bold, intrepid, and fought like heroes, and I do assure you, sirs, our men were equally bold and courageous and fought like men fighting for their all."[14] The Redcoats on the other side of that meadow agreed. "The heavy artillery, joining in concert like great peals of thunder, assisted by the echoes of the woods, almost deafened us with the noise," wrote a British soldier.

"This crash of cannon and musketry never ceased 'til darkness parted us."[15]

Burgoyne then received a message from Sir Henry Clinton, telling him that he would try to reinforce him with about two thousand men in ten days. He trusted Clinton because the general had tried to convince Howe to send his entire army to meet Burgoyne in upstate New York instead of attacking Philadelphia.[16] Gentleman Johnny then decided to dig in behind Freeman's cabin and wait for Clinton's army. It was a mistake. The delay not only gave Gates's army time to rest and regroup, it gave militia commanders throughout New England needed days to raise thousands of men. That was easy because everyone seemed to believe that the defeat of the Redcoats could mean the end of the war. They also wanted to protect their homes against the British.

Dan Granger, a teenager who had finished one enlistment, joined up with dozens of other men and boys when a recruiter staged a rally with bands, singing, and patriotic speakers in his village. The speakers told the people that the British were cornered across the river and could be beaten if enough men joined the fight. Nearly all the able-bodied men in the village marched toward Saratoga, most without even going home to say goodbye to their families.[17]

In addition to the immediate crisis at hand, all of the residents of the Hudson Valley had learned through newspapers that weeks before several of Burgoyne's Indians had murdered a white woman, Jane McCrea.[18] They wanted revenge. By the time ten days had elapsed, Gates's force of seven thousand at Saratoga had swelled to over eleven thousand armed and angry colonists.

The tension between Gates and Arnold had simmered throughout the day on September 19 and reached the boiling point in late afternoon, when Arnold's leadership of the left flank resulted in halting the British advance. Arnold's tough, bold leadership had once more won the admiration of his men. Gates waited three days and then reassigned Morgan's riflemen, the heroes of the battle and among the most reliable troops in the army, away from Arnold's command without even telling him. He had also sent a report to General Washington and Congress about the

September 19 battle and took all the credit for pushing the British army back; he never mentioned Arnold's bravery and never even wrote that he had joined in the fighting. The deliberate insults had the result that Gates knew they would—Arnold stormed into his headquarters, limping as always, and demanded his men back plus a formal apology.

What followed in the large marquee tent that Gates used as his field headquarters at Saratoga was one of the most heated arguments between two generals during the war. Gates not only refused to give Arnold back his men, but told him that his services during the September 19 battle had been inconsequential and that he had, in fact, added nothing to the overall campaign. Gates's aide, James Wilkinson, who was an eyewitness to the argument, wrote that Arnold "was ridiculed by General Gates; high words and gross language ensued."

Gates was relentless in his condemnation of his second in command. He brusquely told him that he had been discussing Arnold's demotion with members of Congress and that he had warned delegates that Arnold should never have been promoted to a major general. He had failed in his invasion of Canada, lost the battle of Quebec, led a chaotic retreat southward into New York in which hundreds of men died, and had a naval fleet under his command destroyed on the waters of Lake Champlain. Looking straight at him, Gates then told Arnold that not only would he continue at Saratoga without a command, but he would be replaced by General Lincoln as soon as he arrived. He did not want Arnold in the army at all, he finished, and suggested he resign and simply go home to Connecticut. Gates said that he would write him a pass on the spot. Enraged by the scathing denunciation, Arnold told Gates he would leave all right, but he would ride to Pennsylvania and report the entire matter to George Washington. Gates sneered and told him to go right ahead and offered to write him a pass to Pennsylvania to see the commander in chief, too.

Benedict Arnold turned and hurried from Gates's tent. Later, he sent Gates a blistering note that Gates ignored. Arnold sent another note that Gates returned with the type of common traveling pass he would issue to any private going home on furlough so that Arnold could leave the army.

The hatred between them was so great, one officer wrote, that he was certain that while Burgoyne sat in his camp pondering defeat the two leading American generals at Saratoga would kill each other in a duel.[19]

The British officers and men knew nothing about the dispute between Arnold and Gates. They had their own troubles. There was nothing but anxiety behind the British lines as the American forces grew each day. The Redcoats were running out of supplies. One messenger informed Burgoyne of Barry St. Leger's retreat back to Canada and another explained that none of the couriers he sent riding off to Henry Clinton, each carrying a plea more desperate than the last for more troops, reached the one man who could save them; all were arrested.

Those days were filled with worry for Wild and the troops waiting for something to happen. "Very dark and foggy this morning," wrote Wild in his diary the day after the September 19 engagement, fearful that the British would attack, aided by the poor visibility. They did not.

The next few days were nerve-racking as Wild and the men in his regiment awaited a British assault. They were constantly moved from one position to another. "Marched off to the earthworks on our right wing," he wrote on the morning of September 20. That night he scribbled, sarcastically, "At sundown the regiment returned and pitched our tents on the same ground they were on before."

Wild's regiment was moved about camp constantly, occupying a hill to their right one day and a wooded area to the left the next. Alarms were sounded after pickets with spyglasses spotted any minor British movement. On September 22, Wild wrote, attack alarms were sounded at 8 a.m. and at 11 a.m. On September 28 there were alarms at 10 a.m., 2 p.m., and 8 p.m.

Wild almost lost his life on September 25. He was ordered to join a scouting party shortly before dawn to check on the latest British troop positions. "We marched within a quarter of a mile of [enemy]. The fog and darkness of the morning prevented our going any further 'til after daylight, when we rushed on the guard and a very hot fire ensued for the space of two or three minutes. The guard ran into their lines as fast as they could. We killed and wounded eight of them and took one prisoner and returned to our camp again about sunrise." He noted that four men in his party were lost in the engagement.

The success of the operation encouraged a commanding officer to send out another scouting party, again including Wild, on a three-day journey around the British encampment to ascertain its strength and its access to forage in the area. On October 1, after a lengthy trip through forests around Saratoga Lake, the men came upon a mill that had fallen into the hands of the British. It was previously owned by General Philip Schuyler.

"We marched upon a rising ground above the mill and ground our arms and a party of us, with axes, went cutting away Schuyler's bridge. After we had destroyed it with axes as much as time would admit of, we set fire to it. We stopped till it got well a-fire and then marched off in a different road."

The next day, again, Wild feared for his life. Under orders to burn buildings that contained grain or other supplies that could help the British, his superior officer ordered an attack on a second mill that was surrounded by several buildings. British soldiers guarded it. To Wild's relief, they surrendered without firing a shot. The buildings, full of grain, were torched and Wild and his comrades marched back to Gates's camp with ten prisoners, three of them officers, twelve horses, and eighteen cattle.

On October 6, Gates was certain Burgoyne would attack. The First Massachusetts, five hundred men including Wild, was sent out as an advance guard. Nothing happened.

The Second Battle of Saratoga

The much-feared attack finally came on October 7, two weeks after the first battle. Burgoyne decided that he might be able to flank the American left wing and move south. The British struck, but despite all of their preparation the First Massachusetts did not engage in the furious fighting.

Benedict Arnold did. The general, still seething from being relieved of his command earlier, had decided to remain in camp. He was with Gates and others at 3 p.m. on the afternoon of October 7 when they heard the sudden sound of cannon. A messenger burst into the tent to announce that the British were attacking.

Arnold leaped up from his chair. "Shall I go out and see what is the matter?" he asked Gates, who told him to go. Benedict Arnold leaped on to a nearby horse and galloped toward the fighting. A man who saw him ride through the woods said that he looked like a "madman." Gates had a change of heart just a few moments after Arnold left his tent. Arnold had been relieved of command and should not be given any now. Gates shouted at an officer to mount a horse, chase down Arnold, and bring him back before he reached the fighting. The aide did so, but never caught up to the galloping Arnold, hell-bent to defeat the British.

Arnold reached the battle between the American left flank and Burgoyne's army a few moments later and started to rally the troops, shouting as loudly as he could over the din of the battle. He told Morgan to ask a sharpshooter to fire at General Fraser, leading his men in the battle while astride a large, gray horse. The man braced himself, aimed carefully, and killed Fraser. Fraser's fall from his horse sent his men into confusion.

The animated Arnold then led a charge on horseback toward a well-fortified redoubt that had just been constructed behind the left flank of the British lines, exhorting his men to follow him as fast as they could. As he approached, he could hear the pounding of his horse's hooves. He shouted for it to gallop faster. Men ran behind him, firing at the enemy. Arnold encountered a thunderstorm of musket fire from the Hessians in and around the redoubt. They sensed they were about to be overrun and rallied for one last defense. General Arnold continued to yell commands and look over his shoulder at the men following him. Suddenly, he was shot in the leg, the same leg that had been hit in the attack on Quebec. His horse had also been shot and fell on top of Arnold's wounded limb, breaking it. The firing around him intensified.

Gates may have hated him but the men and many officers in the fight loved Benedict Arnold. "A bloody fellow he was," wrote private Samuel Downing of New Hampshire. "He didn't care for nothing. He'd ride right in. It was 'come on, boys,' not 'go, boys.' . . . There wasn't any wasted timber in him." An officer, Captain E. Wakefield, agreed. He wrote, "Nothing could exceed the bravery of Arnold on this day; he seemed the very genius of war . . . he seemed inspired with the fury of a demon."[20]

His men, inspired perhaps by Arnold's wounding, took the redoubt a few minutes later, killing or routing the Hessians inside it. As darkness fell, the entire American line advanced quickly, forcing the English and German soldiers to flee. The Americans suffered remarkably few losses.

Burgoyne had failed again, once more defeated by men led by the energetic Benedict Arnold. He did not see any other way to advance as evening began and ordered a general retreat, hoping that Clinton had somehow received his messages. The entire army pulled back. It would march north and then halt. This procedure was followed for a few days. As they retreated, the British also burned down the home of General Schuyler. Burgoyne possessed no intelligence concerning American outposts around his new position. He waited and did nothing. "The greatest misery and utmost disorder prevailed in the army," wrote the Baroness von Riedesel of those days after October 7. She added that her husband wanted a hasty and immediate retreat northward to save the army, but that Burgoyne seemed immobilized. The British "lost everything by his loitering," she added.[21]

As it turned out, Sir Henry Clinton *did* send the troops that Burgoyne had begged him to transport north. He ordered three thousand soldiers to sail up the Hudson to meet Burgoyne at Saratoga, but the voyage went slowly. They received no messages from Burgoyne and dawdled. The ships stopped to bombard and burn Kingston, New York, an easy target. Then the captain in charge of the fleet decided that he did not want to sail any farther north without explicit orders and headed back to New York, leaving Burgoyne without reinforcements.

The one hundred plus wounded American soldiers were transported south to an army hospital in Albany. Their gruesome wounds stunned veteran doctors there. One surgeon wrote of "mutilated bodies, mangled limbs, incurable wounds." One man, he noted, was shot through the face with a musket ball that knocked out some of his teeth and tore off half of his tongue. Another had his face and half his throat blown open by a cannonball. A third was shot in the head with a musket ball and lay on the bed, bleeding profusely. He told the doctor the ball had apparently fallen out of his head and asked him to fix the wound. The doctor examined him and found that the ball was still in his skull, prevented from killing him by a thick bone in which it had lodged. The doctor sat back, told the man what had happened, and joked that it was a good thing that American foot soldiers had skulls too thick for shots to penetrate.[22]

Gates had been busy during the time between the first battle on September 19 and the second on October 7. Using information gleaned from reports from scouting parties such as Wild's, he had moved militia, one unit with eleven hundred men, into positions north of Burgoyne to prevent him from escaping. With the main American army to the south, militia to the north, thick forests to the west, and the Hudson on the east—and supplies dwindling—the British had nowhere to go.

That must have been apparent to Burgoyne on the day after the second battle, October 8, when his camp came under assault from various cannon batteries that surrounded it. The house that General von Riedesel occupied alone was hit with eleven cannonballs.

One of the regiments continually harassing the Redcoats was Wild's. On the morning after the battle, the First Massachusetts was ordered to scout the enemy as well as they could. They marched toward their camp only to find that the Redcoats had moved further north, leaving some cannon and infantry behind to protect them. The First Massachusetts met them head on. Wild wrote, "The enemy had retreated to some works they had in their rear, where they fired from and did us some damage. As we were marching through their [former] lines they fired a number of cannon at us."

The First Massachusetts's commander, Colonel Joseph Vose, ordered the men to disperse as the cannon in front of them erupted, and managed to escape death when his horse was shot out from under him as a cannonball exploded underneath him. The men fled through the woods, regrouped, and moved to Lake Saratoga to form part of a western barrier to prevent a British escape.

Again, on October 10, the First Massachusetts chased the British as they tried to move northward. "We marched within a half mile of the enemy and camped in the woods," wrote Wild. "There was a considerable firing on both sides." On the following day, the First Massachusetts and other regiments tightened the noose around Burgoyne. Now Wild's regiment had advanced to Schuyler's Creek where they engaged in yet another firefight, this time capturing an officer and thirty-six men. On October 12, Wild wrote that there was "considerable smart cannonading the biggest part of the day on both sides, and we fortified against the enemy considerable on the hills all around us." Then again, on the thirteenth, there were more fights. "There was considerable firing on both sides all day. We continue still here in the woods," Wild wrote.

Burgoyne had nowhere to turn and the next day agreed to surrender, accepted a cease-fire, and spent several days negotiating terms. On October 17, Gates ordered all of his men to line the route that the British would take to walk into the American camp to lay down their arms. The morning was dark and foggy, but by noon the sun had risen and bathed the Saratoga area with warmth for a historic event; the total surrender of an entire British army.

"We marched round the meeting house and came to a halt," wrote Wild. By sheer fortune, their spot on the route gave them a front-row seat to the drama. It also offered them an unobstructed view of the size of the British army, with its six thousand men, cannon, camp followers, bands, and wagons. The parade into camp that Wild and his comrades assumed would take an hour or so dragged on all afternoon as company after company of rather grim looking Redcoats walked past their American conquerors.

Wild added, "General Burgoyne and his chief officers rode by us there, and then we marched further down the road and grounded our arms and rested there. At half after three o'clock, General Burgoyne's army began to pass us, and they continued passing 'til sunset."

Private Dan Granger, one of the militia volunteers who had hurried toward the battle, also had a good view of the historic moment. He and his company did not reach Saratoga in time for the final struggle, and on the day of the surrender they were on the other side of the Hudson, near the pontoon bridge that crossed it. They saw the American courier race away from the English camp with the surrender and watched over the river as the American celebration began. Disregarding orders to remain on the west bank of the river, the men in the company ran across the bridge.

"Soon we saw them coming," Granger wrote. "General Gates's troops were arranged on both sides of the road, drums and fifes playing 'Yankee Doodle,' cannon roaring in all quarters and the whole world seemed to be in motion. Officers lost command over the soldiers. I got as near to General Gates's marquee tent as I could for the crowd and saw General Burgoyne and his suite ride up, and dismount and go into General Gates's marquee and soon the van of the prisoners made their appearances. The Hessian troops came first with their baggage on horses that were mere skeletons, not able apparently to bear the weight of their own carcasses. These troops had some women, who wore short petticoats, bare-footed and bare-legged, with huge packs on their backs, some carrying a child and leading another or two. They were silent, civil, and looked quite subdued. The English troops followed and were cross and impudent enough."

Granger felt an enormous sense of satisfaction in the scene. He wrote, "Having seen a large and well-equipped British army of about eight thousand surrender as prisoners of war and leaving on the field the finest and largest park of artillery that ever was seen in America, with all their carts, timbrels, and vehicles for the conveyance of their ammunition, was a great and pleasing novelty indeed."

The British troops could not believe what had happened to them. Perhaps nothing explained their demoralized feelings better than British Lieutenant William Digby's droll recollection of his army's bands, which played one of the Empire's most famous military songs, "The Grenadiers' March," as the troops surrendered. "We marched out with drums beating . . . but the drums seemed to have lost their inspiring sound."[23]

News of the surrender caused jubilant celebrations throughout America. In Boston, Harvard College and dozens of homes were illuminated and thousands gathered around a huge bonfire to cheer the army. Soldiers throughout the army, from Washington's division in Philadelphia to the militia at Bennington to Gates's remaining men at Albany, rejoiced, too, in the astounding turn of events symbolized by the capture of Burgoyne's army in what British historian Sir Edward Creasy, writing nearly one hundred years later, called one of the fifteen most decisive battles in the history of the world.[24]

It was put best by Dr. James Thacher, who treated the wounded from Saratoga at the army's two-story hospital in Albany. "We witness the incalculable reverse of fortune, and the extraordinary vicissitudes of military events, as ordained by Divine Providence . . . the [news] of these events to the British government must affect them like the shock of a thunderbolt, and demonstrate to them the invincibility of a people united in the noble cause of liberty and the rights of man."[25]

The victory at Saratoga had international and historic implications. It made a hero out of Gates, a moderately skilled commander who would soon be talked about as a replacement for George Washington. It stirred up false hopes in most Americans that the war would soon end. Most importantly, though, the victory convinced the French government that the Americans might be able, in time, to defeat the British. The French decided right after Saratoga to conclude treaties with the Americans, recognizing American independence, which led them to come into the war on the American side.

For Private Ebenezer Wild and the men of the First Massachusetts, though, the day after the Saratoga surrender was just another day in the army. There was a false rumor that Sir Henry Clinton was going to attack Albany and Wild's regiment was sent on a grueling one-day, forty-mile march toward that city. As usual, the officers read maps the wrong way and the company became lost, wandering through the woods for an entire day. When they made it to Albany they were told the clothes they expected were not there and the men were given hand-me-down shirts from the Pennsylvania troops. The wagons with their supplies arrived hours late. On the following day it rained heavily and Wild could not sleep because small rivers of water ran through his tent, soaking his clothes.

And on the day after that the men received orders to move out. General Washington had commanded them to spend the winter with his army on a large plateau twenty-three miles from Philadelphia near a small ironworks called Valley Forge.

VALLEY FORGE

Chapter Eighteen

THE HARSH ROAD
TO A WINTER CAMP
The War

*I*n the summer of 1777, General William Howe decided to capture
Philadelphia—the new American capital city, home of the Continental
Congress, and a major port. He was certain that the occupation of that city
would be a major military victory that might just cripple the rebels' willing-
ness to continue the war. Howe took a force of fifteen thousand men down the
Atlantic seaboard on two hundred sixty ships, sailed into the Chesapeake Bay,
landed near what is now Elkton, Maryland, and marched north toward
Philadelphia. There he engaged Washington's main army at Brandywine and
Germantown, near the city.

After those battles, George Washington's force of nearly fourteen thousand soldiers, with their supply wagons and train of cannon, sought a camp
for the coming winter while Horatio Gates's northern army remained in
Albany. Pennsylvania officials insisted that Washington's army establish winter quarters near the Valley Forge, northwest of Philadelphia on the banks

of the Schuylkill River. They wanted the army there to protect southeastern Pennsylvania from any British attack. Several generals recommended Wilmington, Delaware, towns in Pennsylvania, and communities in New Jersey. Washington, under intense political pressure from the politicians, chose Valley Forge.

There was no housing at Valley Forge and the soldiers were faced with the challenge of building a large city on meadows that could, when completed, house all fourteen thousand men, two thousand horses, several slaughterhouses, cattle pens, granaries, offices, parade grounds, privies, stables, wagon barns, blacksmith shops, and several hospitals. To house his men, Washington ordered the construction of log huts, sixteen by fourteen feet in size. Twelve enlisted men would live in each. Every hut had bunk beds for sleeping and a small fireplace in the rear. More spacious huts were built for officers. The cabins were built along neatly planned dirt lanes with soldiers from each state grouped together in their own neighborhoods. The encampment was so large that, in population, it was the fourth largest city in the United States.

The hut city was plagued with problems from the day the army arrived. The misery that the troops encountered there would test their endurance and courage like no other time in the Revolution and, perhaps, no other time in American history.

Sergeant Ebenezer Wild's journey to Valley Forge was ominous. The trip from Morristown, New Jersey, was filled with all of the myriad problems that had plagued the army from the first days of the war. That included a court-martial, mixed up orders, poor intelligence, overly long marches, mismanagement, snowstorms, rain deluges, cold weather, and a lack of both food and supplies. If any soldier's route served as a truly representative preamble for the tangled troubles that would nearly overwhelm the army at Valley Forge, it was Wild's.

The march of Wild's regiment, the First Massachusetts, began in Albany on October 30, just three weeks after the battle of Saratoga. The trek would cover a total of more than two hundred fifty miles and take the soldiers through mountain ranges in northern New Jersey, flat sandy terrain in the central and southern part of the state, and then through the rolling hills of eastern Pennsylvania. The First Massachusetts traveled to Morristown, camped there for several weeks, and then moved south on Friday, November 21, on a narrow dirt highway to Basking Ridge, a tiny village in the foothills of the Watchung Mountains. There, in a brief note that would symbolize much that lay ahead that winter, Wild scribbled in his journal, "Unsettled weather."

Two days later, on November 23, the army camped just outside of Princeton, where it had achieved a stunning victory ten months earlier. Again, in a line that would foreshadow the treacherous months ahead, Wild wrote that the field where they set up their tents was "very full of briers." The prickly brier bushes that dotted the fields and woods around Basking Ridge would be the least of the troubles that the men from Massachusetts would encounter that winter.

The brigade did not move out the next day because a court-martial had to be held so that the regiment's colonel could dispense discipline. The men formed in a large circle to serve as an audience for the judicial proceeding in which two privates and two sergeants were tried for leaving the company without permission. The court-martial board found all four guilty. The privates were to be whipped, one sergeant demoted, and the other admonished in front of the entire company. But the colonel, in a burst of holiday leniency, forgave the privates after they repented and did not have them whipped.

The court-martial proceeding kept the company in the village all morning and they did not leave in time to reach Mount Holly that day. They arrived the next and finally slept in a thick woods outside of the town.

In order to surprise the enemy, the troops were awakened at 3 a.m. The First Massachusetts, with the rest of the army, trudged ten miles in the dark to Moorestown, loaded their muskets, set up pickets, and waited for reinforcements before attacking the British there. But the intelligence the rebels received was wrong. The British had left the area long ago and were already back in Philadelphia.

Wild and his regiment remained in a wooded area outside of Moorestown all of that day, Wednesday. On what the sergeant wrote was

a "very cold and raw" Thursday morning, the men departed for a
Delaware River crossing into Pennsylvania. The bone-chilling weather of
Thursday vanished overnight and Friday morning brought very warm
weather and sunshine, a crazy meteorological mix that would plague the
army all winter. At 9 p.m., the men crossed the river on ferries and
camped at a juncture between two roads that someone with a sense of
humor had dubbed Crooked Billet. The next day the pleasant weather
disappeared and a bad storm hit the area; it was so severe that the men
stayed in their tents the entire following day, trying their best to stay dry
as sheets of rain fell on the region. During the next few days, the temperatures rose and fell and the winds increased and decreased as the men
went about routine camp chores in the uncertain climate.

Twenty-four hours later, on December 5, Wild noted that the company's supplies were vanishing. "We drew some fresh beef and flour," he
noted, "but had nothing to cook in. Was obliged to broil our meat on the
fire and bake our bread in the ashes."

The missing supplies alarmed Wild, but he dismissed his worry the
next day when someone found an iron kettle for cooking. They were
lucky. Throughout Pennsylvania that week and the following week, soldiers complained that their supplies had not been replenished, blankets
and coats had not arrived on schedule, and the usual shipments of food,
much as they complained about its quality, were nowhere to be found.
None of the officers knew why winter coats and other clothing on order
for months had not been delivered and no one knew where to find very
needed shoes. On December 10, Wild and a sergeant, needing coats as
badly as everyone else, walked throughout the camp looking for clothing
but did not find any.

Their situation worsened on December 12, when they crossed the
Schuylkill River and camped in a wooded area as thick flakes of snow began
to fall—hard. The men were told to either pitch their tents or cut down
trees and construct lean-tos for cover as the storm worsened. Crews were
told to cut down trees for firewood. But they could not do so. "We had no
tents nor axes to cut wood to make fires. It was a very bad snowstorm," said
Wild, one of many to notice that the tools they required were also missing.

Some men did manage to build lean-tos and start fires during the week they camped there, but a wind caused flames from a campfire to burn down two of the lean-tos and the men who had planned to sleep in the destroyed structures had to sleep on the ground in the snow with no protection at all. The snowstorm, and days of steady rain that followed, kept the men in their camp in the middle of the forest, unable to travel to wherever the army would spend winter.

They celebrated Thanksgiving on December 18, as ordained by Congress, following another snowfall. It was a disappointing holiday and a harbinger of the winter that was to come. "We had but a poor Thanksgiving," wrote Wild. "Nothing but fresh beef and flour to eat without any salt and but very scant of [beef]."

On December 19, a "clear, cold, and windy" day, the First Massachusetts, along with most of the Continental Army, marched to Valley Forge. Wild and the men in his regiment, and all the other soldiers who were healthy, and there were not many, began what appeared to be the simple construction of the hut city late on the afternoon of December 23, two days before Christmas. They continued the work the following morning.

In early afternoon of December 24, Christmas Eve, all work on the huts for the Massachusetts men, and for thousands of others, was halted.

In a journal note, Wild wrote of the construction shutdown, "There was some misunderstanding." It was a line that would come to represent all of the travails of the Continental Army during that historic and disastrous winter at Valley Forge.

Chapter Nineteen

PRIVATE ELIJAH FISHER AND THE AGONY OF VALLEY FORGE

The American Revolution had been a hard war for Elijah Fisher. The private from Attleboro, Massachusetts, enlisted in the Continental Army for eight months along with his five brothers. At seventeen, the tall, thin Elijah was the youngest. He had joined the army right after the battles of Lexington and Concord, full of love of his country and anger at the British. He soon found himself directly in the line of fire when his regiment was ordered to defend Bunker and Breed's Hills on June 17, 1775.

Thirteen months later, in late July, 1776, after he reenlisted for a year, he came down with a severe case of the putrid fever, which nearly killed him as the army moved from Boston to New York to defend the city. The fever kept the private in bed in a home turned into an army hospital. The medical care provided him, and all the men in hospitals, was minimal, but he survived the fever. Fisher did not feel much better five weeks later when he was released from the hospital, but insisted on rejoining his regiment and did so, despite a sharp pain in his side that remained with him for a long time. Fisher missed the British rout of the Continental Army at Long Island while he was in the hospital, and missed another catastrophe when he arrived back with the army. His regiment did not travel with Washington to White Plains, but was ordered to hold Fort Washington on the northern tip of Manhattan. Fisher's pain in his side became unbearable, however, and a doctor ordered him to another hospital at Kingsbridge, fifteen miles north of the city. He was moved to another hospital in Newark, New Jersey, shortly after his arrival in Kingsbridge and missed the crushing defeat at Fort Washington, in which nearly three thousand Americans were taken prisoner.

Fisher was moved to a private home in Newark after a period of several weeks as the hospital filled up with wounded and sick soldiers. The man he moved in with took him to the residence of a local doctor. The physician was not home but his wife tended to Fisher's medical needs. She asked Fisher what was wrong with him. After a short explanation of the fever and the pains in his side, the doctor's wife told Fisher that she knew from experience that he exhibited all the symptoms of kidney troubles. She nodded knowingly and informed him that she knew how to treat him. She mixed a handful of horseradish roots with a tear dish full of mustard seeds in a quart of gin and told him to drink a glass of the concoction every morning. The mix, a standard potion for kidney ailments in the era, worked. The pain in his side that had caused him so much agony for weeks subsided and Fisher was back with the army nine days later.

There was grim news for him upon his return, however. He visited one of his brothers and learned that another brother, Enoch, had died ten days before. The stress of the news may have aggravated Fisher's kidney and the throbbing pain in his side returned. Horseradish roots and mustard seeds did him no good this time and the pain worsened within days. Despondent over his brother's death and his own poor health, the private asked for and obtained a discharge and went home to Massachusetts. Friends and relatives in Attleboro assumed that the war was over for the spunky teenager.

At home, he was treated by a local physician for several months and was the beneficiary of his mother's care. Neither did much immediate good and Fisher suffered for six more months, spending much time in bed. No one expected him to return to the military. It was during this time, with little to do but think, that Fisher made up his mind to go back into the service. He reenlisted for a full three-year term in January, with the understanding that he could remain at home until his health improved. The army was very happy to oblige him. Recruiters were desperate for men after the waves of desertions and massive expiration of enlistments following the New York defeats. The teenager rejoined the army on August 21. His regiment was not with Washington's army; he had been sent to join the forces under the command of General Horatio Gates at Saratoga. This time Fisher was in the thick of the battle against Burgoyne's army there and, with the others, rejoiced at the stunning victory over the British.

Fisher's regiment was then ordered to join Washington's army at Whitemarsh, Pennsylvania, near Philadelphia, as it prepared to march to Valley Forge for winter camp. It took just four days at Whitemarsh for Fisher, and everyone else in the fourteen-thousand-man army, to realize that they were in for a rough winter. He wrote, "We had no tents nor anything to cook our provisions in and that was pretty poor. Beef was very lean and no salt or any way to cook it but to throw it on the coals and broil it. The water we had to drink and to mix our flour with was out of a brook that run along by the camp and so many a-dipping and washing in it made it very dirty and muddy."

The march to Valley Forge began a week later, December 16, following a snowstorm. The fatigue of the march, the lack of nourishment and shelter, plus stress, brought back the crippling pain in Fisher's side. The pain, he wrote, made daily life "tough to bear."

—◦⟳◯⟲◦—

The creation of the sprawling hut city at Valley Forge was hampered by supply problems from the start. Officers had hoped to obtain the thousands of needed boards for the roofs and doors of the metropolis of huts from area sawmills, but most were inoperable due to frozen streams. The few axes that could be found had to do.

Wrote Major Richard Platt, "If it were not for the scarcity of axes and other necessary tools, most of the troops would have been comfortably covered by this time. But our misfortune in those aspects together with some bad weather and scarcity of wood has prevented the business from being completed."[1]

Men lived in tents and were exposed to several early snowstorms, rain and chilly temperatures for weeks as the erection of the large encampment suffered delay after delay. In an effort to move their men into huts, officers in charge of construction cut corners and many huts were built with openings between logs and roof boards. This negligence resulted in rain seeping into the huts and forming puddles on the uneven dirt floors. As a result, the stagnant water began to breed disease. There were no windows for ventilation.

Soldiers drank dirty water from streams near Valley Forge. They urinated wherever they desired in camp because the digging of the privies in the frozen ground was as slow as the completion of the cabins. Garbage was left outside buildings and rotted; vermin appeared quickly, carrying disease. Horses that died were left where they collapsed; their carcasses brought on more sickness.

The army's supply problems mushroomed at Valley Forge. Washington knew as early as September that he was in the first stages of a clothing crisis that would cripple his "ragged men and half naked soldiers."[2] He knew, too, that he probably did not have as much food as he needed and was warned by commissary official Thomas Jones of "a calamity which I expect here every moment." No one in the army had been paid in over two months. The "thousands" of new and needed soldiers Pennsylvania politicians had promised were nowhere to be found. The commander in chief also had hundreds of wounded and sick men arriving in carts and wagons and nowhere to put them. The army would not be able to live off the land, as the Pennsylvanians had guaranteed, because the farmers in Chester County had little food left in what one of Washington's generals referred to as a "starved country."[3]

No one in the army seemed happy to be at Valley Forge that winter. A Massachusetts army surgeon, Dr. Albigence Waldo, may have put it best, and with a medical double-meaning, when he scribbled in his diary about his arrival there, "A pox on my bad luck."[4]

Ironically, it was not the inclement weather that would be a major obstacle to the survival of the army. The winter, in fact, was relatively mild despite six snowstorms, and many soldiers even referred to the weather on most days as "pleasant."[5] The real dangers were the lack of food and clothing, plus primitive medical care for men crammed into every usable building that the army could find and turn into temporary hospitals.

Elijah Fisher's commanding officer had many sick men under his care in addition to Elijah. Packed tightly against each other in a wagon, they were sent to one of the temporary hospitals at Reading, a town northwest of Valley Forge. The hospital there was full, however. Fisher, his kidney pain growing worse daily, was then dispatched in another crowded wagon down uneven dirt roadways to a second hospital in the tiny village of Ephrata. That hospital was also full. A doctor explained to the men that just about all of the hospitals were overflowing with sick soldiers and they had nowhere to put all of the ill troops who arrived daily. Fisher and another man were told to fend for themselves for care and shelter; there was nothing the army could do for them.

The pair walked several miles through the isolated farmlands until they found a local farmer, a Mr. Miller, who agreed to let them recover in one of the bedrooms in his small home. Fisher had developed a bad cold from the snowstorms and suffered from a lack of food and the long journey by wagon. He contracted the putrid fever again on January 20, 1778, while at Miller's home. It was, he noted, "a severe fit of sickness" and he had to be carried out of the farmhouse, placed in the back of a wooden horse-drawn cart and driven to a hospital. Now, barely able to move from his high fever, his health grave, he was carried from the cart and put in a bed in one of the overcrowded medical facilities.

Fisher was placed in a large open ward with dozens of other men with the putrid fever, dysentery, and other ailments and became even sicker. Men in the ward began to die shortly after Fisher arrived, their bodies carried out to be replaced by other sick men in their beds within minutes—without the sheets being changed and the stench of death fouling the air. Elijah Fisher, fighting for his life, found himself in the center of an unfolding medical tragedy.

The army had many sick and wounded men from the battles of Brandywine and Germantown, and men with diseases such as typhus and dysentery. Army hospital department officials asked ministers in the small villages that surrounded the camp to give them permission to turn their churches into hospitals for the winter. The army simply commandeered those belonging to ministers who objected. Army doctors soon set up hospitals in other buildings too, including linen mills, general stores, courthouses, pottery shops, farmhouses, barns, stables, and a few popular taverns. Even the single men's residence hall run by the Moravian religion at Bethlehem, Brethren House, was turned into a hospital. When those havens reached capacity, carpenters speedily erected Washington Hall, a three-story-high wooden structure with nine foot wide porches that housed thirteen hundred patients, becoming at once one of the largest medical centers in the nation.

The weather, although never overly harsh, was wildly erratic, with temperatures soaring from below freezing to over fifty degrees within twenty-four hours while balmy afternoons were followed by evening snowstorms. The unpredictable weather brought on bad colds that soon turned into bronchitis and other ailments. Hundreds of men came down with "scabies," a medical problem brought on by lice and unsanitary living conditions that causes scabs over much of the body and constant itching. Others had dysentery, influenza, rheumatism, and pleurisy. Many contracted pneumonia from living in their flimsily constructed huts.

The medical facilities soon became hopelessly overcrowded. As an example, there were more than nine hundred soldiers in the three wards of the hospital in Reading that were supposed to hold three hundred sixty patients. Washington then ordered construction of sixteen-by-twenty-five-feet on-site transitional hospitals where soldiers stayed until they could be moved to the larger facilities. In addition to the eleven transitional facilities, the army erected a dozen or more huts just for victims of scabies.

None of the soldiers at the facilities received much medical care because, in a paperwork mix-up, generals had granted furloughs to twelve of the sixty doctors on staff. Another dozen or so doctors became ill themselves. Several, fed up with the lack of care, quit and went home. Medical supplies were short and some regiments had no supplies at all. The lack of medical supplies became so desperate that in April the head doctor at Yellow Springs wrote to his superiors to "beg and pray" that they send him what he required.[6] Dr. James Craig described the hospitals as "mere chaos."[7]

Desperately needing help, Washington asked for the formation of a congressional committee to visit Valley Forge to witness the deprivations there. The congressmen were shocked. "Our troops. How miserable. The skeleton of an army presents itself to our eyes in a naked, starving condition out of health and out of spirits," delegate Gouverneur Morris wrote after his arrival.[8]

Men were not placed in isolation wards and those with one disease would catch another from the man moaning in the bed next to them; men who arrived with a minor wound from a musket ball died a week later from typhus. There were no hospital clothes and men lay ill in their dirty uniforms. Food and water were in short supply.

Dr. Benjamin Rush, the physician general of the army, said that "the hospitals robbed the United States of more citizens than the sword . . . they are an apology for murder." Rush was so fed up with conditions in them that toward the end of the winter he wrote that the worst thing that could happen to a sick soldier was to be put in a hospital and sarcastically suggested that the quickest way to win the war would be to ask the British army to march through Valley Forge so that the diseases there would kill all of them.[9] Describing the numerous calamities at Valley Forge, General James Varnum wrote to a friend that if God determined he had to be punished for his life, he would rather be sent to hell than back to Pennsylvania.

Elias Boudinot, the commissioner general of prisoners, was as angry about conditions as everyone else, but had great admiration for the men of Valley Forge, writing to his brother, "Nothing but suffering for our poor fellows, but they do it without complaint."[10] Adjutant General Alexander Scammel praised "the brave men who experience the severities of a camp life and cheerfully expose their lives with a determination to die or conquer."[11] And Dr. Waldo wrote of them, "The soldier, with cheerfulness he meets his foes and encounters every hardship—if bare-foot, he labours through the mud and cold."[12]

That gritty determination came to not only symbolize the troops at Valley Forge, but the American soldier throughout history. The best example of that was Ebenezer Crosby of Massachusetts, one of the much maligned doctors. He had a recurrence of his asthma as soon as he arrived at Valley Forge and, hacking and wheezing, spent two weeks in the hospital. Even though not recovered, he went back to his regiment and promptly was stricken with pleurisy and bile, which he described as "severe and dangerous." He survived that and, shortly after, came down with pleurisy again and found himself once again bedridden. He wrote that "my constitution was by no means fit to undergo the fatigues, hardships, and irregularities of camp life," and, like so many others, asked to go home with a discharge. It was granted to the quite ill physician.

Some weeks passed and his health improved slightly. Crosby, knowing he was needed and "desirous to see the ensuing campaign," then changed his mind. He turned down the chance to go home to Massachusetts and sit in front of a fireplace in his warm house and eat a fine meal with his family and continued on at Valley Forge, freezing and starving with the rest of the army.[13]

There were so many soldiers in the dozens of hospitals that dotted the Valley Forge camp and the surrounding villages that on March 7 only 3,301 men, out of a force then estimated at 10,200, were deemed fit for duty. Medical help for wounded or sick men in the 1770s was primitive. Ineffective medicine did little good for men stricken with typhus or other diseases and could not stop raging fevers. Men in the hospitals laid in their beds and watched others shake violently under the strains of high fevers before dying. Severe arm or leg wounds suffered in battle almost always resulted in gangrene and there was no medicine to combat it. The only solution was to amputate limbs. Only a very low level anesthetic was available, if at all, and the pain of amputation—by small, crude, handheld saws—was excruciating. Men had to be strapped to wooden operating tables with sticks thrust into their mouth to mute their screams as their limbs were removed. Puddles of blood covered the operating room floors.

The mortality rates were shocking. One-third of all the soldiers sent to the makeshift army hospital in Bethlehem died there, and thirty-seven of the forty men from one Virginia regiment, along with some of their doctors. Half the two hundred forty soldiers at Lititz passed away, along with the Moravian pastor who also served as their doctor, and his five assistants. Hundreds, along with several doctors, could not survive at Yellow Springs. One-fifth of the 1,072 North Carolina soldiers died in the hospitals. Altogether, nearly twenty-five hundred soldiers died at Valley Forge, or nearly one sixth of the entire army.

Washington received letters from men who were desperately ill in his hospitals who requested permission to return to their homes so that they could spend their last days surrounded by their families. Some doctors threw up their hands in frustration because their medicines did little good. "We avoid piddling pills, powders, cordials, and all such insignificant matters whose powers are only rendered important by causing the patient to vomit up his money instead of his disease," wrote one.[14]

A nasty feud between Dr. Rush and Dr. William Shippen, the head surgeon in the army, did not help matters. Rush resigned his post as physician general that winter, charging that Shippen was using hospital funds for his personal gain. Shippen was brought before a court-martial, but merely reprimanded. The result was chaos in the medical department.

Mismanagement was everywhere. Wagons full of medicine chests from Virginia bound for Valley Forge were stopped in Williamsburg and army doctors there took most of the chests to treat their own needy troops. A cask of wine sent from Albany to a camp hospital was kept in the home of a local politician for safety; he stole it. Ships thought to be about ready to land with medicine on board were seized by the British. A driver misunderstood instructions and returned home instead of proceeding to Valley Forge with a wagon full of medicine after waiting several days for a river to recede.[15] Orderlies in the hospitals sometimes stole the clothing of their patients.

The procurement and transportation of supplies, whether medicine, food, or clothing, were not under the jurisdiction of the army, but inept federal administrators in York, Pennsylvania, where the Continental Congress moved when the British occupied Philadelphia, and in Lancaster. There was little congressional supervision of the supply departments. The quartermaster, Thomas Mifflin, quit in October 1777, but Congress did not replace him until March 1778, throwing the entire office into disarray. As an example, Washington was assured that the government had 7.6 million pounds of flour, enough to last the whole winter, but in reality they had just 3.7 million pounds. Supply officers told him just before the winter camp was organized that the army would have enough meat for seven months, but in early December another check showed that there was only enough for eight more days.

Many fumed to Washington about unqualified doctors. Jedediah Huntington suggested, in a cruel remark, that since all the doctors did was bleed "bad blood" from patients, the army should hire local barbers instead because they worked cheaper."[16] Dr. Rush was fed up with the hospitals at Valley Forge, too. "Our hospitals crowded with six thousand sick but [only] half provided with necessaries or accommodations, and more dying in them in one month than perished in the field during the whole of the last campaign," he wrote to Patrick Henry. And Dr. William Brown said that "a large proportion" of the men who died could have been saved if they had enough medicine and recovered under better conditions.[17]

One night, Dr. Waldo rushed to a hut in a vain effort to save the life of an Indian soldier. The man's death seemed to symbolize all of the catastrophes of Valley Forge to the doctor. Waldo wrote, "He was an excellent soldier and a good natured fellow. . . . he has served his country faithfully.

He has fought for those very people who disinherited his forefathers. Having finished his pilgrimage, he was discharged from the war of life and death. His memory ought to be respected more than those rich ones who supply the world with nothing better than money and vice. There the poor fellow lies, not superior now to a clod of earth, his mouth wide open, his eyes staring."[18]

Rush sneered, too, that citizens were not joining the army because of its medical woes. He wrote to Horatio Gates, "The common people are too much shocked with spectacles of Continental misery ever to become Continental soldiers."[19]

Some soldiers reeled from one illness to another. Leven Powell, a lieutenant colonel from Virginia, came down with the "flux," a severe, diarrhea-like bloody discharge, just before Christmas and was taken to the farm house of John Rowland, where he spent nine days recovering with other patients. The flux was followed by a bout of yellow jaundice that lasted nearly three weeks. Toward the end of his struggle with the debilitating jaundice, Powell noticed small sores and a swelling of his right eye that reduced much of his sight in that eye. A few days later he complained of severe headaches and sores that broke out on his face. His left eye then swelled up and both eyes became weak and bloodshot. He feared he would go blind. A doctor told him that he had a bad case of what was called "St. Anthony's Fire" and treated it the best he could.[20]

General Washington was appalled by the medical catastrophe. "I sincerely feel for the unhappy condition of our poor fellows in the hospitals, and wish my powers to relieve them were equal to my inclination," he wrote to Governor Livingston of New Jersey. "Our difficulties and distresses are certainly great and such as wound the feelings of humanity."[21]

The commander took steps to correct the problems. Doctors who had gone home were ordered back to Valley Forge, food and clothing was sent directly to the hospitals and not just to the camp supply officers, pits were dug in which garbage and animal carcasses were buried, urination anywhere except a privy was made a crime punishable by death, officers were put in charge of new cleanliness patrols, more medicine was found in private stores throughout the country and sent to the hospitals, officers were told to make regular visits to the sick, soldiers were ordered to bathe regularly and to wash their uniforms frequently, and windows were cut into the walls of huts to provide much-needed ventilation. The commander also sent chaplains to visit the sick. The work was not easy. The Rev. James Sproat, one of the ministers, wrote in his diary that he saw so many sick soldiers in the hospitals that he "was very much fatigued" at the end of every day.[22]

Washington himself never abandoned his sick soldiers. From time to time, risking his own health, he visited the hospitals and stopped at the beds of soldiers to offer some encouraging words. It "pleased the sick exceedingly," one doctor wrote of the general's visit to his hospital.[23]

Elijah Fisher, lying in his hospital bed, kept track of the daily death toll at the hospital in which he was confined. Fifty of the men in the facility died during just the month that he was there. Fearful for his own mortality as he watched bodies carried out on stretchers, Fisher talked a physician into letting him go back to the Miller farmhouse. He assured him that he felt better and did not need hospital care anymore. The doctor was glad to see him leave; another soldier, from yet another wagon, was given his bed as soon as he left. Miller took him back and there he recovered.

Barely able to walk, Fisher decided to rejoin his regiment at Valley Forge on February 28. As soon as he arrived, he was witness to a smallpox epidemic that had swept into the area. Washington had ordered immediate inoculations for all the soldiers, including any traveling to Valley Forge from other towns or army camps. Elijah Fisher was transported to yet another hospital for his inoculation, his side still hurting, and promptly came down with the pox. The pus-filled pustules formed on his body and his skin turned dark and felt on fire, threatening his life.

At first, George Washington was not overly worried about the smallpox because most of his soldiers had been inoculated the previous year. This time, however, he had hundreds of new soldiers and a quick survey informed him that more than one third of them had never been inoculated. The general could not have the inoculated men recover in the hospitals with all the other sick men; they would give them the pox. He evacuated everyone from the large hospital at Yellow Springs and turned it into a smallpox recovery unit for men inoculated at Valley Forge.

Altogether, doctors inoculated four thousand soldiers at Valley Forge and another one thousand at other army winter camps. The procedures were again a great success and only a few dozen of the five thousand men treated for pox died and some of them passed on from other causes. Elijah Fisher was one of the many who survived. His body fought off the pox and he lived—yet again. By spring, the smallpox epidemic was over.

Another epidemic, starvation, was not.

In mid December, the army found itself with no meat and just twenty-five barrels of flour to be shared by fourteen thousand men. Many men complained to their families that they had little to eat on most days and went several days without any food at all. On the day that the army arrived at Valley Forge, Dr. Waldo wrote "provisions scarce" and wrote that the men wailed, "No meat! No meat!" throughout the day and night and that their cries were like "the noise of crows and owls."[24]

Washington exploded in a letter to Henry Laurens, the new president of Congress. He told him that nearly half his army was sick or in the hospital or did not have enough clothing to report for duty. The other half was starving. He told him in blistering language that the supply departments of Congress impeded him at every turn, that local farmers would not help him and that his soldiers, and he, felt that the government had abandoned them. He went so far as to say that he feared a revolt by the public when they found how badly the soldiers were being treated. On December 23, he bluntly told Laurens that within days the army would "starve, dissolve, or disperse."[25]

Any food that could be procured was difficult to deliver. First, there was a shortage of wagon drivers. And, although the winter was relatively mild, frequent rainfall and thawing snow turned the roadways in southeastern Pennsylvania to mud and wagons with supplies destined for the camp could not move. Rivers flooded over their banks and several boats trying to carry supplies across them capsized and the food was lost. On several occasions soldiers trying to salvage the supplies from the overturned boats drowned in the effort.

Some locals gouged the army, selling what little food they had at high prices, refused to sell on credit, or simply refused to sell at all. The food shortages became a chronic crisis that winter. Jedediah Huntington wrote to his brother in Connecticut that the soldiers "live from hand to mouth."[26] Following another food shortage in mid-February, an assistant in the commissary told his boss that the army had been without beef for five days and that there was no sign of any cattle on their way. "We have been driven almost to destruction," the officer said of the starvation.[27]

The food crisis would continue throughout the winter and into the spring, as would the medical and clothing shortages, threatening the existence of the army. Inflation spiraled once again as American paper money depreciated in value and word of the awful winter brought recruitment to a standstill. There was continued friction among officers and even a failed conspiracy among some officers and members of Congress to replace George Washington as commander in chief with the newly famous Horatio Gates. And, on top of all that, the British army was just twenty miles away in Philadelphia and might attack at any moment.

Chapter Twenty

"THE SOLDIERS OF OUR ARMY ARE ALMOST NAKED . . ."

Lieutenant James McMichael: The Poet

The road to Valley Forge began just before dinner on September 2, 1777, for Lieutenant James McMichael of the Pennsylvania State Regiment, now renamed the Thirteenth Pennsylvania Riflemen. On that day McMichael's regiment camped near Wilmington, Delaware. The men were told to prepare for battle because the British Army, on its way to Philadelphia, appeared to be marching toward nearby Christiana, a village in the northern part of the state.

The armies did not encounter each other there but at Brandywine Creek, south of Philadelphia, on September 11, 1777. McMichael and his regiment were under the command of General William Maxwell and given the assignment of guarding Chadd's Ford, one of several shallow fords that the enemy could use to cross the creek.

The main attack was made by Lord Cornwallis and Howe with seventy-five hundred men three and a half miles west, at Birmingham meeting house, following a flanking maneuver the Americans did not anticipate. Washington's information was faulty, too. He had no idea as to the number of troops and cannon he had. Washington didn't even know the location of the meeting house. The maps given him were not complete either, and the terrain looked different from Washington's spy-glass than it did on his maps.

There, men under General John Sullivan and later Nathanael Greene could not hold back the English attack.[1] Throughout the assault, which came at 4 p.m. and lasted several hours, Washington and Lafayette rode back and forth, rallying all of the men in the area. Lafayette was shot in the thigh and the commander in chief was constantly exposed to fire.[2]

General Wilhelm Knyphausen's Hessians attacked Chadd's Ford around 4:30 p.m. They crossed Brandywine Creek easily and tore into the American defenders, including McMichael, on the other side. It was a hot fight in the afternoon and McMichael knew that he and his men were in trouble from the moment it commenced.

We took the front and attacked the enemy at 5:30 and being engaged with their grand army we at first was obliged to retreat a few yards. We then formed in an open field, where we fought without giving way on either side 'til the [sun] descended below the horizon. It then growing dark and our ammunition all but expired, we ceased firing on both sides . . . This day for a severe and successive engagement exceeded all I ever seen. Our regiment fought at one stand for about an hour with an incessant fire and yet the loss [of men] much less than that of Long Island. Neither was we so [beaten] as at Princeton. Our common defense being about fifty yards. I lost three men in my division, yet Providence preserved me from being wounded.

It had been a horrific encounter. One man wrote, "The batteries at [Chadd's] ford opened upon each other with such fury as if the elements had been in convulsions; the valley was filled with smoke and . . . for an hour and a half this horrid sport continued."[3]

McMichael and his fellow soldiers were disappointed that they had been driven back and forced from the area, and relieved that the British had foolishly decided not to pursue them. All felt like Captain Samuel Shaw, of Massachusetts, who wrote, "No person could behave with more bravery than our troops; but, somehow or other, we were not successful."[4]

The defeat at Brandywine was a stinging setback for the public, though. The Continental Army lost approximately eight hundred men, killed or wounded, and four hundred Americans were taken prisoner. The British lost 577 killed or wounded. Washington's army had failed to halt Howe and permitted him to continue his campaign to capture Philadelphia. Washington came under intense criticism, especially when the English army took the city without a shot being fired in defense of it and paraded through town to the loud cheers of the thousands of Tories who lived there.

Washington learned that after Howe's capture of Philadelphia Howe had divided his army, with three thousand in Philadelphia and about two thousand at Wilmington, Delaware. The remaining seven to eight thousand encamped just northwest of the town at the village of Germantown. The commander decided to attack them there. Recent enlistments had swollen Washington's army to eight thousand continentals and three thousand militia, giving him superior numbers for a single engagement for one of the few times during the war.

On October 3, the battle of Germantown began. Washington decided to copy the Trenton plan of attack and marched the army all night for a surprise assault at dawn. The Americans would hit Howe from four different directions at precisely the same time in a coordinated attack. It would have worked, too, but an early morning fog slowed down the offensive and caused two regiments to collide and fire on each other. Confusion ensued and Washington ordered a retreat. McMichael was angry about the order to turn back. He wrote, "Here we had disagreeably to leave the field when we had nearly made a conquest."

The retreat was slow and difficult. Wrote a drained McMichael that night, "I had previously underwent many fatigues but never any that so much overdone me as this. Had it not been for fear of being taken, I should have remained on the road all night. Considering my march when on picket [the night before], I had in twenty-four hours marched forty-five miles and in that time fought four hours during which we advanced so furiously through buckwheat fields. It was an almost unspeakable fatigue."

Rumors of the Saratoga triumph reached Washington on October 18 and all celebrated. There was not much else to cheer about that fall and winter. Following the double defeats at Brandywine and Germantown, and the loss of Philadelphia, the American forces in Pennsylvania moved from village to village and camped for a night in one location and a week in another. Finally, on December 19, they arrived in Valley Forge for the winter.

McMichael had obtained a furlough just after he arrived at Valley Forge and returned in early January. The lieutenant's hut was finally completed near the end of January; he slept in a tent with others during its construction. By that time, the tragedies of Valley Forge, caused primarily by dysfunction in the commissary and quartermaster divisions—and a lack of assistance from Chester County residents—had already started to unfold. The men had starved from time to time throughout the winter. Many died in the hospitals.

McMichael returned at the height of the clothing crisis that had begun prior to the army's arrival at Valley Forge and continued throughout the winter. Some regiments found they lacked clothing as early as the summer. Colonel Israel Angell, commander of Jeremiah Greenman's Second Rhode Island, complained about it in August 1777, when he wrote a caustic letter to his state legislature. He told them then that his men had been barefoot for weeks and that they gave the appearance of a "ragged, lousy, naked regiment."[5]

The clothes of many other soldiers had been torn badly in the heated battles at Brandywine Creek and Germantown and during hut construction; they needed replacement, but little was available. The clothier department, run by the incompetent James Mease, had not foreseen any great need to buy clothes and Mease had refused several opportunities to do so because he felt that the prices were too high. Added to his recalcitrance was a quartermaster's department, located forty miles away in Lancaster, Pennsylvania, whose administrators seemed to have little knowledge of the clothing woes of the army and did little to transport any. The department had not had a leader for months and clerks there who did try to assist the soldiers often found themselves lost in voluminous paperwork.

No clothing had been set aside either, because no one knew where the army would spend the winter. Shipments of clothes from New York State were lost en route. Another large clothing warehouse had been burned by the British. American officers billeted in other winter camps, such as those in New York and New Jersey, with clothing shortages of their own, halted shipments for Valley Forge and removed many of the uniforms and blankets and gave them to their own badly clad men.

On one occasion, a general obtained five hundred coats for the men of the Pennsylvania regiment, but the clothier general insisted that tailors had to work on the jackets. He then went on vacation, leaving the jackets in a warehouse. It was weeks before the jackets were finally delivered. Troops whose enlistment had ended attempted to take their blankets home with them and had to be ordered to leave them behind for others. Clothing could not be made easily, either. The United States did not have textile mills like England that could produce clothes for fourteen thousand soldiers.[6]

The lack of clothing meant that soldiers received little protection from the weather and came down with bad colds that turned into pneumonia; they wound up in the dreaded hospitals. The clothing crisis also meant that the troops were not available for needed camp drills and work crews throughout the winter.

A Massachusetts general told his superiors that three-quarters of his men could not report for parade because they had no clothes or shoes. "They are naked from the crowns of their heads to the soles of their feet," he wrote.[7] Many of his men wrote to friends and asked them to send clothing and to lobby their state legislatures to do the same. Lt. Archelaus Lewis, of the First Massachusetts, an officer in Ebenezer Wild's regiment, was one. He wrote to a friend, Jesse Partridge, "There is two-thirds of our regiment barefooted and bare-backed, not a second shirt to put on nor breeches to cover their nakedness . . . this is the case with the greatest part of our army." He told Partridge sarcastically that no one back home cared for the troops anymore. "By your conduct, you as good as say why should we trouble or concern ourselves about them? They are tied fast and let them look out for themselves."[8]

One New Hampshire general told a friend about the soldiers that "one half of them destitute of any shoes or stockings to their feet, and I may add many without either breeches, shirts, and blankets . . . living in a cold season in log huts without doors or floors."[9] A Massachusetts officer, Col. Samuel Carlton, wrote that his men had no blankets or coats, but what broke his heart, too, was their lack of footwear. "Ninety men in the regiment have not a shoe to their foot and near as many have no feet to their stockings. It gives me pain to see our men turned out upon the parade to mount guard or to go on fatigue with their naked feet on the snow and ice."[10]

Men without shirts held their overcoats tightly around their bare chests; those without shoes wrapped cartridge box leather around them. Some even sold their clothes and used the money to buy food.[11] One colonel threw up his hands. "The soldiers of our army are almost naked," he lamented in a letter.[12]

Richard Butler, a colonel in the Ninth Pennsylvania, wrote at the end of March that throughout the winter there had been only one blanket for every five men in his regiment. Some men had but one shirt and many none. He added that some of the tents were taken down, cut up, and used as blankets. The clothing crisis was ruining morale. "The want of clothing," he wrote, "is the first thing that makes a soldier think little of himself. Had I clothing for them, I would venture to vouch for their conduct both as to their bravery and fidelity, and am certain it would be very conducive to their health."[13] Some soldiers who found themselves freezing without proper clothing wrote home to ask their families to send them cattle skins they could trade for articles of clothing, but many of these wound up stolen by other soldiers.[14]

The plight of the men was familiar to many who lived in that area of Pennsylvania. Wrote an angry Christopher Marshall, a resident of Lancaster,

> [The] army are now obliged to encounter all the inclemency of this cold weather, as they are . . . living out in the woods with slender covering; our poor friends in town, many of them in want of fuel and other necessities, while internal enemies, under the protection of that savage monster Howe, are reveling in luxury, dissipation, and drunkenness without any feelings for their once happy, bleeding country."[15]

The people who lived in Chester County insisted that they had no spare clothing that they could sell to the army and that the British had seized much of it in September. They had said the same thing about food, that had been confiscated by both British and American forces for months. What infuriated the starving and badly clad soldiers was the sight of those same local residents walking about covered in comfortable great coats with thick woolen scarves wrapped around their necks to keep themselves warm. The residents' refusal to help the army caused great bitterness among the soldiers. On Christmas Eve, 1777, James Gray, a captain in the Third New Hampshire, wrote to his wife Susan of the residents, "In this state we find a people who are (generally speaking) the most unfriendly of any we have passed through."[16]

In a letter to his brother, a furious Elias Boudinot declared, "The inhabitants are only fit for pickhorses," and that "extortion reigns triumphant throughout every part of [Pennsylvania]." He had nothing but scorn for the Pennsylvania troops, writing that as fighting men they were "worse than a company of Jersey women."[17]

Unable to obtain clothing at Valley Forge, many men wrote home and begged family, friends, and neighbors to send them some. A lowly ranking paymaster in a New Hampshire regiment wrote to a friend that he needed a shirt, stockings, white breeches "full large," with a white waistcoat "homespun." He said he would be happy to pay any "agreeable" price and then, in a flush of vanity, asked his friend to get ruffled and not plain sleeves on the shirts.[18] Some men yearned for small pleasures, such as Jonathan Todd, of Connecticut, who asked his father in a letter he wrote on Christmas Day, "Don't forget my shirt and watch; should be glad of a handkerchief."[19]

Many saw the lack of clothing as a lack of patriotism by their states. General Enoch Poor of New Hampshire wrote to the members of his legislature that they had broken their word to the troops: "If any desert how can I punish them when they plead in their justification that on your part the contract is broken?" Henry Laurens, president of the Continental Congress, was even blunter, writing to New Jersey governor Livingston that he believed the army might collapse by the end of the year. He fumed "that we are starving in the midst of plenty, perishing by cold, and surrounded by clothing sufficient for two armies, but uncollected."[20]

George Washington knew that he could simply seize clothing from Americans wherever he found it. Congress had given him dictatorial powers in 1776, since rescinded, and in September 1777 the Pennsylvania State Assembly authorized him to take whatever clothing and supplies he needed from the inhabitants living in the southeastern region of the state. He refused to do so, reminding the state assembly and Congress that martial law was unthinkable to him. He would find another way.

He slowly solved the problem by replacing the key men in charge of the army's supplies. Washington convinced Congress to streamline the quartermaster and commissary departments. He arranged for an excellent administrator, Jeremiah Wadsworth, to be named head of the commissary and the commander in chief's right hand man, General Nathanael Greene, became head of the quartermaster's department and ran it from Valley Forge. Within a month, the crisis ebbed. Wadsworth completely reorganized the department, reduced the corruption within it, and expanded the search for food into the far reaches of each state. Greene tightened up the organization of the quartermaster's department and hired hundreds of new wagon drivers, all civilians, to expedite the delivery of clothing and other supplies.

Unable to procure needed meat in the Valley Forge area to feed his starving troops, Washington sent Generals Wayne and Greene on several foraging expeditions in New Jersey and later ordered officers to disperse throughout the middle Atlantic states to find cattle and bring them to Valley Forge. His scouts located considerable numbers of cattle on farms as far away as Maryland and Massachusetts and brought them several hundred miles to Valley Forge, through inclement weather, down narrow, uneven dirt roads, and over streams and rivers. They also managed to drive every herd except one past the British. The cattle drive, a tenacious undertaking, saved the army.

The state governments that so many cursed at Valley Forge *did* assist the army, even though it took a long time to do so. Colonel William Shepard wrote a heartfelt plea to the Massachusetts legislature complaining that his destitute men lived "barely above a state of want" at Valley Forge due to the inaction of clothing procurers back home. The legislature not only ruled the procurers negligent but ordered the immediate production of new clothing for the troops. Governors in other states ordered clothing for their regiments in the winter camp.[21]

Lt. James McMichael, the poet, was despondent about life in camp throughout the clothing crisis and all of the other disasters of the Valley Forge winter. He missed his wife. On February 2, he wrote a poem that reflected the woes of any soldier who was homesick for the woman he loved. In it he explained that although he preferred to be with her, as a patriot he had to remain in the army and try to survive the brutal winter.

The lieutenant finished his poem, put it down, then picked it up and with his quill added something else that seemed to come directly from his heart to his wife:

Dear creature I must from you go
But yet my heart is filled with woe
I wish you in my absence may

Have all the bliss love can display
Your Jamey must stay in the wars
And try the labors of bold Mars
But yet I hope before I die
In your sweet bosom I shall lie
There whilst I am in your dear arms
Resting secure from war's alarms
This will our absence recompense
By the sweet joy at love's expense

The sicknesses of Valley Forge began to claim his friends, sending McMichael into more depression. One lieutenant whom he knew was killed by another officer in a duel. His friend Captain John Speer, who had fought with valor in several battles, died of a fever on February 8 and McMichael attended his funeral. That night he wrote a poem praising his friend's service to his country and reminding anyone who read it that patriots all went to heaven.

McMichael's journal and collection of poems reflected his increasing unhappiness with life throughout the Valley Forge winter following those incidents. He wrote to his wife often and continually told her how much he loved her and how he desired to be with her.

McMichael and the others were provided with some sports and entertainment to keep their mind off the dreadful conditions in camp. It was discovered that several officers had been amateur actors before the war. They formed a theatre troupe and staged plays in one of the bakehouses; the bakery was filled to capacity for the performances. Part of a meadow was cleared for athletic events. The men played lacrosse, an Indian game, and a type of croquet called wicket. George Washington even participated in some of the wicket contests.

There were fast days to seek God's protection for the army (the men joked that with food supplies low, they fasted every day). Washington's February 22 birthday was celebrated. The first of May, May Day, was celebrated by brigades of men with white blossoms tucked into the bands of their hats. They marched back and forth on the parade grounds in front of wooden poles gaily decorated with ribbons for each brigade. Thirteen men carried bows and thirteen arrows for each state and thirteen drummers and thirteen fifers serenaded the army. All of the privates were drawn up into thirteen platoons of thirteen men each.[22]

McMichael made it through the tough winter, he told his new bride again and again, by reading the many letters she sent him and through the poems he forwarded to her. On March 4, their first anniversary, he composed a short poem that captured both the love of a young couple and the loneliness of the soldier:

> At Lancaster, this was the day I first got my consent
> For to embrace fair hymen, for which I then was bent
> I secondly got the consent of her that's now my wife
> That in cohabitation with me she would spend her life
> We then into the arms of each other sweetly clung
> And soon removed that solitude which on our minds then hung
> We spent some happy time, before that we did part
> But Mars soon us both parted, which grieved us to the heart
> Yet in a short time after, we hoped for to meet
> And for some few days of pleasure that unto us were sweet
> Revolved whilst we together, were all possessed of joy
> But fortune very suddenly did our bliss destroy
> By calling me unto the camp to please great thundering Mars
> There to remain exposed to the alarm of wars

Those alarms would be sounded again in the spring when General Henry Clinton, who replaced Howe, decided what he was going to do with the army of some twelve thousand men he had stationed in Philadelphia. The men at Valley Forge wondered whether he would attack them or whether he would strike at other Pennsylvania towns, or communities in New Jersey. Would Washington assault Philadelphia?

The American commander knew that he had an army that had fought well, despite losing, at Brandywine and Germantown. But he was in charge of a fourteen-thousand-man army weakened and demoralized by the harsh winter. In order to turn his army into a better fighting force he welcomed Baron Friedrich Wilhelm von Steuben, a Prussian army officer and drill master who presented him with a mostly fabricated biography. Von Steuben assured Washington that he could teach the Americans classic European battlefield maneuvers that would enable them to defeat the British in any direct confrontation. Washington needed that assurance. His army had been beaten in most classic, open-field confrontations and registered its victories only in sneak attacks such as Trenton. He might be able to convince Britain to quit the war if they realized the Americans could beat them in direct battle.

At first, most soldiers thought little of the stocky Prussian who barely spoke any English; no one believed the men, so weary from the winter, would have any interest in arduous daily training. They were wrong. Von Steuben was smart enough to turn the drills into contests between regiments, and the men, sometimes as angry with each other as they were with the British, welcomed the competition. He also wrote his own simplified maneuvering manual and the soldiers liked it.

Lt. George Ewing, of New Jersey, described the daily drills that commenced in April with genuine affection. He wrote, "This forenoon the brigade went through the maneuvers under the direction of Baron Steuben. The step is about halfway betwixt slow and quick time, an easy and natural step. I think [it is] much better than the former. The manual also is altered by his direction. There are but ten words of command."[23]

Von Steuben's condensed set of commands for battlefield repositioning and firing were much easier to understand and could be speedily implemented. The contests between the men escalated and within a few weeks the men were even practicing drills and marching maneuvers on their own, without any supervision, determined to do better than other regiments.

On May 6, 1778, the morale of the men at Valley Forge received an enormous boost when it was announced that France had recognized the United States as a sovereign nation and later would come into the war on its side. Louis XVI would supply muskets, cannon, thousands of men, and part of the French fleet to assist the Americans.

The announcement was greeted by a day-long celebration. At precisely 10 a.m. a cannon was fired to alert the brigades. A short time later a second cannon boomed to signal their movement to the parade ground. There they were greeted by a roaring salute by thirteen cannon, one for each state. That salute was followed by the traditional Fue de Joy, in which every man fired his musket three times, one after the other, giving anyone near the camp the joyful sound of more than thirty thousand shots fired into the morning sky. Between each of three Fue de Joys the thirteen cannon boomed again. After the first, the soldiers shouted, "Long Live the King of France." At the conclusion of the second round of cannon they shouted, "God Save the Friendly Powers of Europe." And at the end of the third, they shouted, "God save the American States."[24]

The musketry and cannonading was followed by two receptions, one for the officers and another for the enlisted men. General Washington attended the officers' reception, mingling with as many of his lieutenants, captains, and colonels as he could. Then His Excellency walked to the reception area where all of the thousands of enlisted men were gathered. To their delight, Washington had some food and drink and mingled with them.

Late in the afternoon, Washington left the reception with all eyes on him. He mounted his white horse and reined him to one side. As he did, without prompting, the eleven thousand some men then enrolled in the first American Army cheered him. Genuinely moved, the general turned the horse around, faced the men, took off his hat, and waved it at them in salute. Now they roared, clapping their hands together as fast as they could and then, almost in unison, the soldiers took off their hats and tossed them high into the air as the general rode off.

George Washington marveled at the good cheer of the army. In a letter to his cousin he recounted all of the hardships of the winter, but ended by telling him that "yet the army is in exceedingly good spirits."[25]

James McMichael enjoyed the reception and cheered the commander as loudly as anyone else, but he yearned for his wife. Five days later, on May 11, probably at the repeated urging of Susanna, Lieutenant James McMichael, his time up, finally left the Continental Army after two full years of service. He had participated in some of the greatest battles of the conflict at New York, Brandywine, and Germantown and had survived the harrowing winter at Valley Forge. He wrote that he headed to his wife's home in Stony Brook, New Jersey, on a pleasant spring day filled with the sounds of birds and "their notes of melody in the highest branches of the lofty cedars."

On the night before he departed, McMichael wrote a long, epic poem describing the history and battles of his regiment. In the middle of it, describing the army's arrival at Brandywine Creek, he penned a four-line stanza that captured the attitude of the young lieutenant and, in him, perhaps the entire army:

Our spirits now were roused, we marched without delay
Through Philadelphia, Chester and Wilmington straightaway
We took our post near red clay creek, upon a pleasant field
Where we thought we would rather fight, then unto tyrants yield.

BOSTON

This 1875 lithograph by Heppenheimer & Maurer of New York captured the violence of the Boston Massacre, which took place on March 5, 1770. British soldiers asked the members of a raucous crowd to disperse several times and then fired. Five men were killed in the incident. One of them was Samuel Maverick, seventeen, an apprentice to John Greenwood's father and the teenager's roommate.

—Courtesy of Anne S. K. Brown Military Collection, Brown University

It was never clear who fired "the shot heard 'round the world" at Lexington, Massachusetts, on April 19, 1775, after a Massachusetts militia tried to face down a contingent of British regulars who had marched from Boston in search of hidden ammunition in the area. A. Doolittle, who engraved this scene in 1775, noted underneath that it was a British soldier who fired the shot, as all Americans contended, blaming the start of the war on the Redcoats.

—Courtesy of Anne S. K. Brown Military Collection, Brown University

George Washington arrived in Cambridge in June 1775 to take command of the army. It was an amateurish, undisciplined, and badly organized army, and not the postcard perfect collections of soldiers depicted in this patriotic painting.
—M. A. Wageman, Courtesy of Anne S. K. Brown Military Collection, Brown University

The British finally pushed the hard-fighting Americans off Bunker and Breed's Hills after a third assault and after U.S. gunpowder ran out during the June 17, 1775, battle. English losses were heavy—1,150 men. This painting by Alonzo Chappel shows the death of Dr. James Warren, one of the leading radicals in Boston, during the battle. It also depicts one of the first black soldiers to engage the British, Peter Salem, to the right.
—Courtesy of Anne S. K. Brown
Military Collection,
Brown University

The British evacuated Boston on the evening of March 17, 1776. Here, General William Howe supervises the loading of his eleven thousand troops on to a fleet of ships that would carry them to Halifax and, later, New York.

—Courtesy of Anne S. K. Brown Military Collection, Brown University

The low point of the ill-fated 1775–1776 invasion of Canada was the death of General Richard Montgomery, one of the leaders of the expedition, in the assault on Quebec.

—John Trumbull painting, Courtesy of Anne S. K. Brown Military Collection, Brown University

VALLEY FORGE

Soldiers took wagons into the farmlands that surrounded the Valley Forge encampment to search for wood, food, and clothing, usually without success.

—Courtesy of Valley Forge National Historical Park

This *Harper's Weekly* sketch depicts the spring training of the soldiers at Valley Forge by Prussia's Baron von Steuben. The gruff von Steuben, who spoke little English, turned the brigades into a highly skilled fighting force.

—Courtesy of Valley Forge National Historical Park

These huts at Jockey Hollow, in Morristown, New Jersey, are sturdy recreations of those that were home to the thirteen thousand men in Washington's main army during the winter of 1779–1780, said to be one of the harshest in the history of North America. These type of huts were used at Valley Forge the previous year and in subsequent winter camps.

—Courtesy of the Morristown-Morris Twp. Library

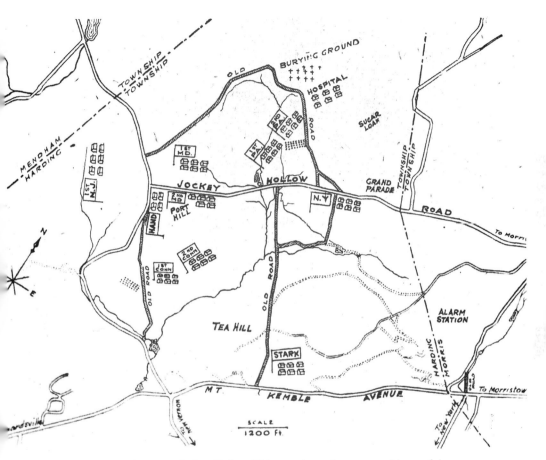

Washington created a city at Jockey Hollow. This map shows the streets and lanes of the town, which in population became the fourth-largest city in the U.S. overnight.

—Courtesy of the Morristown-Morris Twp. Library

The 1851 Emmanuel Leutze depiction of George Washington crossing the Delaware on the evening of Christmas Day, 1776, is one of the most famous paintings in the nation's history. Washington was actually seated. His troops surprised an army of Hessians in Trenton, capturing most, and reversed the fortunes of the war.

—Courtesy of Anne S. K. Brown Military Collection, Brown University

Henry Knox was able to get his artillery into position quickly enough to fire upon the hundreds of Hessians running out of their houses to face the Americans in Trenton. Private John Greenwood was one of the infantrymen who charged the Germans with his sword drawn: "Within pistol shot, they fired point blank at us," Greenwood wrote. "We dodged and they did not hit a man, while before they had to time to reload we were within three feet of them."

—Courtesy of Anne S. K. Brown Military Collection, Brown University

—*inset* Courtesy of Morristown National Historical Park

George Washington, center, rallied his men when they were pushed back early in the battle of Princeton on January 3, 1777, and then led them in a charge straight at the massed British line. A young lieutenant, James McMichael, of the Thirteenth Pennsylvania, was in the middle of the furious engagement. In one volley, the four men to his right fell dead and in the next volley two men to his left died. McMichael did not know why he was the only man standing, but later wrote that he "thanked the kindness of Providence."

—Courtesy of Anne S. K. Brown Military Collection, Brown University

This painting of the 1776 battle of Long Island shows the retreat of American forces under General William Alexander (Lord Stirling) across the Gowanus Canal. In that battle, Lt. James McMichael of the Thirteenth Pennsylvania led his badly overwhelmed men through a nearby pond in which many drowned.

—Courtesy of Anne S. K. Brown Military Collection, Brown University

SARATOGA

This vivid print by L. T. Vernol captured the enemy shooting at General Benedict Arnold as he led his men in a charge against a British redoubt at the battle of Saratoga on September 19, 1777. Arnold, and not Gates, was the real hero in the victory that brought the French into the war on the American side.

—Courtesy of Anne S. K. Brown Military Collection, Brown University

—Courtesy of Morristown National Historical Park

General Horatio Gates, on horseback, looks over the start of the Saratoga battle in 1777. The Americans defeated Gentleman Johnny Burgoyne's forces in two battles and then surrounded him, forcing him to surrender his entire army.

—Courtesy of Anne S. K. Brown Military Collection, Brown University

This woodcut of General William Howe makes him look more like a statue in a London square than a military leader. He is shown, sword drawn, ready to lead his troops in the distant battle. Howe took over for General Thomas Gage as the commander of all British troops in America in 1776 and remained in charge of Her Majesty's forces until the summer of 1778, when he asked to return to England.

—Courtesy of Anne S. K. Brown Military Collection, Brown University

This sketch of Earl, Charles Cornwallis, shows him in a rather casual pose, hand in pocket. Cornwallis was Washington's chief nemesis during the war. Cornwallis coined the phrase "the old fox" to describe Washington, and the American commander continually outfoxed Cornwallis.

—Courtesy of Anne S. K. Brown Military Collection, Brown University

This sketch from the journal of a French officer, Jean Baptist Antoine de Verger, shows a quartet of troops in the Continental Army, including an African American. About five thousand black soldiers fought in the army. This soldier was probably from the First Rhode Island, one of three all-black regiments. The artist seemed to capture the pride of the African American soldier whom both U.S. and British soldiers noted in their letters.
—Courtesy of Anne S. K. Brown Military Collection, Brown University

The First Rhode Island was instrumental in holding off British forces at the battle of Rhode Island at Newport in the summer of 1778 (shown here in a copper engraving from a 1779 issue of *Gentleman's Magazine*), permitting a retreat the next day that saved the army.
—Courtesy of Anne S. K. Brown Military Collection, Brown University

Dozens of black slaves continued their service to their masters when they joined the army or worked as servants to generals. This one is holding the reins of the Marquis de Lafayette's horse.
—Courtesy of Anne S. K. Brown Military Collection, Brown University

Naval battles on the high seas were violent. Ships would engage with cannon but then maneuver as close to each other as possible for close range musket battles and boarding assaults with pistols and swords. The privateers were careful to capture ships, and their valuable cargo, rather than sink them. This scene from the fabled ocean battle between John Paul Jones's *Bon Homme Richard* and the British ship *Serapis* in 1779 is a good example of the fighting on the seas.
—F. C. Yohn, circa 1900 for an insurance broadside, Courtesy of Anne S. K. Brown Military Collection, Brown University

There have been numerous paintings and sketches of the surrender of Cornwallis's army to George Washington at Yorktown. In many, artists erroneously had Cornwallis handing his sword to the American commander. Actually, Cornwallis was too ashamed to come out of the village and had one of his generals, Charles O'Hara, surrender his sword. Someone with a sense of irony ordered the British band to play "The World Turned Upside Down" as the English troops marched out.

—John Chapin, Courtesy of Anne S. K. Brown Military Collection, Brown University

French engineers designed the lengthy trenches that faced Yorktown from the south, cutting off any British escape. The combined French-American land force used about one hundred cannon in a siege that lasted eight days. The most devastating bombardment was on the morning of October 17, 1781, when cannonballs blew up British artillery batteries, hit ships in the river, and knocked down sections of buildings. The siege of Yorktown effectively ended the war, but the peace treaty was not signed for two more years.

—Rufus S. Zogbaum, Courtesy of Anne S. K. Brown Military Collection, Brown University

SOLDIERS

When uniforms could be obtained, later in the Revolution, the riflemen, who began the war clad in buckskin, looked more like regular Continental infantrymen.
—Courtesy of Anne S. K. Brown Military Collection, Brown University

Elijah Fisher, of Massachusetts, served several years as a private before given the honor of joining George Washington's one-hundred-fifty-man life guard. This rare sketch shows the special uniforms and hats worn by members of Washington's bodyguard unit. These men were always with him when he traveled and camped outside his headquarters to protect him.
—Courtesy of Anne S. K. Brown Military Collection, Brown University

Many of the soldiers in the army were teenagers. Private John Greenwood, of Massachusetts, was just fifteen when he joined the First Massachusetts. Many looked like this sketch of a teenaged Continental soldier.
—Courtesy of Anne S. K. Brown Military Collection, Brown University

The clash of Washington's main army and the British at Monmouth, New Jersey, in 1778 was one of the major battles of the war. The Americans had survived the awful winter at Valley Forge and met the Redcoats at Monmouth with renewed spirit. The Continental Army held its own in the fighting on an oppressively hot day and the British retreated the next morning. This scene is from a sketch an issue of *Harper's Weekly* magazine in 1891.

—Courtesy of Anne S. K. Brown
Military Collection,
Brown University

The enlisted men wrote to their families whenever they spotted an important person, such as a state governor or member of Congress, but the ultimate sighting was that of His Excellency, George Washington. An actual meeting with the commander in chief by an enlisted man became family legend for generations.

—Courtesy of Independence National Historical Park

Chapter Twenty-One

PRIVATE ELIJAH FISHER JOINS WASHINGTON'S ELITE LIFE GUARD, 1778

In March 1778, Private Elijah Fisher's luck changed. One of the men from his regiment who was a member of the "life guard" that traveled with General Washington decided to leave just as the unit was increased in size. Fisher's colonel asked him to take his place in the elite military unit, despite his recent illness.

To be chosen for the commander's life guard was a great honor. Washington created the unit for two reasons. First, the guard, usually accompanied by a band, had special uniforms, new hats, the best and fastest horses. They traveled with him wherever he went to create an impressive image for the commander in chief. The members of the guard were a distinguished group and had to meet specific requirements. Each had to be American, not from any foreign power aiding the army. Washington insisted that they had to be good soldiers and men of "sobriety, honesty, and good behavior . . . handsomely and well made . . . neat and spruce." The unit originally consisted of fifty-eight infantrymen and thirty-eight cavalry, but their number grew over the years. They were their own parade and gave Washington an aura of power. Second, the guard, whose members also had to be at least five feet, ten inches in height, was there to protect him from any personal attacks as the army moved. When it rested, they camped right next to his tent or home.[1]

Life was good in the special unit that guarded the commander in chief, the forerunner of the secret service that protected presidents later. The commander took care of the men who served in the guard with warm clothing and ample food. "I like being there much better than being in the regiment," Fisher said. He still experienced kidney pains.

Fisher and the personal guard were always with Washington and the experience gave Fisher a chance to see how Washington conducted himself as he met with foreign dignitaries, other generals and local ministers, farmers and merchants. He was witness to the relationship that Washington enjoyed with his wife Martha, who spent every winter of the war with the general. She, too, was protected by the life guard. Fisher knew about Washington's close relationship with his slave servant, Billy Lee, who spent a considerable amount of time with the general, riding with him many afternoons of the war. Fisher watched as Washington inspected camps and led battles. He saw him during happy times, following a victory in a battle (Washington rarely smiled in public in order to hide his bad teeth) and he saw the flashes of anger that the general kept hidden from the army and the public, especially at Valley Forge when Washington fumed about the lack of clothing and food. Fisher also had a close-up view of the enormous respect and admiration displayed by people who came to see the commander in chief. But Fisher and the men in the life guard served to protect him, not befriend him. Fisher never indicated in his journal that he ever actually talked to Washington.

The personal guard also played a major role in all of the pomp that Washington loved to direct on special occasions. One of Washington's lobbying efforts throughout the war was with the chiefs of various Indian tribes. He wanted their friendship in order to keep them from joining the British. Fisher and the members of the guard would witnesses the arrival of the Indian chiefs at Valley Forge. They came wearing their ornate headdresses and flowing robes for meetings and dinners to cement the friendship with the Continental Army. The guard assembled to greet visiting foreign dignitaries or rode out to greet them with the commander, music playing and flags flying in the breeze. The guard would also assemble in lines to greet American public figures, such as governors or congressional delegates, upon their arrival at Valley Forge and stood near the general in the many anniversary celebrations held to celebrate victories and boost morale.

Their greatest responsibility, of course, was the personal safety of the most important person in the United States—George Washington. They were to protect him from any kidnap attempts or snipers. (There had been one plot to assassinate the general in 1776; an American soldier, Thomas Hickey, was hanged for it.)

On May 30, 1778, Fisher almost lost his life as a member of the personal guard, but it was not during a battle, assassination attempt, or kidnapping. Another member of the guard had crossed the Schuylkill to buy milk and yelled over the river at Fisher, taking a walk with several other men, to fetch a canoe and cross over to pick him up. Fisher procured a canoe and a pole and proceeded to cross the river, whose current was faster than usual. He switched the pole from one side of the canoe to another and pushed down on it, hard. The pole hit a rock underneath the water and then slid off the side of it and plunged further down toward the river bottom. It forced Fisher to tumble out of the canoe and into the rapidly running water.

He later wrote in his journal, "[I] made for shore, but the current was so swift it carried me downstream. Every little while I could touch bottom, the water being up to my middle, but I could not stand in comparison more than I could stand on the side of a house. I tried for shore, but the more I tried the more the current would sweep me downstream. I tried to touch bottom but I could not."

He began to slip under the waters of the Schuylkill. Fisher wrote that each time he tried to push his head out of the water it was held down by the current and he started to go to sleep underwater. The private felt his body go limp and believed that he was drowning. His body, he said, felt "as easy as it ever did in my life."

All of a sudden, he felt arms around him and his head flew up out of the river, droplets of water cascading off of it. His arms were held by something and he could feel them rise above the water level, too. His feet could feel the bottom of the river bed. A friend, Blake, watching him float down the Schuylkill, dove into the river and swam as fast as he could after Fisher, shouting to others to assist him. Blake grasped his friend in a bear hug, his arms under Fisher's armpits, and yanked him hard toward shore; other men on the bank of the river grabbed Fisher and hauled him up out of the river and onto the bank as he gasped for air.

The men dried him off the best they could with their own jackets, wrapped him in a blanket, and took him to one of the barracks in camp to see a doctor, explaining his near drowning to the physician there. The doctor did what every doctor seemed to do in the army. He bled him. Fisher, who probably needed nothing more than some dry clothes and a few hours in bed to recuperate, promptly began to feel very weak and fell ill when several pints of his blood were taken out. "I was very unwell for several days," he reported. Like other men, he was sicker when he left the hospital than when he arrived.

Crime and Punishment

As a member of the elite guard, Fisher was an eyewitness to the harsh punishments, and clemency, meted out by George Washington. On June 4, 1778, Washington approved the hanging of a former soldier in the Tenth Pennsylvania, Thomas Shanks, as a spy. Thousands lined the parade ground to watch the grim execution. On another occasion the commander ordered a firing squad execution for a man who had deserted and rejoined the army seven times, illegally collecting a bonus each time he reenlisted. Fisher witnessed the hanging of another man for robbery. On another occasion, the victims were two soldiers who had, like too many others, fraudulently enlisted for a bounty, then deserted, then reenlisted for another bounty several times. Washington ordered both shot by a firing squad.

But Washington could be lenient, too. On August 21, 1778, sixteen men were sentenced to death for desertion and for illegally enlisting more than once. Washington asked their officers if there was some mitigating circumstance that he could use—character, long service, sterling prior record—to spare them. He pardoned all at the last moment.

George Washington maintained a harsh policy of punishments in the army. He had been notorious for insisting on floggings of one hundred lashes during the French and Indian War. At that time he commanded troops at frontier garrisons in Virginia as head of a colonial company for the British army, which allowed as many as two thousand lashes for infractions. In 1775, Congress set thirty-nine lashes as the toll for punishment of crimes that ranged from first time desertions to striking an officer to petty theft. As the war progressed, and the need for discipline grew, the number again climbed to one hundred by the following year; this pleased Washington, who insisted that harsh punishment deterred further crime. Sometimes as many as a half-dozen men were flogged on the same day for different crimes.[2]

Executions were approved by Washington, too. Capital crimes included murder, excessive robbery or multiple robbery, multiple desertions (usually three), the forging of official papers to permit others to be paid fraudulent bounties, and spying for the enemy. The executions were carried out to warn others not to break the law as well as to punish offenders. They were not only witnessed by thousands of troops, but by large crowds of local residents who streamed to the execution site after hearing about it.

As a member of Washington's personal guard, Fisher had witnessed the executions. He had also witnessed Washington's leniency to men sentenced to die, or for other crimes, carried out with high drama to achieve maximum effect. The general often approved of court-martial punishment for a group of men for a crime, but only punished one and dropped the charges against the others. He would have a group of men who had committed a crime rounded up, but only have the ringleader arrested.

His leniency concerning executions was chilling. Soldiers would spend the morning stacking bales of hay into high walls as a backdrop for a firing squad after people throughout the area were informed that an execution would take place. Large crowds would gather and then the condemned, accompanied by a chaplain reading scriptures, would be brought forth, tied up, and blindfolded. The soldier would be placed on his knees, facing the firing squad, his hands bound behind him. The troops and townspeople gathered around the firing squad would be silent. The officer in charge of the firing squad would shout "Ready . . . Aim . . ."

Suddenly, a rider would gallop up, or an officer would step out of the crowd and shout, "Halt! A pardon from His Excellency!"[3]

One of the most melodramatic pardons concerned the scheduled hanging of eight men found guilty of participating in a ring that forged discharge papers and sold them to several hundred soldiers. Gallows were constructed, coffins built and placed in front of eight freshly dug graves in front of the gallows. The hanging had been advertised on broadsides and a crowd of several thousand townspeople, in addition to a brigade of soldiers, was present for the hangings. The men were led on to the newly built wooden scaffold, the thick ropes were tightened about their necks, and they then spent a few moments listening to the prayers of a chaplain. The clergyman finished his prayers, closed his bible, and stepped back. The hangman walked to the side and put his hand on the lever to spring the trap doors beneath the soldiers, who would then have their necks broken by the rope as their bodies fell or strangled to death.

"Stop! A reprieve from His Excellency!" shouted an officer, stepping out of the front lines of the crowd just as the hangman began to move the lever forward. A shudder went through the throng that had gathered. Seven men were freed and, on Washington's orders, the eighth, the ringleader, was hanged.

The pardoned men were greatly relieved. "The trembling criminals are now divested of [the ropes] and their bleeding hearts leap for joy . . . No pen could describe the emotions which must have agitated their souls. They were scarcely able to remove from the scaffold without assistance," noted someone in the crowd.[4] Washington issued pardons at the last possible moment, he said, "to strike terror into their fellow soldiers."

It worked.

There was nothing on earth that would move him to pardon John Herring though. John Herring was not only a criminal, but he had betrayed Washington's personal trust, the worst thing any man could do. And that betrayal all started with an innocent sixteen dollar loan from Elijah Fisher.

Fisher had given the money to another member of the life guard, John Herrick, and fumed as days went by without any repayment. Finally, after more than two weeks, he returned from a one week furlough to visit his cousin to discover that Herrick was wearing a new suit of clothes. He accused him of purchasing new clothes without repaying his debt to him. Herrick told him that his parents were sending him money and he would pay Fisher when he received it. Then, a moment later, several other members of the guard walked in and they were sporting new suits. Fisher became suspicious.

"Have you had money sent from home, too? I fear that you have taken some other way to get [the clothes] than that," he said. Herrick then blurted out the truth. John Herring, entrusted by Washington to purchase necessary supplies and clothing for the commander and his aides, had attempted to buy clothing from a Tory, Mr. Prince Howland, who lived in Fishkill, New York. Howland, like many Tories, did little to help the army; he turned down the request. Herring noticed several nice suits, shirts, pants, and other pieces of clothing in the home while he was talking to the man. Late that night, Herring and several other members of the guard, Herrick, Elias Brown, and Moses Walton, blackened their faces with burnt cork and with their hats pulled down over their foreheads, broke into the Howland's house and stole dozens of pieces of clothing that they kept for themselves. They also robbed the home of another man in the same neighborhood, John Hoag, stealing hats, coats, shirts, boots, and suits, but this time also helping themselves to $400.

"Whether he be a Tory or not, if it should be found out (which such things as robbery seldom are) some or all of you will be hung," said Fisher, surprising the men with his honesty. In his diary that night, Fisher wrote that "there was no more heard about it" and that the theft, like so many, would not be punished. He was wrong.

Howland complained about the robbery of his home to a member of the life guard whom he knew, John Stockdale. When he described the hats the men wore, Stockdale instantly knew who the thieves were. He went to Herring, Herrick, Brown, and Walton and told them that they might avoid trouble if they sneaked back to the two homes at night and returned everything they had stolen. That was impossible, they said, because some of the clothing was gone. A day later, the second man who was robbed complained to a another man in the guard while the pair had a beer together at a local tavern. A waiter overhearing their conversation told the soldier that Stockdale knew something about the robbery and the soldier confronted him. Stockdale would not talk, but the soldier reminded him that he could be arrested for concealing information and protecting criminals. Stockdale then told him the entire story; the men were arrested and found guilty at a court-martial.

Washington felt betrayed. He expected all of his troops to be law-abiding and honest, but he demanded it above all from members of his own life guard. Like his aides, he considered his personal bodyguards members of his military family. The commander's vengeance was severe. He ordered Herring, Walton, and Brown to be hanged and Herrick to receive one hundred lashes. Walton and Brown managed to escape. Walton was never heard from again but a contrite Brown returned to the army and was pardoned. Herrick was flogged one hundred times and Herring was hanged at Fishkill, on November 22, 1778.

Fisher Returns to Civilian Life

On January 7, his enlistment up, snow covering the roadways and fields of much of the northeast, Elijah Fisher left the army. Needing employment, he rode south to the community of Somerville to visit John Wallace. The Philadelphia merchant's Somerville home had been used by George Washington as his headquarters the previous winter and Fisher had become friendly with the businessman and his wife, whom he referred to as "very clever folks." The Wallaces were looking for a handyman and were happy to employ the ex-soldier. Fisher worked hard for the couple and at night worked on his journal; the Wallaces apparently saw him do so. They cringed at his sloppy handwriting and improper use of punctuation. They offered to tutor him in reading and writing.

Fisher was always eager to learn new things, hopeful that improved reading and writing skills might help him find a good job when he returned home to Massachusetts. He took them up on their offer. For three hours every evening, for the entire month, the couple taught him to read and to improve his writing and penmanship. One of his exercises was to make longhand copies of books that were in the Wallaces' small library and to copy letters and other written documents to perfect his penmanship. The copying in longhand significantly improved his handwriting. He was appreciative of the assistance from educated people and they were happy to help an army veteran on his way home who had helped them with household chores.

Fisher was correct in his assumption that the tutoring in writing would help him land a good job later, but he could not have imagined then, in snow-covered and freezing Somerville, what that job would be and the amazing turn of events that would take him to it.

The former private left the Wallaces in the middle of February and headed home to Attleboro, sometimes walking and sometimes riding. He made it about one-third of the way, to Newburgh, New York, and stopped off at the army barracks there to collect eight days worth of provisions, standard issue for a returning soldier's trip home. Fisher indulged in a little bit of knavery when he arrived at the army encampment at Fishkill, a few miles away, and asked for his eight days of provisions for his trip home, the food he had already drawn at Newburgh hidden in his saddle bags. Unfortunately for him, an officer who saw him draw the original provisions at Newburgh had arrived just before him and watched him from a corner of the warehouse as he made his request.

"Didn't I see you draw your eight days of provisions in Newburgh just two days ago?" he asked the ex-private. An embarrassed Fisher, caught in his trick, tried to talk his way out of his predicament, going into a long explanation of how he had used up some of the provisions and needed more to reach Boston.

"You could get more at Hartford and Litchfield," the officer told him. "But I did not want to do that. With the provisions I am picking up here I won't have to trouble the supply depots at those towns," Fisher said.

It is unknown if his little ruse worked, but he reached home in Attleboro on March 29. He planned to live and work there and found a job with Stephen Pond, a local farmer, agreeing to work six months in exchange for sixty bushels of corn. However, within four weeks he developed a bad sore on his right hand that prevented him from working any longer.

And so, again, he reenlisted in the Continental Army—for the fourth time. Soldiering had become a source of steady income for him, as it was for many other young, unskilled laborers. As soon as Private Fisher reenlisted, he became involved in a heated argument over his pay, a dispute that was common among the soldiers.

He joined a new regiment in Attleboro, pocketing a bounty for his latest service, a six-month tour of duty, and went directly to a military court of inquiry in Boston to collect £54 British sterling in back pay that he had been owed since his departure from the service in January. It was, he speculated, the perfect day for a soldier to arrive to collect money owed him—the Fourth of July.

Many residents of Boston celebrated the holiday, but not Fisher. The board of inquiry informed him that the government owed him nothing. He had been paid £54 as a bounty for his latest enlistment and he had been owed £54—everything was now even. Fisher argued that he had not collected a £54 bounty in January.

Fisher was bitter and wrote, "If that was the way they meant to use the soldiers . . . If I had notice of it before I had engaged I never would have gone the six months. They just use soldiers. They will promise them that they will give them so and so and after they have got them to enlist they are cheated out of one-half they ought to have by one or another of the officers."

He was particularly mad at a government official whom he sneered sat "with his great wig" who said that soldiers sometimes were not owed what they believed. He added that those owed money would get it, but that these things took time. "You are wrong for accusing me and talking as you do," he scolded Fisher, who was not satisfied with his answer and angrily continued to demand his money.

Such disagreements occurred often. Throughout the war, pay and bounties remained hotly contested issues among the enlisted men. They were rarely paid on time; some had no salary for five or six months. An enlisted man's pay was just $6.70 a month at the start of the war, $7.30 for musicians, and it only increased for both to about $13 per month by its conclusion. Soldiers could buy little on pay that could not keep up with runaway inflation. Americans grumbled, too, that the British enlisted men were paid twice their salaries and could buy what they needed at moderate prices, in English pound sterling, through the British army commissaries, sutlers, and supply depots.

American enlisted men collected bounties from the federal government, states, counties, and even towns to join the Continental Army and the state militia. The state bounty was often higher than money offered by the Continental Congress. Those who had accepted the lower federal amount protested that they should have been awarded the state figure. Some were angry because they may have collected a $20 bounty when they enlisted for three years but later, as the state became desperate for recruits, other soldiers from that same state collected bounties that were four times as high (in 1777 the Continental Army offered a $20 bounty and the Massachusetts militia paid $86).

Bounties later soared to $250 and more (with inflation). These later recruits were also often given a clothing bounty (uniform and blanket) and, later, some land. The American paper money they received usually proved worthless as inflation ravaged the United States. States also awarded bounties based on inflation, so $86 bounties worked out to $25, but could be worth less if U.S. money depreciated even further that year. The soldiers often believed they were fighting for no compensation and felt shortchanged whenever they were involved in financial dealings with the government—just like Fisher.

The four-time enlistee from Attleboro received help from an unexpected quarter that day. A black-haired man named Coffern, either a government worker or bystander, overheard the argument at the government office. He stepped forward and told the government official, "The soldiers have been used very ill as this man said, and they are cheated out of a good deal that they ought to have."

Coffern turned to Fisher and acted as an intermediary, holding neither side responsible but offering a solution. "Your selectmen [may have] used you ill in respect of sending in the account of the bounty you have received. It may be that there is a mistake and if you get them to certify what bounty you have received you shall have your [money] made up accordingly."

The representative of the Board of Inquiry said that would be satisfactory. A few days later, Fisher traveled back to Attleboro. Officials in the war recruitment office there checked the records in their books, looked for Fisher's name, written in thick ink, and found the mistake. The £54 bounty was awarded Fisher in 1777, not 1780. They certified that he was, indeed, entitled to £54 in back pay. Fisher was happy as he began the march to his regiment's destination, West Point, and a rendezvous with General Benedict Arnold.

It was an eventful trip. The pain in Fisher's side flared up again, once again sending him to a hospital set up in someone's residence. This time the local physician treating the troops diagnosed his problem as pleurisy, not kidney failure, and kept him bedridden for a week. Fisher discovered that the man and woman who lived in the home where he was told to recover were Catholics. He learned that they had a family catechism among the other books on their shelves and asked to borrow it. He then spent hours each day slowly copying pages from the catechism in longhand, just to practice his penmanship.

He was ordered from the hospital with ten other soldiers as the army abandoned camp and moved out. Other soldiers told him that his stay in the hospital might have saved his life. The regiment, on the eastern side of the Hudson, had to cross the river on barges to reach West Point. The crossing of the river had gone very badly. One of the larger barges overturned in the middle of the river and five yoke of oxen and five men drowned in the accident. Fisher, they said, might have drowned, too. It brought back memories of nearly drowning in the Schuylkill during the Valley Forge winter.

Just before Elijah Fisher's latest enlistment ran out at the end of 1780, a Sergeant Whippel, who was in charge of clothing and supplies for the company, offered a proposition to Fisher, whom he knew practiced reading and writing often. Whippel was eager to return home for a month but had no one to replace him in the supply office. If Fisher agreed to stay one month past his enlistment to fill in for him, Whippel would not only give him lessons on reading, writing, and penmanship, but show him how to write in cipher, or code, and unravel codes in the letters of others.

Fisher kept his end of the deal and took over for Whippel, who left for home on December 4, 1780. However, with someone running his office, Whippel did not keep his end of the bargain. He lingered at home well past the end of the year. One sergeant and one lieutenant in the office were out recruiting and one lieutenant was home on furlough. That left Fisher as the only worker in the busy office. "I had to take care of the whole company and all the returns to sign and clothing to get and state stores and the like," Fisher complained in his journal on February 8.

March arrived and still no sign of Whippel. Fisher told a lieutenant that he believed Whippel would never return and "I would have to spend the whole war in his room." The lieutenant, who must have wondered about the missing Whippel too, told Fisher not to worry, that the sergeant would be back any day.

March turned into April and Fisher continued to complain. Finally, on April 6, four months after he left camp, Sergeant Whippel came back—to Fisher's delight. Fisher was immediately discharged and, to make up his three months of added service, he was promoted to sergeant on his very last day in the army.

On April 23, 1781, Sergeant Elijah Fisher returned home to Attleboro. He began working for a Doctor Johnson in Newton, Massachusetts, for $9 a month on a six-month contract; a sum, he noted with irony, that matched his 1777 bonus of $54 for joining the army. Fisher, now twenty-three years old, put his uniform in a trunk and prepared for civilian life. He had enlisted for four different tours of duty, served nearly six years in the army, had participated in the siege of Boston, survived the winter at Valley Forge, fought at Bunker Hill, Saratoga, and Monmouth, and, he reminded many, was a personal bodyguard for George Washington.

Fisher was certain on May 5, 1781, his first day of employment with Dr. Johnson, that for him the war was finally over. He was wrong.

Chapter Twenty-Two

MONMOUTH, 1778:
Captain Sylvanus Seely's Militia Goes to War

"The whole of the New Jersey militia are cautioned to be ready to march at beat of drum with four or five day's provisions and should the alarm be reasonably given. I think we could turn out men sufficient in the state before General Howe could half perform his route, to make him wish himself back [home] again."
—M. Halstead to Captain Sylvanus Seely

The note was sent in late December 1777 to Seely, head of the five-hundred-man Morris County unit of the New Jersey state militia that protected the northeastern section of the state. It was one of the best organized militia units in the country and had been since the conflict began. Seely was its capable commander.

Seely and the Morris County men were a far cry from the ramshackle militias that sprang up in the early days of the war. The militia units established by the states that supplemented the Continental Army were vital to the success of the Revolution, but most had not performed well. The militia members were drafted by their states to serve short terms of three to eight months; regular Continental soldiers volunteered for terms of one to three years.

Washington needed the militia for several reasons. First and fore-most, he wanted them to join the undermanned army whenever it traveled in spring and summer to fight against the British. The militia was responsible for protecting army supply and munitions warehouses throughout the country and guarding prisoners. Its members often found themselves in small skirmishes with British troops passing through their counties, particularly when British food foraging parties were sent to buy or steal cattle or corn for their vast army. Militiamen also served as guards at roadways and bridges near winter and summer camps and built and repaired wooden beacon towers that were set on fire to warn the army if a British force was on the march.

Regular army troops, generals, and the delegates to Congress often jeered the militias. Militia units from different states were highly criti-cized because at critical junctures in the Revolution they broke and ran in battles and frequently left the service, en masse, when their enlistments were up or simply deserted. Militia would even depart just before a bat-tle, leaving the regular army weakened, because that morning was the last day of their enrollment. Over eight thousand militia participated in the battles in and around New York in 1776, but a week later only two thou-sand remained. In the early days of the war, the militia could not be relied upon to fight well and were poorly armed. The Americans had to retreat from White Plains when New England militia companies ran as the British approached.

They infuriated Washington. "To place any dependence upon mili-tia is, assuredly, resting upon a broken staff," he complained to Congress, and believed that it was difficult to train men accustomed to "unbounded freedom." He was harsher on militia leaders, whose amateurism startled him when he first met them during the siege of Boston. "Their officers are generally of the lowest class of people and, instead of setting a good example to their men, are leading them into every kind of mischief," he said, and throughout the war charged that militia commanders were more interested in promotions than victories.[1]

However, they had also helped the army at key moments of the war. They provided several thousand extra troops for major engagements and often meant the difference between victory and defeat, such as at Bennington, Vermont, where militia led by General John Stark turned back part of Burgoyne's army. It was Ethan Allen's militia that captured Fort Ticonderoga in 1775.

The Morris County division of New Jersey's state militia had already been together for several years when the war commenced and by the time Seely began keeping his wartime diary in May 1778, the Morris militia had shown themselves to be well organized and dependable. They would soon find themselves the critical unit at two of the major battles of the war, Monmouth and Springfield.

Sylvanus Seely was a logical choice for captain of the Morris militia. County officials needed someone with military experience and he was one of the few men in New Jersey who had fought in the French and Indian War. Seely was thirty-five when the Revolution began and had moved to Chatham from Pennsylvania. He ran a small inn, with a general store and tavern (stocked with French brandy and West India rum). The inn was located at the intersection of the two highways that ran through Chatham (today Main Street and Fairmount Avenue). The captain and his family lived in the inn; Seely married Jane Williamson, a local girl. Their first child, John, was born on January 27, 1772. Jane gave birth to Eleanor in 1774. Three more children, Sophia, Elizabeth, and George, were born during the war.[2]

In 1776, Chatham was a small village twenty miles west of New York. The main highway from New York to Chester that then took travelers to Philadelphia ran through Chatham and the Passaic River bisected it. The village could boast of thirty-nine buildings that included a sawmill, a forge, a gristmill, and two taverns. The population consisted of about two hundred forty people, including several slaves. Most of the residents were Presbyterians who worshipped at a church in Bottle Hill (Madison) or traveled to Hanover to another Presbyterian church to hear the fiery patriotic minister, Rev. Jacob Green. Three doctors lived in town. The village children attended school in nearby Morristown.

Chatham was a patriotic community in a patriotic county. Half the men in the village served in the war. Most of them were young; their average age was eighteen. Dr. Peter Smith, twenty-seven, left his practice to become an army doctor just nine months after the war began.[3] Many of the younger boys, from nine to fourteen, formed a mock children's militia. They played soldier, battling each other in nearby fields with wooden guns.

Chatham served as part of the Continental Army's winter camp in 1776–1777. The town let soldiers live in the homes of its residents and in tents in nearby fields. The army brought problems, however. The hundreds of soldiers billeted in the village drained all of the area's food and at times starved when local farmers ran out of it and the army commissary could not find any more to send them. The food crisis there in the winter of 1776–1777 was so bad that Washington mentioned the town in a heated letter he sent to the commissary demanding more food. "The cry of provisions comes to me from every quarter. General Maxwell writes word that his people are starving . . . people could draw none [food]; this difficulty I understand prevails also at Chatham."

The town was hit hard by the smallpox epidemic of 1777 that began in nearby Morristown. Washington took the unprecedented step of inoculating his entire army without the traditional rest and diet formula used all over the world, and offered inoculations for civilians in the area. Some residents were inoculated; some were not. Dozens who did not obtain the inoculation in Chatham died, including young children and a local minister.

Chatham gave the Revolution its young men, one of its doctors, much of its food and supplies, and its townspeople died in the smallpox epidemic. Its citizens, including Captain Seely of its militia, had pledged everything to the cause. The townspeople were so staunchly on the side of the rebellion that people who were on their deathbeds made out patriotic wills, such as Eunice Horton, who in her last days, in 1778, wrote a will that was dated with great pride, "This first day of August, in the year of American Independence."[4]

It was a pretty town. Thousands of acres of fertile land surrounded the farming community where residents grew a variety of crops, such as corn. Dozens of large cherry and apple orchards dotted the countryside. The village lay amid thick forests of hickory, oak, and butternut trees. Chatham was also close enough to larger towns, such as Morristown, Newark, Elizabethtown, and New York to provide business for its merchants. A local farmer praised the community in a newspaper ad, writing that his farm, for sale, was "pleasantly situated in a village of great resort, and excellent situation for business . . . [my] farm is an excellent one for a grazier, is well watered, has thereon a large barn and sheds for cattle and a pretty spot on which a dwelling house might be built . . . a fine prospect."[5]

Seely erected a Liberty Pole in front of his inn and hosted a large crowd there to celebrate the news of the signing of the Declaration of Independence in July 1776. For Seely, the Revolution was not just a celebration; he was eager to fight. Seely applied for a commission in the Continental Army when the war began and was so intent on obtaining one that he had several influential members of the community sign a petition recommending him. It read, "He is an honest man firmly attached to the liberties of his country."[6] He was not given a commission in the regular army, so he won himself the job of captain in the Morris County militia. His ability as a recruiter, administrator, and a superb marksmen who could train others to shoot well earned him a promotion to colonel in just three months.

In the summer of 1776 he took the militia to New York, where they joined George Washington's army in what turned out to be a series of debilitating defeats. Seely and the militia left New York with the army when it fled across New Jersey toward Pennsylvania that fall. They broke off from the main force and went home to Chatham when the army reached New Brunswick and their period of service was up.

The head of any militia company or regiment during the Revolution led a dual life, military and personal. Seely, for example, was required to

live with the militia when it was ordered into service by the governor to
serve with the Continental Army, usually for a period of only a few
months. On duty out of the county, but still in New Jersey, the Morris
militia lived in the army camp.

The militia resided in their own homes when the militia remained in
service to protect northern New Jersey, which was usually the case. Seely's
function changed during those in-county periods. He lived at his residence but spent several days each week working on militia business. He
recruited new men, visited troops stationed at lookout posts, conducted
all militia administrative business, and procured clothing, food, and
munitions for his men. He was also responsible for obtaining clothing
and food for New Jersey prisoners housed on the notorious British prison
ships in nearby New York harbor. Seely was in charge of all repairs to
army fortifications in the area and in 1779 worked feverishly to repair a
series of tall, wooden, pyramid-like towers, filled with dry brush, built to
be lit and serve as beacons to warn the army at Morristown that the
British had invaded the area. As the captain and then colonel, he sent
troops off on assignment out of the county while he returned home.

He worked as a liaison between the army and local courts on crimes
involving soldiers and frequently dined with judges. He was named to a
joint committee that settled civil disputes between the soldiers and local
residents. These disagreements often involved unpaid loans and goods or
tools that were borrowed but not returned or damages to property. From
time to time, he served as one of the judges on a court-martial board. As
the local militia head, he was sometimes asked to suggest honest merchants with whom the army could do business. He also knew from army
sources when certain military goods would be auctioned off to raise extra
revenue for the army. He went to the auctions, hunting for bargains. Sometimes he brought friends, such as Shepard Kollock, who at Washington's
behest would become a newspaper publisher.[7]

At the same time that they tended to army affairs, militia leaders ran
their own businesses or farms; in Seely's case, his inn. Seely spent just as
much time on his personal business as he did on the militia when it was
stationed in-county. He traveled by horseback, a horse-drawn, two-seat

riding chair, or wagon to cities such as Elizabethtown, New Brunswick, or Philadelphia to buy rum, brandy, sugar, cheese, clothing, and other goods for resale at the store in his inn.

These trips were often major undertakings. He would buy several one-hundred-pound barrels of sugar or pepper or some other commodity and transport them more than ninety miles to his home in sturdy wagons. On one trip he purchased ninety-seven gallons of rum and twenty-nine gallons of brandy. Distant trips required him to stay over at an inn somewhere; his trips were often lengthened when ferry service was interrupted by turbulent rivers or ferries under repair. Ferries rarely ran when rains raised rivers, making the passage too dangerous; passengers had to find lodging for a night or two until the river subsided.

Sometimes, despite his best efforts, his business failed. Christmas 1778 was a fine example of how the life of any businessman was dramatically affected by the events of the war and the vicissitudes of the weather. His problems that holiday began on Tuesday, December 22, when he was tied up all day sitting as a judge on the local court of appeals. The next day he was informed that a large load of salt that he had purchased and planned to sell to a Chatham man for $33 had been left in a valley several miles away. He had just sold a second load of salt to Major Sears for the army's use. He spent all of that day and the next, Christmas eve, investigating the missing salt and learned that his friend Jacob Minthorn had forgotten to pick up the salt. Determined to have the salt delivered and to earn the $33, Seely rose early on Christmas Day and spent more time working on the case of the missing salt. He was apparently unable to find anyone to retrieve the load on the holiday and gave up shortly after noon.

Nothing would be done about it for a few days, either, because as Major Sears, Seely, and his wife dined with their friends it began to snow—hard. The snowstorm continued all night and throughout the next day. "Froze me ears," Seely noted.

The weather remained cold. Enough snow fell on Christmas Day and the following day to make the roads impassable. Seely wrote angrily, "Snowed so hard that the teams cannot go with the salt and all hopes of the sale is over."

Seely was a careful businessman, weighing each barrel when he brought it home. He spent much time managing the inn and took care of the needs of the boarders who lived there and locals who drank at his tavern. He had a nineteen-acre farm behind the inn. He and his slave, Prince, tended gardens there and grew crops for sale, along with hay that he sold to local residents for their horses. He collected apples from trees in an orchard and brought them to a local mill where they were turned into barrels of apple cider he would sell at the tavern and store. He rode to the farms of neighbors to buy other fruits, such as peaches, that he sold in his store.

He was a valued member of the Chatham community and was often called upon to serve on juries in civil and criminal matters. He and his wife attended Sunday church services together, visited friends for dinner parties, and drove in his riding chair to the farms of neighbors to pick fruit for their own enjoyment. He often won jugs of cider or money at the shooting matches that were a popular form of local entertainment at the time and attended by many.[8]

It was his work as head of the militia, though, that was critical to the war effort. His diary does not describe his relationship with George Washington, but they must have met from time to time during the two winters that the army spent in nearby Morristown, New Jersey, or during the winter of 1778–1779, when it was fifteen miles south in Bound Brook. He also had a friendly relationship with William Livingston, the fiery governor of New Jersey, with whom he had dinner several times during the Revolution.

The Battle of Monmouth

Seely and the militia were called on to fight in the summer of 1778. On June 21, Seely was ordered to send the five-hundred-man militia fifty miles southward, toward Mount Holly. The unit was to meet up with Washington's force that had left Valley Forge on June 19 and was trying to intercept Sir Henry Clinton's main army. The British had occupied Philadelphia during the winter and decided to return to New York, leaving the Pennsylvania city on June 18. Spies had informed Washington of their route and the commander in chief hoped to engage them, and defeat them, somewhere in Monmouth County.

Washington was full of optimism as he learned that the New Jersey state regiments were headed toward Monmouth. The ranks of the newly trained and resuscitated American army had swollen with new militia units and thousands of new recruits. The army had more cannon than at any time during the revolution. An exchange of prisoners had brought the return of General Charles Lee, whom Washington made his second in command and put in charge of the Monmouth attack. Washington's total force consisted of about 12,600 men, as large as the British army. He was convinced that he could end the war when he intersected Clinton on the highway that meandered through central New Jersey's farmland. He wrote to Robert Morris, "I rejoice most sincerely with you on the glorious change in our prospects . . . The game, whether well or ill, played hitherto, seems now to be verging fast to a favorable issue."[9]

On June 27, British troops were near the tiny village of Monmouth Court House (now Freehold, New Jersey). Rumors that a fight was imminent spread through all the regiments. As night fell, a Rhode Island officer assembled his men to address the rumors. He was blunt. "You have been wishing for some days past to come up with the British," he told them. "You have been wanting to fight. Now you shall have fighting enough!"[10]

The next day, the temperature soared into the high nineties, and the fields seemed like "a heated oven," according to Pvt. Joseph Martin, who added that it was "almost impossible to breathe."[11] Seely had orders "to attack the enemy" that morning and he did, leading his men in an advance against Clinton's rear guard and pushing them back across a wide meadow toward the courthouse. He intended to make certain that the Redcoats in front of him were unable to help flank General Lee's main force. "We drove them back and they formed in a line across the plain from the courthouse."

The Morris militia drove the British back even farther in another sustained attack, overseen by Colonel Seely, and the Redcoats retreated at 8:30 a.m. when it was already sweltering and Seely's men sweated under their shirts and breeches. They did not sweat as profusely as the Redcoats, though, because Washington, realizing how much the heat would affect his men, ordered them to remove their coats before the battle.

Just after 10 a.m., General Lee arrived with some four thousand men. He spent some time studying the area and then ordered the Morris militia to join him in an advance that failed badly. Lee's orders were confusing and contradictory. One advancing regiment would pass another that he had ordered to retreat. One command superseded another. Despite an order to devise one, Lee arrived without a general plan of battle and was unable to mount an orderly assault. Sensing that something was wrong, the British then attacked just before noon. Lee did not know what to do. Confusion reigned on the fields around the courthouse and the Americans, including Seely and his militia, were forced to retreat back toward a white clapboard meeting house, where they stopped.

Washington, with the rest of the army, seven thousand men, arrived just after noon to find the army in retreat as Clinton's army attacked across the field. The commander, sensing disaster, rode to find Lee. He shouted at Lee in scathing language that his soldiers had never heard him use during the first three years of the war and relieved him of command. He later had him arrested. A threatened court of enquiry forced Lee to resign.

Washington sat astride a handsome white horse given to him as a gift by Governor Livingston and then took command himself. He called for an officer from the area, Lt. Col. David Rhea of the Fourth New Jersey, and asked him for a quick description of the terrain. Rhea told him that a slight ridge that overlooked open fields was bordered by a swamp that would prevent a flanking movement by the enemy. He noted, too, that the woods at the top of the ridge could protect reserve troops. A nearby knoll with a relatively flat top with an unobstructed view of the meadow and a nearby orchard, he said, would be a good place for artillery placement.

As Rhea spoke to the commander, British shells exploded around them. Washington noticed, gazing across the meadows, that although his army had retreated, it had done so in great order. No one had panicked. Washington listened to Rhea, looked, nodded, and decided within minutes to do what Rhea suggested, with modifications. He then ordered the army to take up the new positions.[12] Officers and men at Monmouth marveled at Washington's calmness amid the fury of the battle and his ability to make quick decisions and issue crisp and clear orders that not only halted the retreat, but renewed the spirit of the American troops.

Seely then reported a sight that invigorated all of the Americans that morning. George Washington, on his white horse, rode back and forth in front of the American lines to yell out orders and rally the troops, an easy target for British guns.[13] Wrote Lafayette of Washington's bravery, "Never had I beheld so superb a man. [He] rode along the lines, amid the shouts of the soldiers, cheering them by his voice and example and restoring to our standard the fortunes of the fight."[14]

Washington placed Anthony Wayne's regiments, with some two thousand men, just arrived, on a second line of defense farther back up the slope and repositioned the first cannon that he could find on the knoll Rhea had designated. Regiments were stationed along the edges of woods to the right and left of the main force to prevent any flanking movements by the British.

Seely noted that what followed was "a great severe action in which the enemy lost several officers of distinction and left about two hundred men dead on the grounds. Numbers died on both sides." On the other side of the battlefield, Sergeant Ebenezer Wild of the First Massachusetts had been marching with brigades under the Marquis de Lafayette for several days. Washington had at first put Lafayette in charge of the attack, but later changed his mind because he felt that Lafayette's troops were not in the proper position and because the obstinate Lee insisted on being given that job as second in command.

Wild, who always spelled Lafayette's name as "Markis Delefiat," had been drenched in the thunderstorm that broke over the region two nights earlier. Lafayette's brigades slept in the field each night as they moved closer to intercepting the British, with no protection from the elements. Wild wrote, "We took our lodgings in the road, without anything to cover us, or anything to lodge on but the wet ground and we in a very wet condition."

The First Massachusetts marched five more miles the next day, June 27, that Wild said was "excessively hot," and then, on June 28, reached Monmouth Court House just before 2 p.m. He had arrived at the opposite side of the battlefield from Seely and his militia. The Massachusetts men found the fighting severe as soon as they tried to hold a position on top of the slope where Washington had repositioned his army. Wild wrote, "Our division formed a line on an eminence about a half a mile in the front of the enemy and our artillery in our front. A very smart cannonading ensued from both sides."

The Massachusetts men had marched into the middle of the fury and were unable to make much movement. Shells exploded all around them in what one newspaper called "the severest cannonade [that] ever happened in America."[15] Wild wrote, "We stayed here till several of our officers and men were killed and wounded. Seeing that it was of no service to stand here, we went back a little ways into the woods; but the cannonading still continued very smart on both sides for about two hours."

Arriving earlier with Lee was the Second Rhode Island, with Private Jeremiah Greenman. The Rhode Islander, like everyone at Monmouth, complained of the heat, which he described as "hot and sultry." The pullback ordered by Lee that morning was seen from many perspectives. The soldier's view was that of a soldier facing the brunt of the English force directly in front of him. Greenman and his comrades were awed by the size of the British army. He wrote, "They formed in a solid column then fired a volley at us. They being so much superior to our numbers, we retreated. They began a very heavy cannonading and killed a few of our regiment."

The men, scrambling back and away from the lines of Redcoats, found some protection behind a wooden fence, where they made another stand. He noted, "Light horse advanced against us. We fired very heavy. Then the footmen rushed on us." Greenman and his men continued to fight as General Lee panicked. The Second Rhode Island seemed pinned down. "After firing a number of rounds, we was obliged to retreat," Greenman wrote.

Greenman noted with alarm that many of the men running from the British on that unbearably hot day simply collapsed on the field and died of heatstroke. The entire battlefield was covered with men who died from the heat on both sides. "Left the ground with about a thousand killed and wounded, on our side about two hundred killed and wounded and died with heat."

It was during that retreat that Private Greenman's men were turned around by George Washington and ordered to attack the oncoming waves of the enemy. They did. This time they had assistance from sixteen American cannon opening up on each side of them. Amid the bursting shells and the volleys of musket balls in the warm air, Jeremiah Greenman was shot in the thigh and went down.

The American lines held against the constant bombardment of British cannon. Their fire was eventually muted by the return fire of the line of American cannon. The American batteries were not destroyed by the British howitzers, as planned, because the shells continually landed short of their marks. The American infantrymen held off a succession of British charges, large and small, that afternoon. Colonel Stephen Olney's regiment had lost several men during the retreat, but they stopped and formed a solid line when they heard the American cannon erupt behind them and someone arrived, shouting encouragement to them. Olney wrote, "At this instant our main army came up, commanded by Washington himself, and commenced a heavy fire with our artillery and the British found they had got a fresh army to contend with."[16]

The charge that Washington ordered late in the day pushed the British back. The Americans were proud of their work. "Drove the proud King's Guards and haughty British Grenadiers and gained immortal honor," wrote Major Joseph Bloomfield of his men in the Third New Jersey.[17]

The Americans fought with all the appearances of a fine European army as they were trained to do so at Valley Forge by von Steuben. Late in the afternoon, Britain's General Clinton launched a classic flanking movement, but following their Valley Forge training in maneuvering, the American line swung over to stop it and halted the Redcoats in their tracks. That force, led by Anthony Wayne, remained exceedingly cool under the heavy British advance that began just five hundred feet away. Wayne and the officers had the men hold their fire until the last possible moment; then they opened up with a thunderous volley that stopped the attack. The Continentals began to chase the British. A group of Redcoats, pinned down in an orchard, were driven back by Americans and then shredded by Continental cannon as they tried to flee. The army had become, just as Washington had dreamed, a professional force capable of holding its own against, and even defeating, any army in the world.[18]

The intensity of the battle that day was best described by Washington himself in a letter to Congress. He wrote of the British that "they were bravely repulsed and driven back by detached parties of infantry . . . General Wayne advanced with a body of troops and kept up so severe and well directed a fire that the enemy were soon compelled to retire."

The general had nothing but admiration for the regular army and the several New Jersey militia units that had joined it. He declared, "The behavior of the troops in general, after they recovered from the first surprise occasioned by the retreat of the advanced corps, was such as could not be surpassed."[19]

The Americans held the battlefield all night and awoke the next morning to find the British camp vacant. Clinton had had enough of the combined regular army and militia forces; he had departed and headed north, for New York, his original goal. Technically, the battle was a draw, but the Americans claimed victory because they had held the field. American losses were 356 killed and wounded; the British lost 358. More than sixty soldiers on each side died of heat stroke. Monmouth was a military success and a public relations coup for the American army and gave the rebellion new spirit.[20]

That spirit was muted for Sylvanus Seely and his militia company, though, because on the following day, another brutally hot one, he and his men were given one of the grim details of the war; they were told to bury the dead at Monmouth. There were so many dead Americans on the field near the courthouse that it took all day to dig their graves.

Chapter Twenty-Three

THE SECRET LIFE OF CAPTAIN SEELY

Seely was under stress throughout the rest of 1778 and in the early days of 1779. He was trying to buy and sell goods for his store, keep the army supplied, run his militia company, and, at the same time, care for his wife Jane, who was nine months pregnant at Christmas and expecting her child any day. The baby finally arrived two weeks later, on January 11, 1779. Betsy Seely's birth was a very difficult one, however, and Jane was bedridden and sick for weeks.

The militia leader, knowing how poorly she felt, had to leave for Philadelphia for three days shortly after the birth of his daughter to buy things for his store. "Left my wife very sick," he wrote in his diary. He was pleased, though, to discover that she was "mending" when he came home. Jane, or "Jenny," as he called her, was ill for the rest of the month and much of February. Seely did what he could to comfort her and in early February persuaded one of his relatives, a woman, to help him nurse his wife.

The weather improved in mid February 1779, which pleased Seely. He wrote, "We have had so warm a spell that the maple trees are in season and the elm buds are swollen and sundry other buds and the grass begins to start."

The British were pleased with the mild weather, too, because they planned to sneak out of New York and raid Elizabethtown where they would kidnap Governor Livingston as he dined with friends there. The surprise attack came on February 25. The Americans were overwhelmed by the British, who burned the army barracks in that community, along with several residential homes. The governor was having dinner with some military officers and Seely. They were startled, but all managed to escape. David Little, a local freeholder, was not so fortunate. He was seized along with twenty other residents in another part of town.

It was one of a number of attempts by the British to kidnap high-ranking political and military officials. Some succeeded and some did not. They had captured Charles Lee in 1776 and held him for nearly a year and a half. Later, they would arrest Henry Laurens, one of the presidents of the Continental Congress, when they found him on an ocean-going vessel that they seized. The grand prize in these schemes was George Washington and one year later they would stage a raid deep into New Jersey, and into Seely's backyard, in a bold attempt to capture the commander in chief.

Seely was also an eyewitness to another kind of history that winter. His close friend and Chatham neighbor, Shepard Kollock, had been talked into publishing his own newspaper by George Washington and Henry Knox. New Jersey had only one newspaper, the *New Jersey Gazette*, funded by the state legislature and published in Burlington, in the southern half of New Jersey and far from the population centers in the northern half. Washington wanted a newspaper that would be pro-army, a journal that was independent and respected, but one that he knew would praise the army and the country. Kollock, a lieutenant, was the nephew of William Goddard, one of America's most respected editors. Kollock had edited a small newspaper in the West Indies and had recently worked on the newspaper in Burlington. Kollock was also eager to leave the army.

Washington and Henry Knox met with the lieutenant and proposed that he become the editor of a new paper, the *Jersey Journal,* that would be subsidized by the army. He would keep any profits he made from advertising and circulation and the paper would be his when the war ended. He had to promise to promote the interests of the army in its columns.

Washington would also provide him with all the editorial material he needed, including copies of his letters to Congress and his orders, sermons by ministers that the general knew, and political columns and copies of bills in the New Jersey legislature provided by the commander's close friend, New Jersey governor William Livingston.

The army would also provide couriers to deliver the newspaper not only in the Chatham–Morristown area, and to the army camp there, but to other army camps and to towns in New Jersey and New York not occupied by the British. Kollock would also receive an immediate honorable discharge from the army so that he could run the paper as a civilian, permitting him to return to his wife, who lived near Chatham, right away.

Kollock, a tall, large-framed man with shaggy eyebrows, a large nose, and grey eyes, agreed to the arrangement, one that would give him a career after the end of the war. Seely was there in Day's Tavern, Chatham, when Kollock published his first issue and admired it along with his assistant, John Woods, and two young apprentices, Shelly Arnett and Matthias Day.[1]

There was something in Chatham that Seely admired more, though, and that was the lovely Mrs. Stephen Ball.

By the spring of 1778, an affair had been going on for some time between Colonel Seely and the attractive Mrs. Ball, the wife of his friend Doctor Ball. It is unknown how it started or how quickly it caught fire, but the two had deep feelings for each other. The relationship between two friends, in a small town where everyone seemed to know everyone else's business, was dangerous, but the pair seemed to have carried it off without the local gossips finding out. Seely and Mrs. Ball usually rendezvoused in an apple orchard on the outskirts of Chatham; they arranged the meetings during the day in brief conversations with each other. The large apple orchards of the surrounding area, thick with trees in spring and summer, offered the privacy they needed.

Seely was smitten with her and referred to her as his "charmer" and "my jewel" in the cipher code in his diary. She was equally taken by him. They had known each other as friends for over six years since Seely had moved to Chatham. They saw each other in church, at stores in the village, and at dinner parties at the homes of mutual friends. Seely often walked past her residence in the village; the two passed each other constantly when on horseback. Mrs. Ball was friendly with Jane Seely and the women visited each other at their homes.

Little has been written about sex in the colonial era. There have been some works on the large percentages of women who became pregnant and then married, but the married men and women of the era were careful not to write down anything about the sexual liaisons outside of the marriage bed. There were surely a number of extramarital trysts then, just as there are today, and unhappy people sought new partners outside the home. There were few divorces because people had large families and tended to stay together for the sake of their children. Churches also frowned on divorce. There were some and they were messy. Husbands sometimes took out ads in newspapers to announce the split and to remind all that they would not pay any of their spouses' bills. Most unhappy men remained married and some, such as Seely, chased other women.

Seely fancied himself a smooth womanizer, but he was putty in Mrs. Ball's lovely hands. She sent him notes arranging meetings in the orchard and would not show up, leaving him standing alone, seething. She would agree to meet and then break the engagement at the last moment. She would hold what he termed "sweet" conversations with him at her home but then act coldly later in the evening when they met. Then, without warning, she would thaw out and shower him with affections in the apple orchard. The extent of the liaison was never spelled out in Seely's diary, but on at least one occasion he said that she came "to his bed," so it was sexual as well as romantic.

What Jane Seely knew about the affair was never known and throughout the Revolution, as the extramarital relationship continued, she never accused her husband of a liaison. But she knew something was going on. Mrs. Ball and Seely had several meetings in the orchard in July 1778. On August 3, Mrs. Ball visited Jane Seely, unannounced, for another casual visit between friends, but Mrs. Seely was cold and aloof toward her. A nervous Seely, at home when she arrived, scribbled in his diary that his wife "acted imprudently" toward his girlfriend. Mrs. Ball then fretted Jane Seely knew something and cancelled their next meeting in the orchard.

Seely continued his relationship with the doctor's wife, but it was always an uncertain love. She would meet with him but argue about something. At their next meeting they would "share sweet kisses," as he put it. Then she would not show up while he waited on cold nights in the orchard. His nighttime disappearances did not go unnoticed by his wife and throughout the entire fall of 1778, Seely wrote in his secret journal, Jane Seely was cold toward her husband.

In February 1779, following yet another snowstorm, Seely and his lover ended one of their evenings with a horrific argument over something and Seely was shaken. "Had great difference with the delight of my soul, so great that I believe it will never be made up. Oh, my heart. How shall I bear it?" he wrote in his diary.

Then, just four days later, the pair made up.

In the middle of this extramarital jousting, which Seely admitted made him "miserable," his wife Jane appeared to have lived through a bout with breast cancer. She had been to a doctor who prescribed a mixture of roots and herbs, popular at the time, to treat some abnormality in her breasts. A distraught Seely went with his brother Sam to his friend Thomas Gardner's home to obtain some roots to pound into a mixture to treat her breast ailment.

Jane recovered. She resumed her work as a midwife and continued to accompany her husband to dinner parties, church, and receptions. They visited friends and relatives and kept up a public facade of a happy marriage. There was always a chill in the union, though, as the militia leader kept meeting Mrs. Ball. The affair would not continue much longer, however, because Mrs. Ball became more interested in another man.

March and April featured warm days and other days when the temperature fell well below freezing and snowfalls of up to several inches were recorded. On April 18, 1779, Seely wrote in his diary that "it froze so hard as to kill the leave and the ice is half an inch thick." The wild weather also brought diphtheria, whooping cough, typhoid and scarlet fever, and tuberculosis to Chatham and other towns in northern New Jersey.

The rough weather foreshadowed one of the worst winters of American history later that year, a winter that would threaten to destroy the army and end the Revolution.

Chapter Twenty-Four

SPRING 1778:
The African American Soldiers

The War

*T*he victory at Monmouth was the only major engagement in the summer of 1778. Following the battle, the British continued on to New York, fearful that the city might be attacked by the French fleet that had sailed for America. The French admiral claimed that he could not maneuver properly in New York harbor and did not assault the city. Washington set up his summer camp in White Plains, north of New York, to monitor British movements in the area.

Revolutionary activity took place in the west that spring when George Rogers Clark gained authorization from Virginia governor Patrick Henry to lead an expedition west to attack British forces and their Indian allies in the territories of Ohio and Illinois. He captured Kaskaskia, in Illinois, without resistance and then convinced the French settlers at Vincennes to side with the Americans. The British governor of the territory gathered a force of regulars and Indians from headquarters in Detroit and took back Vincennes in

December 1778. The governor sent his Indians home a few weeks later and in February 1779, Clark returned and captured the fort for a second time following a short siege.

One of the Continental Army's continuing problems in the winter and spring of 1778 was the loss of men. Measures taken by George Washington to curb desertions following the large exodus of troops the year before had cut down the number of deserters, but they were still a problem. Officers continued to have difficulty convincing others to reenlist when their time was up. Recruiting new troops always proved difficult and doing so became even harder following the terrible winter at Valley Forge and the recent smallpox epidemic.

One of the answers to the problem was the recruitment of African Americans, both freedmen and slaves. Freedmen would earn salaries and receive cash or land bounties, like white recruits, but slaves would be given something more valuable—their freedom. Any slave who served a full term, ranging from one to three years, would be freed when he left the army; they would also be paid. There were a half million slaves in the southern colonies in 1776, but there were also sixty thousand in the north. They worked for farmers, city merchants, shipping companies and as domestics. Some states, such as New York, had as many as twenty-one thousand slaves.

Black American soldiers were not new; a few had fought for the colonial militias that served with the British army during the French and Indian War from 1756–1763. Prior to the war, and during its early days, several blacks had fought for local state militias. Washington was hopeful that freedom would be a powerful incentive to persuade African Americans to enlist and to remain in the army, thus swelling the ranks for the 1778 summer campaign. And, too, African Americans who joined the service and some white public figures believed victory in the Revolution, fought to end America's slavery to England, would end slavery itself in America.

African American soldiers were needed because in 1778 states found it hard to recruit white residents for troop strengths mandated by Congress. One state, Rhode Island, had such trouble signing up soldiers that it even created an all-black regiment and assigned some of its better soldiers to come home to train its members. It was the most prominent of three black regiments fighting for America. One small group, the American Bucks, was raised in Massachusetts and a third, the Black Brigade of Saint Domingue, from Haiti, fought with the French army in Georgia in 1779.

Sometime during the morning of March 26, 1778, newly promoted Sergeant Jeremiah Greenman, sent home to Providence from Valley Forge to recruit troops, picked up a copy of the *Providence Gazette* and read a notice published in its pages by his commanding officer, Colonel Christopher Greene. Colonel Greene ordered all of the new recruits for Rhode Island's two regiments to report to East Greenwich, twenty miles south on the western side of Narragansett Bay, for the spring campaign. The weather had been unusually mild during the past two weeks, but a few hours after Greenman put down the newspaper the sky darkened and, the sergeant wrote, "it began to snow very fast indeed."

The next day, Jeremiah Greenman found himself marching through several inches of snow in hilly Providence toward East Greenwich to undertake one of the most unusual, and historic, assignments of the war. He had been selected by his commanding officer as one of the drillmasters to train America's first permanent regiment of all-black troops, the First Rhode Island.

Greenman thought little about the assignment. He trained the black recruits on how to parade, maneuver on the battlefield, load, fire, and care for muskets. The more than two hundred men in his regiment were given their guns on April 15. Arming former slaves meant little to Greenman, who remarked casually in his journal that "we got our guns draw'd," and nothing more.

George Washington, who held mixed feelings about freeing slaves all of his life, did not initially want "a black corps," as he later wrote General William Heath and others.[1] Now, though, needing as many trained men as he could obtain, he had changed his mind, albeit reluctantly, and was happy to have men from among Rhode Island's 2,671 slaves.[2]

Washington recognized them as a huge pool from which to enlist much needed troops. He wanted this new all-black unit in Rhode Island to succeed, too, and so he put it under the command of Greene, a relative of his trusted aide, Nathanael Greene.

Washington had seen the reliability of black soldiers during the French and Indian War, when he served as a colonial officer under British General William Braddock, the head of a British army in Virginia in 1755.[3] One New Hampshire black, Robert Miller, fought for the colonial militia that was part of the British army in that war; twenty years later his son fought in the Continental Army against the British.[4]

The coming of the Revolution gave antislavery forces their greatest ammunition. Rev. Samuel Allinson, of New Jersey, used that argument in a letter to Patrick Henry, reminding him that it would be "the lasting disgrace" of Congress not to grant freedom to blacks "if they should spend so much time to secure their own liberties and leave no vestige of their regard to those of their fellow men in bondage to themselves." Congressional delegate James Otis wrote that "those who barter away other men's liberty will soon care little for their own." [5]

One of the voices against slavery belonged to George Washington, who had spoken out against it several times during the previous decade. He introduced a bill to halt the transportation of slaves to Virginia in the 1760s. In 1774, he introduced, with his friend George Fairfax, "resolves," or formal proposals, on the issue. In them, again, Washington called for curbs on slavery, describing bondage as a "wicked, cruel, and unnatural trade." Later, connecting the Revolution to slavery, he wrote that Americans had to free themselves from England or be turned into as "tame and abject slaves as the blacks we rule over with such arbitrary sway," adding that the blacks were "poor wretches."[6] It was no surprise then, when he badly needed troops, that George Washington turned to the slave population of the states and offered freedom as an inducement.

Most African Americans fought in integrated units that were raised in the different states. Their number depended on their geographical location and the population of blacks, freedmen and slaves, in that area. One rural county in Connecticut had just one black soldier, but a company from New York City had eleven on its muster of fifty-nine.[7] A New Hampshire company's roster was 15 percent black.[8] At one point in

1777, nearly one-third of all the American troops at Fort Ticonderoga under General Anthony Wayne were black.[9] By the time the Americans had tightened their noose around the British in Boston in the summer of 1775, there were several hundred black troops in the twenty-thousand-man army.

Hundreds of black freedmen joined the army, too. Some did believe strongly in the cause of independence for America. More importantly, many felt that victory over the British would mean freedom for any relatives still in bondage, and a general freedom for all blacks. Some black soldiers were motivated by a sense of adventure, just like white troops. Money was a reason for the enlistment of the black freedmen, too. Most were recruited after the winter of 1778, when Continental currency had been severely devalued. Congress and the states offered many soldiers who signed up later in the war one hundred acres of land instead of the worthless paper money. That much land was a huge incentive for black freedmen who had no land, little money, and usually had trouble landing jobs.

One of the first Americans to die for independence was Crispus Attucks, a runaway slave, who was one of five men shot and killed during the Boston Massacre in 1770. Black involvement in the war itself began in the very first battle, at Lexington, Massachusetts, as several African American minutemen fought against the British army. Several black soldiers participated in the battle of Bunker Hill. Peter Salem became the most famous of them when he was depicted in the famous painting of the battle by artist John Trumbull.

Blacks were in the first militia raised in the southern states, too. British troops found that out in 1775 in a heated battle at a bridge over the Elizabeth River in Virginia. There they encountered a black freedman named Billy Flora. The American regiment moved back into a breastwork, leaving wooden planks over the river. Flora was the last sentinel to run back over the bridge after firing what he thought was a final volley at the British. He realized that the planks could be used by the British to cross the water, too, and began to pull them up. He soon found himself in a hail of musket balls. Flora dislodged the planks, dragging them to the American side of the river as the English fired furiously at him. As he slowly backed off, he began to fire away at the British. Eyewitnesses said he wound up firing eight volleys at the enemy. Flora, who later purchased the freedom of his family, returned to the army in the war of 1812 as an old man, and fought against the British once more.[10]

The presence of black troops in the military during the early days of the war disturbed many public officials. There were several reasons for this. First, many complained that the black freedmen who signed up were really not free, but runaway slaves who lied about their identity. Second, plantation owners in the South and subsistence farmers in the North said that they could not run their businesses without slave labor. Third, and most importantly, many feared bands of black soldiers with guns would start civil insurrections. This fear was greatest among planters in the South who owned large numbers of slaves. It was so great in Maryland that the governor issued hundreds of muskets and pistols to local counties to distribute to planters to defend themselves in case a slave rebellion began. In South Carolina, the Council on Safety posted warnings against slave uprisings.[11]

The black soldiers in the American army may have earned their freedom, but they rarely garnered the respect of the white officers. Lt. Alex Graydon wrote that the Negroes in a Massachusetts regiment he saw "had a disagreeable, degrading effect" on the entire army.[12] A captain at Fort Ticonderoga wrote that the American regiments comprised "the strangest mixture of Negroes, Indians, and whites, with old men and mere children, which together with a nasty lousy appearance make a most shocking spectacle" and made him "sick of the service."[13] General Philip Schuyler wrote that the black soldiers "disgrace our arms."[14] General William Heath had no complaints about the black troops under his command, but did not believe that they should be mixed with white soldiers.[15] John Adams complained that the army had too many Negroes.[16] One New England company's officer wrote that everyone in his community was opposed to the British except "lunatics, idiots, and Negroes." Another company permitted its men to vote on whether or not blacks willing to enlist would be permitted to do so.[17] Opposition to blacks in the service became so loud that by the end of the summer of 1775 all of the state legislatures took steps to halt their enlistment. Independence was going to be won for white people by white people.

All of that changed toward the end of that year thanks to two former acquaintances, Virginia's royal governor, John Murray, the Earl of Dunmore, and George Washington. The two men had dined together, played cards, and gone hunting for several years before the outbreak of the war. Washington became the head of the American army and Dunmore found himself an embattled royal governor.

As 1776 approached, Lord Dunmore felt threatened as his entire colony appeared to be in rebellion. He was so apprehensive that he fled the lavish brick governor's palace in Williamsburg, with its impressive courtyard and lovely gardens, and took refuge on a British warship in nearby Norfolk harbor. He needed troops, lots of them, to protect the Crown's stake in Virginia.

On November 7, 1775, Dunmore stunned the colonists by issuing a proclamation guaranteeing immediate freedom to all slaves who ran away from their masters and joined his British forces. This was the worst possible event for slaveholders in Virginia and nearby states, whose populations consisted predominantly of black slaves. Not only would the British forces swell tenfold and grow into a slave army, but the planters would be ruined economically without slave labor. And, worse, angry slaves in uniform might kill their former owners, whom all assumed they despised.

Congress, too, was appalled. It was encountering great difficulty raising troops and keeping soldiers in the army. Now Dunmore was giving thousands of slaves a chance to win freedom by soldiering muskets for the enemy. Virginia alone had some two hundred thousand slaves. Congress ordered the committee of safety in Virginia to do all it could to resist Dunmore.[18] Congress asked the same of Washington, who wrote that "if that man [Dunmore] is not crushed before spring, he will become the most formidable enemy America has."[19]

The Virginia slaves fled their plantations and fought for the king in return for freedom, everyone knew but few admitted, because if they stayed where they were they would remain in bondage. Rev. Henry Muhlenberg wrote in his diary of a conversation he overhead between two black servants who worked for an English family leaving Philadelphia. "They secretly wished that the British army might win, for then all Negro slaves will gain their freedom. It is said that this sentiment is almost universal among the Negroes in America."[20]

The patriots in Virginia reacted swiftly, using the pages of the *Virginia Gazette* to carry out a campaign of intimidation against any slaves thinking of joining forces with Lord Dunmore. Slaves were told in a series of letters to the editor that only able-bodied young adult males would be accepted as soldiers and any others who volunteered but were unfit would remain slaves, but now to the British, who would sell them to British planters in the West Indies. Their families might be held hostage. Letter writers reminded slaves, too, that the punishment for running away could be death and that any slave captured in a British uniform would be executed.[21]

Despite these threats, hundreds of slaves fled and traveled to Norfolk to join the British army to gain their freedom. It was worth the risk. Along with them came some twenty thousand other slaves. These men, women, and children were not interested in military service; they simply wanted the Redcoats to protect them. Their departure crippled the labor forces at southern plantations, but the number of refugees dramatically slowed down the Redcoats as they followed the British during the campaign in the southern states.[22]

Dunmore's slaves were honored by the British. They were given an official title, the Ethiopian Regiment, and had a motto: "Liberty for slaves." They fought hard in engagements against local militia and in one engagement two slaves in British uniforms even captured an American colonel. One British company consisted of ninety former slaves and thirty British regulars.[23] These early successes inspired even more slaves to flee their plantations and join Dunmore's forces, housed on his fleet of ships. Within months, nearly eight hundred slaves were in British uniforms.

In the end, Dunmore's slave soldiers were annihilated, but not by the Continental Army. By housing hundreds of men in close quarters on small, badly ventilated ships—and not providing much clothing beyond the uniform—Dunmore had created a classic environment for smallpox.

The dreaded disease that had decimated the American army in Canada earlier that winter struck the slave army the British had recruited in June 1776. The disease spread rapidly in the close quarters of the ship holds and the sick infected the healthy. Dunmore had bombarded and burned Norfolk a few months earlier and was not a popular man there, so he sailed away, desperate to find any harbor to unload his diseased slaves, but no one would take them. Dunmore sent some of his ships with healthy slaves north, to Sandy Hook, New Jersey. Several dozen of those members of the Ethiopian Regiment fought with Sir Henry Clinton's army. The rest of Dunmore's black regiment had to sail all the way to British-occupied Bermuda to find a safe harbor. There, his dream of a slave army dissipated. More than half of his eight hundred slave soldiers had perished from smallpox by the time his fleet anchored and most of the others wound up back in slavery in the West Indies.

Not all of the American slaves who obtained freedom in the ranks of the British army fought for Dunmore. One group of fifteen men enslaved on a Maryland plantation stole a planter's small boat and sailed it to a British frigate. One British regiment in New York had a corps of black drummer boys. Several slaves who were horsemen fought for a British cavalry troop. At the end of the war, the British evacuated their army to Halifax, taking with them several hundred black soldiers.[24]

At the same time that Dunmore was recruiting his army, before Christmas 1775, George Washington made up his mind to overturn the decision of his generals to end black enlistments and permitted recruiters to sign up black soldiers wherever they could find them. He needed men, any men, because nearly half his army had returned home at the end of 1775. The offer of freedom for military service was alluring and from late 1777 on hundreds of black soldiers joined the army. Although there are no reliable figures on black enlistment, it has been estimated that over five thousand black freedmen or slaves fought for the Continental Army. More than seven hundred were said to have participated in the battle of Monmouth alone (about 6 percent of the American force there), one of the critical engagements of the war. In addition, blacks served as boat pilots and spies.

Several African American fathers and sons in slavery signed up together and fought in the same company. Slave brothers enlisted together. Black freedmen fought alongside their white neighbors in county companies. In a few companies a slave given freedom to join the army fought in the same company as his former master.

Most black soldiers served their entire term in the Continental Army, which ranged from eight months in the early years of the war to three years in its second half, but some remained in the army for five or six years and a few for the entire length of the war, even until peace arrived in 1783. Many who fought until the very end were awarded the Badge of Merit and had their discharge papers personally signed by George Washington.

Many black soldiers did not leave the army even when they had an understandable reason to do so. Primas Coffin, said to be a superb violinist while the slave of a New Hampshire minister, joined the Second New Hampshire regiment in February 1777 and fought at Fort Ticonderoga, Saratoga, Monmouth, and the 1779 campaign against the Indians. He was married while on furlough in the spring of 1779, an event that motivated many soldiers to leave the army, but Coffin rejoined the regiment after a few weeks and then, when his time was up, reenlisted and stayed in the army for two more years.[25]

The black freedmen enlisted under their legal names, but most of the slaves enlisted under their actual first name but owner's last name. Some, such as William Griffith, were enlisted as simply "William Negro."[26]

Congress, the army, and state and county governments entered several financial schemes in addition to freedom to procure black troops. Any black freedman who entered the service was given a bounty, just like white recruits. The owner of a slave who left bondage to fight in the Revolution was paid a bounty by either the state or Congress for his loss, usually $100 and sometimes equal to the market value of the slave. Some states, such as New York, even added five hundred acres of farmland as an inducement for owners.

A common practice to recruit as many troops as possible involved the substitution system used by states. Under it, a man drafted by his militia company could pay another to serve in his place. This was sometimes used by many wealthy merchants or southern planters to avoid service. One powerful new inducement to recruit black slaves was to let an owner use his slave as his substitute without paying him.[27]

Some of the slaves who fought in the war never received their freedom, including Peter Bartlett, the slave of well-known congressional delegate and signer of the Declaration of Independence Josiah Bartlett. In fact, some owners were so eager to keep their slaves that they sued each other to retain their services. Peter Blanchard was owned by William Frost, of New Hampshire, who hired him out as a seaman on the *Minerva,* a ship owned by Daniel and Samuel Sherburne and captained by Blanchard's former master. Frost wound up filing suit against all three in order to get his money and his slave back when the *Minerva* returned after a five-month cruise. Some slaves were sold by their owners to other men while they served in the army and had to go to court to win their promised freedom at the end of the war.[28]

One surprise was the high number of runaways who were living free and decided to enlist in the army to fight for their country, even though their enlistment records might be checked by the owners who were looking for them. Another was the continued relationships between the now-free slave soldiers and former owners. Some masters and slaves had always maintained close attachments and during the war this relationship continued. A few slaves kept up a friendly correspondence with their former owners, sometimes to urge them to lobby their states for higher wages for the troops but often just to continue the relationship. One slave who did so was Cato Baker, who kept up correspondence with his former master, Otis Baker. He ended his letters, "I remain your most humble servant until death."[29]

Many blacks in the service were killed, wounded, and taken as prisoners of war. Some, such as Scipio Gray, were captured on the high seas, brought to England, and incarcerated in the notorious Old Mill Prison in Plymouth.[30]

Congress asked some states to make an effort to recruit blacks. The only states that refused to do so were Georgia and South Carolina, where legislators feared that armed black soldiers would foster a slave insurrection. Washington had sent John Laurens, twenty-two, one of his aides and the son of South Carolina's Henry Laurens, to convince the states' legislatures to authorize the recruiting of slaves. Washington hoped to raise three thousand slave troops in the two states; in return, their owners would be compensated at the rate of $1,000 per man. Laurens had written his to father that his mission home to South Carolina not only gave him the chances to raise troops, but to aid "those who are unjustly deprived of the rights of mankind."[31] Colonel Laurens also believed, oddly, that slavery was a beneficial background for soldiering. Referring to slaves, he wrote, "Habits of subordination, patience under fatigue, sufferings and privation of every kind are soldierly qualifications."[32]

The charismatic Laurens was quite unpopular back home though, since his opposition to slavery was common knowledge. The British also let it be known that any slave they captured would be sold into slavery somewhere else, hardly an inducement to owners to relinquish their slaves. Laurens and his father were both disappointed when his mission failed.[33] The young Laurens wrote that his efforts were "drowned by the howlings of a triple-headed monster, in which prejudice, avarice, and pusillanimity were united."[34]

Almost all of the black soldiers served as privates, although some did move up in the ranks to corporals and sergeants. None became officers. Many blacks held menial jobs, such as waiters to generals, but white soldiers held those posts also. Some very young blacks were also held back from battle and placed in fife and drum corps, but so were whites.

Despite George Washington's acceptance of blacks and a desire to keep them in the army, the African American troops received no leniency when it came to punishment. They were given lashes for transgressions like every other soldier. Some, like the black soldier from Virginia who was convicted with three other men of robbing inhabitants of Westchester County, New York, were even hanged.[35]

All of the black volunteers did not serve in the army. When Esek Hopkins took over as the U.S. naval commander in chief in charge of the first four American ships, he brought three of his slaves with him to serve as seamen on two ships under his leadership, the *Cabot* and *Andrea Doria*. They were the first of several hundred slaves that worked on U.S. ships. Several blacks sailed with the legendary John Paul Jones on his first warship, the *Ranger*. One black freedman wanted to fight the British on a privateer so desperately that he took out an ad in a local newspaper imploring any sea captain who read it to hire him.[36]

The slaves who earned their freedom in the navy had an easier time of integrating themselves into the service than their counterparts in the army. The American army was brand new, but American shipping had thrived for one hundred fifty years and black seamen, especially young black cabin boys, had been common. The African American sailors fell into three categories. Some were brought along by their owners, who were sea captains. Some were black freedmen who were experienced sailors on merchant ships before the war. The others were ordinary slaves who were trained to be sailors.

Blacks also enlisted as seamen on ships that sailed in the state navies. These navies offered freedom for shorter terms of enlistment, sometimes just one year, and provided their black sailors the same cut of any booty seized from British ships on the high seas as white seamen. The state navies also operated out of local seaports, such as Boston, Philadelphia, and Newport, so that the sailors had more opportunities to visit relatives. On both the state and federal ships blacks, like whites, had chances for advancement from their original jobs as cabin boys and ammunition carriers; some were made gun captains of crews that fired the cannon.

Some black pilots operated small craft for the state navies in the southern states, especially Virginia and Maryland. These men were slaves on plantations located on the bays and rivers of the region and had piloted their masters' small boats for years. They knew all of the depths, shallows, currents, and the tides and were, according to Thomas Anderson, the Virginia commissioner of provisions, "accustomed to the navigation of the river." They were also reliable. "[They are] as fine fellows that ever crossed the sea," one planter, Stephen Seward, said of his slaves in the Maryland state navy.[37]

The state navies were large; Virginia's had seventy vessels. There were some frigates and schooners, but most consisted of "galley ships." These were seventy feet long, relatively narrow, nearly flat bottom boats with two masts and small sails, like a schooner. The difference was that these galley ships, named after the old Roman galleys, were powered by fifty-man rowing crews. The men, sitting in benches on the main deck, used long wooden oars to propel the vessels swiftly up and down Virginia's rivers and coastline. The flat bottom enabled the pilot to navigate just about any waterway, regardless of its depth.[38] Each ship usually carried one or two slaves as seamen, but some carried as many as ten. Many had black pilots, especially the galley ships. They all won praise for their work during the war. The son of a Virginia commodore who fought with slaves said of one that he was "distinguished for his zeal and daring."[39]

The slaves in the state navies not only fought for America's independence alone; their families did again and again. A black sailor named John De Baptist, of Spotsylvania, Virginia, fought in the U.S. Navy in the Revolution, his son served in it during the war of 1812, and his grandson did the same in the Civil War.

In addition to the men on ships, hundreds of other slaves or black freedmen worked for the navy as laborers on shore. Most repaired ships and some worked with white laborers in building small craft. One integrated work crew was hired on an annual basis to do maintenance at Charleston harbor. Other black freedmen and slaves worked on the privateers sanctioned by the government.

The black men in the navy in the southern states were treated differently from those in the army. Soldiers earned freedom directly, but sailors did not. Some were given freedom for their service. Most were hired out from their owners for service that could range from one day to a year. Some states bought slaves outright from owners and made them the "slaves" of the state navies. Hard-working black sailors were rewarded in many ways, however. Many saw naval work preferable to laboring in the heat on plantations. Some loved the sea. All hoped that victory over the

British would bring an end to slavery. Although many slaves were returned to their owners after the war, or were sold to others by the states if their masters were Loyalists, still others were awarded their freedom for meritorious service to the state navy.

The black pilots engaged the enemy. The *Liberty*, with its heavily black crew, was involved in twenty sea battles. A slave named William Graves was killed in one engagement while at the wheel of his vessel. Another, Minny, was killed while leading a group of men in boarding a British ship during a hot firefight on the waters of the Chesapeake.

Most of the slaves who worked for the Revolution were common laborers. The army needed large groups of workers to build fortifications, toil in mines, ironworks, and shipyards to help manufacture cannon, ammunition, boats, leather goods, clothing, wagons, and lead musket balls. Some were trained as firemen in case their towns were set ablaze in a bombardment. George Washington never had as many soldiers as he needed and could not deploy hundreds of them to work in those capacities.

The slaves who had fled to the British for protection and freedom often lost it if the British army was defeated in a battle. Southern states saw all slaves as contraband, like cargo on ships seized on the high seas, and the property of the victor. Slaves captured from the British were sometimes given away to newly commissioned officers in the American army, along with parcels of land, as their bonus for joining the service.

The slaves who avoided recapture by American forces may have fared worse under the "protection" of the British army. At the end of the Revolution, the British were protecting nearly twenty thousand slaves. They refused to give them back to the Americans, despite Congress' demands for their return to their masters in the United States. The English brought all of them with them as they evacuated between 1781 and 1783. Almost all of the slaves were turned over to slavers in the West Indies, where they spent the rest of their lives.[40]

Chapter Twenty-Five

THE HEROISM OF THE BLACK RHODE ISLAND REGIMENT

The all-black First Rhode Island, trained by Jeremiah Greenman, was not a project to show the world that black slaves could fight as well as whites or that they desired freedom from George III as much as their owners. There was nothing altruistic about it, either. The state legislature simply could not find enough white soldiers to fill the quota insisted upon by Congress and turned to slaves. There were several reasons for that: Rhode Island was a small state with just fifty-two thousand residents (compared to neighboring Massachusetts with 268,000 and Connecticut with 206,000), many of its troops had died at Valley Forge, and its capital, Newport, was occupied by the British.

And so Rhode Island created a black regiment, offering freedom as an inducement. They did so reluctantly because, members of the legislature said, the enlistment of an all-black regiment created two problems. First, the state would have to pay the owners a bounty for the freedom of their slaves (they were eventually reimbursed by Congress). Second, Rhode Island officials would have to explain to America why it needed slaves, who had no freedom, to defend freedom.

The measure passed handily and Governor Nicholas Cooke informed Congress of the vote immediately. Shortly after that, Cooke received a letter from George Washington urging the governor "to give the officers employed in this business all the assistance in your power."[1] That was not difficult. Rhode Island had several hundred male slaves who worked in the shipping industry or for merchants or farmers in and around Providence. Several, such as Barzillar Streeter, had already fought for the state militia. They were eager to reenlist.[2]

Sergeant Greenman and the others who worked with the black troops fighting for their own freedom as well as America's did their job well. The black soldiers not only took great pride in their desire to fight like soldiers, but to look like the best of them, too. A French diplomat who saw the black Rhode Islanders later in the war wrote that "they are strong, robust men and those I saw made a very good appearance." An aide to French General Rochambeau noted that "the regiment is the most neatly dressed, the best under arms, and the most precise in its maneuvers."[3]

The First Rhode Island became one of the Continental Army's best regiments, and quickly, because in August of their first year in arms they were ordered to Newport as part of a massive land and sea invasion to recapture the state capital. They would meet fierce opposition from both British regulars and Hessians firmly entrenched in the seaport city.

Liberating Newport would not only be a military success but a significant public relations coup. The British had evacuated Philadelphia on June 15, 1778, and were forced to retire from Monmouth when Washington's army attacked them there on June 28. That battle, plus the freeing of Newport, would not only rally the Americans to the cause but add fuel to the growing fire against the war among many residents of England, who would read about it in the increasingly antiwar British press.

Washington ordered an all-out campaign against the three-thousand-man army under General Robert Pigot in Newport. The French fleet, under Admiral Charles d'Estaing, had just arrived and was sent to Newport for a sea attack. Washington sent three thousand men under Nathanael Greene and the Marquis de Lafayette to Rhode Island to join John Sullivan and the black regiment in Providence and move against Newport. John Hancock was asked to gather six thousand militia to assist them. It appeared that with a combined force of ten thousand, a three-to-one advantage, and a naval bombardment, that the Americans could not lose.

Other generals were even jealous that Sullivan, as the commander of the attack, had such an opportunity for glory. "You are the most happy man in the world," Nathanael Greene wrote to Sullivan. "What a child of fortune. The expedition you are going on against Newport I think cannot fail to succeed." Lafayette begged Sullivan to share the glory. "For God's sake, my dear friend," he wrote in a nearly giddy letter, "don't begin anything before we arrive."[4]

Sullivan was happy to be there. At fifty-five, the former New Hampshire lawyer was one of Washington's most trusted generals. He was also ambitious but, friends said, rather narrow-minded and had a great need to be admired.

The plan was complicated and relied on timing. Newport sat on the largest of several islands in Narragansett Bay, which was connected to the Atlantic Ocean. The smaller part of the French fleet would attack Newport from the east, moving up a channel there on August 5. The larger part of the fleet would sail into a channel to the west of Newport on August 8 and 9 and land men at the same time that Sullivan's army attacked from the northern end of the city. English general Pigot would not be able to fight the allies off on two fronts. Personalities and plans began to clash, however, and the operation slowly went awry.

The temperamental d'Estaing, a veteran naval officer, was held in low esteem by the Americans for his continued reluctance to battle the British fleet in New York, Halifax, and in the Caribbean. Nor did he get along with the cantankerous Sullivan, whom he claimed treated him as an inferior. He especially did not enjoy Sullivan's dispatches, which gave him orders and not suggestions. The admiral thought little of the Continental

Army troops under Lafayette and Greene and much less of the New England militia.

Back in Providence, some forty miles north, Jeremiah Greenman and his company marched out of town with the rest of Sullivan's army and the First Rhode Island black regiment on August 6 and proceeded south to Tiverton, a town opposite Newport. All day long on August 8 they heard the sounds of the guns from the French ships pounding Newport from a position in the channel to the west of the city. "A very brisk cannonading to the west of Rhode Island and something set on fire but we don't hear what it is," he wrote. The next day, August 9, they ferried across the eastern channel to the island where Newport was located.

"Marched up on the island about a mile and made a halt near one of the enemy's forts and formed a line," Greenman wrote. Several hours elapsed and they moved once more. "We marched about a quarter of a mile and formed a line again where we lay all night."

The British, meanwhile, made quick moves that thwarted the Americans at every turn. Pigot ordered the British ships in the eastern channel scuttled so that they blocked the movement of the French fleet. When Sullivan landed on time, he had no cover from French guns. The French troops never landed. Then, on August 9, as the invasion was underway and Greenman's company moved toward Newport, and the rest of the French fleet had sailed halfway up the western channel for the scheduled assault, Lord Richard Howe's British fleet arrived—unannounced.

The British ships were seen south of Newport just as the French reached the halfway mark toward their destination on the western side of the city, firing cannon at the island and its defenders. The French admiral and his captains, nervous about the presence of Lord Howe's ships, anchored in the channel that night as the weather in the region began to change for the worse. "We lay all night in the rain without tents close to another of the enemy's forts," wrote Greenman.

In the morning, d'Estaing's fleet turned and sailed out to attack the British fleet, two-thirds its size, but there was little action all day except for a few cannon exchanges, as the two fleets maneuvered for position. On land, American commanders did not know what was going on throughout the day and many thought the town was under attack, not realizing a sea battle had started. "Very heavy firing toward the town, the shipping against the batteries. We hear that shipping has gone out and further hear that there is a fleet off but don't hear what it is," wrote Greenman, as perplexed as everyone else.

A ferocious storm hit the Rhode Island coast that night and strong winds and heaving seas battered the ships on both sides. Several ships lost part of the rigging for their sails and all suffered damage as waves whipped up by the winds tossed the ships about in the Newport channel like tiny boxes. The storm continued throughout the evening and into early morning, preventing most of the sailors on them from getting any sleep. Crews had to constantly clear the decks of debris and battle the rough seas.

Sergeant Greenman and his company were lashed by the same storm. It was one of the worst he had ever seen. He noted, "Continued raining and blowing very hard indeed all day. We continued . . . drawing cartridges and fixing our guns for they was in very bad order by the storm blowing down almost all of our tents." The British ships had been pounded just as severely as the French and most of them sailed away in the following days. Howe left only a few ships in case they were needed to protect the British troops on the island.

Two entire days had been lost in the sea battle, delaying the American assault. The Americans finally moved into position to attack on August 15, north of Newport. "Pitched our tents in sight of the enemy about a mile and a half from their lines. Turned out a large picket and a large body of fatigue men, ordered to lay on our arms," Greenman wrote.

The Rhode Islanders, black and white, laid on their arms for quite awhile.

Over the next few days, the Americans sat as British pickets and some artillery fired at them. Greenman told his men that the enemy would attack at any hour. He did not realize that d'Estaing, his ships in dire need of repair, had decided to leave the waters of Rhode Island and sail to Boston. There would be no French gunships to cover the American attack and no French troops landing on the western part of the city as reinforcements. They did see ships on the horizon, but they were British. The news of the French fleet's departure caused panic among the New England militia troops and many deserted.

"It ruined all our operations," wrote Nathanael Greene to George Washington.⁵ Greene wrote to General William Heath that if the French navy had not deserted the Americans, "we might have succeeded with great ease."⁶ "The French fleet is leaving us," Greenman wrote tersely in his diary, feeling just as abandoned by the French as other Americans would say long after the war ended.

Sullivan's army, stranded now, found that the British had far stronger defensive earthworks on Newport than his spies and scouts had reported. He spent August 25, 26, and 27 rallying his troops, but on August 28 decided that an attack would fail and began a general evacuation.

At 7 p.m., orders came to strike tents as quietly as possible and wait. That done, the integrated Rhode Island regiment moved out with others. Shortly after 9 p.m., under the cover of darkness, they began to march northward to the tip of the island. They did not fool the British. The men were fired upon as they departed by two British ships in the channel. Several companies of Hessians were seen following them toward a small fort on Butt's Hill.

The Americans barely made it inside the fortification atop the hill when Pigot and his entire force appeared in front of them, spread out in a long line, on August 29. There was more to be feared. Out in the channel, Sergeant Greenman observed yet more British ships. Three days before, word had reached Newport that a second British fleet had left New York for Rhode Island with transports carrying several thousand men. He assumed the ships he saw were part of that fleet and that his army would soon be attacked by a British army of nearly ten thousand men.

Fortunately, he was wrong. The British fleet was still an entire day away from Newport on Long Island Sound. Their only enemy was right in front of them, and the enemy would not go away. General Pigot sensed victory and threw all of his British regulars at the middle of Sullivan's army and ordered his well-trained Hessians to charge against the right wing, where the black First Rhode Island regiment was dug in. The Hessians waited until after a heavy bombardment from the British ships created havoc in the American lines as shells exploded all around the soldiers and smoke filled the air. Pigot then sent his Hessians against the black regiment's side.

The Germans were surprised, though. Their assault was stopped cold and their lines shattered by the 125 black troops behind the earthworks. They met "a more stubborn resistance than expected" and had to pull back, suffering high casualties. The regulars attacked the center of the American line at the same time that the Hessian charge began, but they were repulsed too. Greenman had to be pleased as he looked to his right to see the troops in the black regiment that he had helped to train turn back the ferocious Hessian assault.

The German commander was not pleased, however, and after his men had been stopped, shot up, and turned back, he ordered them to attack yet again. He was confident that the black troops could not hold off his veteran soldiers any longer. His second attack failed, as did a third. The Hessians could not dislodge the black troops from their position on the right. After four solid hours of fighting, the Germans ended their charges. Pigot's regulars fared no better, turned back again and again by Greenman's Rhode Islanders and the main force commanded by Sullivan. The British attacks ended as night fell; the Americans moved a short distance to another hill.

The soldiers in the First Rhode Island felt both relief and pride at the end of the day. "Balls, like hail, were flying all around me. The man standing next to me was shot by my side," said a Doctor Harris, reportedly one of the troops in the black regiment, whose brother was killed in the Revolution. "They attacked us with great fury, but were repulsed. They reinforced and attacked us again, with more vigor and determination, and were again repulsed. Again they reinforced, and attacked us the third time, with the most desperate courage and resolution, but a third time were repulsed. The contest was fearful. Our position was hotly disputed and hotly maintained."[7]

The commanders at Butt's Hill marveled at the courage of the white troops and especially the bravery of the black soldiers. The British encountered "chiefly wild looking men in their shirt sleeves, and among them many Negroes," wrote one. Lafayette called the stand at Butt's Hill "the best fought action of the war." General Sullivan heaped praise upon his black troops and cited the entire regiment for honors in his report on the battle to George Washington. Nathanael Greene, who watched the black regiment up close, agreed. Discussing the men under him, including the blacks, he wrote to Washington, "We soon put the enemy to rout and I had the pleasure to see them run in worse disorder than they did at Monmouth." He added that the troops fought with "great spirit" and "great honor" and "stood the fire of the enemy with great firmness."[8] A Rhode Island historian wrote later that "it was in repelling these furious onsets that the newly raised black regiment, under Col. Greene, distinguished itself by deeds of desperate valor."[9]

The Hessians, who suffered the most that day, agreed. "No regiment is to be seen in which there are not Negroes in abundance; among them are strong able bodied and brave fellows," wrote one.[10]

The following day, August 30, the Americans evacuated, departing across the channel on small craft. They had suffered 211 casualties in the battle versus 260 for the British. There would have been far more if Sullivan had been trapped on the island or waited to evacuate; the British fleet arrived the following day with five thousand troops.[11]

Americans everywhere were relieved. "I never in general saw people more anxious than my acquaintances under the present suspense," wrote Henry Laurens about the pullback.[12] There was a sense of loss by some, such as congressional delegate James Smith, who wrote forlornly that perhaps a victory at Newport "would have put an end to the war." The country's top propagandists, such as Richard Henry Lee, dismissed naysayers like Smith and told one and all that the Americans at Newport had actually won the battle and had given the British "a drubbing."[13]

The First Rhode Island, mobilized in February of 1778, fought on until the victory at Yorktown in the fall of 1781, participating in numerous engagements, providing one of the longest service records in the Continental Army. It was led by Colonel Greene throughout the war until he was killed in a British ambush in the spring of 1781.

The states honored their promise to give freedom to all of the five thousand slaves who served as soldiers and sailors during the Revolution, as well as land that had been guaranteed to some. The victory in the Revolution did not bring about the end of slavery in America, as the black soldiers had hoped. No one freed their slaves to celebrate victory at Yorktown or the signing of the peace accords in 1783. The new Constitution, approved in 1789, did not eradicate slavery either. In fact, the booming cotton market meant an even greater increase in slavery in the southern states in the years following the war.

Life was often harsh for blacks in the North as well as the South after the Revolution. Black veterans awarded their freedom for military service had an even harder time finding work than whites. In 1796 one, Pomp Peters, unable to make ends meet, sold the one hundred acres of land the United States had given him as his bounty to fight for his country for just $20 in order to pay his bills.[14] Another, George Knox of New Hampshire, faced such financial woes that in 1784 he and his wife gave up their freedom and became indentured servants for five years in order to be given food and shelter and to collect a promised $100 worth of land or cattle at the end of the term.

Black private Michael Sudrick, who enlisted and reenlisted five different times and fought until the very end of hostilities in 1783, spent the rest of his life in such terrible financial shape that he was constantly sued for nonpayment of bills.[15] Another army veteran, Prince Light, who fought at Saratoga, had such financial trouble in the years following the war that when he died in 1821 his recorded estate was worth just $2.20.[16] Some, such as Joseph Mun of Connecticut, felt betrayed. His owner, and the Connecticut legislature, agreed to free him if he served the full three-year term in the army. Mun suffered a broken arm in a battle and had to be discharged short of his three years. The Connecticut courts ruled that he had to go back into slavery because he had not served his full term.[17]

An ironic footnote to part the black soldiers played in the Revolution, and the smashing of their dream of universal freedom at its end, was the story of the three grown sons of Jude Hall. Black freedmen James, Aaron, and William Hall, of New Hampshire, were all mistaken for runaway slaves or deliberately kidnapped by groups of slave catchers traveling through New England in the early nineteenth century, taken South, and sold into bondage. Their father, Jude Hall, had fought for eight years in the Revolution, longer, in fact, than George Washington, certain that the war would bring an end to slavery in America.[18]

That would not come for another eighty years and yet another war.

Chapter Twenty-Six

JOHN GREENWOOD, PRIVATEER

Two years after he left the army in January 1777, following the crossing of the Delaware and the victory at Trenton, private John Greenwood felt "uneasy" and wanted to fight in the Revolution again. He had spent three months of 1778 with the Boston Light Infantry when they were assigned the duty of guarding some of the British soldiers captured at the battle of Saratoga. There, he worked once more as a fifer, not as an infantryman. Now, in the winter of 1779, Greenwood turned his back on the army and decided to go to sea to do what he could to win the war. It was a natural choice. Young Greenwood, who had just turned nineteen, had spent most of the previous two years working in Cape Cod fisheries in Falmouth, Massachusetts. He had been on boats constantly and befriended many seaman, some of whom had sailed on the American privateers that preyed on British shipping in the Atlantic Ocean and the Caribbean Sea.

Privateering was a lucrative industry. Congress had no navy when the war began. By the summer of 1775, Rhode Islanders had transformed two ships into warships by adding some guns and Congress had ordered the refitting of several more, but that was a meager fleet.[1] America needed a substantial sea force to combat Great Britain's hundreds of ships and their flotillas of merchant ships carrying millions of dollars worth of supplies to and from America and ports in the West Indies. British privateers also preyed on American merchant ships. The English vessels were equipped with "avarice and enmity," congressional delegate Richard Henry Lee charged, and America needed the privateers to "clear our coast" of the British villains.[2] Building new ships was incredibly expensive and time consuming, so in order create an "instant navy" Congress authorized private shippers that did not already carry cannon for protection to refit their vessels with them to prey on English boats. The refurbishing was completed in American harbors such as Boston, Marblehead, and Newburyport in Massachusetts, New London, Connecticut, or in Caribbean ports.

The owners of every type of ship—brigs, schooners, sloops—refitted their vessels for high seas combat. Most of the sailors on these ships, guaranteed a portion of any booty, signed on when the ship became a privateer.[3] The captains of these ships were given "letters of marque" that acknowledged that they fought for America but were entitled to the goods they captured. Some called it a patriotic license to steal.

The heavily armed merchant-turned-privateer vessels were necessary because neutral nations, such as Holland, were willing to trade with America. That meant American ships could sail to a Caribbean island, such as Dutch-held St. Eustatius and there trade their cargoes of tobacco and corn for gunpowder brought to the tiny island by Dutch captains. The gunpowder was essential to the American Revolution. But the laws of neutrality also permitted any belligerent nation (the British) to sink or capture any ship carrying arms for their enemy.[4]

Privateering became popular because there were so many cargo-laden ships that could be taken on the high seas in a region that stretched from Halifax, Canada, all the way to the coast of Brazil; others sailed off the coasts of Ireland, Scotland, and England itself, using French ports as their home. About seventeen hundred American privateers put to sea, six hundred from Massachusetts alone, from 1776 until 1783. As many as 449 sailed at any one time. The privateers ranged in size from one to five hundred tons and carried between four and twenty cannon. Crew sizes averaged about one hundred men, half with muskets for armed engagements, but some ships carried as many as three hundred. The ships carried more than ten thousand seamen with them over the seven years of the war, captured or sank six hundred British vessels (American ships sunk or captured twice as many vessels as the British and five times the value in cargo) and seized goods worth between $18 million and $66 million, according to different records.[5]

Life on board the privateers could be very lucrative for the ordinary seamen. The ship's owner received the largest share of the prize booty and the U.S. government received a small cut, but the captain and officers received shares and each seaman was awarded a share. A seaman's percentage of the booty from a single voyage of a few months, if the prize ships taken were loaded with expensive goods, could provide him with an income for a year or more. The opportunity to make fast money attracted so many investors that merchants sold off shares of their ships. Some ships were owned by a dozen shareholders, but one merchant sold off 196 shares to eager subscribers.[6]

Newspaper advertising for sailors to serve on privateers emphasized the windfall profits to be earned on the rolling waves of the Atlantic. A Connecticut newspaper ad said that ship owners were looking for "all gentlemen volunteers who are desirous of making their fortunes in eight weeks," and a *Boston Gazette* ad sought out "all those jolly fellows who love their country and want to make their fortune at one stroke."[7] Patriotic privateers also had the satisfaction of sinking or disabling one of Her Majesty's ships or seizing supplies on their way to the British army, bringing the end of the war that much closer.

This combination of patriotism and profit made privateering quite attractive. One British officer held as a prisoner of war in Boston wrote that "Boston harbor swarms with privateers and their prizes." America had gone privateering mad, crazed with the profit and wealth that privateering promised.

And the British knew it. The *London Chronicle* reported in 1777 that American privateers terrorized Scottish officials. "Our seas so full of American privateers that nothing can be trusted upon this defenseless coast," one said.[8] A British writer commented in 1778 that commercial British ship owners now had to employ a fleet of small combat ships just to protect their large, cargo-heavy merchant ships from attacks by Americans, adding "The coasts of Great Britain and Ireland were insulted by the American privateers in a manner which our hardiest enemies had never ventured in our most arduous contentions with foreigners." British and Scottish parents were so fearful of the American naval commander John Paul Jones that they told their children to stay away from the beaches for fear his crew would kidnap them.[9]

It was not just the safety of shipping near Great Britain that the Crown worried about, either. The privateers seemed to be everywhere in the Caribbean, too. The governor of British-held Jamaica reported "a constant track of American schooners" in his waters.[10] And especially in the Caribbean, small fleets of American privateers set out to capture specific large British ships, often successfully. "A great number [of privateers] in these seas fitted out on purpose to take the *Greyhound*," wrote Captain Henry Byrne of one large ship to the British Admiralty just before Christmas, 1776.[11] The American raids became so successful that in one single week in Caribbean waters American ships captured fourteen British vessels.[12]

The ships were extraordinarily successful at harassing British merchant ships. John Adams wrote that the captains and sailors all deserved the fame that they had received. He noted, "Some of the most skillful, determined, persevering, and successful engagements that have ever happened upon the seas have been performed by American privateers."[13]

Some American officials opposed the sanctioning of privateers because their owners could use their booty to pay sailors an average of five times what the Continental Navy could offer on its few ships. The privateers, some said, also took on board thousands of men who might have fought for the always recruit-desperate army. American general Charles Lee even suggested that no privateers should be allowed to sail until all army regiments were filled with men.[14] The money made many congressional delegates also wonder about the sailors' true patriotism. William Whipple wrote that the income earned on the privateers would bring about "the destruction of the morals of the people." He said that sailors would "soon lose every idea of right and wrong." [15]

Whipple, and others, worried that the privateers would seize cargo from friendly ships, too, for the money, and that some would wind up behaving no better than pirates. In a letter filled with sarcasm, John Pickering wrote to his brother Timothy, a congressional delegate, just after the war ended that many sailors and port workers seemed demoralized by the peace because it ended their opportunities to make money on privateers.[16]

Of course, the punishments for those captured on privateers were severe. Those not killed or drowned in hotly contested sea battles were imprisoned in the wretched British prison ships in New York harbor or, if captured in the waters of the Caribbean, put in irons in hot, rancid jails on malaria-infested islands held by the British there. Some went to prisons in England.

None of this concerned John Greenwood. The young private had survived the invasion of Canada, smallpox, and the crossing of the Delaware; he would not worry about being captured on the high seas. As every sailor he knew who had sailed with the privateers assured him, the small, sleek American boats could always outrun the lumbering British warships.

In 1778, he signed on to the *Cumberland,* bound for Barbados in the Bahamas with one hundred thirty men, as a steward but worked as a midshipman. At first, the men were nervous because sea combat was dangerous. Men were killed and their ships sunk or wrecked. One vivid description was written by John Paul Jones after his *Ranger* took on the *Drake:* "The *Drake* being rather astern of the *Ranger,* I ordered the helm up, and gave her the first broadside. The action was warm, close, and obstinate. It lasted an hour and five minutes, when the enemy called for quarters, her fore and main top sail yards being both cut away, and down on the cap; the fore top gallant yard and mizzen gaff both hanging up and down along the mast; the second ensign which they had hoisted shot away and hanging over the quarter gallery in the water; the jib shot away and hanging into the water; her sails and rigging entirely cut to pieces, her masts and yards all wounded and her hull also very much galled."[17]

Captain Nathaniel Fanning was just as graphic in recounting his sea battle with the British ship *None Such,* a privateer that not only carried valuable cargo, but 127 British soldiers bound for America. He wrote, "We soon got within reach of her guns, when she began to fire upon us. But we after this soon got astern of her . . . We now [fired on] the privateer, brought our broadside to bear upon her stern and poured it into them."[18]

The *Cumberland's* first encounter was easy pickings. The vessel seized a sinking British ship, wrecked by a storm that suddenly appeared, and, with an officer appointed as prize master, repaired her, and sent her on to French-held Martinique for the sale of her goods so that the crew could pocket the money. The *Cumberland's* crew, delighted at such early and effortless success, could not wait until it reached the busy shipping lanes of the Caribbean, where British vessels carrying valuable cargo could be found rather easily. For days they moved over the water with no other ships in sight, the men lounging on the deck of the ship as its sails filled up with wind and its boards creaked. The hot winter sun of the region beat down on them, their hats and rolled up bandanas covering their foreheads giving them little refuge from it. Their idyll amid the rolling waves of the Atlantic south of Florida ended suddenly just after dawn on January 26, 1779, however, when they spotted the *Pomona,* a thirty-six-gun British frigate with three hundred men, one of the Crown's most famous ships. The *Pomona* bore down on them, its mast continually bobbing up and down as the ship cut through the waves.

The *Pomona* began firing her decks of cannon several hours later, their smoke nearly engulfing the sides and deck of the vessel. The cannonading killed an officer sitting on top of the *Cumberland's* main mast with his spyglass. The captain of the *Cumberland* knew that his ship was no match for the British ship and wanted to sail away with as much speed as his ship could muster. To lighten the vessel, he ordered eight of the ship's eighteen heavy cannon tossed into the water, but the *Pomona* was already too near, sailing in behind her, and closing fast.

Greenwood wrote, "The frigate, being right in our wake within short distance, kept her course and shooting close up under our larboard quarter, gave us four or five double headed and round shot. Some flew among our rigging and one ball striking us abaft the forechains, went through and through the ship, making her shake again."

The captain of the *Cumberland* devised a desperate plan that depended on ingenuity and sheer luck. He would let the *Pomona* crash right into the *Cumberland*'s side. That would enable the men of the *Cumberland*, armed with cutlasses, muskets, and pistols, to quickly board the *Pomona* under the cover of the smoke from the cannon and capture the British frigate in a bold maneuver.

When the weapons cabinet doors were thrown open, however, the men of the *Cumberland* found less than thirty swords and only a few muskets. There would be no fight. The captain decided to surrender, striking his colors when the captain of the *Pomona* yelled across the water for him to do so.

The boarding of the *Cumberland* was delayed by the distance between the ships and high waves that tossed both vessels up and down and made it difficult to close the space between them. A comedy followed, according to Greenwood. The men of the *Cumberland*, resigned to capture and prison, decided to have one last fling. They broke open the liquor casks in the hold and began to pour the contents down their throats; many became drunk. The drunken sailors then raced to the storeroom where the captain had put dozens of British uniforms taken from the men of the ship they captured earlier. The inebriated men were certain that if they dressed like the Redcoats they would not be jailed. Unable to distinguish coat and trouser sizes in their stupor, they put on uniforms that did not fit, their pants legs dragging across the deck and their arms sticking through short sleeves of coats designed for much smaller men. Many of the inebriated "Redcoats" then collapsed on the deck and had to be tossed into the boats to take them to the *Pomona*, "like hogs," Greenwood wrote. The officers of the *Cumberland* rowed over to the *Pomona* but the rough waves upended their boat at the last moment, smashing it against the side of the frigate. The British had to lower their own boat and fish the Americans out of the ocean.

"It would have made a saint laugh to see the men tumbling about," Greenwood observed.

The last laugh was on Greenwood. He carefully wrapped up several pounds of chocolate, some sugar, and some biscuits in a handkerchief, put some of his clothes in a small bag with the sweets and climbed into the longboat to be taken to the *Pomona*. There, a teenage British sailor just as young as Greenwood told him that the captain would seize his candy and biscuits. He offered to take them and hold them for Greenwood until they could split the sweets later. Greenwood breathed a sigh of relief, thanked the teen, and handed him the handkerchief. He never saw the sweets again.

The Americans were rushed into the dark hold of the ship that was already filled with supplies. "Here we were stowed so close that we had no room to stand, sit, or lie, except partly on each other, for with the exception of the captain, doctor, first and second lieutenants, and captain's clerk, we had all officers and men, to the number of 125, been placed indiscriminately together."

Their prison in Barbados was awful. Greenwood wrote, "Our dungeon consisted of three apartments connected together, the floors of which were nothing but mud and clay, and, on account of the heavy rains prevalent in the West Indies, the water had settled in the center of these to the depth of two inches. Every part of the place was wet and damp yet here on the ground we were obliged to lie, having been robbed of everything except what we had on our backs. No bread was furnished us, nor do I recollect that they gave us a particle during the five months we were kept on the island."

It was in that jail that Greenwood was scarred for life. Another prisoner, assigned to assist with the kitchen facilities, stumbled while carrying a large pot of scalding hot soup as he walked through the yard. The soup pot tipped over and its contents spilled over Greenwood, barechested, lying on the ground to relax. The soup burns left a permanent scar on his shoulder and chest.

A few days later, word spread that on the following morning British navy and English privateer captains would arrive to choose men to be placed on their ships as impressed seamen for the remainder of the war. Greenwood and five others attempted to escape to avoid that fate, but they were caught. Greenwood then came up with another scheme. He talked a doctor into giving him a double dose of an emetic designed to make men purge themselves. His timing was perfect and just as the prisoners were led into the yard for sea assignment his systems erupted; he became violently ill and then fell down in the dirt courtyard.

His scheme almost backfired. Somehow, Spanish inmates in their prison obtained knives and used them during an altercation among themselves on the floor above the dungeons where the Americans were held. Guards, local police, and a mob of townspeople rushed the jail to put down the revolt and some charged toward the American cells, thinking they were responsible for the melee.

"Prepared to sell our lives as dear as possible, we prepared to meet them," Private Greenwood wrote. "We first brought close up to the door a half barrel or tub which had been placed in the room for the accommodation of several of our men who were at the time very sick and five or six of us stood ready with tin pots to greet the enemy if they attempted to unlock the door. We were likewise armed with junk bottles which, holding by the necks, we intended to dash against the grated door so that the fragments would fly among them. They saw our warlike preparations and when we stirred up our ammunition, afraid . . . they soon left the doorway clean."

That stroke of bad luck was offset by another of good fortune a short time later when the prisoners were ordered released and put on a schooner bound for Martinique. By chance, on that island Greenwood was spotted by an old schoolmate from Boston who was an officer on a ship bound for New York. That ship's captain turned out to be a cousin of Greenwood's father. He took Greenwood to New York, where he was certain he could hide from British troops occupying the city.

The voyage was a nightmare. The old and battered ship, badly in need of repairs, continually took on water and had four feet in the hold during most of the trip north. The crew was struck by yellow fever halfway up the coast; most fell ill and several men died. Then, off of Long Island, they were intercepted by a British privateer carrying numerous guns. Greenwood's ship had port holes for guns, but no cannon on board. The ingenious private scampered about the deck in search of all the wood he could find and then, wielding an axe and hammer with as much agility as he could muster, he built fake wooden cannon that jutted out of the port holes enough to look believable. He and other sailors took extra jackets and nailed them near the cannon and on the deck rails to make it appear that the ship's crew was several times its actual number. The ruse worked. The English vessel sailed close enough so that it's captain could see what appeared to be a long train of cannon and a large crew and turned away.

Once on shore in Boston a few days later, free at last, Greenwood was relieved. "No emperor or king could feel so happy as I then was, and there is a good and true saying that no person ever knows what happiness or pleasure is without first seeing adversity," he wrote.

Restless as always, Private Greenwood could not relax. He was soon hungry for the war again. "I could not long content myself while my fellow countrymen were abroad, contending for their freedom," he wrote.

He signed on for another voyage aboard a privateer, this one the well-armed *Tartar* (there were several ships of that name), with twenty-eight guns and a crew of one hundred fifty, commanded by Captain David Porter of Boston. It was Porter's third ship in two years. After a storm-tossed sail south, the *Tartar* moved into the warm waters of the Caribbean and immediately began to take British ships. It was a small miracle, because the *Tartar* was a war-weary vessel. Greenwood lamented, "Our ship was so old, crazy, and leaky that we were obliged to nail strips of rawhide over the sides of her upper works in order to keep the oakum in place."

To make up for its lack of speed, the captain of the *Tartar* and his crew relied on ingenuity. Every few weeks they painted the hull of the ship a different color. Sometimes they appeared to sail as a merchant ship, hiding their guns. At other times, the captain hid the guns and struck most of the sails to appear disabled to lure a prize ship close before opening up with his cannon. One very successful trick was to fly an American flag on the top mast of small schooner they captured and a British flag on the *Tartar*. The schooner would chase ships that would turn and sail toward the "British" warship for protection—and be captured.

The *Tartar* soon became one of the chief targets of the British fleet in Jamaica and three warships were sent out with the sole mission of sinking her. They found her, too, and Porter, knowing he could not take on three ships at once, raced for French-held Port-au-Prince, in Haiti, but did not make it. The three ships closed in on him and he turned into an inlet short of Port-au-Prince. There the *Tartar* ran around on some rocks and sank; the crew fled.

Greenwood found passage on another privateer, the *General Lincoln*, bound for New York, but the *Lincoln* was stopped at sea by a British warship. Prior to its seizure, the captain had asked if any of the crew could help repair the ship. The private volunteered and spent the entire voyage trying to fix the leaks that caused several feet of water to spill into the hold of the *Lincoln* every day. The crew started to good naturedly call him "the carpenter."

When the British seized the ship, their captain asked around for the man everyone called "the carpenter" and told Greenwood, when he found him, that he needed someone to stay with the *Lincoln* to keep up with repairs as the British sailed it to New York as their prize; the rest of the crew would be put in irons. Greenwood, by then tired of prisons of any kind, kept up his appearances as "the carpenter" and stayed with the *Lincoln* all the way up the coast. A crowd of several hundred curious people waited for the *Lincoln* to dock at Manhattan, preparing to board her for the ritual inspection of the public that the British permitted because they thought it built up Loyalist morale. Greenwood waited until half the curious crowd had surged across the gangplank and on to the deck and then slowly, unobtrusively, slipped between them and walked away in a calm and very successful escape to the congested streets of Manhattan.

He had fled into British occupied New York, though, and had to avoid capture. The English would soon be looking for "the carpenter."

There were only two New Yorkers whom he knew, Ahasuerus Turk Jr., the instrument manufacturer who had sold him several fifes just before he traveled north to Canada with his regiment in 1776, and a friend of his father's named Francis Hill. Turk offered him refuge until he located Hill. He lived in New York for six weeks, constantly ducking any British soldiers he saw, always trying to figure out a way to get out of the occupied city and back to Boston. Finally, Hill and a chaplain that he knew concocted a ruse. The chaplain persuaded someone in the military to simply add Greenwood to a group of prisoners scheduled for immediate parole and about to sail to Boston. Young Greenwood was free again.

Cleverness seemed to run in the family. Greenwood's older brother Isaac, who served on the crew of another privateer, was captured and imprisoned in the West Indies. He escaped by feigning sickness to enter and then escape from a prison hospital and then, dressed as a British naval officer, made it on board a merchant ship and fled to the U.S.

Despite his numerous escapes, John Greenwood had yet to learn his lesson about the dangers of sailing on privateers. Upon his return to Boston, he sought out more privateers and signed on as a seaman on the *Aurora* with his former captain, David Porter, at the helm, for an expedition to Port-au-Prince that nearly resulted in his death. This time it was not at the hands of the British or local jailers, but misfortune.

The *Aurora* sailed to Port-au-Prince without incident, but an explosion in port sunk her. Private Greenwood, ill, had earlier taken medicine that made him groggy. Unable to work any longer, he had climbed into his hammock, below deck and near a cannon port hole, and fell asleep. The roar of the explosion awakened him. He opened his eyes and felt his body sliding toward the other side of the boat. He looked toward that side and saw the boat begin to roll away from him. The cannon on that side crashed into the port hole and water gushed in. He saw that water was coming into every port hole on the far side of the ship and felt her start to sink. He rolled out of the hammock, grabbed the cannon next to him and climbed up its barrel, out of the port hole and scrambled off the ship to save his life.

The tragedy was quickly followed by comedy. Back in Boston a few months later, Greenwood signed on with the *Race Horse,* captained by

Nathaniel Thayer, bound for the West Indies. In the middle of the night, serving as watch, he saw a ship sailing toward him. He summoned the captain, who always feared capture, and the commander ordered sails rigged for a getaway. It turned out that the vessel was a prize captured by the British and captained by a woefully inexperienced sailor trying to bring her to a port. The ship had been floating around the Caribbean for days, completely lost. Captain Thayer seized the ship himself, promising the grateful British officer that he would get his crew to Barbados and release them.

He told Greenwood to serve as the new captain and take five crewmen to bring the ship to port. That night Greenwood nearly ran into a huge British man-of-war sailing nearby. He knew he could neither outfight or outrun the ship, but might trick her commander. In the dark, their captain knew just as little about "Captain" Greenwood as the American knew about him. The novice captain had a man-of-war trumpet on the ship and a single, small, swivel-gun cannon. He sounded the trumpet and shouted with convincing bravado that he would sink the British ship if its commander did not heave to and surrender. There was no response from the man-of-war's captain, trying to figure out what ship was out there in the dark, and if it was in range for his guns.

Greenwood then loaded the tiny swivel gun with two cannonballs and a strong gunpowder charge and fired in the direction of the ship. The sound was similar to that of a large cannon and it was loud enough, and menacing enough, to scare the British captain, who turned and sailed away as quickly as the night wind could carry his vessel. He must have thought he had engaged John Paul Jones himself.

On board Greenwood's ship there was a combination of fright and laughter. The charge and double load had blown the small gun out of its locks and sent it sailing across the deck, crashing into everything in its way. When Greenwood related the story to the captain of his mother ship, whom he met in port, the captain howled with merriment.

"Captain Greenwood," who had recently turned twenty, decided to become a real captain just a few weeks later. He took the money he had earned from privateering and with a ship's mate, Myrick, purchased a schooner in Baltimore and won a contract to carry a load of corn to an ironworks on the Patapsco River, nine miles southwest of Baltimore on the Chesapeake Bay.

The two rookie captains then embarked on one of the most inept cruises of the Revolution. They were supposed to sail behind another schooner to the ironworks, but left port late when Greenwood lingered too long at a nearby tavern. Lost in the middle of the Chesapeake, the sailing "expert" had to ask directions to the mouth of the river from the captain of another schooner that passed by them, much to the embarrassment of Myrick.

No sooner did they start up the river when, according to Greenwood, a "monstrous" storm arose. Instead of heading for a safe inlet on the river, or simply anchoring and lowering their sails to ride out the furious winds, the two captains tried to sail through it. They soon lurched into each other on the deck when the ship ran aground on a sandbar. Greenwood was determined to keep sailing. Instead of waiting for the light of morning and the tide to attempt to move off the sandbar, he rode out in a flat bottomed boat they had secured on deck in the pitch black night. Thunderclaps boomed and lightning crackled all about him. He brought a coil of rope along, intending to pull the larger craft back into the river with his small boat. As soon as he yanked on the thick rope, his boat overturned and he was unceremoniously pitched into the river.

Greenwood spotted a farmhouse on shore when another bolt of lightning hit and illuminated it and went there to get help for his ship. The farmer would not go out into the storm and told Greenwood to sleep in his home. By morning, the tide had lifted the boat off the sandbar and the captains prepared to sail to the ironworks. The men soon discovered that they never secured the corn ears, which had now floated into the pumps and clogged them, preventing any movement. Finally, the corn removed and the pumps fixed, the ship limped upriver to the ironworks with its battered cargo and similarly battered crew. The voyage had been such a catastrophe that Myrick quit and sold his share of the boat to another man in Baltimore.

Private Greenwood made one last voyage and it should have been a calm one. He was the first mate for a repugnant captain on the *Resolution,* a six-gun schooner bound for St. Eustatius with a load of flour and orders to buy salt to bring back for Maryland merchants. The voyage took place without incident and upon his return Greenwood was happy to hear that the obnoxious captain had been fired and he had been given charge of the schooner for another run to St. Eustatius.

This trip was no pleasure cruise, however. In the middle of their passage between the islands of Antigua and Saint Bartholomew a large, fast ship bore down on them. Greenwood let out all of his sail in an effort to outrun the monster ship coming at him. "I let out the reefs of the mainsail and clapped her away four points free," he wrote. "She sailed like a bird, but in two or three hours the pursuing vessel came up with us, firing, one after another, seven shots at us, and at last got so close that I could see the buttons on the men's coats."

The ship, the *Santa Margaretta,* looked fearsome. Originally a Spanish ship, the *Santa Margaretta* was a sleek, fast-moving, forty-four gun warship that carried two hundred twenty sailors, half of them musket men. She had been cruising up and down the Atlantic seaboard, bagging several prizes, before departing for the warmer waters of the Caribbean. Suddenly, the guns of the *Santa Margaretta* opened up.

"They then got ready a six-pound cannon from the quarterdeck loaded with grapeshot and fired point blank into us, cutting away our jib sheet blocks, forepeak tie, and other rigging forward," a frantic Greenwood noted.

The *Resolution* had been turned into the wind and toward the British warship. Greenwood was certain that if he did not surrender, the huge ship would ram his, cutting the *Resolution* in half and sinking her and his crew. He struck his colors and gave up.

The captain and officers of the *Santa Margaretta* were a casual crew, far more interested in their prize cargo than prisoners. They let all of the crew of the *Resolution* go free when they anchored in Kingston, Jamaica. In fact, it was the British, not the Americans, who brought Greenwood home. The sailing master of the *Santa Margaretta* knew Captain Henry

Nicholls, in charge of the British privateer *Barracouta*, headed for New York in a few days. He told him Nicholls would take him on as a passenger (probably for a price).

Several weeks later, "Captain" Greenwood said goodbye to the commander and crew of the *Barracouta* in New York and made his way back to Boston in the spring of 1783 on board one of the ships carrying prisoners to their homes as the war wound down.

Greenwood worked as a mate on merchant ships sailing out of Boston and was the captain of a schooner out of Baltimore on three trips during the last few months of the Revolution. The end of hostilities meant an end to privateering and, for awhile, the profitable merchant trade between New England and the West Indies. There was no work for the hundreds of wartime sailors like Greenwood, so he left Boston and traveled to New York. There, Greenwood, only twenty-three, planned to move in with his brother Isaac and, with him, take up dentistry, their father's profession.

The veteran soldier and sailor left Boston just as he had arrived there eight years before, in the summer of 1775 at the age of fifteen, carrying fifes in his backpack, bragging to all at a roadside tavern where he entertained patrons with his fife that year that he was there "to fight for my country."

He certainly had done so, and there was still one more chapter left in his story.

Chapter Twenty-Seven

1779–1780:
The War's Worst Winter and Mutiny

The War

*T*he Crown, determined to destroy Washington's main army, sent more than six thousand troops up the Hudson toward West Point, where he was headquartered, in the spring of 1779. The British force seized and held Fort Lafayette and a garrison at Stony Point, both twelve miles south of West Point on the banks of the Hudson. In a daring nighttime raid, Anthony Wayne's men retook Stony Point on July 16, ending the British threat against the army. A month later, on August 19, Light-Horse Harry Lee captured the British garrison at Paulus Hook (Jersey City).

The major battle between British and American troops in 1779 was the failed attempt by a combined American and French forces to recapture Savannah, seized by the British at Christmas, 1778. A September 1779 siege to take Savannah, aided by French troops who arrived with Admiral d'Estaing's fleet, failed and residents complained that the Americans had destroyed half the town in the process. D'Estaing insisted that he could not stay and forced an early final assault on October 9 that was easily repulsed by the British.

British forces in Georgia captured several towns and then Augusta, and administered a devastating defeat to an American force that tried to reclaim it. In May, Redcoats in Virginia easily captured Suffolk, Portsmouth, and a naval shipyard at Norfolk, where they seized or wrecked 137 American ships.

Indian raids on rural towns in Pennsylvania and New York infuriated Congress, who had been courting tribal leaders. In the summer of 1779, Washington sent Generals John Sullivan and James Clinton and a force of thirty-seven hundred men to upstate New York and western Pennsylvania with orders to destroy the Six Nations of the Iroquois Confederation and capture as many Indians as possible. Troops sent to the Pittsburgh area burned ten Indian villages while Sullivan's main force campaigning through New York destroyed forty, including the entire community of Genesee, New York with its 128 buildings. The devastation of the communities made it difficult for the Indians to find much shelter for the coming winter. Sullivan's men also ruined corn fields and apple orchards to make it impossible for the Iroquois to live off the land.

The alliance with the French had not been as productive as Congress had hoped. The massive numbers of troops promised by Paris had not arrived and those that did saw meager action. The French navy had so far contributed little to the American cause. Its admirals were strongly criticized for leaving the battle of Newport, refusing to attack New York, and leaving too soon in the aborted effort to retake Savannah. In 1779, the U.S. received some more international help when Spain declared war on England, seized several towns from the British along the northern shores of the Gulf of Mexico and helped financially with some small loans. The Spaniards could not be convinced to contribute much needed troops, however, and a promised combined Spanish-French sea assault on the British navy in waters near England, to be followed by an amphibious attack, never materialized.

Sea battles between America, France, and Spain against England raged in the Caribbean throughout the year. American ships successfully harassed British warships and merchant task forces around Great Britain and in a *much heralded battle, John Paul Jones's* Bon Homme Richard *defeated the British* Serapis *in a lengthy battle off the coast of England.*

The victory at Monmouth in the summer of 1778, the apparent end of the smallpox epidemics, and mild weather throughout 1779, plus more clothing, caused an increase in enlistments and a decrease in desertions for Washington's army in the north.

It had been a year when Washington's spy network, started in the early days of the war to provide him with solid information about the enemy, had grown to hundreds of informers. Spies had tipped him off to the exact route of the British toward Monmouth 1778 and in 1780 would once again prove invaluable.

Washington's strategy had been to fight the British head-on when he could, such as at Monmouth and Brandywine, but to avoid confrontations when his prospects were not good. He needed to convince the British press and public that the Crown could not win what was becoming a lengthy war, and should quit. The plan began to pay off in 1779 as more and more British periodicals criticized the conflict, some publishing "body counts," lists of the casualties, in their columns. Groups called "patriotic societies" were formed throughout England to protest the war in America and an increasing number of influential members of Parliament spoke out against it. The city of London refused to tax its residents for the war. One British army regiment had even mutinied when told they were going to fight in America. Even the prime minister, Lord North, began to consider shifting the focus of the war from America to Europe and the French and Spanish.

Still, there was no end to the war in sight. The British maintained posts in New York, Savannah, Charleston, and Newport and sent an endless supply of British troops and hired mercenaries, cannon, and warships to America. Their treasury appeared bottomless and King George III was determined to triumph.

Some thought that an American victory would only come if the British believed that they could never truly win, that they would fight for years with no result—and at great cost. Others were convinced victory for the rebels could only be realized if the conflict escalated into a full-blown world war, with Spain sending hundreds of ships and thousands of men to America, in addition to the promised French forces. Either way, the Continental Army and its thousands of enlisted men had to hold together as a fighting force. Their ability to do that was severely tested in the brutal winter of 1779–1780.

It began to snow early on Sunday morning, December 5, 1779, and continued into Monday, the snow piling up throughout the village of Chatham and throughout Morris County, New Jersey. Militia Colonel Sylvanus Seely wrote that it "snowed hard all day." So much had accumulated over the two days, nearly nine inches, that the roads were impassable to all but horse-drawn sleighs. In Philadelphia, where the storm hit even harder, residents measured the snowfall at eighteen inches.[1]

In Danbury, Connecticut, that morning the storm did not stop the Second Rhode Island, with Jeremiah Greenman, now a lieutenant, from starting its march to winter headquarters in Morristown, New Jersey. The regimental commander, Colonel Israel Angell, pushed his men to trudge eighteen miles to Cortlandt Manor, Colonel Phillip Van Cortlandt's large estate on the eastern bank of the Hudson River, in a storm that blanketed the Hudson River Valley. The Second Rhode Island then marched a few miles each day until they were stopped by another severe storm on December 12. The men were wet and hungry. They were so hungry that, Greenman said, a group of them, wielding muskets, chased a pair of fleet-footed deer through a woods but did not catch them.[2]

Washington's main army traveled through the falling snow and arrived in Morristown from Newburgh, New York, on December 13. Colonel Seely had turned his wagon into a sleigh, taking off its wheels and fastening ski-like runners to it. On the day that Washington arrived, it snowed again. The temperatures remained low.

Everyone feared the weather would be severe, but no one anticipated one of the most brutal winters in American history. From November 1779 until the spring of 1780, New Jersey would be pounded by twenty-six snowstorms, six of blizzard proportions. It was so cold that the temperatures in the region that January remained below freezing during all but two days. The Delaware River froze over by the end of December and remained so until March 4. The Schuylkill River in Pennsylvania, which intersected with the Delaware just below Philadelphia, froze and the ice was so thick that every day residents of the city rode horses and sleds over it. The York River in Virginia was frozen solid for several months. The water in Baltimore harbor was covered with a thick sheet of ice for twelve weeks. Most of the Chesapeake Bay froze over. New York harbor froze, and remained so for several months, permitting sleds to travel back and forth between New York City and New Jersey. It was the only time in recorded history that the deep harbor had frozen solid.[3]

Washington selected Morristown, where the army had camped during the winter of 1776–1777, for several reasons. He again wanted to be stationed near Clinton's army, warm and comfortable in New York City, in case the British decided to move out of the city and attack anywhere on the east coast. Morristown was at the intersection of two highways that he could use to move the army quickly if necessary. It was protected from a British surprise attack by several mountain ranges. It sat in the middle of thousands of acres of farmland with, he thought, plenty of food and cattle for his thirteen thousand man force. (A few hundred men would be billeted in towns a few miles away.) The county was patriotic and he was told that its local militia, led by Colonel Seely, was reliable.

His three thousand man army of 1776–1777 had caused problems in Morris County because the men had been quartered in private homes. As many as a dozen soldiers had stayed with families in small houses built to hold just four or five residents. The people complained of constant drinking, gambling, and cursing by the soldiers. This time, with a much larger army, Washington decided to build a sprawling city of huts in Jockey Hollow, near Morristown, as he had done at Valley Forge in the winter of 1777–1778 and at Bound Brook, New Jersey, the previous year. The massive hut encampment would, again, in population, take its place as the fourth largest city in the United States, behind Philadelphia, New York, and Boston.

Washington designed the huts and the city himself. The log cabins were similar to those at Valley Forge, but this time the huts were built on the sides of hills to provide drainage for water and melted snow. The walls and roofs were solid to prevent seepage. Each had a window cut into a wall for ventilation later, when the weather turned mild. The lack of drainage and haphazardly built walls in the Valley Forge huts, and little ventilation, helped to bring about diseases there. All of the Morristown huts were built in planned neighborhoods, New Yorkers together in one section, Pennsylvanians in another, and along carefully laid out streets. Warehouses, cattle pens covering several acres, and slaughterhouses were erected after the residential huts were completed.

The regiments that arrived early, in milder weather, had more luck with construction and were living in their cabins within two weeks. The men from other states, who came later, took much longer to complete hut construction because they had to battle the elements. Those without huts slept in tents; some had nothing.

On the day after the storm of December 5 and 6, Dr. James Thacher arrived in Morristown with his Massachusetts regiment. They had no cover. Thacher wrote in his diary,

> The snow on the ground is about two feet deep and the weather extremely cold; the soldiers are destitute of both tents and blankets and some of them are actually barefooted and almost naked. Our only defense against the inclemency of the weather consists of brushwood thrown together. Our lodging last night was on the frozen ground. Having removed the snow, we wrapped ourselves in great coats, spread our blankets on the ground and lay down by the side of each other, five or six together, with large fires at our feet. We could procure neither shelter or forage for our horses and the poor animals were tied to trees in the woods for twenty-four hours without food, except the bark which they peeled from the trees.[4]

One week later, a cold front moved into northern New Jersey, sending the already low temperatures in Jockey Hollow plunging. Lieutenant Erkuries Beatty, of the Fourth Pennsylvania Regiment, wrote to his brother, "Colder weather I never saw." Captain Walter Finney, of Pennsylvania, freezing like everyone else, remembered that Jockey Hollow's pre-war nickname was "Pleasant Valley." In a sarcastic note in his journal, a freezing Finney wrote, "We did not find it answered to its name."[5]

The day after Beatty wrote his letter, the Second Rhode Island Regiment arrived in Morristown, exhausted from their long march over snow- and ice-covered dirt highways. One soldier wrote that "very early that winter the cold came. And such cold! There had been nothing like it in the memory of the oldest inhabitants. Roads disappeared under snow four feet deep."[6] Johann Kalb, an officer who had come to America with Lafayette, wrote that Morristown was worse than Valley Forge and that "it is so cold that the ink freezes in my pen while I am sitting close to the fire."[7]

Jeremiah Greenman was not only irritated by the harsh weather but by the discovery that the land set aside for the Rhode Islanders had already been taken by the New Yorkers. Lieutenant Greenman's regiment was ordered to march another mile through thick, snow-covered woods to a new piece of land. There, over the next two weeks, the Rhode Islanders labored through several snowstorms and the cold to build their huts. They had to live in flimsy tents on the outskirts of Morristown and march more than a mile to their construction site each day; they had little food.[8] Greenman wrote, "Very cold and almost starved for want of provisions."

Freezing as hut construction went slowly, Greenman remembered that he was now a lieutenant and decided to pull rank. He told a sergeant to leave his finished hut and Greenman took his place. He told the unhappy sergeant that it was only temporary, until Greenman and the others finished their own huts. The sergeant had to wait a very long five weeks for that to happen.

They faced another clothing shortage. There were no shoes, either, for men walking in snow five inches deep. "The deficiency of shoes is so extensive that a great proportion of the army is totally incapable of duty and could not move," Washington complained to a quartermaster at Newburgh. The commander fumed about the shortages to all later, when he could not send a five-hundred-man regiment to assist in the defense of Charleston because none of the men had footwear.[9] The southern city then fell to the British under Sir Henry Clinton on May 12; the entire

American army of fifty-five hundred men was captured and four thousand muskets seized. It was a terrible blow to the American cause.

The bitter cold was not the biggest worry of the enlisted men and their officers, though; they were starving. An autumn-long drought had caused a bread and flour shortage and many of the men who arrived in Morristown had not eaten any meat or bread in days. The snowstorms prevented the transportation of cattle to slaughterhouses so that the animals could be turned into meat for the soldiers. The cold and snow in New Jersey further hampered food and shelter operations. Gristmills that depended on fast-running water from rivers and streams for power had to shut down when all the waterways froze over, and could not produce bread.

The army soon discovered that not only was there little food in the area but that the residents there were as reluctant as those near Valley Forge had been to sell the army food and clothing following yet another currency depreciation. Runaway inflation had crippled the national economy and now it took $30 in continental scrip to purchase what one hard dollar (gold or silver) could buy. Most farmers and merchants would not accept credit, as the Pennsylvanians at least had done. Many local merchants complained that the army still owed them money from the winter of 1777. The citizens who refused to feed the army were as angry as the soldiers who were starving. General Greene wrote Colonel Daniel Broadhead that he was afraid "the people will pull us to pieces."[10]

Private Joseph Martin wrote, "We were absolutely, literally starved. I do solemnly declare that I did not put a single morsel of victuals into my mouth for four days and as many nights, except a little black birch bark which I gnawed off a stick of wood, if that can be called victuals. I saw several of the men roast their shoes and eat them."[11] Men were again reduced to eating their pets. Major James Fairlie wrote, "I ate several meals of dog and relished [them] very well."[12]

An angry Washington complained to state governors and wrote to Congress that "unless some expedient can be instantly adopted, a dissolution of the army for want of subsistence is unavoidable."[13] The governors were enraged by price gouging and the reluctance of the citizens to support the troops. None was angrier that New Jersey's Governor

William Livingston. He wrote "that America, after having so long been the admiration of Europe and having an army on foot that defies the power of Great Britain should at last be compelled to disband her troops by the artifices and practices of Tories and speculators and monopolizers and scoundrels of all sorts and sizes could go very near to deprive me of my senses."[14]

The governors, and Congress, responded to the general's pleas and within days dozens of wagons arrived with food and clothing that would carry the troops through another few weeks. But it seemed that no matter what Washington did, he was thwarted by the unending snowfalls that continually made the roads impassable and forced the cancellation of the food deliveries. A brutal storm dropped eighteen inches of snow on December 18, and again halted all hut construction at Jockey Hollow and again ruined any chance to obtain food.

Sawmills throughout the state that the army relied upon to produce boards for the completion of the soldiers' huts had been shut down by the ice and snow just like the gristmills. The shortage of boards became so acute that a supply officer, Joseph Lewis, a local man, ordered soldiers to tear down area barns for their wood and even had latrines pulled apart for their boards. Lewis begged area farmers to give the soldiers straw to make bedding for those who had managed to move into their huts.

There was little joy on Christmas Day. Most men still slept in tents that sagged under the weight of snow and ice. They existed on one-third rations. Their meager meals had been supplemented a bit in mid December, when Washington sent the emaciated horses to Pennsylvania and gave the men the animals' corn. The soldiers had little clothing or shoes and found the little money they had was worthless.

Their commanders felt badly for them and noted that soldiers had often gone four or five days without food. "I was extremely shocked," General von Steuben wrote to New York governor George Clinton. "[It was] the greatest picture of misery that was ever seen."[15] Governor Livingston told the New Jersey Assembly that the military situation was "deplorable," and that "the army [is] reduced for want of provisions and that the magazines are everywhere exhausted."[16]

If all of that was not enough to cause consternation throughout the army, Benedict Arnold was court-martialed that winter for malfeasance during his term as the military governor of Pennsylvania the previous year. He was convicted of illegally appropriating army wagons to haul goods that he reportedly sold for personal profit. General Washington, Arnold's lone supporter in the army, simply admonished him. That rebuke, though, enraged Arnold and started him on his road to treachery.

Then, on December 27, yet another storm arrived and dropped yet another eighteen inches of snow, halting any food delivery. Desperate, many of men sneaked out of camp and plundered the local farms of food, clothing, kettles, knives, shovels, stockings, and anything else they could lay their hands on.

An appalled Washington issued orders barring any further theft and promised harsh punishments for those caught stealing, but he did not carry them out. The people had not helped the army in its hour of dire need, he reasoned, and so he let them suffer.

On January 2, a Sunday, a blizzard that continued for three days hit northern New Jersey, dumping more than a foot of snow on the Morristown area. Baron de Kalb remembered measuring drifts at twelve feet. The storm created havoc. Dr. Thacher, who still had no hut, wrote, "Several [tents] were torn asunder and blown down over the officers' heads in the night, and some of the soldiers were actually covered while in their tents and buried like sheep under the snow. My comrades and myself were roused from sleep by the calls from some officers for assistance; their [tent] had blown down, and they were almost smothered in the storm; before they could reach our [tent] only a few yards, and their blankets and baggage were nearly buried in the snow."[17]

Thacher wrote too soon. Just two days later, a second blizzard hit the area, dropping another six inches. This storm, too, was accompanied by high winds and chilly temperatures. On the morning of January 6, General Washington, who had watched the storm for four days, wrote in a weather diary he kept, "Night very stormy. The snow, which in general is eighteen inches deep, is much drifted. Roads almost impassable."[18]

Greenman and the Rhode Islanders, like the other soldiers, found themselves trapped by the storms. The lieutenant worked with his men in digging out their tents and huts. They found piles of wood for their fireplaces beneath the thick blanket of snow that seemed to cover the whole world. They were freezing and starving to death at the same time. Dr. Thacher put it best when he wrote, "The sufferings of the poor soldiers can scarcely be described. While on duty they are unavoidably exposed to all the inclemency of storms and severe cold. They are badly clad and some are destitute of shoes. We are frequently for six to eight days entirely destitute of meat and then as long without bread. The soldiers are so enfeebled from hunger and cold as to be almost unable to perform their military duty or labor in constructing their huts."[19]

No one realized this more acutely than George Washington. He rode through the snow to Jockey Hollow from time to time to visit the camp and supervise the work crews as they dug out. He only had admiration for his soldiers. "The troops, both officers and men, have born their distress with a patience scarcely to be conceived. Many of the latter have been four or five days without meat entirely and short of bread," he wrote to Continental Congress president Samuel Huntington on January 5.[20]

The situation was desperate and everyone knew it. Congressional delegate William Ellery wrote with alarm that "we are at the very pinch of the game."[21] Washington did not want to declare martial law and seize food from residents, even though Congress had urged him to do it and that seemed the army's only salvation. He knew martial law would set a terrible precedent. But after those January storms he had to consider doing so. His soldiers were trapped by a blizzard and starving to death. The general asked Nathanael Greene to call an emergency meeting of the Morris County freeholders, the area's governing body, on the night of January 8. Greene had already told friends that he feared the worst, writing to one, "Unless the good people immediately lend their assistance to forward supplies, the army must disband."[22] That night, Greene read the men a letter from Washington in which he begged them to give the army the cattle, food, and clothing he needed, on credit, trusting him to pay them at some point in the future. If they did not, he seemed to say between the lines, and Greene surely indicated, they would force him to declare martial law and take what he needed to save his men.

It was a short meeting. Fully realizing the plight of the men, the freeholders assured the general that they would quickly find food and direct the residents to somehow open up the roads. Over the next two days, in a miracle of engineering, hundreds of local militiamen and farmers worked tirelessly to break open more than eight miles of roadway. Those same farmers, and others, then sent Washington hundreds of head of cattle, straw, wheat, corn, anything they had, on just credit, to save the army. A week later, a correspondent wrote in the *Jersey Journal*, "The army is now exuberantly supplied with provision and every other necessary to make a soldier's life comfortable."[23]

The soldiers were stunned by the generosity of the people that day. Wrote one, "The inhabitants of this part of the country discovered a noble spirit in feeding the soldiers; and to the honor of the soldiery, they received what they got with thankfulness."[24]

Another Winter Surprise Attack

The weather, food, and clothing catastrophes did not stop the Americans from planning yet another surprise winter attack. Washington had startled the enemy at Trenton three years before with his crossing of the Delaware in a snowstorm; why not do it again? The target was the British garrison on Staten Island, across the harbor from New York City, with its one thousand men.

Washington placed twenty-six hundred men under one of his veteran generals, Lord Stirling. Washington had to get the army to Staten Island quickly, so he decided to use hundreds of horse-drawn sleds to transport the army in what would be one of the most unusual attacks in military history.

Still, Washington worried. What if the caravan of sleds was seen? What if a thaw hit in the morning and the ice bridge to Staten Island from New Jersey melted, stranding the soldiers? What if the British forts were impregnable? Eager to stage the attack, and assured by Lord Stirling that it would succeed, Washington finally relented.[25]

Jeremiah Greenman arrived at the staging area for the raid, on the south side of the Morristown green, at 8 a.m. sharp on the morning of January 14 and waited with the twenty-six hundred other troops selected for the attack for the sleds promised by local farmers. Many of the soldiers wore hats and mittens that they had to borrow from the clothing warehouses. They had to return them when the attack ended. The sleds, each drawn by two horses, were delayed, but by 10 a.m. over four hundred had arrived and Lieutenant Greenman and seven others boarded one. Their sled followed the others in creating a lengthy train of sleighs that left Morristown in the early afternoon and traveled silently across the snow-covered roads thirty miles to Elizabethtown, where the soldiers slept overnight.

The attack on Staten Island commenced early the next morning. Greenman wrote brusquely in his journal, "Crossed the river on the ice. Came to Staten Island and proceeded on toward the enemy's forts . . . five miles."

The element of surprise that the Americans had enjoyed when they crossed the Delaware had been lost; the army had been seen. The British had time to dig in behind ten-foot-high snow and ice walls and barricade themselves in houses and barns. They were ready for the assault and easily turned back the American forces after a series of thunderous musket and cannon volleys.

To Lieutenant Greenman's surprise, Lord Stirling did not order a retreat back to Morristown. He kept the army on Staten Island overnight on what turned out to be one of the coldest evenings of the year. "We took a post on a hill half a mile from one of the forts where the snow was about two feet deep. Here we dug the snow off the ground and built up fires and tarried all night. Very cold with a number of our men's feet froze." Doctors later reported nearly five hundred men suffered frozen feet.

An angry Greenman wrote the following day, after the retreat finally began, that one-third of the men in his own regiment had suffered frostbite on their feet during the night. The trip back to Morristown on the sleds began after disheartening news that some local residents had followed the army to Staten Island and looted some of the homes there.[26] Sylvanus Seely was a witness to that. He had not been ordered to participate in the attack, but rode to Staten Island with a friend anyway to watch. He noticed with disgust people rummaging through homes of British sympathizers. Seely wrote that "the residents of the island are sorely plundered." The looting would mushroom into a public relations disaster for the Continental Army and cost Lord Stirling his command.

The British retaliated for the raid in early February by attacking both Elizabethtown and the nearby community of Bergen. They burned several buildings in each community, captured more than a dozen officers and, in a bold move, abducted Joseph Hedden, one of the Essex County freeholders.[27]

By that time, all of the huts at Jockey Hollow were completed, but continual clothing, food, and supply problems continued to plague the soldiers. The currency shortage that drove the price of a horse up to $20,000 eased somewhat when Congress decided to collect and burn existing money and create a new, limited supply to curb inflation.

Several more storms hit the area, delaying shipments of clothing and food. The population that had saved the army in January was reluctant to do so again and throughout February and March merchants and farmers constantly argued with army purchasing agents over prices and credit. At one point General de Kalb wailed, "These are the people who talk about sacrificing their all in the cause of liberty!" And Nathanael Greene lamented that "there was never a darker hour in American politics than this."[28]

The Militia Colonel under Arrest

Sylvanus Seely, now a colonel, spent the winter of 1780 as he had spent most of the winters of the war. Since the army was in camp, the militia was not called to join it and Seely's military business was limited to overseeing the posting of guards around the Morristown area and maintaining the complicated beacon and alarm gun lookout network that Washington had devised three years earlier. He continued to run his small inn, but the dreadful weather curtailed business. The colonel continued to engage in business deals, traveling to purchase items for his store that he would try to sell at a profit. He again entered into small business deals with army officers. They would provide cash for some transaction with him, and he would take care of the business and split whatever profit there was. He became sick from the bad weather from time to time.

His life fell apart in early April. The militia leader had gone out to settle some financial debts in a snowstorm that dumped three inches of snow on the area on Friday, March 31. Seely became ill from exposure and on the following Thursday saw a doctor, who bled him. The bleeding did not hurt as much as what happened to him later that day—he was arrested.

The charges against him were serious—trading with the enemy. It was alleged that as leader of the militia while it was posted in Elizabethtown he permitted local residents to illegally purchase British goods taken by the American army from a captured ship. He was also accused of permitting residents to illegally sell goods to the British, as well as transporting goods from ships to his quarters and later selling them. It was charged that he permitted loyalists to illegally travel back and forth between Elizabethtown and New York. Finally, it was alleged that Seely juggled his militia payroll books to permit friends who were just privates to receive officers' pay.

The arrest came at a time when illegal colonial–English sales, called "London trade," had become an epidemic; Governor Livingston called any such transaction "a piece of villainy."[29] American currency was practically worthless and many Americans found it more beneficial to sell goods to the British for their far more valuable pound sterling. It was also difficult to find goods in American stores and British soldiers were happy to sell what they had at a tidy price. Several American officers had been convicted for participating in these illegal transactions during the winter. Seely found himself one of many people sought in a widening effort to stop the business, which hurt the local and national economy.

The next day, Friday, brought even more trouble for the militia colonel. He learned in the morning that a friend, William Crowell, had been killed by a musket ball from a British gun that had accidentally discharged. Then, that night, he saw Mrs. Ball again and they got into a terrible fight. "Believe I shall never be able to get her affection again, and that she hates me," he wrote in his secret diary.

Despite these personal woes, Colonel Seely worked hard to prove himself innocent at his court-martial, which was eventually held on May 4 in Bernardsville. He asked a friend to gather evidence that would prove him innocent and he himself testified that he had done no wrong and offered the court-martial board all the assistance they requested in looking at his orders and his militia payrolls. The court-martial board only took one hour to acquit Seely of all charges.

In an extraordinary move, Governor Livingston issued an official proclamation noting the acquittal that was published in both the *Jersey Journal* and the *New Jersey Gazette*. It was no ordinary proclamation, though. It listed the charges and the not guilty verdict but then, at the end, the governor wrote that Seely "is entitled to the character of a good soldier, a vigilant officer, and faithful citizen, and as such deserves the gratitude of his country."[30]

Seely was relieved; the court-martial had worried him for weeks. He wrote, "Cannot help remarking that I felt very heavy when I was called to answer guilty or not guilty although I knew my innocence." He was relieved, too, that his friend Governor Livingston had written the special proclamation. The governor and the militia leader had become friends during the war, sometimes dining together, and the governor knew that at some point the New Jersey militia might be instrumental in defending the state.

That day came sooner than Livingston anticipated.

Mutiny

The month of May did not bring much happiness to the troops camped at Morristown. There was not much of a harvest following the dreadful winter. Farmland had been ruined by the cold and snow, fruit trees were destroyed, and corn fields frozen. Hundreds of cattle died from a lack of fodder. Food supplies were short and the soldiers complained continuously. In addition to the lack of food, there was a lack of money since many of the soldiers had not been paid in months. At the same time, soldiers talked bitterly about the profits being earned by the thousands of men working as sailors for the privateers that preyed on British merchant ships while the soldiers at Jockey Hollow starved.

The enlisted men were just as angry with black market entrepreneurs who purchased salt for $15 a bushel in south Jersey and sold it in Morristown for $35 a bushel. The lower-ranking officers, some of whom had risen from the ranks of enlisted men, were bitter about problems with promotion. The states had consolidated lowly enrolled companies and regiments into new regiments. Captains and lieutenants were then forced into the consolidated companies at the lowest rank. Officers who had been prisoners, and there were many, were told that their time imprisoned in warehouses or ships would not count toward their time in the army; they fumed as men with less time in service than they were promoted ahead of them. All starved.

"The men were now exasperated beyond endurance; they could not stand it any longer," wrote Private Joseph Martin.[31] Their anger boiled over on May 25, a rather pleasant day, and exploded in a mutiny, the very event that George Washington feared the most. That evening, a hungry Connecticut soldier complained about some orders to a sergeant. The sergeant called him "a mutinous rascal." The soldier slammed the butt of his musket into the ground. "Who will parade with me?" he yelled. His entire regiment, including Private Martin, rushed to his side, shouting at the sergeant that they would all join him, march out of camp, and go home. Another regiment joined them. Someone said that many other regiments would join and that they should take a band with them as they left for home.

There were several versions of what happened next. According to most, a popular officer, Colonel Return Meigs, was accidentally wounded by a bayonet. That prompted an officer to order other officers to put down the mutiny. They approached the group and one officer apparently seized a man. Another officer shouted that the men should not move. Instead, the Connecticut men turned on the officers, brandishing their bayonets, and pushed them back.

A Pennsylvania officer quickly brought up a regiment of his men, armed with their muskets, to put down the mutiny but many of the troops thought they had been brought up to join it. Their officers then ordered them back to their quarters. Confusion reigned.

Finally, according to Martin, the Connecticut soldiers quieted down and broke into small groups to argue their grievances, still uncertain what action to take. They were "venting our spleen at our country and government, then at our officers and then at ourselves for our imbecility in staying there and starving in detail for an ungrateful people."[32]

The soldiers abandoned the mutiny and returned to their huts after Colonel Walter Stewart wrote down their complaints and promised to take them to General Washington. The commander was angry, but fully understood the reasons why the men revolted. He could not bring himself to have all of the mutineers executed, or even the instigators. He chose one of the leaders and had him shot. The rest were eventually forgiven. The mutiny, which followed a few smaller ones in other posts, deeply disturbed Washington.

News of the dissension in the ranks, a feeling that the Americans were too hungry to fight, plus an assessment that the members of the local militia were not skilled and would not turn out for a battle, prompted the British to launch an invasion of New Jersey that they believed could smash the American army. A victory over Washington's force, coupled with the capture of Charleston, would surely force the Continental Congress to surrender and end the war.

Chapter Twenty-Eight

SPRINGFIELD:
The Militia Saves the Revolution

General Wilhelm Knyphausen was left in charge of the eight-thousand-man British force in New York when Sir Henry Clinton sailed south to take Charleston. The veteran Prussian general, in charge of all Hessian troops since January 1777 and second in command of British forces to Clinton, was a slender man who walked and sat ramrod straight. The sharp-featured Prussian was a gentleman and esteemed by his men. In the beginning of June, Knyphausen decided to attack the Americans at Morristown by landing at DeHart's Point, Elizabethtown, and then marching west through Connecticut Farms (now Union) and then Springfield. He would surprise the Americans by landing at night, overcome what he believed to be a skeleton lookout force in the area, and then march to Morristown the next morning with five thousand troops.

The attack surprised no one. Washington expected such a campaign and had carefully prepared for it. His beacon fire towers and alarm guns had been manned twenty-four hours a day for more than a week when the British landed on June 7. Couriers were ready to ride to militia leaders to alert them to the attack. The number of lookouts had been increased. On June 2, Washington had asked Governor Livingston to call out the entire state militia and have them march to the Morristown area.[1] Elizabethtown *was* protected by Continentals under Colonel Elias Dayton.[2]

Knyphausen was also wrong about the loyalty of the militia. They responded immediately upon hearing the alarm guns. Militia leaders rode as quickly as they could to mobilization points and waited for their men, who arrived soon after, in force and eager to take on the Redcoats.[3]

The British moved over the water from Staten Island on the evening of June 6 and arrived at Elizabethtown about 3 a.m., expecting no resistance. They were surprised by Dayton's men. The Americans, realizing that they were engaged with a very large army, held back the British the best they could in a brief skirmish and then began an orderly retreat toward Connecticut Farms, firing at the British as they went. This harassment slowed the British force considerably. By the time they arrived at Connecticut Farms, the Americans there had time to assemble enough men to do battle. General William Maxwell's brigade formed a line near the Presbyterian meetinghouse and held off the British for several hours as more Americans arrived. The British finally pushed the Continentals back and out of the village. The Redcoats then set fire to a dozen buildings in the village, including the meetinghouse, and, in the melee, it was charged that a British soldier shot and killed Hannah Caldwell, the wife of Rev. James Caldwell, a beloved local minister and patriot. The British denied one of their soldiers had shot Mrs. Caldwell.

The Americans withdrew westward and set up another line. One of the keys to victory for the British was a small bridge that crossed the Rahway River, a narrow tributary only slightly wider than a brook. Dayton's regiment, with a single cannon, defended the bridge. They were already in place as the British appeared. Ordered to assist them was the Morris militia under Seely, but to do so the men had to cross an open meadow as the British artillery was put in position.

Seely had been the head of the militia for four years by then and was an accomplished leader. Cursing as loudly as he could to get his men to move faster, the colonel led the militia into and across the meadow. They soon became targets of a heavy cannon and musket bombardment and scrambled for cover behind any large rock or thick tree trunk they could find. Ashbel Green, a seventeen-year-old volunteer who later became a minister, was caught in the middle of the shelling. He wrote later, "Cannonball and grape shot . . . swept over us like a storm of hail, the ground trembling under us at every step. No thunderstorm I have ever witnessed, either in loudness of sound or the shaking of the earth, equaled what I saw and felt in crossing that meadow."[4]

Dayton's Continentals and Seely's militia held the bridge and the line that Greene had put together held off the entire British army during heavy skirmishing that lasted several hours. Late in the afternoon, Washington's wing of the army arrived and the commander in chief aligned them in a north-south arc at the foot of the Watchung Mountains to await another British advance. There was none. Knyphausen knew he had been defeated and withdrew to Elizabethtown.

The Second Rhode Island saw little action that day, but did the next. Washington assumed that Knyphausen might be preparing to move northward, toward West Point, a target Washington always believed key for the Redcoats.

To protect himself, Washington sent a fifteen hundred man force under General Edward Hand, including the Second Rhode Island, to DeHart's Point to harass the enemy. The Rhode Islanders walked directly into the five-thousand-man British and Hessian force. Greenman wrote, "Marched forward in this position to attack the enemy. Fired two rounds at them."

Sylvanus Seely and the Morris militia stood right next to the Rhode Islanders. The several hundred militiamen had been ordered to join the Continental Army force and advanced as the center column. When they encountered fire, along with the Second Rhode Island, the militia, Seely wrote, "behaved exceedingly well." Some men fell back after the shock of the first volley, but moved toward the enemy on Seely's orders. The Morris County men took twenty British prisoners in that first engagement and, with the Rhode Islanders, moved forward into the woods in an effort to claim more. They were stopped cold. "The enemy opened up on us with a number of field pieces," Seely wrote.

The Rhode Islanders and the local militia had no chance in face-to-face combat against what Greenman labeled a "far superior" force and the enemy cannon; the Americans retreated back into the woods in an orderly manner and waited for the British to attack. The enemy, though, had no plans to do anything except leave. When he returned from the victory at Charleston on June 17, Sir Henry Clinton declared that the British were not finished with Springfield. Knyphausen's plan had been solid. Clinton would try, too.

The Rhode Islanders had been expecting something would happen following the return of Clinton's fleet. Washington had left them to guard the Springfield area and they heard numerous rumors that the British were about to attack again. They spotted seven large British ships in New York harbor. On the twentieth they were again told to be prepared. "ordered to hold ourselves in readiness to march at a moment's warning."

That same day a very nervous Baron von Steuben, hearing reports of a huge British force being assembled for an invasion, begged Governor Livingston for as many militia units as he could raise. Livingston had prepared for just such a situation. Within just twenty-four hours, he had armed troops on the highways headed north as fast as they could march. He wrote to a relieved von Steuben that morning, "The militia from the lower counties of this state are on their way in considerable numbers."[5]

The situation became even more intense the next day. Early in the morning, Washington ordered Seely to draft as many men as necessary to swell his militia unit to its largest size ever, 1,248 men, and to get them into the service immediately. The commander took the main army and started toward West Point, fearful that the British fleet was getting ready to sail up the Hudson. Nathanael Greene assumed command of the twenty-five-hundred-man army in the Springfield area. On the twenty-second, more rumors flew and Greenman wrote that "this day a number of boats and small craft passing from New York to Elizabeth, which we imagine the enemy was reinforcing and their approach might be speedily expected."

He was right. The British, now under Clinton, attacked the next morning, June 25, with a force of six thousand regulars and a long train of cannon against Greene's far smaller army. The British had massed in

Elizabethtown and at 5 a.m. again headed toward Springfield along two roads, Springfield and Vauxhall. The Second Rhode Island was at first ordered into the village of Springfield, with its fifty buildings, to defend a meetinghouse as part of Maxwell's brigade. But then the Rhode Islanders were rushed back, over a bridge, into an orchard at a second bridge that crossed one of tributaries of the Rahway River—the scene of a hot fight during the June 8 invasion—to prevent the British from crossing and moving toward Morristown. The Second Rhode Island had only a single field piece for artillery. In the distance, they could hear cannonading coming from the British line and watched as shells hit several buildings in the area, setting them on fire. The Americans knew they were outnumbered by more than two to one.

Lieutenant Greenman wrote of the Rahway River that it was "not passable only by the bridge as it appeared swampy on each side. A field piece was posted on a hill just in our rear, our right wing on the right of the bridge and the left wing on the left of the bridge, where we thought the enemy must pass." The British were soon in view, surging toward them. Lieutenant Greenman wrote, "A firing of muskets immediately took place by the enemy's right column advancing for the other part of the town which they approached with little difficulty. We then discovered their left column approaching us very fast."

Colonel Israel Angell ordered the men of his artillery battery to fire their lone cannon as rapidly as they could, filling the early morning air with explosions and clouds of thick smoke as the British bore down on the Rhode Islanders. "The field piece back of us played very briskly on them. The enemy opened with five field pieces on [our] one, which they compelled to retire with the loss of a captain and a few men."

The British troops fired volley after volley into the Rhode Islanders at the same time that their five cannon shelled the regiment, explosions erupting throughout the area near the bridge, cutting the Americans down in a near-slaughter. Greenman, in the thick of the fight and surrounded by the smoke, wrote of the British artillery pieces that "they leveled them at our regiment and by this time their infantry was not more than a musket shot from us and advancing very fast for the bridge. Their troops [were] Jaegers [Hessians] and advanced for the brook and each flank which they soon gained. The musketry at the same time playing very smartly on the bridge. They being also far superior in number, they crossed it."

The Rhode Islanders' bold but costly stand at the Rahway—they lost one quarter of their men—had held up what had been the fast-moving British army for a precious forty minutes and gave Generals Maxwell and Greene time to bolster their defenses as thousands of New Jersey militia arrived, some having marched four hours to the battle. The newly arrived and well-organized militia from around the state, totaling five thousand and eager for a fight, joined the Continentals in lines in the woods behind the Rahway and waited for the British.

The Second Rhode Island was ordered to fall back from the bridge. The span's wooden planks were now splintered and shot up with cannon firing and musket balls and drenched in the blood of men from both sides. As the Americans retreated, the British had splashed through the waist deep water and swarmed around the American right flank. They were soon right on top of the Rhode Islanders. "Our left wing fought them on a retreat at every fence knoll," wrote Greenman of the heated battle that morning.

As the Rhode Islanders backed up, firing away at the English as they did so, Greenman was shot in the shoulder. Wounded and bleeding, he continued to fire his musket as the unit moved out and back to a better position with the militia in the nearby woods. No one was safe in the retreat and the Rhode Islanders looked out for each other, determined to get the wounded off the battlefield.

All of the men seemed to have been withdrawn when Dr. James Thacher was spotted riding *to* the battlefield, not away from it like everyone else. He had seen an American fall and wanted to treat him. He dismounted, tied his horse to a wood rail fence, grabbed his medical pouch, and ran to the wounded soldier's side, kneeling next to him. Suddenly, a cannonball exploded within a few yards of the horse, ripping up the rail fence and huge chunks of grass and dirt. Several soldiers raced to Thacher and screamed at him to get off the battlefield—fast. They pulled the wounded man back to the woods with them and the brave but frightened doctor ran to his horse, mounted it, and, his spurs digging into the side of steed, raced into the woods and safety.

The enormous outpouring of militia now gave Greene seventy-five hundred men, more troops than the British, and he was no longer at a disadvantage. The Americans were arrayed throughout the woods at the foot of the Watchung Mountains, where they could look down at the British with their muskets and cannon. They were thus able to stop the British advances. George Washington had been marching toward West Point, where he was convinced the enemy would attack. General Knyphausen learned Washington had been alerted and had turned his army southward. The Americans were moving quickly and would be at Springfield within an hour or two. The British general, thwarted already by Greene and the militia, would not risk a major defeat in a battle with Washington. He retreated, ordering the burning of most of the village of Springfield as he went. The Americans' view of the British army fleeing to New York was soon blocked by columns of black smoke rising into the sky from the torching of Springfield.

The Americans only lost fifteen killed and sixty-one wounded in both battles of Springfield. British losses were not reported, but villagers said they saw several wagons filled with dead soldiers rolling down the highway as the soundly beaten British retreated.[6] Later, in a report that would have made the Morris militia and other militia units proud of themselves, General Knyphausen wrote to George Germain, head of Britain's colonial office and in charge of the war, "I found the disposition of the inhabitants by no means such as I expected; on the contrary they were everywhere in arms."[7] Even more pleasing was Washington's assessment of the militia. The general had been critical of them since he took command of the army three years earlier. The militiamen fought in the two Springfield engagements, he wrote to General Robert Howe, "with admirable spirit."[8]

Washington praised the Second Rhode Island, too, writing that "the gallant behavior of Col. Angell's [men] on the 23 instant, at Springfield, reflects the highest honor upon the officers and men. They disputed an important pass, with so obstinate a bravery, that they lost upwards of forty killed, wounded, and missing before they gave up their ground to a vast superiority of force."

The Rhode Island Assembly was even more effusive in its praise. An official proclamation conveyed "sincere thanks to the officers and soldiers in general, belonging to the regiment, for that bravery, patriotism, and perseverance and those military virtues manifested on all occasions so similar to those exhibited by the famous legions of ancient Rome, in the shining periods of the history of that republic."[9]

The battles for Springfield have usually been dismissed by historians, but they were two of the most important encounters of the war. If the Americans had not turned the enemy back both times, the British might have defeated Washington, decimated the American army, and moved into Morristown to capture all of the Continental Army's supplies, food, and ammunition. The French had agreed to send ships, cannon, ammunition, and several thousand soldiers in 1780, but their fleet and troops had not yet arrived. So a defeat at Springfield, coupled with the loss of Charleston, lack of provisions, and the reeling U.S. economy might have resulted in American capitulation.[10]

The awful winter and spring had brought about a mutiny, starvation, inflation, the loss of Charleston, the defeat at Staten Island, the corruption trial of Arnold, and animosity between the people and the troops. But in an odd way, these travails had somehow rekindled the spirit of many in the service. Wrote one foot soldier in a long and passionate letter to the *Jersey Journal*:

> At least half the whole family of mankind may be interested in our success; a prize as important was never before disputed on the stage of the world. We have every virtuous, every great and noble idea to animate our exertions; the superior Beings who inhabit other worlds may behold our efforts with pleasing admiration—and the Eternal may look down with approbation and pleasure, while we contend for the rights of creation and refuse to part with our divine inheritance.[11]

Chapter Twenty-Nine

1781:
Victory at Yorktown

The War

*T*he Revolution, its critics claimed, was about to collapse as a series
of events worked against the American cause throughout 1780
and 1781.

All of America was enraged at the defection of Benedict Arnold in September 1780. The disgruntled Arnold, thirty-nine, had just married the nineteen-
year-old daughter of a Philadelphia Tory. He still fumed about his conviction
on corruption charges in the winter and shortly thereafter defected to the British
after selling them the military plans for the American fortifications at West
Point; his connection, British Major John Andre, was captured and hanged.
Arnold's betrayal hurt Washington deeply, but it also infuriated every soldier
who had served with Arnold, including Ebenezer Wild, at Saratoga, John
Greenwood, and Jeremiah Greenman, plus Dr. Lewis Beebe, and Rev. Ammi
Robbins, now at home (Greenman was present at Andre's execution).

The army was hurt again in January 1781 when a large-scale mutiny
took place at Morristown, where another uprising had occurred the previous

winter. This time nearly fifteen hundred unhappy Pennsylvania troops mutinied, presenting grievances connected to lack of food, clothing, back pay, and enlistment time, and marched out of camp. The mutineers planned to travel to Philadelphia to plead their case to Congress, but wound up in Princeton, where they seized the town. The mutiny ended when Congress agreed to pay troops who wanted to leave—almost all of them—and give proper clothing and food to those who remained. All were pardoned. The leaders of another mutiny three weeks later in Pompton, New Jersey, were not so lucky. Washington had the mutiny put down with force and ordered the three leaders shot by their closest friends in the regiment. The mutinies strengthened British belief that support for the Revolution was fading fast.

American finances were also at a low point and recruitment was difficult. The French alliance had not been as successful as most hoped and British commander Henry Clinton had just asked the home office for ten thousand more men and more warships to win the war.

Furthermore, the British had established a near stranglehold in the southern states, where they had the support of thousands of Loyalists. The Redcoats' capture of Charleston, along with five thousand American soldiers in May 1780, and the continued occupation of Savannah, solidified their dominance in the lower half of the country.

At first, efforts to end British control of the South failed. Blithely overriding Washington's recommendation of Nathanael Greene, Congress named Horatio Gates, the "hero of Saratoga," to lead forces there. His leadership proved a disaster. Cornwallis promptly routed Gates's army of two thousand regulars and two thousand militia on August 16, 1780, at Camden, South Carolina. Gates foolishly matched his poorly trained militia up against Cornwallis's best troops; the militia folded quickly, most of the men dropping their guns and running. Hundreds of Americans were killed, wounded, captured, or went home. Within two weeks, his army shrank to just seven hundred men.

Two events then helped the Americans. Militia defeated a large Loyalist army under Col. Patrick Ferguson at King's Mountain, South Carolina, on October 7, 1780. Ferguson was shot dead. This severely undercut the Loyalist movement. Then, in early December, Greene replaced Gates.

Greene knew that he was an underdog in any battle he entered against Cornwallis and his savage cavalry leader, Lt. Col. Banastre Tarleton. Greene cagily engaged in a hit and run strategy, trying to inflict huge losses on the British in every battle and then escape to fight another day. Cornwallis was so eager to destroy Greene's army that he chased it all over the South. Cornwallis could do so because the home office gave him total freedom of movement; he no longer had to clear any decisions with Henry Clinton, whom he despised.

The Americans surprisingly defeated the British at the Cowpens, South Carolina, January 17, 1781, capturing five hundred British regulars, and immediately fled. Cornwallis pursued them to get his men back, but could not catch the Americans. Later, on March 15, the two forces met again at Guilford Court House, in North Carolina. The British won this time, but suffered heavy losses. Throughout 1781, Greene had the assistance of nearly two thousand local militia led by shrewd backcountry partisan commanders, such as South Carolina's Francis Marion, "The Swamp Fox." They all engaged the British in skirmishes, sometimes winning and sometimes losing, and inflicting heavy losses on Cornwallis's army. At Eutaw Springs, in a bloody confrontation, the Americans again lost but killed 693 of Cornwallis's men, nearly one quarter of his army, the highest percentage loss of men in the entire Revolution.

Cornwallis finally joined forces with General Benedict Arnold in Virginia. Arnold was ordered back to New York. On August 1, Cornwallis took his combined forces of six thousand to Yorktown, a port on the York River, close to the Chesapeake Bay, where he hoped to establish a defensive position near a harbor.

At that same time, George Washington held several meetings in Connecticut with the head of the French army, Lt. General Donatien Marie Rochambeau. The French had arrived in force in the summer of 1780, too late to see any major action, but now Rochambeau wanted to put together a plan of action with Washington to strike a major blow against the English. Its result would be a final campaign to defeat Cornwallis.

Washington had long dreamed of reclaiming New York City, where his army had been beaten so badly in 1776. Upon news that the French fleet, under Admiral Comte de Grasse, with three thousand troops, could sail from the West Indies to Virginia in early September, Rochambeau instead suggested moving their combined force southward all the way to Virginia to attack Lord Cornwallis and end the war. The plan was to merge with forces already in the south under Lafayette and Anthony Wayne, surround Cornwallis by land, and have the French ships blockade the mouth of the Chesapeake so that he could not escape by ship or be rescued. Washington quickly saw it as a golden opportunity.

The Americans did feign an assault on New York to make Sir Henry Clinton believe an attack on him was imminent; Clinton was also certain that the British navy would annihilate de Grasse's fleet. Then the American-French army marched southward to Maryland. French transports and American ships carried the army from Elkton and Annapolis, Maryland, to Virginia for the attack. Washington and Rochambeau together had nearly eighteen thousand soldiers and one hundred cannon, making it one of the largest American forces of the war. Would the plan work? Could they defeat the well-entrenched Cornwallis? Would the British fleet rout French admiral de Grasse? Could they achieve victory before October 15, when de Grasse said he had to leave?

The journey of the First Massachusetts and its newly promoted lieutenant, Ebenezer Wild, to York, Virginia, or Yorktown, as it was also called, began in earnest on April 21, 1781, when the regiment crossed the Potomac River from Maryland into Virginia. The regiment was now attached to the combined French-American forces led by the Marquis de Lafayette. A month later, on the evening of May 21, the First Massachusetts was met by two regiments of Virginia militia on the northern bank of the James River, just outside of Richmond, where they had camped overnight. The next day, the First Massachusetts, with the others, crossed the James.

Wild's confidence in the army was given a jolt a few days later when a sudden thunderstorm broke over the Virginia countryside following a day of excessive heat. The storm hit while the army was marching down a roadway. The thunder was so loud and so quick that the local militia troops that had just joined the column thought the noise was enemy cannon and fled into the woods for protection. It took the officers ninety minutes to bring the frightened militia back to the road.

Wild, who had been in the service for six years, had just been promoted and he seemed delighted to be an officer. He wrote that he was pleased to have been invited to Colonel Vose's tent for a dinner of his officers just outside of Richmond and seemed to enjoy spending time with his fellow officers, among them a new acquaintance, Captain Stephen Olney. Now he would receive more pay, live in a better tent in summer, and larger hut in winter. He was also satisfied that since he was an officer he could be a member of courts martial boards. Ebenezer Wild was now a man to be respected.

Throughout the march, supplies the men had been clamoring for since winter arrived. On June 3, the angry enlisted men were quieted when a man who had ridden all the way from Boston trotted into camp on a horse with large bags of hard money consisting of gold and silver to distribute to the enlisted men in salary. A week later, on June 10, a wagon train loaded with twelve hundred shirts for the soldiers pulled up to the column as the men marched. For some, these were the first new shirts they had been given in a year.

Sometimes everything seemed to go wrong, though. Wild and his company were about to capture a herd of horses but the steeds ran off at the last moment. A doctor and two privates drowned while bathing in a river. Somehow, many of the tents of the First Massachusetts were lost during the march and the men had to sleep in the open meadows. Directions were poor and once the men marched all day to wind up at a local meetinghouse where they had started that morning. A surprise attack on a British force General Anthony Wayne had spotted at Green Springs backfired and the First Massachusetts and the Pennsylvanians had to retreat. Promised food shipments were late. The crossings of rivers took all day because there were not enough boats.

On September 1, Wild heard the news that his "tiny army," as he called it, would not only join forces with George Washington's main army, but that the French fleet, with twenty-eight ships carrying four thousand troops, had arrived in Chesapeake Bay, blocking the entrance to the York and James rivers. By September 6, various elements of the plan to surround the British were falling into place. Wild's regiment had been sent to Williamsburg, twelve miles southwest of Yorktown. The French army, under the Marquis de St. Simon, had arrived five days before. The next day, Lieutenant Wild heard that more ships had arrived and the French now had thirty-seven vessels anchored in the bay. The day after that two regiments from Maryland trudged into Williamsburg as the American and French forces camped in the Virginia capital began to swell. And finally, on Sunday, September 14, George Washington arrived and took command. He asked to greet as many officers as he could that day, and at 2 p.m. he met Ebenezer Wild (oddly, Wild wrote nothing about the encounter). "The arrival . . . of General Washington gave new hopes and spirits to the army," noted Lt. Col. St. George Tucker of Rawson's Brigade, a Virginia militia group, who also met Washington that day.[1]

The commander in chief had lots of good news. He had just returned from a meeting with Admiral de Grasse, head of the French fleet, on board his flagship, the *Ville de Paris*, said to be the largest warship in the world. De Grasse informed him that his ships would remain in the Chesapeake Bay until the end of October, giving the combined American and French forces plenty of time to defeat Cornwallis. Washington's army and the French force had arrived practically intact, with very few desertions and a small number of sick men. The cannon he brought with him over the great distance from the New York area were in good order and few had suffered any damage on the lengthy journey. His spies assured him that British supplies in Yorktown were low. The French had given him just about everything—in men, cannon, and supplies—that they had been promising for more than two years.[2]

Yorktown was situated on land originally owned by an ancestor of George Washington's, Nicholas Martiau, who acquired it in 1691. Over the years, its location on the York River close to the Chesapeake and in the heart of tobacco country had turned it into a busy port. Its zenith as a trading town was reached in the 1740s, when British visitors remarked that the homes of merchants in the community of three thousand people were as large and as fine as those in the best neighborhoods in London. An explosion in the tobacco trade in other areas of the Chesapeake area near ports, such as Norfolk and Baltimore, soon undercut the importance of Yorktown. The war and British blockades also hurt Yorktown's business, and by 1781 it turned into a small, depressed community.

Yorktown still possessed the remnants of its former importance. There were three hundreds homes, three churches, and an ornate red brick courthouse located on its one main street and four cross streets. The town sat on a wide, high bluff that overlooked the river. The small wharf that had been built beneath the bluff still had ships that anchored there on trading excursions and was now home to Cornwallis's warship, the *Charon,* and several supply ships. Merchants, farmers, and workers from nearby plantations conducted business in some of its stores and frequented a local tavern.

The townspeople had embraced the Revolution. In 1774, local men raided British ships in action similar to the "tea party" in Boston. The community elected its leading patriot, Thomas Nelson, to the Continental Congress. Throughout the war, Yorktown was home to a three-hundred-man militia company

The community looked like a ghost town by the time Cornwallis made it his headquarters. The militia had fled, along with dozens of area shopkeepers, plantation owners, and local residents. Many had moved to the interior when the British invaded the state. Some homes, stores, and stables were empty and uncut grass overran walkways and streets.[3]

The enlisted men began to believe that it might be possible to defeat Cornwallis's army of some six thousand men, which appeared bottled up, and take the fabled British general and all of his men prisoners. True, the British still had other armies in the U.S., in New York, Charleston, Savannah, and Wilmington, North Carolina. But the capture of Cornwallis's brigades would cripple British forces and their surrender would be perceived as a tremendous public relations coup throughout America, in England where sentiment against the war had grown over the last two years, and the world. It just might be the final blow necessary to force the Crown to quit the war.

American hopes were high in Williamsburg, indeed so optimistic that some soldiers began pools, similar to contemporary sports betting pools, with each participant choosing the date upon which Lord Cornwallis would surrender. Men who frequented the capital's taverns, such as Christiana Campbell's, wagered money, silk stockings, coats, and beaver hats on the date. Lafayette predicted September 22. Others chose dates ranging from September 23 to October 14.[4]

At dawn on September 28, in a grand spectacle, Washington and Rochambeau led their joint army out of Williamsburg—down the pretty, wide, tree-lined Duke of Gloucester Street with its many taverns, gardens, yards, stores, and hitching posts, and headed northeast toward Yorktown. Lt. Wild counted just over sixteen thousand men, along with hundreds of cannon and wagons.

The young lieutenant was impressed. "About sunrise the army began their march [in one column] toward York. The light infantry, with some cavalry and one regiment of riflemen, formed the vanguard. In this order, we proceeded about seven miles, where the roads parted; the Americans taking the right and the French the left, we proceeded within about two miles of York, where the French army encamped on a plain with a large morass in their front. The American army proceeded further toward the river."

Cornwallis had decided to defend the town against a siege and had built numerous wide ditches, a lone line of earthen walls, and two large redoubts of wood and earth to serve as ramparts to hold soldiers and cannon. These defenses were guarded with newly built abatis (tree branches sharpened like spears stuck into the earth to stop rushing hordes of troops). The well-defended redoubts and protective walls at times curved and at times zigzagged so that the British could fire at attackers approaching from any angle.

For one of the few times during the war, the American forces—ninety-five hundred Americans and eighty-eight hundred crack French regulars—substantially outnumbered the British force of about six thousand men. Most of the British were in Yorktown and a few hundred were in the village of Gloucester directly across the river. Cornwallis made up for his lack of men with his seemingly impregnable defensive walls.

When Rochambeau and Washington first discussed an attack on Yorktown, Washington worried that the only way to defeat the British would be to mount a series of frontal assaults that would cost the lives of many men. Could these assaults be carried out by the time de Grasse had to leave? Would de Grasse be attacked by the British navy? He worried, too, that Cornwallis would sneak away in the night, just as he would do. The Redcoats certainly had the opportunity. De Grasse had blocked the entrances to both the York and James Rivers, but he refused to sail up the York to moor directly opposite Yorktown. He was afraid British guns in the town would sink his ships. With the river behind him clear, Cornwallis might try to cross it to the village of Gloucester, quietly march his troops northwest, and escape.

General Rochambeau had told Washington earlier, before they met with de Grasse, that the only way to defeat Cornwallis was to lay siege to Yorktown, using short, fat mortars that could fire cannonballs in high arcs to fly over the defensive redoubts and come down in the town. He himself had been involved in fourteen sieges and his engineers were experts at designing and constructing trenches for a long siege. On the same day the army arrived in the plain in front of Yorktown, work began on the lengthy trenches, designed in a semi-circular arc around the community one half mile away, and out of artillery range, or so Rochambeau said.[5]

The men building the trenches certainly disagreed. They became instant targets as they worked with pickaxes and shovels. "The enemy have kept a constant fire on our working parties all day," wrote Wild, who toiled on the trenches with his soldiers. "Several of our men were killed or wounded in the night by shot and shells which the enemy fired very briskly." Another soldier complained, "The firing from the enemy's works was continued during the whole night at the distance of fifteen or twenty minutes between every shot . . . [in] morning, the firing has been much more frequent, the intermissions seldom exceeding five minutes and often not more than one or two minutes."[6]

The siege began on October 9 when Rochambeau asked Washington to do the honor of firing the first cannon. It was followed by dozens of others barking away, over and over. Pennsylvania lieutenant William Feltman wrote that "this whole day we cannonaded the enemy, and sent them a number of shells and drove their artillery from the embrasure and they had not the spirit to return one shot."[7] The hundreds of cannonballs, especially the mortars, found their mark and there was considerable damage to the British fortifications and a significant loss of life. Dr. Thacher, watching the bombardment, wrote that "I have more than once witnessed fragments of mangled bodies and limbs of British soldiers thrown into the air by the bursting of our shells."[8]

By the end of the second day, the French found by sheer chance that cannonballs that overshot Yorktown were hitting the British ships below the bluffs, tearing huge holes in their sides and decks and setting the rigging of many on fire.[9] Several ships sank so deeply into the river that only their masts could be seen. It was nonstop bombardment, too. Lt. Wild wrote that "a very brisk fire, both of shot and shells, are kept from them on the enemy, who returns theirs with equal spirit."

One thing that worried the enlisted men was the continued persistence of George Washington to expose himself to enemy fire. He had done so in just about every major battle of the war. Wild remembered him riding back and forth directly in front of him across the plains of Monmouth to rally the men as the British fired away with muskets and cannon. Others remembered him, atop his magnificent horses, leading attacks in other places. Now, at Yorktown, he was again oblivious to danger, again vulnerable to a sniper's musket ball.

On the first day that the commander was shown the plain in front of Yorktown, and told to stay off of it because it was within the range of British guns, he stood at the edge of the meadow to talk to a local minister. The British saw them and an artillery battery opened fire. An explosion tore up the earth a few yards from the two men, sending soil and rocks flying into the air. The minister, Rev. Evans, was startled when dirt flew up, hit him, and landed in his hat. "See here, General!" he exclaimed, flustered. Washington, nonplussed, told Evans to take his hat home "and show it to your wife and children."[10] At another juncture, one of Washington's aides thought he was standing too close to the artillery bombardment and might be hit. He asked the commander to "step back a little." Washington dryly told him, "Colonel Cobb, if you are afraid, you have liberty to step back."[11]

The American and French guns fired from the first set of trenches had been effective, but Washington wanted to move them even closer, to within a few hundred yards of the town. An artillery pounding from that close would inflict so much damage that he believed Cornwallis would give up. The problem was how to get that close. The answer, Rochambeau said, was a second line of trenches.

Those trenches could not be dug, however, because the British maintained two well-defended fortified redoubts, Numbers 9 and 10 on their maps, that ran parallel to the town and guarded the plain close to it. The only way those redoubts could be taken, Washington decided, was by a direct assault. That attack was dangerous because the men would come under artillery and musket fire from British well-entrenched on the fortifications. So he decided to launch another of his famous nighttime surprise attacks. Soldiers would move quietly, using bayonets. They were forbidden to fire their guns. He chose his chief of staff, Alexander Hamilton, to lead the American soldiers, giving Hamilton his long-sought battlefield command, and Colonel Guillaume, Comte de Deux-Ponts, to lead the French.

Washington gave a short speech to the men as they lined up in the darkness for the attacks on the two redoubts, urging them to be fearless, but the soldiers were scared. Captain Olney was assigned to the attack on Number 10, in the battalion led by Colonel Jean Joseph Gimat, Lafayette's top aide. Olney's knees shook as he listened to Washington. He wrote that the column marched toward the British positions forlornly. The men were certain that many of them would be killed, especially since they were under orders not to fire their muskets.

When they were close to the British lines near redoubt Number 10, just after 7 p.m., they were spotted and the one hundred twenty British defenders opened up with a musket volley. Olney's men immediately shouted a loud "huzzah" and heard other cheers along the field. The silence had been broken and there would be no more of it. Gimat ordered Olney's men and others to use axes to widen gaps between pointed tree branches of the abatis. This decision not only caused the attack to stall, but resulted in many men being shot dead or wounded as they tried to hack their way through the branches. Olney and others, realizing the folly of what they were ordered to do, slipped between the tree branches and scrambled down into the twenty-five-yard-wide ditch behind them and then mounted the parapets of the fortifications. There, in the dark, they encountered a group of defenders, bayonets fixed, who rushed them.

"I had not less than six or eight bayonets pushed at me," wrote Olney later. "I parried as well as I could with my espontoon [a spear], but they broke off the blade part and their bayonets slid along the handle and scaled my fingers; one bayonet pierced my thigh, another stabbed me in the abdomen just about the hip bone. One fellow fired at me and I thought the ball [hit] my arm."

Olney fought back in a fury, stabbing one of the Redcoats in the middle of his forehead with his broken espontoon. His men rushed to his side, bayoneting the group of British soldiers who had surrounded and bayoneted their captain. Sergeant Edward Butterick was stabbed in the stomach. Another sergeant was stabbed in the hand. Colonel Gimat was shot and carried off the field. Olney, bleeding badly from his bayonet wounds and the musket ball in his arm, somehow managed to keep leading the men attacking the fort. By then, more than two hundred Americans and Frenchmen were encountering horrific fire as they swarmed through the abatis—the French at Number 9 and the Americans at Number 10.

Private Joseph Martin was one of them. Stumbling through, he wrote that as the soldiers reached it, "the enemy discovered us and . . . opened a sharp fire upon us. We were now at a place where many of our large shells had burst in the ground, making holes sufficient to bury an ox in. The men were . . . falling into these holes. I thought the British were killing us off at a great rate . . . I could not pass at the entrance we had made, it was so crowded. I therefore forged a passage at a place where I saw our shot had cut away some of the abatis. Several others entered at the same place. While passing, a man at my side received a ball in his head and fell under my feet, crying out bitterly. While crossing the trench, the enemy threw hand grenades [small bombs] . . . into it. They were so thick that I at first thought them cartridge papers on fire, but was soon undeceived by their cracking."[12] Martin and others told friends later that there was so much musket fire from both sides that the entire trench and the British fort walls were illuminated by it.

The Redcoats fled. Total French and American losses in the attack were twenty-four killed and one hundred two wounded; the British had eighteen killed and seventy-three wounded.

Captain Olney's detachment secured the redoubt within a half hour and he was soon carried away with the rest of the wounded to Williamsburg, twelve miles away, and placed alongside other badly injured and bleeding men in a home that had been turned into a hospital. By the next day the upper half of his arm had turned completely black, but it was the bayoneting in his stomach, and the extreme loss of blood, that concerned surgeons. One looked down at the captain with great sadness and told him that he would not live and would die there in the hospital.[13]

At the same time that Olney was bayoneted, Ebenezer Wild was in the middle of a charge against the second redoubt, Number 10. The lieutenant's company had been joined by light infantry and ordered to advance through the darkness. Wild's regiment moved much faster than Olney's toward their goal because their commanders told them to ignore the abatis branches and simply race between or over them as quickly as possible. Wild did so, writing, "We advanced from the battery on our right in one column to the redoubt on the enemy's left, which we attacked and carried by storm. A detachment of French Grenadiers carrying the one on our left about the same time (& in the same manner). We had nothing but the enemy's fire from their main works to hinder our completing our second parallel, which we proceeded to do with all possible expedition."

The quick victory was satisfying to Wild, who noted in his diary the following morning that the parallels they now held extended all the way to the York River and put their newly arrived cannon just two hundred yards from Yorktown—easy shelling range. Defending the captured redoubt was a dangerous affair, though. The British would still not give it up. Wrote Wild, "We are much troubled with their small shells, which they now throw into our trenches exceeding fast. The fire, both of shot and shells, on both sides, has been exceeding hot all day."

The next day Cornwallis sent a force of just over three hundred men to recapture the two redoubts. They convinced some officers that they were French soldiers and were able to capture several cannon, spiking them with bayonets. The ruse did not last long. "The enemy were made to retire to their works with precipitation and considerable loss, both of killed and wounded," Wild noted.

That night, on land just two hundred yards from the British lines, the American cannon opened up with hundreds of shells in a heavy barrage. "The cannon and bombardment from ours and the French batteries were kept up with little intermission," wrote St. George Tucker, a Virginia militia leader. "Red hot balls being fired at the shipping from French battery over the creek; the *Charon,* a forty-four-gun ship, and another ship were set fire to and burnt during the night and a brig in the morning met with the same fate. Our batteries have continued incessant firing during the whole day."[14]

The capture of the two fortifications permitted Washington to array cannon in a large semicircle so that the artillery could commence enfilade firing (hitting targets from different angles). Lord Cornwallis was trapped. He tried to move his men out of Yorktown across the York River on the night of October 16, but he had few boats and a sudden rainstorm ended his plans. The next day, the seventeenth, the fourth anniversary of Burgoyne's surrender at Saratoga, guns in position, Washington ordered yet another bombardment of the British lines at Yorktown, utilizing practically every available cannon.

Ebenezer Wild stood right in the middle of the bombardment that started with the sounds of multiple explosions at dawn. "At daylight," he wrote, "we found the enemy had stopped up the embrasures of most of their batteries and the fire from their cannon became almost silenced; but they continued to throw small shells very brisk. By this time, the fire from our works became almost incessant as new batteries are opening from almost every part of the line."

More than one hundred cannon were used in the bombardment and they were close enough to hit individual buildings within the town as well as the ships in the river and the defensive lines. It was a murderous cannon fire. Chaos reigned in Yorktown. A Hessian, Stephen Popp, wrote, "Their heavy fire forced us to throw our tents in the ditches. The enemy threw bombs, one hundred, one hundred fifty, two hundred; their guns were eighteen-, twenty-four-, and forty-eight-pounders. We could find no refuge in or out of the town. The people fled to the waterside and hid in hastily contrived shelters on the banks, but many of them were killed by bursting bombs. More than eighty were thus lost, besides many wounded, and their homes utterly destroyed."[15]

Cornwallis had the combined American and French armies in front of him, the York River behind him, the French fleet down the river, and nowhere to turn. The only British fleet that could rescue him was far away in New York. Explosions ripped through the community; smoke was everywhere. Just before 10 a.m., on October 17, Cornwallis sent an officer with a white handkerchief to Washington to discuss his surrender.[16]

The British commander asked for twenty-four hours to work out a proposal for surrender; Washington gave him two. The next two days were spent in heated arguments over the exact terms of the surrender. The final document, signed by Washington and Cornwallis, was gracious: although the British soldiers would be taken prisoner, the officers and Cornwallis would be sent back to England and would keep their side arms.

The surrender discussions ended the constant bombardment that had shaken the Virginia town for eight long days. The night of October 17 was one to remember for the enlisted men at Yorktown. St. George Tucker wrote, "A solemn stillness prevailed. The night was remarkably clear and the sky was decorated with ten thousand stars. Numerous meteors gleaming through the atmosphere afforded a pleasing resemblance to the bombs which had exhibited a noble firework the night before, but happily divested of all their horror."[17]

Finally, at 3 p.m. on October 19, a scene transpired that few in the world ever expected to take place back in 1775, when the first shots of the war were fired in the village of Lexington, Massachusetts. On that day and hour, the entire British and Hessian army of nearly six thousand men began to march out of Yorktown down Hampton Road to the surrender ground, parading in front of the soldiers in the victorious American and French armies. Reportedly, someone with sense of humor ordered the British military band to play "The World Turned Upside Down." It seemed an ironic selection on a day that the greatest professional army in the world surrendered to an army of former farmers, blacksmiths, and shopkeepers.

In a bit of good fortune, Lieutenant Ebenezer Wild's company found itself stationed right at the beginning of the parade route. Wild and his comrades were up-close eyewitnesses to one of the great surrenders in military history—and for a second time, since they had witnessed the surrender of Burgoyne at Saratoga. Wild wrote of the Yorktown surrender, "They began to march out with shouldered arms and drums beating, but were not allowed to beat any French or American march; neither were they allowed to display their colors. In this order they were conducted [by General Lincoln] to a large plain in front of the American encampment, where they grounded their arms."

Lord Cornwallis was not with his men. The humiliated military leader, outwitted and outgeneraled yet again by George Washington, stayed in Yorktown and sent word to the Americans that he was "sick." Someone had to surrender, so he told his blustery Irish general, Charles O'Hara, to do it (The unlucky O'Hara had been with Burgoyne at Saratoga, too). O'Hara then tried to surrender to Rochambeau to insult the Americans by pretending that the French alone had defeated the British. The French general would not talk to him and pointed across the road to Washington. O'Hara then tried to surrender to him, offering Cornwallis's sword. The American commander would not accept the sword from a second in command, and told him to hand it to General Lincoln, sitting astride a horse next to him. O'Hara did so. Abiding by protocol, Lincoln, who himself had been forced to surrender his army at Charleston in 1780, touched the sword and handed it back to O'Hara.[18]

Some observers believed that many British soldiers had been drinking that day. Others said that their line of march was ragged and undisciplined and that even the sober men seemed wildly disoriented. A New Jersey officer standing near Joseph Martin may have put it best when he told those around him that "the British officers in general behaved like boys who had been whipped at school. Some bit their lips, some pouted, others cried. Their round, brimmed hats were well adapted to the occasion, hiding those faces they were ashamed to show."[19]

Washington never said anything about Cornwallis's refusal to lead his army out of Yorktown, but almost everyone in the American army chortled over his Lordship's humbling. Dr. Thacher was one. The doctor, who always thought the British generals pompous, skewered Cornwallis. He wrote, "But there is no display of magnanimity when a great commander shrinks from the inevitable misfortunes of war; and when it is considered that Lord Cornwallis has frequently appeared in splendid triumph at the head of his army, by which he is almost adored, we conceive it incumbent on him cheerfully to participate in their misfortunes and degradations, however humiliating; but it is said he gives himself up entirely to vexation and despair."[20]

News of the surrender thrilled America. Nearly five days later, the news arrived at 3 a.m. on October 24 in Philadelphia and by order of the president of Congress, Thomas McKean, men began to ring the Liberty Bell and kept ringing it until dawn. Thousands awakened by the pealing of the bell crowded into the streets with candles to celebrate the victory. In New Jersey, ministers of churches throughout the state ordered their bells to be rung most of the day. When the news reached Boston a day after that, the city was engulfed in wild celebrations and church bells rang for hours. In Fishkill, New York, residents enjoyed a daylong barbecue and at night celebrated with a huge bonfire and fireworks display.

Couriers rode as fast as their horses could carry them along New England highways, shouting, "Cornwallis is taken! Cornwallis is taken!" to anyone they passed. Villages through which they rode erupted in immediate celebrations that lasted all night. A special courier brought the news to Mount Vernon, where it was received with joy by Martha Washington and Henry Knox's wife Lucy, preparing to give birth to her fourth child there.[21]

On the British side, one of the first to receive word of the defeat was Rear Admiral Samuel Hood, with the British fleet, who, shocked, said the loss was "the most melancholy news Great Britain ever received . . . a heartbreaking business."[22] Upon hearing the news in London, British prime minister Lord North was far more direct. "Oh God!" he said, pacing back and forth in his apartment, "It is over. It is all over."[23]

The war did not actually end at Yorktown. It would take another two years before the peace treaty was finally signed, but nearly everyone at the surrender of Cornwallis's army was certain that the outcome of the six year conflict, with considerable help from the French, was now certain— independence for America.

AFTERWORD

The Revolutionary War did not end with the British defeat at Yorktown. England still had armies in New York, Savannah, and in North Carolina. British forces engaged in several small skirmishes on land and on the high seas after Yorktown and England could have continued militarily. However, the capture of Cornwallis's army at Yorktown brought about antiwar riots in London, strident calls for a cessation of activities in the London press and would cause the resignation of Lord North, the prime minister. The Crown, in effect, decided to end the war and grant the colonies independence after Cornwallis's defeat in the fall of 1781. Negotiations toward a peace treaty took nearly two years, however, and the war did not technically conclude until the fall of 1783.

What happened to the soldiers of the first American army when the war finally ended?

The return to civilian life was difficult for most of them. The army did not disperse en masse in November of 1783, when the British left. The enlisted men went home throughout 1781, 1782, and 1783. There were thousands of them. Those who were not going back to family farms had no guarantees of returning to their old jobs and neither the

Continental Congress or the states had job **programs** for them. Some veterans, particularly craftsmen, did find **work or** went back to their old employers. Others only landed positions that paid less than they earned before the war; many could not find employment at all. The end of the war also meant the end of the privateering business and thousands of seamen found their careers on the high seas over. Many had to pursue new lines of work.

That's what happened to Elijah Fisher. The cantankerous Fisher, who had problems getting along with people throughout the war, was never able to find long term employment in the Boston area after he left the army in 1780. He worked as a laborer and bounced from one job to another, sometimes being dismissed and sometimes quitting. Each job seemed to end in a heated dispute over work rules and pay.

Disgusted, Fisher signed on as a seaman on a merchant ship out of Boston in 1783 while the war still continued. The vessel was captured by a British ship on the high seas shortly thereafter and the crew was incarcerated on the notorious prison ship *Jersey*, anchored in New York harbor. There, at long last, Fisher's penmanship studies and practice finally did him some good. The captain of the *Jersey* needed a prisoner with good handwriting to serve as a clerk. Fisher won the post. He continued as a prisoner, and still slept in the dreary hold with the men. As a much-needed clerk, though, he spent the day working in his own office and received decent meals—missing all of the daily misery of the other prisoners. He was on the prison ship when the war ended.

Fisher had little luck finding a job upon his return to Boston after the peace treaty. Fed up, he moved to the wilderness of Maine, where he met and married Jerusha Keene in 1784. They had eight children. He settled into the village of Livermore and lived out his days as a farmer there.

Ebenezer Wild remained with the army until the very end of the war in 1783. He was so devoted to the military that he became one of the founding members of the Massachusetts Society of Cincinnati, founded by officers to memorialize the war throughout their lifetimes. Wild moved to Boston in 1789 and became a shopkeeper on Merchants Row, one of the city's most prominent business streets. He had married Abigail

Hayward in 1786. They had two children, Harriot and Ebenezer.

Shepard Kollock, who founded the *Jersey Journal,* continued to serve as the editor of the newspaper the rest of his life and made it one of the finest publications in early America.

Stephen Olney, bayoneted at Yorktown in 1781 and told by doctors that he would not live out the week, died fifty long years later.

Dr. Lewis Beebe had been greatly influenced by his wartime friend, the Rev. Robbins. Beebe himself became a minister in the Congregational Church in Vermont in 1787. The pastorate was not a good choice for the highly opinionated Beebe though, and he left the ministry four years later. He moved to Lansingburgh, New York, where, ironically, the staunch critic of drunkenness at Fort Ticonderoga opened up a liquor store that he ran until his death in 1816.

Rev. Ammi Robbins stayed in the ministry all of his life, continuously preaching the word of the Lord and the righteousness of the Revolution. He moved from Canaan to Litchfield, Connecticut, after the war and later became a member of the local school board.

Colonel Sylvanus Seely remained the head of the Morris County militia through the end of the war. He and his wife attended the December 4, 1783, fireworks extravaganza in New York that celebrated the signing of the peace treaty. Seely's tempestuous affair with Mrs. Ball ended sometime in the winter of 1782 but his womanizing continued. He tumbled into an affair of several weeks with Betsy Barnet, a doctor's wife from the Philadelphia area, whom he met at a vacation resort in northwestern New Jersey. Following that, he became romantically involved with the wife of his friend, Shepard Kollock.

Seely ran inns in Chatham until 1800 and then, at age fifty-three, decided that New Jersey was too congested. Seely and his family moved to an undeveloped region of eastern Pennsylvania, where he built a sawmill and a gristmill. Other settlers followed and a town was created; the locals named it Seelyville in honor of its founder and Revolutionary War hero. His secretly coded diary indicated that his womanizing wound down after he moved to Pennsylvania. Colonel Seely lived there until his death in 1820. His wife Jane stayed with him despite his unfaithfulness and in 1819 they celebrated fifty years of marriage.

Young John Greenwood, the fifteen-year-old who worked as a fifer, soldier, and sailor, had the most unusual post-war career of all. Greenwood, unable to find much work in Boston after the war, moved to New York and became a dentist, just like his father. He was a good one, too. Greenwood pioneered the use of foot-powered drills and tooth implants. His specialty, though, was dentures. He invented adaptable springs for dentures and became renowned for creating porcelain false teeth out of ivory from hippopotamus.

Greenwood knew that George Washington suffered from his bad teeth and that the general was unhappy with the various false teeth dentists had given him. He offered his services once more to the commander in chief, now the president of the United States. Washington was very pleased with the ivory dentures that Greenwood fashioned for him and wore them for the rest of his life, visiting his former private's Manhattan office on occasion for care. The president also let Greenwood advertise himself in newspapers as "Dentist to His Excellency, George Washington."

A few of the lower ranking officers and enlisted men mentioned in this account went on to some prominence. Sam Shaw, a major by the time the fighting ended, was later appointed America's first consul to China. Joseph Bloomfield, who made out his will soon after he enlisted and was shot at Brandywine, plunged into politics and served as the governor of New Jersey for ten years and later spent two terms in the U.S. House of Representatives. At the age of fifty-nine, he abruptly left the governor's mansion and enlisted in the army to fight the British yet again in the war of 1812.

Lt. James McMichael, the poet, joined his wife at her home in Stony Brook, New Jersey, in the spring of 1778 after his discharge. Then, after some time with her, he returned to the army on July 1, 1778, with the Seventh Pennsylvania. That unit was consolidated with the Fourth Pennsylvania in 1781 and became the First Pennsylvania in 1783. McMichael saw combat at the battle of Monmouth and in several skirmishes and remained in the army until the peace treaty in 1783, but kept no further diaries. He received two hundred acres in land bounties for his service and moved to back to his hometown, Lancaster, Pennsylvania, with his wife Susanna. After the war the McMichaels moved to Philadelphia. The lieutenant, who joined the Society of Cincinnati, too, died there in 1791.

Perhaps Jeremiah Greenman's post-war life was representative of most of the unheralded soldiers who fought in the first American army. Greenman, shot twice during the Revolution, had no skills when he entered the army at age seventeen and despite some experience as a regimental clerk, had none when he left on the day the army took possession of New York City in 1783. He drifted for a few years after he returned to Providence and then worked as a sea captain from 1790 to 1805, but never really enjoyed it. Then, with his family, he moved to Marietta, Ohio, in 1806 to run a farm.

He died there in 1828 at the age of seventy-one. On his tombstone his sons carved an inscription that might have served for all the soldiers in the first American army:

"Revolutionary Soldier—in memory of Jeremiah Greenman Esq an active officer in that army which bid defiance to britons power and established the independence of the United States."

ACKNOWLEDGMENTS

The writing of *The First American Army: The Untold Story of George Washington and the Men behind America's First Fight for Freedom,* was a long journey through original diaries, journals, and letters of nearly one hundred soldiers who fought in the American Revolution. It was a joyous journey because along the way I had the assistance of many fellow lovers of history.

Many people aided me in the work on this book. The most helpful was historian Joseph Lee Boyle, the author of a five volume series of books on Valley Forge and an expert on the American Revolution. Lee served as the official historian at Valley Forge National Historical Park for many years. He read through the book and offered numerous helpful suggestions for its historical structure.

Of considerable help in my research were Kathy Ludwig and Greg Johnson, librarians at the David Library of the American Revolution, at Washington's Crossing, Pennsylvania. They spent an entire summer helping me locate the enlisted men whose stories comprised the bulk of this book and then were of invaluable assistance through a long winter and spring on other research.

Librarians everywhere were of assistance. These included Marie Heagney at the Morris County Free Library, in Whippany, N.J., Kim Nusco at the Massachusetts Historical Society, in Boston, and the library staffs at New Jersey City University, Rutgers University, the New York Public Library, and the New York, New Jersey, Pennsylvania, Rhode Island and Connecticut Historical Societies.

I owe a debt of gratitude to New Jersey City University, especially Jo Bruno and Liza Fiol-Matta, for giving me travel grants to complete the research on the book.

I had generous help in finding photos to accompany the book. I owe an enormous debt to Peter Harrington, the curator of the S.K. Brown military history collection of paintings and prints at Brown University, in Providence, Rhode Island. He gave me access to the University's vast collection and helped in the production of photos. I am grateful, too, to Scott Houting of the museum services office at Valley Forge National Historical Park, Andrea Ashby-Leraris at Independence National Historical Park, in Philadelphia, Johnni Rowe at the Morristown National Historical Park, and Christine Jochem and Suzanne Gulick at the Morristown- Morris Township library.

I would like to thank Hillel Black, the executive editor of Sourcebooks, who urged me to write *The First American Army* and did a superb job of editing the manuscript. Thanks also to Peter Lynch and Michelle Schoob, other editors at Sourcebooks, and Vicky Brown and Terri Rieck, the Sourcebooks publicists.

Many thanks to my literary agents, Elizabeth Winick and Henry Williams, of McIntosh & Otis, both history lovers, who were so enthusiastic about this book. Finally, thanks to my wife Marjorie, who helped with the research.

BIBLIOGRAPHY

All of the quotes from Dr. Lewis Beebe, Rev. Ammi Robbins, Elijah Fisher, John Greenwood, Jeremiah Greenman, Ebenezer Wild, James McMichael, and Sylvanus Seely, the central figures in the book, were from their diaries. To cite each of the hundreds of quotes from the same sources would be futile, so the single sources for each man's quotes are listed below. The citations from the more than one hundred other people in the work are listed separately.

Central Figure Sources

Beebe, Lewis. "Journal of a Physician on the Expedition Against Canada, 1776," *Pennsylvania Magazine of History and Biography* 59, October, 1935, pp. 320–361.

Bray, Robert and Paul Bushnell. Eds. *Diary of a Common Soldier in the American Revolution, 1775–1783: An Annotated Edition of the Military Journal of Jeremiah Greenman*, Dekalb, IL: Northern Illinois University Press, 1978.

Greenwood, John. *A young patriot in the American Revolution, 1775–1783: The wartime service of John Greenwood: a record of events written during the year 1809 at such leisure moments as the arduous duties of a professional life permitted the dentist to his Excellency, George Washington*. New York: DeVinne Press, 1922, reprint, Westvaco, 1981.

Lapham, William. Ed., *Elijah Fisher's Journal While in the War for Independence and Continued Two Years After He Came to Maine, 1775–1784*, Augusta, Me: Press of Badger and Manley, 1880.

McMichael, James. "James McMichael's Diary." *Pennsylvania Magazine of History and Biography 16*, 1892.

Robbins, Rev. Ammi. *Journal of the Rev. Ammi Robbins, a Chaplain in the American Army in the Northern Campaign of 1776*, New Haven: B. L. Hamlen, 1850.

Wild, Ebenezer. "The Journal of Ebenezer Wild," *Proceedings of the Massachusetts Historical Society*, 1890, vol. 6, pp. 78–161.

Archival Sources

Avery, David. Papers. Princeton Theological Seminary.
Force, Peter. Papers. David Library of the American Revolution.
Huntington, Jedediah. Connecticut Historical Society.
Valley Forge Historical Park Collection, Valley Forge.

Newspapers

Boston Gazette, 1781.
Freeman's Journal, 1777.
Jersey Journal, 1780.
London Chronicle, 1777.
New Jersey Gazette, 1778.
New York Gazette, 1775–1778.
New York Packet, 1783.
Pennsylvania Evening Post, 1776.
Pennsylvania Journal, 1775–1777.
Virginia Gazette, 1775.

Pamphlets and Articles

Bayley, Frye. *Colonel Frye Bayley's Reminiscences.* Burlington, Vermont.
Beebe, Lewis. "Journal of a Physician on the Expedition Against Canada, 1776." *Pennsylvania Magazine of History and Biography* 59. October, 1935.
"Colonel Thomas Johnson's Letters and Documents." *Proceedings of the Vermont Historical Society,* 1923–1925. Below Falls, Vt.: P.T. Gobie Press, 1926.
Fitch, Jabez. "Jabez Fitch Diary." *Massachusetts Historical Society Proceedings,* 1894–1895. 2d series. Vol. 9.
Gerlach, Larry. "Smallpox Inoculations in Colonial New Jersey." *The Journal of the Rutgers University Library,* 1967.
Linn, John and William Hegle. Eds. Captain Joseph McClellan and Lieutenant William Feltman, "Diary of the Pennsylvania Line." *Pennsylvania Archives.* 2d series. Vol. XI. Harrisburg, Pa.: Lane Hart State Printer, 1880.
Lobdell, Jared. Ed. ""Revolutionary War Journal of Sgt. Thomas McCarty." *Proceedings of the New Jersey Historical Society.* No. 16. January, 1964.
Ludlum, David, "The Weather of Independence, Trenton and Princeton." *Weatherwise,* August, 1975.
McKee, Charles. "Letters of a Soldier of the American Revolution." *Connecticut Magazine,* vol. 10, 1906.
McMichael, James. "James McMichael's Diary," *Pennsylvania Magazine of History and Biography* 16. 1892.
Parker, Robert. "The Journal of Robert Parker." *Pennsylvania Magazine of History and Biography* 28. 1904.
Popp, Stephen. "Journal: 1777–1781." *Pennsylvania Magazine of History and Biography* 26. 1902.
Powell, William. "A Connecticut Soldier under Washington: Elisha Bostwick's Memoirs of the First Years of the Revolution." *William and Mary Quarterly,* series 3, vol. 6, 1949.
Quaife, M. M. "A Boy Soldier under Washington: The Memoir of Daniel Granger," *Mississippi Valley Historical Review,* vol. 16, 1929–1930.
Rau, Louise. Ed. "John Smith's Diary of 1776." *Mississippi Valley Historical Review.* XX. 1933–1934.
Seely, Sylvanus. *Diary of Sylvanus Seely.* Mss. Morristown National Historic Park, Morristown, NJ.
Seller, Horace. "Charles Wilson Peale, Artist-Soldier." *Pennsylvania Magazine of History and Biography* 38. 1914.
Tucker, St. George. "Journal of the Siege of Yorktown." *William and Mary Quarterly.* 3d series. July, 1948.
White, Joseph. "The Good Soldier White" American Heritage, June, 1956.
Wild, Ebenezer. "The Journal of Ebenezer Wild," *Proceedings of the Massachusetts Historical Society,* 1890, vol. 6.

Books

Alen, Gardner. *Massachusetts Privateers of the Revolution.* Massachusetts Historical Society, 1927.
Anderson, Enoch. *Personal Recollections of Captain Enoch Anderson, an Officer of the Delaware Regiments in the Revolutionary War, with Notes by Henry Hobard Bellas, L.L.B., Captain of the U.S. Army.* Wilmington, DE: Historical Society of Delaware, 1896.

Barber, Dan. *History of My Own Times*. Washington, D.C. S.C. Ustick, 1827.

Barnes, John. Ed. *Fanning's Narrative: Being the Memoir of Nathaniel Fanning, an Officer of the Revolutionary Navy, 1778–1783*. New York: New York Times-Arno Press, 1968.

Baxter, James. Ed. William Digby, *The British Invasion from the North*. Albany, 1887.

Binger, Carl. *Revolutionary Doctor, Benjamin Rush, 1746–1813*. New York: W. W. Norton, 1966.

Bingham, Hiram Jr. *Five Straws Gathered from Revolutionary Fields*. Cambridge, Massachusetts, 1901.

Blumenthal, Walter. *Women Camp Followers of the American Revolution*. New York.: New York Times-Arno Press, 1974.

Boatner, Mark. *The Encyclopedia of the American Revolution*. Mechanicsburg, Pa: Stackpole Books, 1994.

Bodle, Wayne and Jacqueline Thibault. *The Valley Forge Historical Report*. 3 vols. Valley Forge National Historical Park, 1980.

Bolton, Charles. *The Private Soldier under Washington*. New York: Charles Scribner's Sons, 1902.

Boyle, Joseph Lee. *Writings from the Valley Forge Encampment of the Continental Army, December 19, 1777—June 19,1778*. 5 vols. Bowie, MD: Heritage Books, 2000–2004.

Bray, Robert and Paul Bushnell. *Diary of a Common Soldier in the American Revolution, 1775–1783: An Annotated Edition of the Military Journal of Jeremiah Greenman*. Dekalb, Illinois: Northern Illinois University Press, 1978.

Burg, David. Ed. *An Eyewitness History: The American Revolution*. New York: Facts on File, 2001.

Butterfield, L. H. Ed. *Adams Family Correspondence*. 6 vols. Cambridge: Belknap Press of Harvard University, 1963–1993.

Chadwick, French. *The Graves Papers and Other Documents Relating to the Naval Operations of the Yorktown Campaign, July to October, 1781*. New York: DeVinne Press, 1916; reprint New York: New York Times-Arno Press, 1968.

Chase, George. Ed. *Diary of David How, a Private in Colonel Paul Dudley Sargent's Regiment of the Massachusetts Line, in the Army of the American Revolution . . . with Illustrative Notes by Henry Dawson*. Morrisania, New York, 1865.

Chase, Philander. Ed. *The Papers of George Washington*. 45 vols. Charlottesville: University of Virginia Press, 1983–2004.

Clark, William. Ed. *Naval Documents of the American Revolution*. 10 vols. Washington, D.C.: Department of the Navy, Naval History Division, 1976.

Claussen, W. Edmund. *Patriots of the American Revolution*. Boyerstown, PA: W. Claussen, 1975.

Codman, John. Ed. *Arnold's Expedition to Quebec*. New York: MacMillan, 1902.

Commager, Henry Steele and Richard Morris, Eds. *The Spirit of 'Seventy Six*. 2 vols. New York: Bobbs-Merrill Company, 1958.

Creasy, Edwin. *The Fifteen Decisive Battles of the World*. London, 1851.

Davis, Burke. *The Campaign that Won America: The Story of Yorktown*. New York: Dial Press, 1970.

Dodd, William. *John Branch Historical Papers of Randolph-Macon College*. Richmond: Everett Weoddry Co, 1902.

Duane, William. Ed. *Extracts From the Diary of Christopher Marshall, 1774–1781*. Albany: Joel Munsell, 1877.

Dwyer, William. *The Day Is Ours*. New York: Viking Press, 1983.

Elting, John. *The Battle of Saratoga*. Monmouth Beach, NJ: Philip Freneau Press, 1977.

Ewing, George. *The Military Journal of George Ewing, 1754–1824, a Soldier at Valley Forge*. Yonkers, NY: Thomas Ewing, 1928.

Fenn, Elizabeth. *Pox Americana: The Great Smallpox Epidemic of 1775–1782*. New York: Hill and Wang, 2001.

Fields, Edward. *Esek Hopkins: Commander in Chief of the Continental Navy During the American Revolution, 1775–1778, Master Mariner, Politician, Brigadier General, Naval Officer, and Philanthropist*. Providence: Preston and Rounds Co., 1898.

Fields, Edward. Ed. *The Diary of Israel Angell, Commanding the Second Rhode Island Continental Regiment During the American Revolution, 1778–1781*. Providence, 1899.

Fitzpatrick, John. Ed. *The Writings of George Washington*. 38 vols. Washington, D.C.: United States Government Printing Office, 1932.

Fleming, Thomas. *Beat the Last Drum*. New York: St. Martin's Press, 1963.

Fleming, Thomas. *The Forgotten Victory: The Battle for New Jersey, 1780*. New York: Reader's Digest Press, 1973.

Flexner, James. *George Washington in the American Revolution*. Boston: Little Brown and Company, 1967.

Flexner, James. *The Traitor and the Spy: Benedict Arnold and John Andre*. New York: Harcourt, Brace and Company, 1957.

Foot, Caleb. *Reminiscences of the Prison Letters and Sea Journal of Caleb Foot*. Salem, MA: Essex Institute Collections, 1889.

Force, Peter. Ed. *American Archives*. 9 vols. Washington, D.C.: 1837–1853.

Ford, Worthington. Ed. *Correspondence and Journals of Samuel Blachley Webb*. 2 vols. New York, 1893. New York Times-Arno Press, 1969.

Ford, Worthington. Ed. *Journals of the Continental Congress, 1774–1789*. 34 vols. Washington, D.C. Government Printing Office, 1904.

Frothingham, Richard. *The History of the Siege of Boston*. 3d ed. Boston,1872.

Furneaux, Rupert. *The Battle of Saratoga*. New York: Stein and Day, 1971.

Gibson, James. *Dr. Bodo Otto and the Medical Background of the American Revolution*. Springfield, IL: Charles Thomas, 1937.

Greenwood, John. *A young patriot in the American Revolution, 1775–1783: The wartime services of John Greenwood: A record of events written during the year 1809 at such leisure moments as the arduous duties of a professional life permitted the dentist to his Excellency, George Washington*. New York: DeVinne Press, 1922; reprint, Westvaco, 1981.

Guild, Reuben, *Chaplain Smith and the Baptists: or Life, Journals, and Addresses of the Rev. Hezekiah Smith, D. D., of Haverhill, Mass., 1737–1805*. Philadelphia: American Baptists Society, 1885.

Hallahan, William. *The Day the Revolution Ended, October 19, 1781*. New York: John Wiley & Sons, 2004.

Hansen, Richard. *The Glorious Hour of Lieutenant Monroe*. New York: Athenaeum, 1976.

Harwell, Richard. Ed. Douglas Southall Freeman. *George Washington*. Abridged ed. New York: Collier Books, 1992.

Haws, Samuel. *The Military Journals of Two Private Soldiers, 1758–1775*. New York: DeCapo Press, 1971.

Henry, J. J. *Arnold's Campaign Against Canada*. Albany: Joel Munsell, 1877.

Henshaw, William. *Orderly Books . . . October 1, 1775 through October 3, 1776*. Worcester, MA: 1948.

Hutchinson, Thomas. Ed. *Diary and Letters of Thomas Hutchinson, with an Account of His Administration*. Boston: Houghton, 1889–1896.

Isaac, Rhys. *The Transformation of Virginia, 1740–1790*. Chapel Hill: University of North Carolina Press, 1982.

Jones, John Paul. *Memoirs of Rear Admiral John Paul Jones*. Edinburgh, Scotland: Oliver and Boyd Publishers, 1890.

Ketchum, Richard. *Victory at Yorktown: The Campaign That Won the Revolution*. New York: Henry Holt, 2004.

Ketchum, Richard. *Winter Soldiers*. Garden City, NY: Doubleday & Company, 1973.

Knouff, Gregory. *The Soldiers' Revolution: Pennsylvania in Arms and the Forging of the Early American Identity*. University Park, PA: Pennsylvania State University Press, 2003.

Langguth, A. J. *Patriots: The Men Who Started the American Revolution*. New York: Simon & Schuster, 1988.

Lapham, William. *Elijah Fisher's Journal While in the War for Independence and Continued Two Years After He Came to Maine, 1775–1784*. Augusta, ME: Press of Badger and Manley, 1880.

Lauber, Almon. Ed. *Orderly Books of the 4th New York Regiment, 1778–1780, the 2d New York Regiment, 1780–1783 with the Diaries of Samuel Tallmadge, 1778–1780, and John Barr, 1779–1782*. Albany: University of the State of New York, 1932.

Laurens, John. *Army Correspondence of Colonel John Laurens*. New York: New York Times-Arno Press, 1969.

Lender, Mark and James Kirby Martin. Eds. *Citizen Soldier: The Revolutionary War Journal of Joseph Bloomfield*. Newark, NJ: New Jersey Historical Society, 1982.

Littell, John. Ed. *Alexander Graydon's Memoirs of His Own Time*. Philadelphia: Lindsay & Blakiston, 1846; reprinted, New York: New York Times-Arno Press, 1969.

Mayer, Holly. *Belonging to the Army: Camp Followers and Community During the American Revolution*. Columbia, SC: University of South Carolina Press, 1996.

Miller, Nathan. *Sea of Glory: A Naval History of the American Revolution*. Annapolis: Naval Institute Press, 1974.

Mintz, Max. *The Generals of Saratoga: Horatio Gates and John Burgoyne*. New Haven: Yale University Press, 1990.

Nelson, Paul. *General Horatio Gates, a Biography.* Baton Rouge: Louisiana State University Press, 1976.

Newell, Timothy. *Journal of Timothy Newell.* Boston: Massachusetts Historical Society Collections, Boston.

O'Connor, Thomas. *Bibles, Brahmins, and Bosses: A Short History of Boston.* 2d ed. Boston: Public Library of the City of Boston, 1991.

Patterson, Samuel. *General Horatio Gates, Defender of American Liberties.* New York: Columbia University Press, 1941.

Pickering, Octavius. *The Life of Thomas Pickering.* 2 vols. Boston, 1897.

Quincy, Josiah. *The Journals of Major Samuel Shaw, the First Consul at Canton.* Boston: William Brosby and H. P. Nichols, 1847.

Randall, Willard. *Benedict Arnold: Patriot and Traitor.* New York: William Morrow, 1990.

Randall, Willard. *George Washington: A Life.* New York: Henry Holt, 1997.

Rankin, Hugh. Ed. *Narratives of the American Revolution, as Told by a Young Soldier, a Home-Sick Surgeon, a French Volunteer, and a German General's Wife.* Chicago: R. R. Donnelly and Sons Company, 1976.

Robbins, Rev. Ammi. *Journal of the Rev. Ammi R. Robbins, a Chaplain in the American Army in the Northern Campaign of 1776.* New Haven: B. L. Hamlen, 1850.

Roberts, Kenneth. Ed. *March to Quebec: Journals of the Members of Arnold's Expedition.* New York: Doubleday and Company, 1938.

Roberts, Lemuel. *Memoirs of Captain Lemuel Roberts, Containing Adventures in Youth, Vicissitudes Experienced as a Continental Soldier, and Escapes from Captivity with Suitable Reflections on the Changes of Life.* Bennington, VT: Anthony Haswell, 1809; reprinted, New York: New York Times-Arno Press, 1969.

Rodney, Thomas. *Diary of Captain Thomas Rodney, 1776–1777.* Wilmington, DE: Historical Society of Delaware, 1888.

Royster, Charles. *A Revolutionary People at War, the Continental Army and American Character, 1775–1783.* Chapel Hill: University of North Carolina Press, 1979.

Salsig, Doyen. Ed. *Parole: Quebec; Countersign: Ticonderoga; Second New Jersey Regimental Orderly Book, 1776.* Cranbury, NJ: Associated University Presses, 1980.

Scheer, George and Hugh Rankin. *Rebels and Redcoats.* New York: World Publishing, 1957.

Scheer, George. *Private Yankee Doodle: Being a Narrative of Some of the Adventures, Dangers and Sufferings of a Revolutionary Soldier.* Boston: Little Brown and Company, 1962.

Senter, Isaac. *The Journal of Isaac Senter, Physician and Surgeon to the Troops Dispatched from the American Army Encamped at Cambridge, Mass. On a Secret Expedition against Quebec under the Command of Col. Benedict Arnold, in September, 1775.* Philadelphia: Historical Society of Pennsylvania, 1846; reprinted, New York: New York Times-Arno Press, 1969.

Shipton, Nathaniel and David Swain. Eds. *Rhode Islanders Record the Revolution: The Journals of William Humphrey and Zuriel Waterman.* Providence: Rhode Island Historical Society, 1984.

Showman, Richard. Ed. *The Papers of Nathanael Greene.* 12 vols. Chapel Hill: University of North Carolina Press for the Rhode Island Historical Society, 1976.

Shy, John. *A People Armed and Dangerous: Reflections on the Military Struggle for American Independence.* New York: Oxford University Press, 1976.

Smallpox in Colonial America. New York: New York Times-Arno Press, 1977.

Smith, Paul. *Letters to the Delegates of Congress, 1774–1789.* 26. Vols. Washington, D.C.: Library of Congress, 1976.

Smith, Samuel. *The Battle of Trenton.* Monmouth Beach, NJ: Philip Freneau Press, 1965.

Stevens, James. *The Journal of James Stevens, of Andover, Massachusetts, a Soldier in the American Revolution.* Salem, Massachusetts, 1911.

Stiles, Ezra. *Literary Diary.* 3 vols. New York: Franklin Dexter, 1901.

Stone, William. Trans. *Friederich Riedesel, Letters and Journals Relating to the War of the American Revolution,* Albany, 1867.

Stryker, William. *The Battles of Trenton and Princeton.* Boston: Houghton and Mifflin Company, 1895.

Symmes, Rebecca. Ed. *A Citizen Soldier in the American Revolution: The Diary of Benjamin Gilbert in Massachusetts and New York.* Cooperstown, NY: New York State Historical Association, 1980.

Syrett, Harold. Ed. *The Papers of Alexander Hamilton.* 27 vols. New York: Columbia University Press, 1961.

Thacher, James. *Military Journal of the American revolution, from the Commencement to the Disbanding of the American Army; Comprising a detailed account of the principal events and Battle of the revolution with Their Exact Dates, and a Biographical Sketch of the most Prominent Generals, to which is Added the Life of Washington, His Farewell Address, the Declaration of Independence and the Constitution of the United States.* Hartford, Conn.: Hurlbut, Williams & Company, 1862.

Thayer, Theodore. *Nathanael Greene: Strategist of the American Revolution.* New York: Twayne Publishers, 1960.

Trussell, John. *Birthplace of an Army: A Study of the Valley Forge Encampment.* Harrisburg, PA: Pennsylvania Historical and Museum Commission, 1998.

Tucherman, Bayard. *The Life of Philip Schuyler, 1733–1809.* New York: Dodd, Mead and Company, 1903.

Tuchman, Barbara, *First Salute: A View of the American Revolution.* New York, Alfred Knopf, 1988.

Ward, Christopher. *The War of the Revolution.* 2 vols. New York: MacMillan, 1952.

Wharton, Francis. *The Revolutionary Diplomatic Correspondence of the United States.* 6 vols. Washington, D.C.: U. S. Government Printing Office, 1889.

Wheeler, Daniel. *The Life and Writings of Thomas Paine.* 10 vols. New York: Vincent Parker Company, 1908.

Whitehill, Walter. *Boston's Topographical History.* 2d ed. Cambridge: Belknap Press of the Harvard University, 1968.

Wilkinson, James. *Memoirs of My Time.* 3 vols. Philadelphia: Abraham Small, 1816.

Williams, Catherine. *Biographies of Revolutionary Heroes, containing the life of General William Barton and also of Captain Stephen Olney.* Providence: Catherine Williams, 1829.

Wood, Gordon. *The Creation of the American Republic, 1776–1787.* New York: W. W. Norton, 1969.

Zobel, Harry. *The Boston Massacre.* New York: W. W. Norton, 1970.

NOTES

Abbreviations
GWW = *Writings of George Washington*
GREENE = *Papers of Nathanael Greene*
VFHP = Valley Forge Historical Park Collection

Chapter One
1. James Thacher, *Military Journal of the American Revolution, from the Commencement to the Disbanding of the American Army; Comprising a detailed account of the principal events and Battles of the Revolution, with Their Exact Dates, and a Biographical Sketch of the most Prominent Generals, to which Is Added the Life of Washington, His Farewell Address, the Declaration of Independence and the Constitution of the United States.* Hartford, CN: Hurlbut, Williams & Company, 1862, p. 68, p. 23.
2. Peter Brown to his mother, June 28, 1775, in Ezra Stiles, *Literary Diary,* New York: Franklin Dexter, 1901, 3 vols., I: 595.
3. Rev. David Avery, David Avery Papers, Princeton Theological Seminary.
4. Samuel Webb to Joseph Webb, June 19, 1775, Worthington Ford, Ed., *Correspondence and Journals of Samuel Blachley Webb,* 2 vols., New York, 1893, New York Times-Arno Books, 1969, I: 63–65; Samuel Ward to Mary Ward, August 17, 1775, Samuel Ward Papers, Rhode Island Historical Society, Providence.
5. Robert Steele to William Sumner, July 10, 1825, Samuel Swett Papers on Bunker Hill, New York Historical Society, in George Scheer and Hugh Rankin, *Rebels and Redcoats,* New York: World Publishing Company, 1957, pp. 59–60.
6. Scheer and Rankin, *Rebels and Redcoats,* p. 61.
7. William Prescott to John Adams, August 25, 1775, Richard Frothingham, *History of the Siege of Boston,* 3rd ed., Boston, 1872, pp. 395–396.
8. Peter Brown to his mother, June 28, 1775, in Stiles, *Literary Diary,* I: 595.
9. Amos Farnsworth, June 17, 1776 entry in "Diary of Amos Farnsworth," in Henry Steele Commager and Richard Morris, Eds., *The Spirit of 'Seventy Six,* 2 vols., New York: Bobbs-Merrill Company, 1958, I:122–123.
10. Thacher, p. 27.
11. Scheer and Rankin, p. 55–64.

Chapter Two

1. Harry Zobel, *The Boston Massacre,* New York: W. W. Norton, 1970, p. 191.
2. Walter Muir Whitehill, *Boston's Topographical History,* 2d ed., Cambridge: Belknap Press of the Harvard University Press, 1968, pp. 3–45.
3. Thomas O'Connor, *Bibles, Brahmins and Bosses, A Short History of Boston,* Public Library of the City of Boston, 1991, 2d ed., pp. 38–52.
4. *Pennsylvania Journal,* August 2, 1775.
5. Thomas Hutchinson, Ed., *Diary and Letters of Thomas Hutchinson, with an Account of His Administration,* Boston: Houghton, 1889–1896, in Commager, *Spirit of Seventy-Six,* I: 117–118.
6. Elijah Fisher, *Elijah Fisher's Journal While in the War for Independence and Continued Two Years After He Came to Maine, 1775–1784,* Augusta, ME: Press of Badger & Manley, 1880, p. 5.
7. James Stevens, *The Journal of James Stevens, of Andover, Massachusetts, a Soldier in the American Revolution,* Salem, Mass., 1911, p. 7.
8. From a letter in *Rivington's Gazette* (NY), June 20, 1775.
9. Stevens, *The Journal of James Stevens, of Andover, Massachusetts, a Soldier in the American Revolution,* p. 6.
10. August diary notes of Sam Haws, Abraham Tomlinson, *The Military Journals of Two Private Soldiers, 1758—1775,* New York: DeCapo Press, 1971, pp. 64–70.

Chapter Three

1. John Littell, ed., *Alexander Graydon's Memoirs of His Own Time,* Philadelphia: Lindsay & Blakiston, 1846, reprinted by the New York Times-Arno Press, 1969, p. 152.
2. George Wingate Chase, *Diary of David How, a Private in Colonel Paul Dudley Sargent's Regiment of the Massachusetts Line, in the Army of the American Revolution . . . with illustrative notes by Henry Dawson,* Morrisania, N.Y., 1865, entry May 27, 1775, p. 19.
3. George Ewing, *Military Journal of George Ewing, 1754–1824, a Soldier of Valley Forge,* Yonkers, NY: Thomas Ewing, 1928, p. 26.
4. Nathan Avery to David Avery, June 19, 1775; Papers of David Avery, Princeton Theological Seminary.
5. Fisher, *Elijah Fisher's Journal While in the War for Independence and Continued Two Years After the War in Maine, 1775–1784,* p. 5.
6. Tomlinson, Haws, *Military Journals,* p. 82.
7. Tomlinson, Haws, *Military Journals,* p. 77.
8. Rev. David Avery, David Avery Papers.
9. Leven Powell to Sarah Powell, February 24, 1776, William Dodd, Ed., *John Branch Historical Papers of Macon-Randolph College,* Richmond: Everett Weoddry Co., 1902, pp. 29–31.
10. GW to John Hancock, September 24, 1776, GWW VI:110–111; GW to William Livingston, January 4, 1777, GWW VII: 56; GW to Jack Custis, January 22, 1777, GWW VII: 52–53; GW to Lund Washington, Aug. 20, 1775, GWW III: 433; Scheer and Rankin, p. 81.
11. Scheer and Rankin, p. 87.
12. Jesse Lukens to John Shaw Jr., September 17, 1775, in Scheer and Rankin, p. 88; Richard Harwell, Ed., Douglass Southall Freeman, *George Washington,* abridged ed., p. 236.
13. GWW III: 357.
14. Scheer and Rankin, p. 78.
15. Avery, Papers.
16. Charles Bolton, *The Private Soldier Under Washington,* New York: Charles Scribner's Sons, 1902, p. 112–113; Stevens, *Journal.*
17. Chase, *Diary of David How,* entry of March 1, 1775, p. 9.
18. John Lacey, *Memoirs,* PMHB, XXV, 1901, p. 12.
19. William Richardson to William Smallwood, April 12, 1777, Papers Relating to the Maryland Line, p. 91.
20. Joseph White, "The Good Soldier White," *American Heritage,* June, 1956, pp. 5–6.
21. Harwell, *George Washington,* abridged ed., p. 350.
22. GW to Lord Stirling, January 19, 1777, GWW VII: 33.
23. Jedediah Huntington to Jabez Huntington, Nov. 23, 1775, Huntington Papers, Connecticut Historical Society.
24. John Adams to William Heath, October 5, 1775, Paul Smith, *Letters to the Delegates of Congress, 1774–1789,* 26 vols., Washington, D.C.: Library of Congress, 1976, II: 112.

25. Silas Deane to Elizabeth Deane, Dec. 15, 1775, Smith, II:488–489.

26. John Hancock to the colonies, December 18, 1775, Smith, II: 444.

27. Josiah Bartlett in Peter Force, Ed., *American Archives V,* six series, 9 vols., Washington, D.C., 1837–1853, I: 404; Bolton, *The Private Soldier Under Washington,* p. 31.

Chapter Four

1. *Pennsylvania Evening Post,* March 30, 1776.

2. Timothy Newell, *Journal Kept During the Time That Boston Was Shut Up, 1775–1776,"* Massachusetts Historical Society Collections, Fourth Series, 2 vols., Boston, 1852. I: 274–275; Manasseh Cutler, *Life, Journals and Correspondence of the Rev. Manasseh Cutler, LLD,* Cincinnati: Robert Clark & Co., 1888.

Chapter Five

1. *Virginia Gazette,* July 28, 1775.

2. Scheer and Rankin, p. 128.

3. Chase, ix.

4. Gregory Knouff, *The Soldiers' Revolution: Pennsylvania in Arms and the Forging of the Early American Identity,* University Park, PA: The Pennsylvania State University Press, 2003, pp. 77–79.

5. Mark Lender and James Kirby Martin, Eds., *Citizen Soldier: The Revolutionary War Journal of Joseph Bloomfield,* Newark, NJ: New Jersey Historical Society, 1982, p. 111.

6. John Adams to Abigail Adams, September 2, 1777, L. H. Butterfield, ed., *Adams Family Correspondence,* 6 vols., Cambridge: Belknap Press of Harvard University, 1963–1993, II: 336.

7. Mark Boatner, *The Encyclopedia of the American Revolution,* Mechanicsburg, PA: Stackpole Books, 1994, pp. 263–264.

8. Orderly Book of the First Pennsylvania Regiment, August 15, 1776.

9. Knouff, *The Soldiers Revolution: Pennsylvania in Arms and the Forging of the Early American Identity,* pp. 84–89.

10. James Thomas Flexner, *George Washington in the American Revolution,* 1775–1783, Boston: Little Brown and Company, 1967, p. 35.

11. Charles Royster, *A Revolutionary People at War, The Continental Army and American Character, 1775–1783,* Chapel Hill: University of North Carolina Press, 1979, p. 59.

12. *Boston Gazette,* April 22, 1776.

13. When Joseph Reed, an aide to Washington, left the army he was elected "President" of Pennsylvania.

14. George Fleming to Sebastian Baumann, January 21, 1778, Baumann Papers, New York State Historical Society.

15. *New Jersey Gazette,* March 18, 1778.

16. Sam Shaw to his father, May 13, 1777, Josiah Quincy, *The Journals of Major Samuel Shaw, the First Consul at Canton,* Boston: William Brosby and H. P. Nichols, 1847, p. 91.

17. Boyle, Joseph Lee, *Writings from the Valley Forge Encampment of the Continental Army, December 19, 1777–June 19, 1778,* 5 vols., Bowie, MD: Heritage Books, 2000-2004, II: 16.

Chapter Six

1. Isaac, *The Transformation of Virginia, 1740–1790,* Chapel Hill: University of North Carolina Press, 1982, p. 269.

2. April 20, 1775, "Farnsworth's Journal," Mass. Hist. Soc. Proc. 2d Series, XIII (1898, p. 79).

3. Royster, *A Revolutionary People at War: The Continental Army and American Character,* pp. 16–17.

4. Knouff, *The Soldiers' Revolution,* 44.

5. Samuel Cooper to his wife and children, July 18, 1775, Charles McKee, "Letters of a Soldier of the American Revolution," *Connecticut Magazine,* X, (1906), p. 25.

6. Royster, *A Revolutionary People at War,* p. 30.

7. Quoted in petitions of Pennsylvania soldiers for pensions after the war, Knouff, p. 44.

8. John Shy, *A People Armed and Dangerous: Reflections on the Military Struggle for American Independence,* New York: Oxford University Press, 1976, p. 168.

9. "George Morison's Journal," Kenneth Roberts, ed., *Marching to Quebec: Journals of the Members of Arnold's Expedition,* New York: Doubleday and Company, 1938, p. 505.

10. Dan Barber, *History of My Own Times,* Washington, D.C.: S.C. Ustick, 1827, pp. 13–14.

11. "James McMichael Diary," *Pennsylvania Magazine of History and Biography,* no. 16 (1892), pp. 129–159, p. 3.

12. William Powell, "A Connecticut Soldier Under Washington: Elisha Bostwick's Memoirs of the First Years of the Revolution," *William and Mary Quarterly,* Series 3, vol. 6 (1949), p . 99.
13. George Scheer, Ed., *Joseph Plumb Martin, Private Yankee Doodle,* Boston: Little Brown and Company, 1962, p. 17.
14. Avery Papers.
15. *Jersey Journal,* March 29, 1780.
16. Lemuel Roberts, *Memoirs of Captain Lemuel Roberts, , Containing Adventures in Youth, Vicissitudes Experienced as a Continental Soldier, and Escapes from Captivity with Suitable reflections on the Changes of Life,* Bennington, VT: Anthony Haswell, 1809; reprinted, New York: New York Times-Arno Press, 1969, p. 21.
17. Holly Mayer, *Belonging to the Army: Camp Followers and Community During the American Revolution,* Columbia: University of South Carolina Press, 1996, p. 32.
18. John Laurens, *Army Correspondence of Colonel John Laurens,* New York: New York Times-Arno Press, 1969, p. 136.
19. Nathanael Greene to GW, GWW IV: 441.
20. William Dwyer, *The Day Is Ours,* New York: Viking Press, 1983, p. 249.

Chapter Seven

1. John Codman, Ed., *Arnold's Expedition to Quebec,* New York: Macmillan, 1902, pp. 6–8.
2. Commager and Morris, *The Spirit of '76,* I: 583.
3. Willard Stern Randall, *Benedict Arnold: Patriot and Traitor,* New York: William Morrow, 1990, pp. 84–87.
4. Randall, *Benedict Arnold: Patriot and Traitor,* pp. 135–137.
5. Scheer and Rankin, *Rebels and Redcoats,* pp. 115–118.
6. Benedict Arnold, "Col. Arnold's Journal of His Expedition to Canada," entry of September 29, 1775, in Kenneth Roberts, *March to Quebec: Journals of the Members of the Arnold Expedition,* 1938, p. 45.
7. George Morison, "George Morison's Journal," in Roberts, *March to Quebec,* p. 511.
8. Isaac Senter, "Journal," in Roberts, pp. 202–203.
9. Arnold, "Col. Arnold's Journal of His Expedition to Canada," entry of October 12, 1775, in Roberts, p. 50.
10. Codman, *Arnold's Expedition to Quebec,* pp. 70–73.
11. Randall, *Benedict Arnold: Patriot and Traitor,* p. 182.
12. Scheer and Rankin, p. 119.
13. Abner Stocking's "Journal," in Roberts, pp. 555–556; Morison, "Journal," in Roberts, pp. 525–526.
14. Randell, p. 188.

Chapter Eight

1. Codman, *Arnold's Expedition to Quebec,* p. 128.
2. "George Morison's Journal," in Roberts, *March to Quebec,* pp. 536–537.
3. Stocking's Journal," in Roberts, *March to Quebec,* p. 565.
4. Nathaniel Shipton and David Swain, eds. *Rhode Islanders Record the Revolution: The Journals of William Humphrey and Zuriel Waterman,* Providence: Rhode Island Publications Society, 1984, pp. 32–34.
5. John Henry, "Journal," Roberts, *March to Quebec,* pp. 389–90.
6. Boatner, *The Encyclopedia of the American Revolution,* pp. 894–895.
7. *Colonel Thomas Johnson's Letters and Documents,* Vermont Historical Society, 1923–25, 1926, Proceedings of the Vermont Historical Society, Below Falls, VT: P.T. Gobie Press, 1926.
8. Caleb Foot, *Reminiscences of the Prison Letters and Sea Journal of Caleb Foot,* Salem, MA: Essex Institute Collections, Vol. XXVI, 1889, pp 8–9.
9. Pension request affidavit of Greenman, in Bray and Bushnell, *Diary of a Common Soldier in the American Revolution,* pp. 300–301.

Chapter Nine

1. Benedict Arnold to the Congressional Commissioners, June 2, 1776, Peter Force, *American Archives,* 5th Series, I:165.
2. Randall, *Benedict Arnold: Patriot and Traitor,* pp. 235–236.
3. David Burg, ed. *An Eyewitness History: the American Revolution,* New York: Facts on File Inc., 2001, pp. 107–109.

4. Benedict Arnold to Philip Schuyler, April 20, 1776, Peter Force. Ed., *American Archives*, 6 series in 9 vols., Washington, D.C., 1837–1853, 4th Series, V:1098–1100.

Chapter Ten
1. Isaac Senter, *The Journal of Isaac Senter, Physician and Surgeon to the Troops Detached from the American Army Encamped at Cambridge, Mass., on a Secret Expedition Against Quebec under the Command of Col. Benedict Arnold, in September, 1775,* Philadelphia: Historical Society of Pennsylvania, 1846,; reprinted by New York Times Books-Arno Press, 1969, pp. 38–39.
2. Codman, *Arnold's Expedition to Quebec,* p. 285.
3. Elizabeth Fenn, *Pox Americana: The Great Smallpox Epidemic of 1775–82,* New York: Hill and Wang, 2001, pp. 62–68.
4. Arnold's general orders, March 26, 1776, in Doyen Salsig, ed., *Parole: Quebec; Countersign: Ticonderoga; Second New Jersey Regimental Orderly Book, 1776,* Cranbury, NJ: Associated University Presses, 1980, pp. 55–56.
5. Fenn, *Pox Americana,* p. 113.
6. *Smallpox in Colonial America,* New York: New York Times-Arno Press, 1977, section four; Larry Gerlach, "Smallpox Inoculations in Colonial New Jersey," in *The Journal of the Rutgers University Library,* December, 1967, pp. 21–28.
7. Dan Barber, *History of My Own Times,* p. 25.
8. Fenn, pp. 68–72.
9. Lemuel Roberts, *Memoirs of Captain Lemuel Roberts, Containing Adventures in Youth, Vicissitudes Experienced as a Continental Soldier, His Sufferings as a Prisoner and Escapes from Captivity With Suitable Reflections on the Changes of Life,* Bennington: Anthony Haswell, 1809; reprinted by New York Times-Arno Books, 1969, p. 34.
10. Lewis Beebe, "Journal of a Physician on the Expedition Against Canada," *Pennsylvania Magazine of History and Biography,* Vol. LIX, No. 4, October, 1935, p. 328.
11. J. J. Henry, *Arnold's Campaign Against Canada,* Albany, Joel Munsell, 1877, pp. 134–139.
12. James Gibson, *Dr. Bodo Otto and the Medical Background of the American Revolution,* Springfield, Ill.: Charles Thomas, 1937, pp. 96–97.
13. Frye Bayley, *Colonel Frye Bayley's Reminiscences,* Proceedings of the Vermont Historical Society, 1923–1925, P. H. Gobe Press, 1926, pp. 34–35.

Chapter Eleven
1. Roberts, *March to Quebec,* p. 26.
2. Jonathan Trumbull to George Washington, July 9, 1776, quoted in Gibson, *Dr. Bodo Otto and the Medical Background of the American Revolution,* p. 99–100.

Chapter Twelve
1. W. Edmund Claussen, *Patriots of the American Revolution,* Boyertown, PA: W. Claussen, 1975, p. 73.
2. "John Henry's Journal," "James Melvin's Journal," in Roberts, *March to Quebec,* p. 443–444.
3. July 21, 1776, note, *Diary of Matthew Patten of Bedford, NH,* Concord, NH: 1903, frame 1039.
4. Benedict Arnold to Phillip Schuyler, October 12, 1776, Peter Force, *American Archives,* 5th Series, III: 253–254.

Chapter Thirteen
1. Dwyer, *The Day Is Ours,* pp. 152, 213.
2. Louise Rau, ed., "John Smith's Diary of 1776," *Mississippi Valley Historical Review,* XX, 1933–1934, pp. 247–270.
3. Jared Lobdell, ed., "Revolutionary War Journal of Sgt. Thomas McCarty," *Proceedings of the New Jersey Historical Society,* No. 316, January, 1964, pp. 36–43.
4. Powell, "A Connecticut Soldier under Washington: Elisha Bostwick's Memoirs of the First Years of the Revolution," *William and Mary Quarterly,* pp. 94–107.
5. Dwyer, p. 243.
6. Richard Ketchum, *The Winter Soldiers,* Garden City, NY: Doubleday & Company, Inc., 1973.
7. William Stryker, *The Battles of Trenton and Princeton,* Boston: Houghton and Mifflin Company, 1898, p. 133.
8. Theodore Thayer, *Nathanael Greene: Strategist of the American Revolution,* New York: Twayne Publishers, 1960, pp. 140–143.

9. David Ludlum, "The Weather of Independence: Trenton and Princeton," in *Weatherwise* (August, 1975), 75–83.

10. Christopher Ward, *The War of the Revolution*, 2 vols, New York: MacMillan, 1952, I: 295.

11. Samuel Smith, *The Battle of Trenton*, Monmouth Beach, NJ: Philip Freneau Press, 1965.

12. Richard Hansen, *The Glorious Hour of Lieutenant Monroe*, New York: Athenaeum, 1976, p. 153.

13. Sgt. Joseph White memoir, "The Good Soldier White," *American Heritage*, June 1956, pp. 74–79.

14. James Flexner, *George Washington in the American Revolution*, Boston: Little Brown, Co., pp. 176–179; *Pennsylvania Journal*, July 9, 1777.

15. John Polhemus narrative, Leach Collection, Genealogical Society of Pennsylvania, Philadelphia.

16. James Wilkinson, *Memoirs of My Time*, 3 vols., Philadelphia: Abraham Small, 1816, I: 131.

17. GW to John Cadwalader, Dec. 27, 1776, GWW VI: 446.

18. White, 77.

19. Powell, "A Connecticut Soldier Under Washington: Elisha Bostwick's Memoirs of the First Years of the Revolution," 102.

20. Dwyer, p. 293.

21. Rau, *Mississippi Valley Historical Review*, p. 269.

Chapter Fourteen

1. Ward, *The War of the Revolution*, I: 310.

2. Quincy, *The Journals of Major Samuel Shaw, The First American Consul at Canton*, pp. 30–33.

3. Dwyer, *The Day Is Ours*, p. 325.

4. Dwyer, p. 333.

5. Catherine Williams, *Biographies of Revolutionary Heroes, containing the life of General William Barton and also of Captain Stephen Olney*, Providence: Catherine Williams, 1839, p. 196.

6. William Thompson to Leven Powell, January 10, 177, Dodd, *John Branch Historical Papers of Randolph-Macon College*, pp. 120–121.

7. Wilkinson, *Memoir of My Time*, I: 138.

8. Richard Wheeler, *Voices of 1776*, New York: Crowell, 1972, pp. 183–185; Dwyer, *The Day is Ours*, White Diary, Williams, Olney Memoir.

9. George McIntosh to John Muir, January 5, 1777, Dodd, pp. 119–120.

10. Horace Wells Sellers, "Charles Wilson Peale, Artist—Soldier," *Pennsylvania Magazine of History and Biography*, v. 38, 1914, p. 280.

11. Thomas Rodney, *Diary of Captain Thomas Rodney, 1776–1777*, Wilmington, DE: Historical Society of Delaware, 1888, p. 35.

12. Powell, *William and Mary Quarterly*, p. 105.

13. Dr. David Griffith to Leven Powell, Dec. 27, 1776, Dodd, *Branch Historical Papers*, pp. 46–47.

14. *Freeman's Journal*, January 21, 1777.

Chapter Fifteen

1. Boatner, p. 654.

2. Colonel Jonathan Fitch to Governor Trumbull, August 13, 1776, in Force, *American Archives V*, I:938.

3. GW to John Hancock, January 31, 1777, GWW VII:80–81.

4. GW to Joseph Reed, November 28, 1775, GWW IV: 124–125.

5. GW to Major General Philomon Dickinson, January 21, 1777, GWW VII: 45–46.

6. Nathanael Greene to a friend, January 4, 1776, Richard Showman, Ed., *The Papers of Nathanael Greene*, 12 vols., Chapel Hill: University of North Carolina Press for the Rhode Island Historical Society, 1976, hereafter cited as GREENE, I: 126–127.

7. Littell, ed., *Alexander Graydon, Memoir of His Own Time, with Reminiscences of the Men and Events of the Revolution*, p. 147.

Chapter Sixteen

1. Powell, *William and Mary Quarterly*, p. 100.

2. Hugh Rankin, Ed., "Abilgence Waldo Diary," *Narratives of the American Revolution, as Told by a Young Soldier, a Home-Sick Surgeon, a French Volunteer, and a German General's Wife*, Chicago: R.R. Donnelly and Son Company, 1976, p. 173.

3. Jabez Fitch Diary, *Massachusetts Historical Society Proceedings, 1894–1895*, 2d series, vol. 9, pp. 53–61.

4. Jabez Fitch Diary, p. 53.

5. Almon Lauber, ed., *Orderly Books of the Fourth New York Regiment, 1778–1780, the 2d New York Regiment, 1780–1783, with Diaries of Samuel Tallmadge and John Barr, 1779–1782*, Albany, University of the State of New York, 1932, p. 633.

6. Scheer, *Yankee Doodle*, p. 123.

7. General orders, Aug. 22, 1775, GWW III: 444.

8. William Henshaw, *Orderly Books . . . October 1, 1775, through October 3, 1776*, Worcester: Mass., 1948., p. 131.

9. Diary of Lt. Walter Finney, Chester County Historical Society.

10. Walter Hart Blumenthal, *Women Camp Followers of the American Revolution*, New York: Arno Press, 1974, p. 187–188.

11. Loammi Baldwin to his wife, June 17, 1776, Baldwin Papers, Harvard College Library, quoted in Douglas Southall Freeman, *George Washington: A Biography*, New York: Charles Scribner's Sons, 1952, 7 vols., IV, p. 85.

12. Blumenthal, *Women Camp Followers of the American Revolution*, pp. 225–226.

13. Rebecca Symmes, ed., *A Citizen Soldier in the American Revolution: The Diary of Benjamin Gilbert in Massachusetts and New York*, Cooperstown, NY: New York State Historical Association, 1980, p. 30.

14. Symmes, p. 33.

15. Blumenthal, p. 59.

16. General Orders, GWW, IX: 129:30.

17. Blumenthal, p. 86; John Hyde Preston, *Revolution, 1776*, New York, 1933, p. 170.

18. Wheeler, *The Life and Writings of Tom Paine*, I: 90.

Chapter Seventeen

1. Bayard Tucherman, *The Life of General Philip Schuyler, 1733–1809*, New York: Dodd, Mead and Company, 1903, pp. 230–234.

2. Max M. Mintz, *The Generals of Saratoga: Horatio Gates and John Burgoyne*, New Haven: Yale University Press, 1990, p. 181.

3. Entry of November 25, 1777, Walter Finney Diary, Chester County Historical Society, West Chester, Pa., p. 20.

4. Return Meigs, "Journal of Return J. Meigs," in Roberts, *March to Quebec*, p. 181.

5. Robert Parker, "Journal of Lieutenant Robert Parker," *Pennsylvania Magazine of History and Biography*, v. 28, 1904, p. 15.

6. M. M. Quaife, "A Boy Soldier under Washington: The Memoir of Dan Granger," p. 555.

7. Quaife, "Boy Soldier," p. 555.

8. John Burgoyne to George Germain, Aug. 20, 1777, in John Burgoyne, *The Remembrancer*, 1777, p. XXV.

9. Paul Nelson, *General Horatio Gates: A Biography*, Baton Rouge: Louisiana State University Press, 1976, pp. 114–115.

10. John Elting, *The Battle of Saratoga*, Monmouth Beach, NJ: Philip Freneau Press, 1977, p. 51.

11. Samuel Patterson, *Horatio Gates, Defender of American Liberties*, New York: Columbia University Press, 1941, pp. 150–153.

12. James Flexner, *The Traitor and the Spy: Benedict Arnold and John Andre*, New York: Harcourt, Brace and Company, 1957, pp. 170–173.

13. Boatner, p. 974.

14. John Glover to J. Glover and A. Orne, September 21, 1777, in Essex Inst., Hist. Coll. V, June, 1863, pp. 101–102.

15. James Baxter, ed., William Digby, *The British Invasion from the North*, Albany, 1887, p. 274.

16. John Elting, *The Battle of Saratoga*, p. 35.

17. Quaife, p. 544.

18. Horatio Gates to John Burgoyne, September 2, 1777, Papers of Horatio Gates, in Mintz, p. 182.

19. Randall, *Benedict Arnold*, pp. 368–361.

20. From Samuel Downing's pension statement, in Bolton, p. 244; Wakefield in Reuben Aldridge Guild, *Chaplain Smith and the Baptists: or Life, Journals and Addresses of the Rev. Hezekiah Smith, D.D., of Haverhill, Mass., 1737–1805*, Philadelphia: American Baptist Society, 1885, p. 213.

21. William L. Stone, trans., *Friederich Riedesel, Letters and Journals Relating to the War of the American Revolution*, Albany, 1867, pp. 125–127.

22. Thacher, *Military Journal of the American Revolution*, pp. 112–114.

23. Rupert Furneaux, *The Battle of Saratoga*, New York: Stein and Day, 1971, p. 268.

24. Boston celebration in *Boston Gazette*, November 1, 1777; Sir Edwin Creasy, *The Fifteen Decisive Battles of the World*, London, 1851.

25. Thacher, pp. 109–110.

Chapter Nineteen

1. Major Richard Platt to General Alexander McDougall, Dec. 29, 1777, Lee Boyle, *Writings from the Valley Forge Encampment of the Continental Army, December 29, 1777—June 19, 1778*, II: 9–11.

2. GW to Congress, October 13, 1777, Philander Chase, ed., *Papers of George Washington*, 45 vols. Charlottesville, VA: University of Virginia Press, Revolutionary War Series, II: 497–501; GW to Thomas Nelson, November 11, 1777, GWW X: 27.

3. Jedediah Huntington letter, Dec. 25, 1777, VFHP.

4. Hugh Rankin, Ed., "Albigence Waldo Diary," *Narratives of the American Revolution, as Told by a Young Soldier, a Home-Sick Surgeon, a French Volunteer, and a German General's Wife*, p.182.

5. Diary of Ebenezer Wild, January 1–14, 1778, *Proceedings of the Massachusetts Historical Society*, 1890, vol. 6, pp. 78–161.

6. James Craig to Jonathan Potts, April 26, 1778, VFHP.

7. James Craig to Jonathan Potts, May 2, 1778, VFHP.

8. Gouverneur Morris to John Jay, February 1, 1778, Smith, 9:4.

9. Benjamin Rush to George Washington, Jan. 1, 1779, VFHP; Rush to Washington, December 26, 1778, Washington Papers, Library of Congress; Rush to Greene, February 1, 1778, GREENE II: 267.

10. Elias Boudinot to Elisha Boudinot, March 15, 1778, Lee Boyle, *Writings from the Valley Forge Encampment of the Continental Army, December 29, 1777—June 19, 1778*, I: 78–79.

11. Alexander Scammell to Timothy Pickering, March 17, 1778, Boyle, I: 83–88.

12. Rankin, "Waldo Diary," *Narratives of the American Revolution*, p. 182.

13. Ebenezer Crosby to Norton Quincey, April 14, 1778, Boyle, I: 103–104.

14. Rankin, "Waldo Diary," December 25, 1777.

15. A. Craigie to Jonathan Potts, April 4, 1778; John Cochran to Jonathan Potts, March 22, 1778; Thomas Herbert to Jonathan Potts, March 25, 1778; J. B. Cuttings to Jonathan Potts, March 16, 1778, VFHP.

16. Jedediah Huntington to GW, January 1, 1778, VFHP.

17. Benjamin Rush to Patrick Henry, January 12, 1778, in Carl Binger, *Revolutionary Doctor, Benjamin Rush, 1746–1813*, New York: W. W. Norton & Co. 1966, p. 133; Dr. William Brown letter to unknown friend, January 20, 1778, VFHP.

18. Rankin, "Waldo Diary," p. 201.

19. Benjamin Rush to Horatio Gates, February 4, 1778, VFHP.

20. Leven Powell to Sarah Powell, January 21, 1778, Dodd, *John Branch Historical Papers*, pp. 36–38.

21. GW to William Livingston, December 21, 1777, GWW X: 233.

22. James Sproat, *Journal of Rev. Dr. James Sproat*, Pennsylvania Historical Society Library, in Gibson, p. 326.

23. James Craig to Jonathan Potts, May 15, 1778, VFHP.

24. Rankin, "Waldo Diary," p. 185.

25. GW to Henry Laurens, December 23, 1777, GWW X: 192–198.

26. Jedediah Huntington to Jabez Huntington, Jan 7, 1778, VFHP.

27. Thomas Jones to Charles Stewart, Feb. 16, 1778, Charles Stewart Papers, NYHS.

Chapter Twenty

1. Enoch Anderson, *Personal Recollections of Captain Enoch Anderson, an Officer of the Delaware Regiments in the Revolutionary War, with Notes by Henry Hobard Bellas, L.L.B., Captain of the U.S. Army*, Wilmington, DE: Historical Society of Delaware, 1896, pp. 36–37.

2. James Flexner, *George Washington in the American Revolution, 1775–1783*, pp. 219–224.

3. Joseph Clark, *Diary of Joseph Clark*, NJ Historical Society Proceedings, VII: 96, 98–99; Elias Dayton narrative, Elias Dayton Papers, New Jersey Historical Society, Newark, NJ.

4. Quincy, *Journals of Major Samuel Shaw*, pp. 34–35.

5. Edward Fields, Ed., *Diary of Colonel Israel Angell, Commanding the Second Rhode Island Continental Regiment During the American Revolution, 1778–1781*, Providence, 1899, pp. xii-xiii.

6. John Trussell Jr., *Birthplace of an Army: A Study of the Valley Forge Encampment,* Harrisburg: Pennsylvania Historical and Museum Commission, 1998, pp. 34–35.

7. John Paterson to Thomas Marshall, Feb. 23, 1777, Boyle, II: 66–68.

8. Archelaus Lewis to Jesse Partridge, February 1, 1778, Boyle I: 39–40.

9. Peter Force Mss., Series E., New Hampshire Council, David Library of the American Revolution; Library of Congress.

10. Samuel Carlton to General William Heath, January 28, 1778, Boyle I: 37–38.

11. Charles Scott to George Washington, January 14, 1777, Boyle I: 22–23.

12. Richard Platt to Alexander McDougall, January 24, 1778, VFHP.

13. Richard Butler to Thomas Wharton Jr., March 26, 1778, Boyle, II: 94–95.

14. John McDowell to Col. David Grier, January 16, 1778, Boyle II: 24–25.

15. William Duane, Ed., *Extracts from the Diary of Christopher Marshall, 1774–1781,* Albany, NY: Joel Munsell, 1877, pp. 161–162.

16. James Gray to Susan Gray, December 24, 1777, Boyle I: 4.

17. Elias Boudinot to Elisha Boudinot, September 23, 1777, George Adams Boyd, *Elias Boudinot: Patriot and Statesman, 1740–1821,* Princeton: Princeton University Press, 1952, reprint, New York: Greenwood Press, 1969, p. 43.

18. Anonymous letter of William Weeks, Feb. 16, 1778, Hiram Bingham Jr. *Five Straws Gathered from Revolutionary Fields,* Cambridge, MA, 1901, pp. 23–25.

19. Jonathan Todd to Jonathan Todd Sr., Dec. 25, 1777, Boyle, II: 6–7.

20. Enoch Poor to Mesech Weare, January 21, 1778, Force MSS, series 7-E, New Hampshire Council, Library of Congress; Wayne Bodle and Jacqueline Thibault, *Valley Forge Historical Report,* Valley Forge, PA: Valley Forge Historical Park, 1980, 3 vols., I: 160–161; Henry Laurens to William Livingston, Ibid. III: 142.

21. Governor and Council Letters, Massachusetts State Archives, Force Mss., Series 7E, David Library; Library of Congress.

22. George Ewing, *The Military Journal of George Ewing, 1754–1824, a Soldier at Valley Forge,* Yonkers, NY: Thomas Ewing, 1928, pp. 44–45.

23. Ewing, *The Military Journal of George Ewing,* p. 34.

24. Ewing, pp. 49–51.

25. GW to John Augustine Washington, June 10, 1778, GWW XII: 43.

Chapter Twenty-one

1. George Washington to Caleb Gibbs, April 22, 1777, GWW, VII: 452–453, GW to Alexander Spotswood, April 30, 1777, GWW VII: 494–495.

2. Maurer Maurer, "Military Justice Under General Washington," *Military Affairs,* vol. 28, no. 1, 1964, p. 8.

3. Scheer, *Yankee Doodle,* pp. 45–46.

4. Thacher, pp. 195–196.

Chapter Twenty-two

1. George Washington to John Hancock, September 24, 1776, GWW VI: 110–111.

2. Ambrose Ely Vanderpoel, *History of Chatham, New Jersey,* Chatham: Chatham Historical Society, 1959, pp. 82–91; John Cunningham, *Chatham: At the Crossing of the Fishawack,* Chatham: Chatham Historical Society, 1967, pp. 19–21.

3. Donald White, *A Village at War: Chatham, New Jersey, and the American Revolution,* Cranbury, NJ: Associated University Presses, 1979, pp. 23–28.

4. White, *A Village at War,* p. 103.

5. *New York Gazette,* June 3,1778.

6. Papers of the New Jersey Provisional Congress.

7. Theodore Thayer, *Colonial and Revolutionary Morris County,* Morristown, Compton Press, for the Morris County Heritage Commission, 1975, pp. 255–256.

8. Thayer, *Colonial and Revolutionary Morris County,* pp. 85–87.

9. George Washington to Robert Morris, May 25, 1778, GWW XI: 453.

10. Scheer, *Yankee Doodle,* p. 126.

11. Scheer, *Yankee Doodle,* p. 127.

12. Boatner, pp. 719–725.

13. Flexner, *George Washington in the American Revolution,* pp. 303–309.
14. Earl Schenk Miers, *Crossroads of Freedom,* New Brunswick: Rutgers University Press, 1971, pp. 156–157.
15. *New York Journal,* July 13, 1778.
16. Williams, *Biographies of Revolutionary Heroes,* pp. 214–215.
17. Lender and Martin, *Citizen Soldier,* pp. 136–137.
18. Randall, *George Washington,* pp. 357–360.
19. Washington to Congress, GWW XII: 143–145.
20. Boatner, p. 725.

Chapter Twenty-three
1. Thayer, *Colonial and Revolutionary Morris County,* pp. 214–215.

Chapter Twenty-four
1. George Washington to William Heath, June 29, 1780, GWW XIX: 93.
2. Boatner, p. 883.
3. Edward Braddock to Robert Napier, March 17, 1755, Stanley Pargellis, ed., *Military Affairs in North America, 1748–1765,* New York, 1936, p. 78.
4. Glen Knoblock, *"Strong and Brave Fellows": New Hampshire's Black Soldiers and Sailors of the Americans Revolution, 1775–1784,* Jefferson, North Carolina: McFarland and Co., 2003, pp. 149–151.
5. Samuel Allinson to Patrick Henry, October 12, 1774, Allinson Papers, Rutgers University Special Collections; James Otis, *The Rights of British Colonists Asserted and Proved,* 3rd ed., Boston, MA, 1766, pp. 43–44.
6. Fairfax Resolves, in *Virginia Gazette,* July 24, 1774; Washington on "tame and abject slaves," George Washington to Bryan Fairfax, August 24, 1774, *Papers of George Washington,* Colonial Series X: 154–156.; "poor wretches," George Washington to Lund Washington, GWW IV: 147–149.
7. *Connecticut Military Records,* 1775–1848, Hartford, 1889, p. 85, 90.
8. Knoblock, *"Strong and Brave Fellows,"* p. 20.
9. Knoblock, p. 22.
10. Sidney Kaplan, *The Black Presence in the Era of the American Revolution, 1770–1800,* New York: Graphic Society for Smithsonian Institution, 1973, pp. 20–21.
11. Benjamin Quarles, *The Negro in the American Revolution,* Chapel Hill: University of North Carolina Press, 1961, pp. 13–15.
12. Graydon, *Memoirs,* p. 131.
13. General Persifor Frazer, "Some Extracts from the Papers of General Persifor Frazer," *Pennsylvania Magazine of History and Biography,* 31, 1907, p. 134.
14. Philip Schuyler to George Washington, July 14, 1777, Jared Sparks, ed., *Correspondence of the American Revolution, Being Letters of Eminent Men to George Washington from the Time of His Taking Command of the Army to the End of His Presidency.* 4 vols., Freeport, NY: Books for Libraries Press, 1979, I: 398.
15. William Heath to Samuel Adams, August 27, 1777, Heath Papers, Massachusetts Historical Society Collection, 7th Series, 4 (1904), p. 148.
16. Quarles, *The Negro in the American Revolution,* p. 16.
17. Knoblock, p. 13.
18. Worthington Ford. Ed., *Journals of the Continental Congress, 1774–1789,* 24 vols., Washington, D.C.: U.S. Government Printing Office, 1904, III: 395, 403.
19. George Washington to Richard Henry Lee, December 26, 1775, in *R. H. Lee, Memoir of the Life of Richard Henry Lee,* Philadelphia, 1825, II: 9.
20. Henry Muhlenberg, *Muhlenberg Diaries,* quoted in Kaplan, *The Black Presence in the Era of the American Revolution, 1770–1800,* p. 66.
21. *Virginia Gazette,* Nov. 17, 1775; Nov. 24, 1775.
22. William Foster, *The Negro People in American History,* New York: International Publishing Company, 1954, pp. 48–49.
23. Quarles, pp. 26–28.
24. Kaplan, pp. 66–69.
25. Knoblock, pp. 96–97.
26. Ibid., p. 118.

27. Ibid., pp. 53–54.
28. Ibid., pp. 83–84.
29. *Jeremy Belknap Papers*, Massachusetts Historical Society, Boston.
30. *Jeremy Belknap Papers*, p. 117.
31. John Laurens to Henry Laurens, January 14, 1778, William Gilmore Simms, *The Army Correspondence of Colonel John Laurens in the Years 1777–1778*, New York: New York Times-Arno Press, 1969, p. 108.
32. John Laurens to Henry Laurens, February 2, 1778, *Army Correspondence of Colonel John Laurens in the Years 1777–1778*, pp.114–118.
33. Alexander Hamilton to John Jay, March 14, 1779, HAM II: 17–18.
34. John Laurens to George Washington, May 19, 1782, Sparks, *Correspondence of the American Revolution*, III: 406.
35. Walter Finney Diary, Chester County Historical Society, p. 18.
36. Knoblock, p. 88.
37. Thomas Anderson quoted in Quarles, p. 87, Stephen Steward to the Maryland Council, March 7, 1781, William Browne, ed., *Archives of Maryland, 1883–1952*, 65 vols., II: 362.
38. Ed Riley, ed., Charles Cross, Jr. *A Navy for Virginia: A Colony's Fleet in the Revolution*, Yorktown: Virginia Independence Bicentennial Commission, 1981, pp. 22–23.
39. James Barron, "The Schooner Liberty," *Virginia Historical Register*, 1848, I: 80.
40. Quarles, p. 171–173.

Chapter Twenty-five

1. Bartlett, ed., *Records of the Colony of Rhode Island*, VIII, p. 641.
2. Knoblock, p. 300.
3. Kaplan, pp. 55–58.
4. Nathanael Greene to John Sullivan, John Sullivan, *Letters and Papers of Major General John Sullivan*, 3 vols., Concord, NH: New Hampshire Historical Society, 1930–39, II: 103, 101–102.
5. Nathanael Greene to George Washington, August 28, 1778, GREENE, II: 499, a British sailor with Howe that day wrote that the French left because of fierce British opposition, but admitted that Howe and the officers were surprised at their departure, Thomas O'Beirne, *Narrative of the Fleet Under Lord Howe*, New York: New York Times-Arno Press, 1969, pp. 40–41.
6. Nathanael Greene to William Heath, August 27, 1778, GREENE II: 497.
7. William Nell, *Colored Patriots of the American Revolution*, New York: New York Times-Arno Press, 1968, pp. 128–130.
8. Theodore Thayer, *Nathanael Greene: Strategist of the American Revolution*, pp. 256–257.
9. Kaplan, pp. 55–56.
10. John Hope Franklin. *From Slavery to Freedom*, New York: Alfred Knopf, 1947, p. 136.
11. Boatner, pp. 788–794.
12. Henry Laurens to New Jersey Governor William Livingston, September 1, 1778, Smith, X: 546–547.
13. James Smith to his wife Eleanor Smith, September 4, 1778, Smith, X: 572.; Richard Henry Lee to Adam Stephen, September 5, 1778, Ibid., X: 574.
14. Knoblock, p. 285–286.
15. Ibid., pp. 173–174.
16. Ibid., pp. 137–138.
17. David White, *Connecticut's Black Soldiers*, 1775–1783, Chester, CN: Pequot Press, 1973, p. 22.
18. White, pp. 120–121.

Chapter Twenty-six

1. Edward Field, *Esek Hopkins: Commander in Chief of the Continental Navy During the American Revolution, 1775–1778, Master Mariner, Politician, Brigadier General, Naval Officer and Philanthropist*, Providence: Preston and Rounds Co., 1898, p. 45.
2. Richard Henry Lee to John Page, March 29, 1779, Smith, XII: 160–161.
3. Gardner Weld Allen, *Massachusetts Privateers of the Revolution*, Massachusetts Historical Society, 1927, p. 18.
4. Barbara Tuchman, *First Salute: A View of the American Revolution*, New York: Alfred Knopf, 1988, p. 20.

5. Boatner, pp. 896–898. Boatner estimated $18 million, but adding total worth of cargo a $66 million figure was set by Nathan Miller in *Sea of Glory: A Naval History of the American Revolution,* Annapolis: Naval Institute Press, 1974, pp. 260–264.

6. Miller, *Sea of Glory,* p. 262.

7. Miller, p. 282.

8. *London Chronicle,* September 2, 1777.

9. Annual Register, XXI, 1778, p. 36.

10. Governor Valentine Morris to Vice Admiral James Young, William Bell Clark, Exec. Ed., William Morgan, Ed. Vol. VII, *Naval Documents of the American Revolution,* 10 vols., Washington, D.C.: Department of the Navy, Naval History Division, 1976, VII: 1184–85.

11. Henry Byrne to Vice Admiral James Young, December 4, 1776, in Morgan, *Naval Documents of the American Revolution,* VII: 372–373.

12. Miller, p. 261.

13. Francis Wharton, *The Revolutionary Diplomatic Correspondence of the United States,* 6 vols., Washington, D.C.: U.S. Government Printing Office, 1889, III: 650.

14. John Langdon to John Hancock, November 4, 1776; Charles Lee to Mescheh Weare, November 27, 1776, Morgan, *Naval Documents,* VII: 31.

15. *Historical Magazine,* March 1862.

16. Allen, *Massachusetts Privateers of the Revolution,* p. 16.

17. John Paul Jones, *Memoirs of Rear Admiral John Paul Jones,* Edinburgh: Oliver and Boyd Publishers, 1890, pp. 80–81.

18. John Barnes, ed., *Fanning's Narrative: Being the Memoir of Nathaniel Fanning, an Officer of the Revolutionary Navy,* 1778–1783, New York: New York Times-Arno Books, 1968, pp. 194–195.

Chapter Twenty-seven

1. David Ludlum, *History of Early American Winters, 1604–1828,* Boston: Boston-American Meteorological Society, 1966, pp. 120–121.

2. *Diary of Colonel Israel Angell,* New York: New York Times-Arno Books, 1971, pp. 101–102.

3. *Diary of Colonel Israel Angell,* pp. 114–115.

4. Thacher, pp. 180–181.

5. Erkuries Beatty to Reading Beatty, December 29, 1779, *Pennsylvania Magazine of History and Biography* 14, 1890, p. 205; Finney journal entry, December 2, 1780, Finney Diary.

6. Christopher Ward, *War of the Revolution,* 2:612, quoting N. W. Stephenson and W. H. Dunn, *George Washington,* New York: Oxford University Press, 1940, 2 vols., 2:121.

7. Miers, *Crossroads of Freedom,* p. 202.

8. *Diary of Colonel Israel Angell,* December 13, 1779, p. 101.

9. George Washington to James Wilkinson, Dec. 22, 1779, GWW XXVII: 300.

10. Nathanael Greene to Daniel Broadhead, December 8, 1779, GREENE, V: 182.

11. Scheer, *Yankee Doodle,* p. 172.

12. Major James Fairlie to Charles Tillinghast, January 12, 1780, Dennis Ryan, Ed., *A Salute to Courage: The American Revolution as Seen through the Wartime Writings of Officers of the Continental Army and Navy,* New York: Columbia University Press, 1979, p. 178.

13. George Washington to Samuel Huntington, Dec. 25, 1779, GWW XXVII: 272–273.

14. William Livingston to George Washington, December 21, 1779, *Livingston Papers,* 5 vols. III: 277.

15. Baron von Steuben to George Clinton, Thayer, *Colonial and Revolutionary Morris County,* p. 224.

16. William Livingston to the New Jersey Assembly, December 20, 1779, *Livingston Papers,* III: 273–274.

17. A. E. Zucker, *General De Kalb: Lafayette's Mentor,* Chapel Hill, University of North Carolina Press, 1966, p. 190; Thacher, pp. 214–216.

18. George Washington's Weather Diary, entry of January 6, 1780.

19. Thacher, p. 185.

20. George Washington to Samuel Huntington, January 5, 1780, GWW XXVII: 358.

21. William Ellery to Nathanael Greene, December 21, 1779, Smith, XIV: 288.

22. Nathanael Greene to Benoni Hathaway, January 6, 1780, GREENE V: 243.

23. *Jersey Journal,* January 15, 1780.

24. "A soldier's letter," *Jersey Journal,* January 22, 1780.

25. Thayer, *Colonial and Revolutionary Morris County,* pp. 228–230.

26. *Jersey Journal,* January 16, 1780.

27. *Jersey Journal,* February 2, 1780.
28. De Kalb quoted in Miers, p. 209; Nathanael Greene to Alexander McDougall, March 1, 1780, GREENE V: 428.
29. William Livingston to Rensalaer Williams, December 12, 1779, *Livingston Papers:* III: 282.
30. Proclamation, May 27, 1780, from Seely Diary.
31. Scheer, *Yankee Doodle,* p. 182.
32. Ibid., p. 186.

Chapter Twenty-eight

1. William Livingston to George Washington, June 7, 1780, *Livingston Papers,* III: 435.
2. White, *A Village at War,* p. 173; Boatner, p. 1045; Thayer, *Colonial and Revolutionary Morris County,* pp. 247–248; Miers, *Crossroads of Freedom,* pp. 217–220.
3. Thomas Fleming, *The Forgotten Victory: The Battle for New Jersey, 1780,* New York: Reader's Digest Press, 1973, pp. 132–136, Miers, pp. 220–221.
4. Joseph Jones, *The Life of Ashbel Green,* New York, Robert Carter & Brothers, 1849, pp. 112–114.
5. William Livingston to Baron von Steuben, June 21, 1780, *Livingston Papers,* III: 438–439.
6. Boatner, pp. 1045–1047.
7. Wilhelm Knyphausen to George Germain, July 3, 1780, K. G. Davis, Ed., *Documents of the American Revolution, 1770–1783,* (Colonial Office Series), 21 vols., Shannon: Irish University Press, 1976, XVIII, pp. 112–113.
8. George Washington to Robert Howe, June 10, 1780, GW XVIII: 494–496.
9. Washington's note, GWW XIX: 96–97; *Diary of Colonel Israel Angell,* p. 169.
10. Notes on the battles of Springfield from Thayer, *Colonial and Revolutionary Morris County,* pp. 246–255; White, pp. 171–177; Joseph Jones, *The Life of Ashbel Green,* pp. 112–114; Scheer, *Yankee Doodle,* 188–189; Thacher, p. 201–202; *Jersey Journal,* June 14, 1780; Scheer and Rankin, p. 374; William Wilcox, Ed., *Sir Henry Clinton, the American Rebellion: Sir Henry Clinton's Narrative of His Campaign 1775–1782, With an Appendix of Original Documents,* New Haven: Yale University Press, 1954, p. 194; Miers, pp. 217–225; *See Also* Thomas Fleming, *The Forgotten Victory,* Boatner, pp. 1045–1047.
11. *Jersey Journal,* March 29, 1780.

Chapter Twenty-nine

1. St. George Tucker, "Journal of the Siege of Yorktown," *William and Mary Quarterly,* 3rd Series (July 1948), p. 378.
2. Richard Ketchum, *Victory at Yorktown: The Campaign That Won the Revolution,* New York: Henry Holt, 2004, pp. 211–213.
3. Thomas Fleming, *Beat the Last Drum,* New York: St. Martin's Press, 1963, pp. 61–65.
4. John Linn and William Hegle, Eds., Captain Joseph McClellan and Lieutenant William Feltman, *Diary of the Pennsylvania Line,* Pennsylvania Archives, 2d Series, vol. XI, Harrisburg: Lane Hart, State Printer, 1880, p. 689, 691, 693.
5. James Thomas Flexner, *George Washington in the American Revolution, 1775–1783,* pp. 448–455; Freeman, *George Washington: A Biography,* VI: 365–371; Randall, *George Washington: A Life,* pp. 391–393.
6. St. George Tucker, "Journal of the Siege of Yorktown," p. 382.
7. Linn and Hegle, *Diary of the Pennsylvania Line,* p. 694,
8. Thacher, p. 284.
9. *The Journal of Lieut. William Feltman, of the First Pennsylvania Regiment, 1781–1782,* Philadelphia: Historical Society of Pennsylvania, 1853; reprint, New York: New York Times-Arno Press, 1969, p. 18.
10. Thacher, p. 280.
11. Thacher, p. 285.
12. Scheer, *Yankee Doodle,* pp. 235–236.
13. Williams, *Biographies of Revolutionary Heroes,* pp. 276–279.
14. Tucker, "Journal of the Siege of Yorktown, 1781," p. 386.
15. Stephen Popp, "Journal, 1777–1783," PMHB, XXVI, pp. (1902), pp. 25–41.
16. For details on the battle of Yorktown, see Boatner, pp. 1230–1250.
17. Tucker, p. 391

18. William Hallahan, *The Day the Revolution Ended, October 19, 1781,* New York: John Wiley & Sons, Inc., 2004, pp. 199–201.
19. Burke Davis, *The Campaign That Won America: The Story of Yorktown,* New York, Dial Press, 1970, p. 267.
20. Thacher, p. 289.
21. Hallahan, pp. 229–249.
22. Admiral Samuel Hood to George Jackson, October 29, 1781, French Ensor Chadwick, *The Graves Papers and Other Documents Relating to the Naval Operations of the Yorktown Campaign, July to October, 1781,* 10 vols., New York: Printed for the Naval History Society, DeVinne Press, 1916, VII: pp. 144–145.
23. Fleming, *Beat the Last Drum,* p. 343.

INDEX